Handy Household

PROBLEM SOLVER

2013

www.jerrybaker.com

Other Jerry Baker Books:

Jerry Baker's Solve It with Vinegar!
Jerry Baker's Speed Cleaning Secrets!
America's Best Practical Problem Solvers
Jerry Baker's Homespun Magic
Jerry Baker's Supermarket Super Products!
Jerry Baker's It Pays to Be Cheap!

Healing Fixers Mixers & Elixirs
Grandma Putt's Home Health Remedies
Nature's Best Miracle Medicines
Jerry Baker's Supermarket Super Remedies
Jerry Baker's The New Healing Foods
Jerry Baker's Amazing Antidotes
Jerry Baker's Anti-Pain Plan
Jerry Baker's Oddball Ointments, Powerful Potions, and Fabulous Folk Remedies
Jerry Baker's Giant Book of Kitchen Counter Cures

Jerry Baker's The New Impatient Gardener
Jerry Baker's Supermarket Super Gardens
Jerry Baker's Dear God...Please Help It Grow!
Secrets from the Jerry Baker Test Gardens
Jerry Baker's All-American Lawns
Jerry Baker's Bug Off!
Jerry Baker's Terrific Garden Tonics!
Jerry Baker's Backyard Problem Solver
Jerry Baker's Green Grass Magic
Jerry Baker's Great Green Book of Garden Secrets
Jerry Baker's Old-Time Gardening Wisdom

Jerry Baker's Backyard Birdscaping Bonanza
Jerry Baker's Backyard Bird Feeding Bonanza
Jerry Baker's Year-Round Bloomers
Jerry Baker's Flower Garden Problem Solver
Jerry Baker's Perfect Perennials!

To order any of the above, or for more information on Jerry Baker's
amazing home, health, and garden tips, tricks, and tonics, please write to:

Jerry Baker, P.O. Box 1001
Wixom, MI 48393

Or, visit Jerry Baker online at:

www.jerrybaker.com

Handy Household PROBLEM SOLVER

2013

By Jerry Baker

Published by American Master Products, Inc.

Executive Editor: Kim Adam Gasior
Managing Editor: Cheryl Winters-Tetreau
Writer: Vicki Webster
Copy Editor: Nanette Bendyna
Production Editor: Debby Duvall
Interior Design and Layout: Nancy Biltcliff
Indexer: Nan Badgett

Publisher's Cataloging-in-Publication Data
(Provided by Quality Books, Inc.)

  Baker, Jerry.
      Jerry Baker's handy household problem solver 2013.
      p. cm.
      Includes index.
      ISBN 978-0-922433-80-3

      1. House cleaning. 2. Storage in the home.
  3. Orderliness.   I. Title. II. Title: Handy household
  problem solver 2013.

  TX324.B35 2013   648'.5
               QBI12-600214

Printed in the United States of America
2 4 6 8 10 9 7 5 3 1 hardcover

CONTENTS

INTRODUCTION.....................vi

CHAPTER ONE:
THE BEDROOM

Deal With the Drawers 1
Sleeping Beauty.................................. 17
End Bedroom Closet Chaos 28

CHAPTER TWO:
THE KITCHEN

Free Up the Fridge and Freezer 42
Conquer Cabinet Clutter.................. 56
Clear the Decks!................................ 78
Pare Down the Pantry....................... 86

CHAPTER THREE:
THE LIVING ROOM

The Big Picture 99
That's Entertainment! 114

CHAPTER FOUR:
THE HOME OFFICE

Dig Out the Desk 133
The Paper Chase 151

CHAPTER FIVE:
THE BATHROOM
AND LINEN CLOSET

Bathroom Brainstorms 168
Behind Closed Doors 197

CHAPTER SIX:
THE LAUNDRY ROOM

Action Central 211
Supplies 'R' Us 228

CHAPTER SEVEN:
THE BASEMENT
AND ATTIC

Dig in Downstairs............................ 242
Under the Eaves 263

CHAPTER EIGHT:
THE GARAGE AND SHED

Auto Motives................................... 282
A Place for Everything..................... 305

CHAPTER NINE:
THE WORKSHOP
AND HOBBY ROOM

Nail Down a Plan 318
Create A Masterpiece....................... 338

CHAPTER TEN:
DOWNSIZING

Getting Ready.................................. 351

INDEX 366

INTRODUCTION

If clutter is taking over your home and life, then it's time to fight back and clear it out once and for all. This year, I've developed a simple SOS method—Sort, Organize, and Store—so you can clear out the clutter, stow your stuff, and reclaim your home, your time, and your sense of well-being.

HOLD EVERYTHING!

Whether your entire house is in a state of chaos, or you have just one room that needs de-cluttering, my SOS strategy will show you how to find a place for everything and keep everything in its place. In each chapter you'll learn how to tackle a specific part of your home using this revolutionary three-part plan. As you'll soon see, it can be fast, fun, and easy to weed out unwanted junk, reorganize your space, and store your stuff in the way that works best for you.

SORT

This is the first step on the road to clutter-free living. In each Sort section you'll discover surefire solutions for determining what to keep and what to toss. But your sorting spree doesn't stop there: I'll share some terrific tricks for banishing visual clutter, so your rooms look serene and spacious. Finally, you'll learn some no-fail techniques that'll keep the clutter from creeping back in (as it tends to do) and re-staking its claim on your home, sweet home.

ORGANIZE

Even after you've sorted through your belongings and gotten rid of things you don't need, your home can still seem cluttered—until you organize the keepers in such a way that clutter-free living becomes a no-brainer. That's where the smorgasbord of ideas in this section comes in. I'll guide you through the process of analyzing your available space, focusing on areas where clutter tends to collect. You'll find lots of clever ways to take advantage of every square inch, whether you're working with a kitchen that sees lots of daily activity, or an attic that's used only for storage.

STORE

Each area has its own special challenges, ranging from dampness and pests in the basement to wildly fluctuating temperatures in the garage. Well, never fear, ol' Jer is here! Using the third part of my SOS strategy, you can conquer those perplexing problems—and a whole lot more! You'll discover new ways to use your existing storage space, and learn how to turn potential trash into handy helpers that'll stow all kinds of things. Plus, I'll clue you in on how to store everything from ship models to shirts and books to broccoli, so they're out of the way when you're not using them and easy to grab when you need them.

TO EACH HER OWN To banish clutter once and for all, you have to understand what caused the mess in the first place. That's why, throughout this book, you'll find special **Alert** boxes that focus on the three usual suspects when it comes to cluttering things up:

1. Collectors, who deliberately acquire things ranging from free-for-the-taking beach stones to priceless Fabergé eggs

2. Pack rats, who hang on to anything and everything long after the items have served their useful purpose

3. Mess-makers, who create clutter simply by not putting things back where they belong
   Once you identify which kind of clutterer you are (or live with), I'll share the steps that you'll need to break the cycle and conquer the chaos for good.

NOW, THERE'S AN IDEA! Make that plenty of ideas! I've added two recurring features in this book that will help you clear the clutter creatively. **Out of the Box** helps you solve de-cluttering dilemmas by saying "No thanks!" to sloppy old habits. (Sneak peek: Believe it or not, you can actually make your bedroom less cluttered if you ditch the dressers.) And that's not all—**Making Space** shows you how to find storage space in places that you never dreamed existed.

HELP FROM THE PROS, AND JERRY As an extra-special bonus, each chapter also contains right-on-the-money tips from full-time professional organizers who really know their stuff. I call them the **Clutter Buster Pros**, and they're here to do what they do best: provide expert advice to help minimize clutter while maximizing storage space. If you follow their terrific tips, I guarantee your life will be simpler, more productive—and a lot more fun!

And speaking of advice, you'll find even more of my practical de-cluttering tricks in the **Ask Jerry** boxes. That's where I tackle your toughest problems with some commonsense solutions.

WHY BOTHER AT ALL? It's as clear as the nose on your face: A clutter-free home is a happy home, and you want your home to be delirious! By following my SOS plan, you'll be well on your way to success. For starters, you and your family will feel more relaxed. (Just think: no more searching high and low for car keys every morning!) You'll also have more free time because you won't have to sift through piles of stuff to find what you're looking for. Plus, imagine the pride you'll feel when someone visits and compliments you on how beautiful, well organized, and peaceful your home looks.

So what are you waiting for? This is the year to shout out "SOS!", roll up your sleeves, and dig in. And before you know it, you'll tame the clutter monster, clear out your excess stuff, and be able to enjoy your home, sweet home.

CHAPTER ONE

THE BEDROOM

I t's the first room you see in the morning and the last one you see at night, and it's the very room where you'll spend at least a third of your life. Not only will a clutter-free bedroom provide a peaceful place to start your day and a restful haven at the end of it, but it can even promote better sleep, and more sex! By tackling this room first, you'll realize just how wonderful de-cluttered surroundings can be, and that will keep you motivated to conquer the rest of the house. Start by setting aside a chunk of time—a few evenings in a row, or an entire weekend—to devote to de-cluttering your bedroom. Then divide the room into three sections—drawers, sleeping area, and closet—and let our SOS strategy be your guide.

DEAL WITH THE DRAWERS

In This Section:
✔ Dresser
✔ Bureau
✔ Night table
✔ Armoire

Drawers can be super organizing tools, but if you're not careful, they can turn into disaster areas. Don't worry, though. By putting SOS to work in them, you'll be well on your way to a serene—and junk-free— bedroom.

SORT

There's no doubt about it: Combing through bedroom drawers can be a daunting task. That's because, chances are, you've crammed them with more things than you need to keep there. So muster up all of the determination and willpower you can and dive right in, using the guidelines you'll find here.

DIVVY IT UP. No law says you have to tackle all your drawers in one fell swoop. If you have a lot of them in your bedroom, you'll find the going easier—and you'll be more likely to actually finish the job—if you spread it out over several evenings or weekends. But no matter how long it takes to complete the project, don't work on more than one drawer at a time. That way, you won't wind up with mountains of stuff to deal with all at once.

START SMALL. For all you natural-born pack rats out there, my advice is to take that "divide and conquer" tip above one step further: Begin your de-cluttering campaign with the smallest drawer in your bedroom. Whether that's a drawer in your nightstand or the top one in your dresser, it shouldn't take you more than 10 or 15 minutes—max— to sort through the contents and put back the stuff that really belongs there. And once you see how neat and orderly it looks, you'll be all fired up to tackle the rest of the room.

CLEAR THE DECK! Or rather, clear the floor. Once you've chosen a drawer to reorganize, you'll need enough space for five boxes (or piles, if you prefer). Then, as you pull each item out of the drawer, assign it to one of these categories:

1. Trash

2. Keep Here

3. Take Elsewhere (see the note below)

4. Donate or Sell

5. Recycle

Note: Bear in mind that some of the things in the Take Elsewhere box may remain in the bedroom—but simply not in their current space.

PACK RAT ALERT!

Problem: Sweaters riddled with moth holes.

Solution: As long as the sleeves are hole-free, cut them off just below the shoulder seams, and stuff them with old socks or panty hose. Then stitch the ends closed, and put them to work blocking drafts under your doors.

THINK BEFORE YOU TRASH. As you're pulling out potential castoffs, keep in mind that what's nothing but drawer-cluttering trash to you may be true treasure to someone else. Even garments or accessories that are worn, torn, or paint-spattered may be welcomed with open arms by a whole lot of creative folks who use small pieces of fabric in their work. So tuck those defective duds into your Recycle box. Then ask around your neighborhood or search the Internet for nearby artists or craftsmen who make any of these:

• Cat toys

• Collages

• Doll clothes

• Dollhouse accessories

• Fancy scrapbooks

• Hooked, woven, or braided rugs

• Quilts

HERE AND NOW. Ideally speaking, bedroom bureaus and dressers should hold only the clothes, accessories, and other things you use in order to dress and prepare for your day. After all, who wants to rummage through a pile of wool sweaters in August in search of a bathing suit? Anything that's out of season, or that you wear only once in a blue moon—like the sweater with the big Santa Claus on the front that only sees action at your neighborhood Christmas party—needs to go in the Take Elsewhere box.

MAKING SPACE | Some things in your drawers will be obvious candidates for the Trash box—for instance, a pocket pack of tissue with one paper hanky left in it, or a half-empty box of three-year-old cough drops. But don't forget about any T-shirts, sweaters, scarves, or underclothes that are torn, frayed, stained, or stretched out of shape. Getting rid of them is guaranteed to free up a fair amount of room.

ENOUGH IS ENOUGH. Do you really need six pairs of cuff links when you have only one shirt with French cuffs? Probably not. Is it necessary to keep three flashlights in the drawer of your nightstand when only you and your spouse share the bedroom? I don't think so. Weed out all of the things that you have just too many of, and put them into your Donate or Sell box. And if you can use them someplace else in the house (as in the case of that third flashlight), pop them into your Take Elsewhere box.

SOCK 'EM TO IT. Is your search through your drawers turning up orphaned socks galore? Or do you just have more pairs of socks than you know what to do with? Well, don't throw 'em out! Instead, toss 'em into your Recycle box, and give them new careers as household helpers. Just look at this handy half-dozen ways you can put your former foot covers to work around your home, sweet home.

1. Back savers. Instead of lifting heavy furniture to move it around a room, slip a soft, thick sock over each leg, and slide that piece to its new location.

2. Car window de-fogger. Carry an orphaned sock in your car, and slip it over your hand when you need to wipe away the fog from the windows and mirrors.

3. Dust cloths. A cotton sock, pulled over your hand, is just the ticket for dusting knickknacks, blinds, or shutters—or anything else, for that matter! To extend your reach, or to get into tight places (say, under the couch or clothes dryer), slip the sock over a yardstick or broom handle.

4. Jewelry holders. Toss a sock into your gym bag. Then, when you take off your jewelry at the pool or health club, tuck it into the sock and

Ask Jerry

Q. My husband has a drawer full of fraying underwear that he refuses to part with because he says it's just starting to get really comfortable. (But I know he'd be horrified if he were to end up in the emergency room wearing any of it!) Any suggestions?

A. Tell your hubby to do what I do with pairs of underwear (and socks, too) that are getting toward the end of their careers: I take them along on a trip and after I've worn a pair, I throw it away. That way, I get rid of drawer clutter and make my suitcase lighter at the same time!

knot it closed. You'll be able to retrieve your treasures quickly. What's more, they're all but guaranteed to stay safe— after all, what thief is likely to steal a sock?

5. Moth chasers. Fill 'em with cedar shavings, or bug-repelling herbs like lavender or thyme, and tie the tops shut. Then tuck 'em among your clothes and linens to fend off moths and silverfish.

6. Shoe bags. When you're heading off on a trip with children, pack their shoes in grown-ups' socks. And men's roomy athletic socks are just the right size for holding women's dress shoes.

ALL TIED UP. If you need tiebacks for some new curtains, or you'd just like to replace your plain old fabric tiebacks with something a little snazzier, look no further than your bureau drawers. Most likely, they hold quite a few things that you haven't worn in years, but will give you the best-dressed windows on the block. Good candidates include scarves, sashes, leather shoelaces, and fabric or chain belts.

ACCESS YOUR ACCESSORIES. We all know the old saying "Out of sight, out of mind." Well, that's exactly what things like belts, scarves, and purses tend to be when they're buried in bedroom drawers. Weed out anything that doesn't match any of your clothes, isn't flattering to you, doesn't fit, or is no longer worn, for whatever reason, and fling it into your Donate or Sell box.

MESS-MAKER ALERT!

Problem: Orphaned socks are piling up like crazy!

Solution: Buy a mesh lingerie bag for every member of your household, and write each person's name on it with a different color of indelible marker. Then hang one in the closet of each bedroom, and issue orders that as soon as socks are removed from the owner's feet, they go directly into the bags. When it's time to do laundry, zip the bags closed, toss 'em into the washer, then into the dryer. Your stray sock problems will be a thing of the past!

DE-JUNK YOUR JEWELRY COLLECTION. When it's time to sort your costume jewelry, take it all out of the box or drawer at the same time. Spread it out on your bed or the dining room table, and go to town using these two guidelines:

1. Examine any broken pieces. If the damage can be repaired, and the item has either real or sentimental value (say, your grandmother's favorite brooch that needs a new clip), take it to a jeweler ASAP. If a fix-up isn't possible, or it would cost more than the piece is worth, get rid of it. *Note*: That doesn't necessarily mean tossing it into your Trash box. Many artists who make found-object sculpture (also called assemblage art) would love to take it off your hands. If you don't happen to know any such folks, contact the nearest art school or the art department of a local high school or community college.

2. Pull out everything you don't wear anymore, for whatever reason, and get rid of that, too. Either put it into your Donate or Sell box, or give it to a child who likes to play with grown-up jewelry.

PACK RAT ALERT!

Problem: A jumbled pile of post earrings that you rarely, if ever, wear.

Solution: Haul them out of your drawer or jewelry box, and pull off the backs. Then use the little baubles as decorative pushpins on a bulletin board.

WHEN YOUR GEMS ARE THE REAL McCOY. Even jewelry that's made of fine metals and precious stones is nothing but clutter if it's just taking up space in a drawer or jewelry box. Now don't get me wrong—I'm not talking about family heirlooms that you intend to pass on to your children or grandchildren! I'm talking about gifts you've received over the years, or that you've splurged on for yourself, but that you no longer wear—and maybe never did. Even if you think you know what the pieces are worth, have them appraised by several reputable dealers. (Just like the stock market, the metals markets fluctuate daily and so, therefore, does the value of anything that's made of gold, silver, platinum, or even nonprecious metals such as copper.) If the price appeals to you, sell your treasures to one of those dealers. If not, you still have a couple of options:

• Place your jewelry in an upscale consignment shop, or advertise it for sale on the Internet or in your local newspaper. You'll reap the reward of extra cash in your pocket, and gain a little extra drawer space in your bedroom.

• Hang on to your treasures, and keep an eagle eye on the precious metals markets (just crank up your favorite Internet search engine and type in those three words). When the price hits a figure that pleases you, go for it! In this case, your reward could be a little more space in your drawers and a *lot* more bucks in your bank account!

ORGANIZE

Think about it: Frantically rummaging through cluttered drawers every morning to find this scarf or that matching sock is enough to start anyone's day off on the wrong foot. On the other hand, having a system of drawers in which you can find exactly what you want, when you want it is the key to stress-free dressing in the morning—and will put a smile on your face for the rest of the day.

Ask Jerry

Q. *I've been sorting through my drawers for a couple of weeks now, and I'm finding all kinds of things I don't need anymore. My Donate or Sell box is filling up fast. The trouble is that every time I look in it, I see something that just might come in handy someday, so I put it back where it came from. Do you have any ideas for stiffening my willpower?*

A. I sure do—and it couldn't be simpler! As you finish each sorting session, place your castoffs in a box and tape it shut. That way, you'll be less tempted to dig back in and reclaim your goods. Then toss all your boxes into the car and deliver them to their new homes as soon as you can. Or, if you're planning a yard sale, stash the sealed cartons where you won't have to look at them every day.

TO EACH HIS OWN. Ideally, if you share a bedroom with a spouse, you should each have your own dresser. If that's not possible, assign the highest drawer to the taller of you, then alternate on down to the bottom. And whatever you do, make sure you stick to the arrangement. That way, your belongings won't "wander" into your roomie's drawers, and vice versa.

NIX THE NECKLACES. No, I don't mean you should get rid of them all! Just don't shove them back into a drawer—or even a jewelry box—once you've sorted out the ones you want to keep. If you do, you'll be all but guaranteed to wind up with a tangled mess. So instead, as long as your closet doors aren't the bifold or sliding type, screw some cup hooks into the back of the door and drape one or, at most, two necklaces over each hook. Don't add any more than that; otherwise you'll have to pull a handful of them off to reach the one you want to wear *now*. And they may well get all tangled together, just as they were in the drawer, and you'll be right back to square one.

NIX THE NECKLACES, TAKE TWO. You say you'd rather not make holes in your closet door? No problem! Just get a wooden clothes hanger and screw cup hooks into it at intervals of 1 inch or so. Then hang it in the closet and drape your beads, chains, and pendants over the hooks.

MAKING SPACE

If you have any long, low dressers in your bedroom, consider trading them in for tall chests of drawers. These thinner, vertical bureaus hold just as much stuff as their horizontal counterparts, while taking up less room. You could even have two of them in the space occupied by a single, shorter piece. Plus, tall chests have more—and often smaller—drawers than the low units have. This gives you the chance to divide your clothes into more categories, thereby keeping them better organized. For instance, in a low dresser with only a few drawers, your socks and underwear might have to mix and mingle. In a taller chest, you can give them separate quarters.

By the way, this method also works great for organizing belts.

PUT 'EM ON DISPLAY. If your jewelry collection includes especially beautiful (and substantial) pieces like strings of handmade beads, ornate Navajo silver necklaces, or big, colorful wooden or plastic bracelets—don't keep them behind closed doors. Instead, make them part of your bedroom decor using one or more of these arty ideas:

- Buy an attractive wall rack and hang chains or strings of beads from the hooks. Your choices range from the classic, Shaker-style peg rack to the colorful, funky metal kinds you can find in craft galleries, gift shops, and housewares stores.

- Show off an extra-special, individual piece of jewelry in a shadow-box display case with a hinged opening. You can find them at picture-framing and art-supply stores, and on the Internet. Simply attach your treasure to the case's backing (which is usually velvet) using a T-shaped craft pin, and hang the case on the wall. Depending on the size of your collection, your available wall space, and your personal preference, you can either give each necklace or bracelet separate quarters, or group several together in a single, large display case. Now you have a work of art! Whenever you want to wear your prized possession, just open the door and take it out.

- Bracelets made from Bakelite (an early type of plastic) are hot collectors' items these days. If you're lucky enough to have some

Use an old shoe bag to hold your jewelry. Just pick up a shoe bag that has clear plastic pouches. Hardware and housewares stores and even many supermarkets sell them, in both hook-mounted and over-the-door versions. Give each necklace, bracelet, or large pin its own "room," and you can instantly grab whatever you need as you're dressing. *Note*: This system works best for jewelry that is on the chunky side, as opposed to delicate chains, which could become just as tangled in the bag as they would in a drawer.

of them—or any other big, brilliantly colored bangles, keep them in a large, clear glass bowl, where you can enjoy them even when you're not wearing them. No space for a bowl? Then get one of those vertical wooden holders that are meant for paper towels, and pop the bracelets over the center post.

PUNT THE PINS. Even though these little adornments are not as tangle-prone as necklaces and bracelets are, even a modest collection of pins can add up to big-time clutter when you stash them in a drawer. To free up space, and make a decorative statement at the same time, run down to your local fabric store and buy a length of grosgrain ribbon. (It'll cost pennies a yard.) Use a hole punch to make an opening in one end, and hang the ribbon from a hook on the back of the closet door or (if you have the space) on a wall of the closet. Then arrange your pins in a pleasing pattern along the length of the ribbon.

Instead of placing your furniture evenly around your bedroom walls, try putting your dressers close together near your closet. This way, you won't have to dart from one part of the room to another as you get dressed in the morning. Plus, with all of your clothing storage in one place, it'll take you less time to put the laundry away.

A MIRROR IMAGE. Have you ever heard of a jewelry mirror? Neither had I until recently, but you can find them in housewares catalogs and on the Internet, and they're a shining example of efficient bedroom organizing. What you see on the outside is a mirror, but it swings open to reveal a cabinet with designated spaces for holding bracelets, necklaces, rings, and earrings. These dandy things come in many sizes, finishes, and price ranges, in both wall-hung and freestanding models. What makes them so useful is that you can just reach in and grab the piece you want to wear, then put it on and use the mirror to see how it looks. Now that's what I call a picture-perfect solution!

ALL TOGETHER NOW. If you have certain pieces of jewelry that you always, or nearly always, wear together, then store them together. For instance, keep your gold necklace(s) in the same place as any matching bracelets, rings, and earrings. That way, when it's time to put them on, they'll all be right at your fingertips.

A TIP OF THE HAT(BOX). One of the easiest ways to organize all the small stuff that you've pulled from your bedroom drawers is to stash it in decorative hatboxes. You can pick them up for peanuts at thrift shops, flea markets, and yard sales. Or if you prefer fresh, new ones to vintage models, buy some from a discount craft-supply store. Even there, they'll set you back by only a few dollars each. Fill them up with gloves, scarves, sewing supplies, or whatever you want to keep close at hand. Then stack them in a corner, under a table, or on a shelf or tabletop. They'll add a decorative touch to your bedroom—and provide neat, dust-free storage at the same time.

A DROP IN THE BUCKET. Believe it or not, buckets can help you corral all kinds of former drawer clutter, from matchbooks to mittens and socks to small change. Use various sizes of containers if you like, but to avoid visual clutter, choose a single material. Your choices range from sleek stainless steel pails, available in pet-supply shops and housewares stores, to weathered sap buckets that were—and in some places, still are— used in the maple sugaring business. (You're most likely to find these at flea markets and junk shops in New England, but they also show up on Internet auction sites.) Another good option, especially for children's rooms,

COLLECTOR ALERT!

Problem: You like to wear a different pin every day, so you want easy access to your whole collection—but it's a *big* collection.

Solution: Attach your pins to a T-shirt, and hang it from the rod in your closet. (If you need even more room, use two or three T-shirts!) Your collection will be close at hand, and it'll be a snap to choose the piece you want to wear.

is the colorful, enameled-metal or plastic sand buckets that supermarkets and toy stores carry in the summertime.

BUTTON UP. If you have beautiful old or new buttons taking up valuable real estate in your dresser drawer, don't keep them hidden away. Turn a vest or jacket into a one-of-a-kind creation by sewing buttons all over the front of it. (Just don't put 'em on the back, or you'll get a rather uncomfortable surprise the first time you lean back in a chair!)

BOWL 'EM OVER. Pottery bowls are hot collectibles, whether they're vintage models from the '30s, '40s, and '50s, or handmade creations fresh from the potter's wheel. If you've got some of either kind, don't keep them hidden in a cupboard. And don't let them sit empty on a display shelf, either—at least not all of them. Instead, choose a few of your favorites, and distribute them around your bedroom in strategic spots, like the top of your dresser, your bedside table, or a wall shelf. Then use them as catchalls for small stuff like safety pins, hair clips, and any jewelry that you wear every day. *Tip:* To keep piles of clutter from building up in the bowls themselves, use each one to hold a single kind of object. For instance, put pins in one bowl, buttons in another, and so on.

BOWL 'EM OVER, PART TWO. You say you don't have a collection of beautiful bowls to stash your tiny

Ask Jerry

Q. *I have a large collection of earrings that are just too pretty to hide in a drawer or jewelry box. Do you have any ideas for displaying them in my bedroom?*

A. I have a picture-perfect idea! First, find an attractive picture frame that blends with the decor of your room. (You can pick up fabulous frames for next to nothing at thrift shops and garage sales.) If the backing and glass are still intact, remove them. Next, get some flexible window screening at your local hardware store, and cut it to fit the opening in the frame. Hot-glue the mesh onto the back of the frame, and hang your earrings from the screen. Hang the frame on the wall, or set it on top of your dresser and prop it against the wall.

treasures and trinkets in? No problem! Just trot off to a flea market, thrift shop, or housewares store, and buy some that appeal to you and that blend well together.

THE STUFF OF DAILY LIFE. Most likely, you have at least a few pieces of jewelry that you wear every day, like your wristwatch and maybe certain rings or a special locket. Well, do yourself a favor: When you take them off at night, put them in a small dish or box on your dresser. This way, you'll be able to grab them instantly in the morning—and they'll stand no chance of falling off the dresser top onto the floor or into a drawer.

THE BIG COVER-UP. Quilts, coverlets, throws, and afghans are handy things to keep in the bedroom, but they take up a lot of drawer space. And besides that, a lot of them are too attractive to stay tucked away out of sight. So instead of stashing them in a dresser, show them off with one of these display aids:

- A quilt rack. They come in styles to complement any decor, and they'll show off anywhere from three to six of your blankets, depending on their size and how you fold them.

- A stepladder. Either track down an old ladder at a flea market or antique shop, or buy a new wooden one at your local hardware store. If you like, paint it to match the style of your furnishings. Then lean it against a wall, fold your throws in thirds or quarters, and drape them over the ladder's rungs.

OUT OF THE BOX

No law says you have to have any drawers in your bedroom at all. In fact, one of the most organized people I know (a self-proclaimed clutterphobe) keeps all of her sweaters, T-shirts, sweat suits, and other foldable clothes on shelves. This way, she can see everything at a glance and instantly find the garment she wants. Smaller wearables, like socks, underwear, scarves, and panty hose, "live" in rectangular baskets that also sit on shelves. If you'd like to try this organizing system, simply trade in your dressers for armoires; lower, dresser-height cabinets; or both.

HELP FROM THE OL' DRUGSTORE. In days gone by, pharmacists (a.k.a. apothecaries) kept their powdered medicines in wooden chests that had scads of small drawers. When a customer came in with a prescription, the ingredients were always close at hand. Now you can often find these apothecary chests in antique stores and flea markets or—if you're very lucky—in your grandparents' attic or basement. If you do come across one, don't hesitate for a minute: Take it home and make it a focal point in your bedroom. It's just what the doctor ordered for corralling all kinds of potential clutter, from shoe polish and shoe horns to hair clips, combs, and even spare bulbs for your bedside lamps.

COUNT YOUR PENNIES. If you're like most folks, you end up with a pile of loose change on your dresser top after emptying your pockets or purse. Keep it neat by dropping your change into a clear glass jar or bowl. This way, you'll have the satisfaction of watching how quickly those coins add up. When the container is full, deposit the contents into your investment account, or use the cash to buy yourself a special treat.

STORE

Now that you've cleared everything out of your bedroom drawers and decided what doesn't belong there, it's time to restash the stuff that does. But remember: If you're not careful, those drawers will turn into black holes where your things will disappear, and before you know it you'll be right back in Clutterville again. So before you so much as tuck a single sock into your dresser, take some time to peruse the storage tips in this section. They'll help you make the most of your newly freed-up space.

MAKING SPACE

Corner cupboards are old standbys for adding storage space to kitchens and dining rooms. Well, guess what? They can work just as well in your bedroom. If you find one that has glass doors or open shelves on top, use that space to hold books, quilts, or decorative storage containers. Stash less attractive stuff like jeans, T-shirts, and everyday bedding behind the closed doors down below.

OUT OF THE KITCHEN AND INTO THE BEDROOM.

When it comes to storing jewelry and other small, clutter-prone objects in a drawer, three of the most useful helpers you'll ever find are right in your kitchen (or your local kitchen gadget store). What are they? This versatile trio:

1. Plastic egg holders (the ones that are designed to store eggs in the refrigerator)

2. Plastic ice cube trays

3. Divided cutlery holders

EGG 'EM ON. If you'd rather not go out and get a plastic egg holder, the next time you buy hen fruit, just save the container, and use it to hold rings, earrings, and other tiny doodads. Either paper, plastic, or foam egg cartons will work just fine.

THINK INSIDE THE BOXES. Shoe boxes, that is. They're exactly the right size for corralling small items like panty hose, underwear, socks, scarves, gloves, and small purses. Just load up the boxes (one type of item in each) and line them up neatly in a drawer that's just deep enough to hold them.

PAY THE PRICE. If shoe boxes and egg cartons aren't your style, trot off to a housewares store and buy a diamond drawer organizer. It's made up of plastic strips that interlock diagonally to form a diamond pattern, and you can cut it to fit any drawer. The little cubbyholes are intended to hold socks—one pair per diamond—but they're ideal for storing anything that's small enough to fit inside, from cuff links to earmuffs.

MESS-MAKER ALERT!

Problem: The mirror over your dresser makes it look like you've got twice as much stuff in the room.

Solution: Get rid of that mirror and replace it with a full-length version that's attached to the back of your closet or bathroom door. It'll cut visual bedroom clutter in half, and you'll be able to see yourself from head to toe—not just from the hips up as you do in a dresser-top mirror.

GET ON A ROLL. If your dresser has two shallow drawers on top, count yourself lucky! You've got the perfect place to store belts, sashes, scarves, and/or neckties. In each case, just roll them up, and arrange them inside the drawers. When you need any one of them, it'll be in full view and ready to wear.

DON'T HAVE A BALL. There's nothing more irritating than having to plow through a drawer in search of two matching socks. So most folks keep their foot covers paired up by folding the tops over together, forming a sort of ball. Well, take my advice: Don't do that! Granted, it does keep your socks together, but it also stretches the elastic, thereby reducing their life span. Instead, clip the two mates together with a safety pin or spring clothespin.

WHAT GOES WHERE? When it comes to assigning drawer space to your various belongings, you have a couple of options. Consider these methods, and try the arrangement that seems most appealing. If it doesn't work, try the other one.

• Keep like things together. For instance, store all your sweaters in one drawer, T-shirts in another, blue jeans in still another, and so on.

• Separate your duds by their purpose. Here, the categories might consist of the clothes you wear to work, your casual weekend attire, and dressier outfits. If you have clothes that you wear for particular activities—for instance, golf, tennis, or cycling—keep those items together in a separate drawer.

OUT OF THE BOX

Accessories aren't the only things in your wardrobe that lend themselves well to being rolled up. Consider rolling blue jeans, sweaters, T-shirts, polo shirts, and cotton turtlenecks, and placing them in a single layer in a shallow drawer. They'll stay wrinkle-free and, best of all, you won't have to dig down through a stack of garments to find the one you want to wear.

SLEEPING BEAUTY

Nothing beats a good night's sleep. Not only do we feel better when we've had our eight hours, but scientific research shows that when we get a good night's sleep we're more apt to fend off everything from heart disease to extra weight to wrinkles. And there's nothing like the sight of a calm, clutterless bedtime area to promote sound slumber. Here's how to get it.

In This Section:
✔ On the bed
✔ At the foot
   of the bed
✔ Under the bed
✔ Bedside

SORT

If you've gotten into the habit of letting stuff pile up in the area around your bed, I have just two words to say to you: Stop it! With the help of these hints, you can make your sleepy-time zone a serene place where nothing gets between you and your z's (with the possible exception of a little, er, recreation with your spouse).

MAKE ROOM TO BREATHE. It is true that home decor is a highly subjective matter. What one person sees as a homey, cozy retreat, another may see as a cluttered mess. But, as designers know, a space that contains just a few large objects looks and feels more spacious and serene than one that's filled with a lot of small things—no matter how beautiful they may be. The bottom line: Keep stuff to a minimum in your sleeping area.

TA-TA, TINY TREASURES. The bedroom is no place to keep small collectibles, whether they're whimsical souvenirs you've picked up in your travels, or valuable brand-name figurines. So gather 'em up and get 'em outta there! You'll enjoy them more—and sleep a whole lot better—if you move them to a display cabinet somewhere else in the house.

PUT AN END TO LITERARY LITTER. Your bedside table is not a bookcase. Remove any books or magazines that you are not currently reading, and put them on the shelves where they belong.

WORKS IN PROGRESS. Even magazines and paperback books that you are reading can make quite a mess when they're just piled up on your nightstand or on the floor beside your bed. The simple solution: Pick 'em up and put 'em in a basket. It'll take just seconds—and you'll be amazed at how much more restful and inviting your sleeping area looks!

BUCK THE TREND. When you pick up any home decorating magazine, you're likely to see beds piled sky-high with dolls, stuffed animals, and decorative pillows in just about every size, shape, and fabric you can think of. Well, that more-is-more look may appear charming in a photograph, but in real life it creates visual busyness that makes your sleeping quarters feel anything but restful. What's more, that jumble of stuff creates *real* busyness for you because you have to take it off the bed every night, and rearrange it all the next morning. So whittle the inventory down to the pillows you actually use, with at most a couple of your favorite adornments. They'll stand out more anyway—and you'll have less work to do at the start and the end of each day.

TRASH THE TRASH. If you keep a wastebasket beside your bed, empty it on a regular basis. That one simple step will ease the visual clutter in your sleeping space.

Ask Jerry

Q. I have a stationary exercise bike that I use every day. It's certainly not the most attractive thing in the world, but the only place I have room for it is in my bedroom. Any ideas on how I can make it look less, well, prominent?

A. First, put your bike in the most out-of-the-way spot you have in your bedroom. An alcove is perfect, but a corner will do in a pinch. Then get a lightweight, folding room screen with panels that are made of fabric or rice paper, and place it so that it will conceal the bike. Then anytime you want to climb aboard and pedal, just move the screen out of the way. *Note:* A freestanding screen is also great for concealing other unsightly but essential gear, like a treadmill, vacuum cleaner, or television set.

STOP INVADERS FROM THE BATHROOM. Tired of seeing wet towels slung on the bed or dropped on the bedroom floor? Then try this simple trick: Hang a wall-mounted quilt rack on the back of the bedroom or bathroom door, or on a wall (or use a freestanding one if you have the room), to catch wet towels.

DON'T PAY YOUR BILLS. Not in bed, that is. Not only is it an extremely unrestful thing to do, but it's also a surefire way to clog your sleeping area with envelopes, stamps, receipts, and other odds and ends—and get ink stains on your sheets, besides! So gather up any finance-related material and take it elsewhere. As for how to organize your bill paying and other money matters, see Chapter Four, "The Home Office," starting on page 133.

NIX THE NIGHTSTANDS. Just because you bought (or inherited) a matched set of bedroom furniture that came with a couple of nightstands doesn't mean you have to use the things. In fact, they can make a small room seem even more cramped. So increase your space by hanging a wall shelf on one or both sides of your bed, and use it (or them) to hold your phone, alarm clock, and whatever else must remain at arm's reach. On the other hand, if you do have a little space to spare at your bedside, check out the tips beginning on page 21 (see "Depend on Drawers"). They'll help you make the most of every inch!

SOOTHE YOUR SOUL.
It may seem that the decor you choose for your bedroom has nothing to do with clutter, but that's not the case at all. In fact, with one simple move, you can eliminate visual clutter and

COLLECTOR ALERT!

Problem: Your snapshot collection is cluttering your nightstand—and every other horizontal surface in the bedroom.

Solution: Put your best photographs in frames that are all the same size and color, and hang them on the wall in a single grouping. You'll streamline your surroundings and still have your family, friends, and vacation memories to cherish every day.

make your whole room seem more restful and serene. How? Simply weed out any bold colors and busy prints—in bedding, curtains, wallpaper, or what have you—and replace them with solid colors in soft, soothing tones. If you absolutely must have at least one pattern in the room, confine it to one place. For example, use a fancy print for the curtains, and pick up one of the colors for the bedspread, or vice versa.

ORGANIZE

Everyone needs to have certain objects within easy reach of the bed. For just about all of us, that includes an alarm clock, a telephone, and a lamp. You'll probably also want to include other things, too—like reading glasses, your TV remote, an eye mask, and the book you're currently reading. The key to making your bedtime area a place for rest and relaxation is to have only the gear that really matters to you, and to organize it so that it's accessible, but doesn't clutter up the space.

ONE "SIZE" DOES NOT FIT ALL. As you start to organize your sleeping area, gear the arrangement to your personal habits. For instance, if you watch television in bed every night, position the set directly across from you. If you like to listen to music as you fall asleep—or you sometimes need it to mask noise coming from the street or the adjacent apartment, then keep your CD player close at hand, along with a few of your favorite, snooze-inducing recordings.

AS YOUR MOTHER ALWAYS TOLD YOU... Get your clothes off the floor! Or make sure your spouse and/or children pick theirs up—without having to constantly nag them. How? Simply hang a coatrack on the bedroom wall. Then you (or your loved ones) can toss pajamas, hats, or shirts over the hooks instead of dropping them on the rug.

MAKING SPACE To gain a lot more space on your bedside tables, simply get rid of your freestanding lamps and replace them with wall-hung versions. And if you like to read in bed, opt for the swing-arm kind that lets you direct light anywhere you want it.

MAKE YOUR BED. Even a bedroom that's as neat as a pin looks like a disaster area when the bed is dressed in rumpled sheets and caved-in pillows. So do yourself a favor: Take a few minutes every morning to smooth the sheets, plump up the pillows, and pull up the bedspread. You'll be amazed at how much more welcoming the room will look when you're ready to turn in for the night!

MAKE A STATEMENT. Exercise your creative urge and neaten up your z's zone at the same time by making your own hanging rack. Here are two easy, inexpensive options:

- Pick up an old wooden shutter at a flea market, or buy a new one at a local lumberyard or home-improvement center. Screw clothes hooks (available at your local hardware store) into the frame, and attach the shutter to the wall using nails, screws, or picture wire and hooks.

- Paint or stain a wood board to complement your decor, and screw old doorknobs into the wood. Then fasten your new rack to the wall, using any of the methods described above.

OUT OF THE BOX

If you like to watch television while you're in bed, this tip has your name written all over it: Instead of keeping the remote on top of your nightstand, where it can easily tumble off, attach it to the side with Velcro™ tape. Then it'll always be within easy reach.

LAZY DOES IT. Tired of having to stretch across your bedside table to snag something that's almost out of reach? Then head to the kitchen (or the closest kitchen-supply store) and grab a lazy Susan. Set it on the table, arrange your stuff on top of it, and presto—whatever you want is only a quick spin away!

DEPEND ON DRAWERS. When it comes to organizing your bedside stuff and enhancing the uncluttered appearance of your room, a small chest of drawers can work wonders. Choose one that is the right height for your bed and the right width for the available space. If it doesn't complement the room's decor, and you lack the time or inclination to paint or refinish it, just toss a tablecloth over the top—that is, of course, after you've filled the drawers with out-of-season clothes and other odds and ends that you don't need very often. Keep your reading glasses, a water glass, and the other usual "suspects" on the surface.

ROLL OUT THE BARREL. Trade your nightstand in for a wooden barrel. Either scout up an old one at a flea market or junk shop, or buy a fresh new one at a lumberyard, home-improvement center, or anyplace that sells wine-making supplies. Then follow this five-step routine to convert that big keg into an organizational superstar:

1. Make sure the inside of the barrel is clean and spotless.

2. Clean up the outside, too, and decorate it to suit your taste.

3. Cut a piece of wood (either round or square) to cover the top, or have the folks at your local lumberyard cut it for you.

4. Fill the barrel with whatever you want to store in there—perhaps beach towels and such in the winter, and bulky down comforters during the summer months.

5. Toss a tablecloth over the top, and bingo: You've got a hardworking and elegant bedside helper!

OUT OF THE BOX

If your decor is on the rustic side, you can find some fabulous nightstand substitutes at the closest farmers' market—or even your local supermarket— for absolutely nothing. What are they? Empty wooden produce crates. Just stack 'em two or three high on one or both sides of your bed, and use 'em to hold everything from books and magazines to your alarm clock and bedside box of tissues.

MORE BEDSIDE OPTIONS. For my money, when you're setting out to organize your sleeping area, there's no such thing as too many good ideas. Here are a few of my favorite ways to use space more efficiently:

- An old piano bench with a flip-top lid makes a perfect nightstand for small quarters (provided your bed isn't too high). Keep your nightly necessities on top, stash less frequently used things inside, and tuck a basket underneath to hold books and magazines.

- Instead of a conventional nightstand, use a wall-hung cupboard. Find a veteran performer at a flea market or antique store, or pick up a sleek new one at a home-improvement center. If the cupboard has a drawer on the bottom, so much the better. Hang it within reach, then arrange your clock, box of tissues, bedtime reading material, and what have you on the shelves. Use the drawer to keep things like your medications, flashlight, and extra batteries secure and out of sight.

- Tables come in all shapes, sizes, and materials—and just about any one of them can make an outstanding bedside partner. Choose the one that best suits the space you have and the job you want it to do. For instance, if all you need is a flat surface to keep a few key items on, a table with a decorative pedestal would work just fine. On the other hand, if your bedside area has to hold any more than that, go with a table that has a drawer, one or more shelves, or space below that'll hold your stuff.

STORE

There's plenty of storage space in your sleeping area—it's just playing hide-and-seek. Where can you find it? Try looking under the bed, in front of the bed, and on the walls, for starters.

SKIRT THE ISSUE. Every night you sleep on top of one of the best storage areas you have in your bedroom—or anywhere else in your house, for that matter. The space under your bed is the perfect place to tuck away everything from out-of-season clothes to nonbedroom gear like the silver flatware that you use only on special occasions. Just put your storables in shallow containers, shove them under the bed, and hide them with a bed skirt or dust ruffle.

THIS MAY SEEM OBVIOUS, BUT... Whatever you choose to stash under your bed, be sure you put it in some sort of covered container. Otherwise, you're just asking for a mess because even in the best-kept house, under-bed dust bunnies can multiply like, well, bunnies.

MAKING SPACE One of the simplest ways to gain more storage space in your sleeping area is to buy a set of bed risers, and put one under each leg of your bed. Depending on the height of the risers you choose, you'll increase your vertical storage area by anywhere from 3 inches to a foot. (Of course, you will need to get a longer bed skirt to hide all the stuff under there, but that's a small price to pay for all that extra room.) To find some of these dandy devices, crank up your favorite Internet search engine and type in "bed risers."

THE CONTAINMENT POLICY. Housewares stores and catalogs (both paper and Web-based) sell containers made of plastic, stiff fabric, and fabric-covered cardboard that are especially designed to fit under beds. But any of these will do the trick, too:

- Large, zippered plastic bags (like the kind blankets and bedspreads come in)
- Shallow, covered baskets
- Suitcases
- Vacuum-sealed, space-saver bags (available from catalogs and housewares stores)

BEST BETS FOR UNDER-BED STORAGE.

If it's time to shop for a new bed, consider looking for an old one. Antique bed frames sit higher off the floor than most modern ones do—thereby providing more under-bed storage space. Check around at thrift shops, flea markets, and (of course) antique stores for old frames. On the other hand, if you prefer your decor on the modern side, maybe one of these two trim-looking options is your answer to better bedroom storage:

1. Platform beds are designed to hold a mattress without the need for a box spring. They're about the same height as a conventional, modern bed frame—so you get a good foot or more of storage space that would otherwise be occupied by the box spring.

2. A captain's bed won't actually give you any more storage space than a regular bed, but it does offer a big organizational bonus: built-in drawers. This style of bed is on a platform with the drawers underneath. So you can stow your gear neatly out of sight.

There is no rule that says you have to keep all of your bed linens or clothes in your sleeping quarters. If you have a tiny bedroom, you can cut a whole lot of clutter by finding someplace else to store things that you don't need every day. For instance, you might keep bulky sweaters in a trunk that doubles as a coffee table in your living room. Or fold extra blankets neatly, and stash them in the bottom of a dining room hutch. Just let your creative juices flow, and you can find a whole lot of storage space you never knew you had!

ZONED FOR ACCESS. Regardless of how much under-bed storage space you have, it's important to organize it carefully. Otherwise, your belongings can just vanish into that cave, and you'll have to go on a spelunking expedition every time you want to get something out. So before you shove anything under your bed, ask yourself exactly how you want to use that space. To be more specific, do you:

1. Want to push out-of-season clothing and gear out of sight and out of mind?

2. Want to keep frequently used things out of the way, but within easy reach?

3. Need storage space for items in both of those categories?

DON'T MIX AND MINGLE! If your answer to question number 3 is yes, whatever you do, make sure you divide the space into two zones:

• One should be within easy reach for things that you may want to grab at any moment, such as wrapping paper, in-season sports equipment, or extra bed linens.

• The other should be farther back for things that you won't need for months, like winter blankets or Christmas decorations in the summer, or badminton rackets and beach towels in the winter.

PLAY FOOTSIE. The foot of your bed is a terrific place to add extra storage to your sleeping area. And you have plenty of options that are just as attractive as they are useful. Choose a piece of furniture that fits along the foot of your bed and is no taller than your mattress. Use it to hold blankets, sheets, extra pillows, or Christmas presents that are waiting to be turned over to Santa Claus. Excellent choices include:

Ask Jerry

Q. I know that under the bed is a great place to store things, but every time I want to get something out from under there, I spend too much time on the floor digging around to find what I need. Any tips?

A. Put all that stuff on wheels! Visit your local lumberyard or hardware store, and pick up a sheet of finished plywood, four casters, a couple of eye hooks, and some rope. Cut the plywood to the size you need (or have the store do it for you). Screw a caster to each corner, and attach a length of rope to each side, using the two eye hooks. Load the platform with the things you're storing, and roll it under the bed. Then, whenever you need something, grab onto a rope and pull it out.

- ✔ Bench with a lift-up top

- ✔ Blanket, a.k.a. hope, chest

- ✔ Extra dresser

- ✔ Old footlocker or steamer trunk

- ✔ Wicker hamper (or a couple of them, stacked up or placed side by side)

BRING IT TO THE TABLE.
A long, narrow table with a drawer or two at the foot of the bed is perfect for storing things that are less bulky than blankets and pillows. Put small odds and ends in the drawers and in decorative boxes on the tabletop. Tuck attractive baskets underneath it to provide even more stowaway space.

CREATIVE CASES. A low bookcase at the foot of your bed can hold books and magazines (of course), along with storage containers like baskets, boxes, and bowls. But if that arrangement won't work for you, use a small bookcase in place of a nightstand. Or go all out, and build floor-to-ceiling shelves on either side of your bed, and connect them with one or two shelves running all the way across at the top.

DON'T GET BOOKED. In almost every furniture store, you can buy headboards with built-in shelves. It is true that they give you plenty of extra storage space in a very handy spot. The trouble is that when you pile up your pillows and lean back to enjoy your bedtime reading or

MAKING
S P A C E

What do you do when you have a bedroom that's so small that the bed itself is clutter? Depending on the circumstances, you have a couple of excellent options. In a guest room that doubles as your home office or hobby room, go with a Murphy bed. This clever device can disappear completely during the day, folding up into the wall or into a freestanding cabinet. Plus, because it has a conventional mattress, a Murphy is much more comfortable than a sleeper sofa.

If you need additional sleeping space for your kids' pals who stay overnight, get a trundle bed. When it's not in use, it rolls right under the regular bed.

your favorite TV show, you'll probably shove everything out of place, or even knock something over. My advice is to stick with a good, solid headboard, and stash your stuff elsewhere.

LOOK UP. Instead of hanging a picture on the wall above your headboard, as lots of folks do, use that space for storage. Just hang one or two shelves and use them to hold boxes or baskets filled with out-of-season accessories or other small things that you don't use very often. To make the arrangement even more decorative, use a mantel top instead of simple shelves. Look for an old one at antique shops, architectural salvage dealers, and flea markets, or buy a new one.

END BEDROOM CLOSET CHAOS

In This Section:
✔ Clothes
✔ Shoes
✔ Accessories

In most homes, the closet is the bedroom's worst clutter culprit, and it can strike fear in the heart of even the most determined anticlutter crusader. Well, don't fret! Whether you're lucky enough to be planning a new closet, or you just want to make the most of the one you've got now, help is close at hand. Even a closet that's been crammed to the hilt for decades can be transformed. Just follow our SOS plan, and you'll have the closet of your dreams—or close to it—in no time at all.

SORT

When it comes to a bedroom closet, there's no doubt that deciding what to keep and what to lose is the most crucial but difficult part of the whole operation. Start by clearing the decks (the floor, rather) to make room for the same five boxes or piles that you designated for your drawer-declogging project: Trash, Keep Here, Take Elsewhere, Donate or Sell, and Recycle. Then charge ahead, and let the following tips be your guide.

A PAINLESS WAY TO START. Maybe you're dreading
the thought of sorting through your clothes because you haven't
really examined your wardrobe since the last time you bought bell-
bottom, hip-hugger jeans in a size 4. Or perhaps you simply have
trouble making decisions about what to keep and what to pitch.
Either way, I know a simple trick that will get you into pitching mode
in a hurry: Before you even touch a single garment, gather up all of
the empty hangers in your closet, and
get them out of there. Chances are,
you'll be amazed at how much space
you'll free up.

HANGER HANDLING 101. So
what do you do with all those hangers?
For starters, toss 'em into your Take
Elsewhere box. Then as soon as you
can, return any wire ones to the dry
cleaner they came from. As for the high-
quality wooden or plastic ones, here's a
trio of terrific ways to keep them from
cluttering up your closet:

MAKING SPACE If you've managed
to accumulate
more nice-looking
hangers than you
can possibly use
anywhere in your
house, put the extras into your
Donate or Sell box. Any thrift
shop will be delighted to take
them off your hands. And good
hangers—especially vintage
wooden ones—sell like hotcakes
at yard sales.

• Take some hangers to a closet in a
  guest room or entryway, where they're
  always in demand.

• Stash a supply in your laundry room, so they'll be ready to use for
  clothes coming out of the washer or dryer.

• If there's enough room in your bedroom closet, install a short rod just
  for empty hangers. Otherwise, hang them together in one section of a
  regular rod.

CUT YOUR LOSSES. No matter how much you may have paid
for it, any article of clothing that falls into one or more of the following

categories needs to go into either the Trash or the Donate or Sell box—pronto!

- Hopelessly stained
- Worn or frayed
- Too revealing
- Not age-appropriate
- Too dowdy
- Too big
- Too small
- Not comfortable

SEPARATE THE BEST FROM THE REST. To take your de-cluttering to the highest possible level, don't hang on to anything that's simply okay. Instead, take a tip from the most well-organized—and best-dressed—women I know, and keep only those garments, shoes, and accessories that meet these criteria:

- ✔ It fits perfectly.
- ✔ You absolutely love it.
- ✔ It flatters your figure and your complexion.
- ✔ It makes you feel good every time you put it on.

BACK TO REALITY. Of course, in real life, most of us have at least a few things in our wardrobes that we're not crazy about—or even dislike—but that we need to wear from time to time. For instance, maybe you have an outfit or two for formal evening events, or for especially dressy daytime

OUT OF THE BOX

A rule of thumb for sorting clothes—and shoes, too—is that if you haven't worn something in a year or more, you should get rid of it. By and large, that's good advice, but what if you come across some things that fall into that category, but you're pretty sure you'll want to wear them again? In that case, cut yourself a little slack. (After all, this is supposed to be an exercise in organization, not deprivation!) Gather up those duds, and put them into a box labeled "Maybe." Tape up the box, write today's date on it, and store it in a spare closet or wherever else you have room for it. Then make yourself a note on your calendar to check on your stash in one year. If 12 months go by, and you still haven't wanted anything that's in the box, pack it off to a thrift shop or consignment store.

occasions, like weddings, funerals, and graduations. And, if you're like a lot of folks, you probably bought those duds on short notice, and didn't have time to find something that suited you to a T. Well, here's my advice: Hang on to them for now, because you're bound to need them again. But whenever you're out shopping, especially at a thrift shop or consignment store, keep an eye out for possible replacements that fit my four criteria for wardrobe "keepers" (see "Separate the Best from the Rest" at left). Then, when you come across a winner, snap it up, and get rid of its so-so counterpart in your closet.

GIVE SHOES THE BOOT. Go through your shoes, boots, and bedroom slippers using the same criteria you used for sorting your clothes. Get rid of any footwear you don't like or haven't worn in heaven knows how long, and anything that isn't comfortable, doesn't flatter your legs, or is worn beyond repair.

PITCH IT OR GO SHOPPING—NOW. A classic piece of clutter-control advice is to get rid of any garment or accessory that does not go with anything else you currently own. In most cases,

MAKING SPACE

One of the simplest ways to increase the space in your closet is to clear out any garments or accessories that are out of season or that you seldom wear (formal clothes, for instance). Either move them to a spare closet, or tuck them into appropriate containers and stash them under your bed, in the attic, in a dry basement, or anyplace else you have room for them.

that is exactly what I recommend, too. But if you bought (let's say) a one-of-a-kind vest or jacket that you fell madly in love with at an art fair or craft shop, it may deserve a second chance. On the other hand, it may not. To make the call, ask yourself these four questions:

1. Do I love it as much now as I did when I bought it?

2. Does it still fit?

3. Does it still look good on me?

4. Do I have the time and inclination to find something that works well with it?

If the answer to all four questions is "yes," then put the search for a match at the top of your to-do list—and start looking *tomorrow!* If the answer to any one of those questions is "no," then send the thing packing. Either give it to a friend who will love it as much as you do, place it with a consignment store, advertise it for sale over the Internet, or give it to a thrift shop and take a tax deduction.

GET A SECOND OPINION.

Sometimes it's hard to know for sure how you really look in a particular piece of clothing—especially if it's something you bought simply because it was "your" color, or because it was (and maybe still is) at the height of style. In that case, enlist the help of a friend whose taste you respect and whom you trust to give you an honest, objective opinion. Invite her over and model the things you're undecided about. Besides getting some good advice, you may find a happy home for some of your castoffs!

LOOK A GIFT HORSE IN THE
MOUTH. A whole lot of folks I know
just cannot bring themselves to part with anything they got as a gift—even if it doesn't fit, it doesn't go with anything else they own, or they simply don't like it. Well, if that description fits you, do yourself a favor and change your ways. Remember, as the old saying goes, it's the thought that counts. So take a picture of the thing—or have one taken of you wearing it—and tuck the snapshot into a photo album or scrapbook. This way, you can keep fond memories of

Ask Jerry

Q. *I have some special-occasion dresses that I know I'll never wear again, but I just can't bear to part with. What can I do with them?*

A. First, take a picture of each garment. Then do what resourceful women have been doing for centuries: Cut the dresses into pieces and use them to make a quilt. Or commission an expert to do the job for you. To find a first-class quilter in your area, check with the folks who run the closest quilt-supply shop. Keep the photos in an album, and put the quilt on display where it will bring you joy every time you look at it.

the giver's thoughtfulness, while you get rid of the unwanted gift in one of these ways:

- Give it to a thrift shop that benefits your friend's favorite charity.

- Sell it yourself and donate the proceeds to a cause your pal cares about.

HELP 'EM GIVE A SHOW. It's always easier to part with something when you can give it to someone who will really enjoy it. If you know any kids who love putting on shows or playing dress-up, earmark some of your closet castoffs for them. Any items that are brightly colored, silky, sparkly, fuzzy, or feathery will be perfect. Put them all in a toy chest or vintage suitcase, and present it to the young entertainers. You'll get rave reviews—and so will they—guaranteed!

'TIS THE SEASON. Cleaning out your closet is not a one-time event—that is, not unless you want it to become a jumbled mess again! The key to a truly clutter-free closet is to sort through your clothes at the beginning of each new season. Check every piece for moth holes, mildew, or other damage that may have occurred, and get rid of any items that can't be repaired. If you've gained or lost weight, weed out anything that no longer fits. And if you even look at something and think, "Why on earth did I buy that?" give it the boot without another thought.

PACK RAT ALERT!

Problem: You have clothes you like that fit just fine, but need minor repairs.

Solution: Tuck those duds into a box, and write the date on the outside. If you do your own mending, carry the carton to your sewing room. Otherwise, put it in the trunk of your car, so you can take it to a tailor or seamstress who can make the necessary repairs. Whatever you do, don't put those clothes back into your closet until they're in wearable condition again. Set a realistic time limit, based upon the time you have to do the work, or the money your budget will allow for professional help. When the deadline arrives, get rid of anything that's still sitting un-mended in the box.

GAIN ONE, LOSE ONE. Let's say you get your closet all neat and orderly, but in no time at all, it's jam-packed again. Here's how to solve that little problem: Make a rule that every time you buy (or you're given) a piece of clothing, you give another item to a thrift shop. You'll prevent "creeping clutter" in your closet and help someone else at the same time!

ORGANIZE

Now that you've pared down the stuff that was clogging up your closet, it's time to organize what's left. And take it from me: When your closet has a place for everything, and everything is in its place, you'll feel like a million bucks! So ponder this passel of possibilities, and pick the ones that seem most likely to work for you.

TAKE INVENTORY. The first step is to sort everything in your Keep Here box into categories, and then count the individual items in each category. These should include:

- Bathrobes and lingerie
- Dresses
- Jackets and vests
- Pants
- Shirts and blouses
- Shoes and boots
- Skirts
- Suits

COUNT THESE, TOO—MAYBE. If you store foldable clothes like T-shirts, sweaters, and pajamas on shelves in your closet, include them in your tally. And don't forget any accessories, such as scarves, belts, gloves, and handbags, that "live" in your closet now, or that you'd like to make room for.

When you're organizing the space in your closet, make room for one essential piece of "furniture" that's guaranteed to stop future clutter in its tracks. What is this miracle worker? A simple box. As you come across any clothes, accessories, or jewelry that you don't want to keep— for whatever reason—toss them into the box. When it's full, take it to a thrift shop or women's shelter.

REORGANIZING OPTIONS. When it comes to reconfiguring that nice, empty space you've got in your closet (regardless of how much of it there is) you have three choices:

1. Leave the basic design as it is, and add individual storage pieces, such as shoe racks, specialized hangers, or even bins, boxes, and baskets that you may already have around your house. This won't give you a dream closet, but with a little creativity, you can come pretty close while spending very little money.

2. Essentially "gut" the closet and build yourself a custom storage system (or hire someone else to do the job). If you've looked at any decorating or home-improvement magazine lately, you know there are more custom-closet builders than you can shake a coatrack at. This option can be very time-consuming if you do the work yourself, and hiring a specialist will cost you a pretty penny. On the plus side, if it's done well, you will end up with exactly the arrangement you— and your wardrobe—need.

3. Opt for a premade organizing system. At many local hardware stores, you can buy either entire kits or individual pieces, including vinyl-coated wire shelves, brackets, hooks, hangers, bins, and racks of various types and sizes. You simply attach them to the walls, and to each other, in just about any configuration you like. For anyone who's handy with tools, the installation process is fairly simple. As for the cost, the price will vary considerably, depending on the size of your closet and the components you choose—but any way you slice it, you'll pay a lot less than you would for a custom-built system.

MAKING SPACE

Does your bedroom have an alcove that isn't earning its keep? Then turn it into a closet. Hang a wall-to-wall rod for your clothes—or use two rods, one below the other, if your ceiling is high enough. To make "doors," attach a curtain rod just below the ceiling, and hang curtains or draperies from it.

MEASURE THE SPACE. This step is crucial to the success of your closet de-cluttering mission, because not only will you have to match your storage methods and containers to the kinds of clothes and accessories you have—but you'll have to make the whole shebang fit into your available space. Before you start measuring, draw a sketch of your closet, writing the numbers down as you go. And don't forget to include the height of the walls!

MEASURE YOUR STUFF. Boots and bulky accessories like hats and handbags can take up a fair amount of room—and they can vary so much in size and shape that it's a good idea to measure them individually to be sure they'll fit neatly. Fortunately, for garments on hangers there's a simple rule of thumb: For each one, you need to allow $1/2$ to 1 inch on your clothes rod.

Ask Jerry

Q. I have a lot of work clothes that are navy blue and black, and I have a dickens of a time telling them apart in my closet. Any suggestions (short of installing extra-bright spotlights)?

A. I have a system that works like a charm: Just use different-colored plastic hangers. For instance, hang your navy clothes on white hangers and your black clothes on black hangers. Never again will you show up at work wearing a navy blazer with a black skirt!

FAR AND WIDE. If you're planning to add a rod or two to your closet, you'll need to decide how far from the wall it should go—and that depends on the width of the things you'll be hanging from it. Most clothes will have plenty of room on a rod that's 21 inches away from the wall. On the other hand, bulky winter coats will need an additional 2 to 3 inches.

THE LONG AND SHORT OF IT. How high your clothes rods need to be depends—of course—on the length of the clothes you intend to hang from them. Once you've grouped your duds into categories (dresses, skirts, and so on), measure the longest garment in each group, from the top of the hanger to the bottom of the hem.

Add another 6 inches for "breathing" room, and that's how much vertical space you'll need for each category.

HOW THINGS STACK UP. To figure out how much shelf space you'll need for T-shirts, sweaters, and so on, first divide your foldables into stacks that are no more than 12 inches high. Then simply line them up and haul out your tape measure. (Be sure to allow an inch or so between stacks so you have room to maneuver.)

DOUBLE YOUR PLEASURE. Or at least the hanging space in your closet. How? Simply hang two rods: one up high, and the second one below it. The exact measurements will depend on the height of your ceiling, the lengths of the garments in your wardrobe, and how high you can reach comfortably. (Of course, you can always keep a step stool in the closet to snag hard-to-reach hangers.)

REFINING THE SYSTEM. Organizing your clothes according to their length is a great way to maximize space in any closet. But if you have the room, go one step further by grouping your duds in whatever way makes it easiest for you to find them. Any of these category breakdowns might work for you:

- Color

- Function (work clothes, casual clothes, dressy clothes)

- Type of garment (skirts, dresses, pants, jackets, shirts, suits)

WEIGHTY MATTERS. Does your weight tend to fluctuate enough that you keep two different sizes of clothing on hand? If so, then this organizing tip has your name written all over it: Store

MAKING SPACE

If your ceiling is too low to allow for a second rod, make the most of the one you've got by hanging all your long garments on one side, and all your short ones on the other. Then use the space underneath the short things to hold a few shelves, a large shoe rack, or even a small dresser.

your "skinny" wardrobe in one part of your closet and your "plump" garments in another area. If your space simply won't allow for that plan, then use different-colored hangers for the larger and smaller sizes.

STORE

There is no such thing as a closet that's too big. No matter how much stuff you've gotten rid of, or how well you've organized the space in your closet, there's always room for more, well, room! So check out these clever ways to increase your storage space—and make your life simpler, to boot.

Even though you don't want to put your clothes on wire hangers, it is a good idea to keep one or two of them in your closet—that is, if you have any skirts or dresses that tend to cling to your legs. To get rid of static cling without resorting to smelly chemical sprays, just run the flat side of a wire hanger over the outer surface of your skirt, and then repeat the process on the underside.

GET UNWIRED. After you've pared your wardrobe down to the things you love to wear, and you've carefully reorganized your closet, don't you dare put your treasured duds back in there on wire hangers! Even with their $0 price tag, they're no bargain because they can stretch garments out of shape, or send them slipping off onto the floor, where they then lie in a wrinkled heap. Instead, protect your clothing by opting for these:

• Hangers with either clips or spring-type bar clamps for pants and skirts

• Padded hangers for delicate silk and lightweight cotton dresses and blouses

• Wooden or heavy-duty molded plastic hangers for jackets, suits, and shirts

• Wooden or lightweight plastic hangers with notched shoulders for dresses or tops that have thin straps

BEHIND CLOSED DOORS. If the back of your closet door is just standing there, as bare as a newborn's bottom, shame on you!

From a storage standpoint, that space is some of the most valuable real estate in your bedroom. Just take a gander at some of the space-stretching superstars you can hang on that door. (You can find all of them at just about any housewares store.)

✔ Racks or individual hooks for robes, purses, belts, hats, or tote bags

✔ A shallow cabinet to store cosmetics, shoe polish, or containers of pins, buttons, or other tiny trinkets

✔ A shoe rack that's specially designed to store from 20 to as many as 40 pairs of footgear

✔ A shoe bag to hold scarves, socks, jewelry, small odds and ends, or (of course) shoes

✔ A trouser rack that can hold up to 20 pairs of pants on separate dowels that swing out from the door

HOMEMADE HELP. If you'd rather *make* storage devices for your closet door than buy them, consider these two ultrasimple options:

> ## MAKING
> ### S P A C E
>
>
>
> Do you always wear a certain jacket and shirt with the same pants or skirt? If so, then combine all three garments on one sturdy wooden hanger. But don't stop there! If you always wear certain accessories with that outfit, add them to the group, too. For instance, hook a belt, necklace, and/or bracelets over the top of the hanger, and drape or loosely tie a scarf around the hanger's neck. Bingo—you'll have a complete ensemble rarin' to go. You'll save closet space and put an end to last-minute accessory searches in one fell swoop.

1. Hang several brass or stainless steel chains from hooks on the inside of the door. Attach S-hooks to each chain, about 6 inches apart, and use them to hang belts, bags, or chunky necklaces.

2. Scout around in your attic or basement for an old towel bar, or buy a basic new one from your local hardware store—for a lot less than you'd pay for a fancy tie rack at a housewares store. Screw it to the back of your closet door, and drape scarves, sashes, or ties over the bar.

PASS BY PLASTIC BAGS. We all have clothes in our closets that we don't wear every week, or even every month. And it's always a good idea to keep them covered up so they don't collect dust. But whatever you do, don't store them in plastic bags. Moisture will be trapped inside the plastic, and can eventually damage the fabric beyond repair. So instead, either invest in garment bags that are made of breathable material, or make your own dust deterrents from old sheets. Simply cut a hole in the middle of the sheet for the hanger, and drape the cloth over your clothes.

ABOUT THOSE SHOES...

Shoes that are sitting loose on a closet floor can turn into a jumbled mess before you know it. Shoe storage units, commonly called shoe cubbies, are divided into compartments, each of which holds a single pair of shoes. But you have other good options, too—for instance:

1. Freestanding floor racks. These come in a variety of materials and function just like the door-mounted models.

2. Revolving carousels. These come in both two- and three-tiered models, and can hold up to 18 pairs of shoes in the floor space occupied by two pairs.

> **MAKING SPACE**
>
> At just about any housewares store, you can buy hangers that are made to hold multiple pieces of clothing, one below the other. They come in versions for shirts, skirts, and pants. Besides enlarging your storage space in the blink of an eye, these hard workers perform another service that's especially valuable if you have a small closet: Not only do they store up to five garments in the space of one, but they also lessen the wrinkling that often occurs when you cram too many filled hangers onto a closet rod.

ARMOIRE, ANYONE? If no amount of reorganizing can give you all the closet space you need, go shopping for an armoire. In the days before built-in closets became the norm, these freestanding versions were fixtures in houses large and small—and they can still perform as storage superstars. You can find genuine old-timers in antique shops, thrift stores, and flea markets. Retail furniture stores carry modern versions. Find one that fits your budget and your bedroom decor, and outfit it to suit your needs. For instance, install a closet rod inside it for hanging clothes, attach hooks for belts and purses, or fit it with shelves for T-shirts and sweaters.

CLUTTER BUSTER PRO

If you have children, the mere thought of de-cluttering their rooms—much less keeping them neat and orderly—may be enough to send you into a full-scale panic attack. Well, here's some good news, courtesy of Rosanne Larkins, a professional organizer and owner of Defining Time & Space (www.dtsorganizing.com) in Atlanta, Georgia. "The key to getting kids' rooms organized, and keeping them that way, is to include the youngsters in the action, rather than doing the job for them," she says. Here's a starter checklist of projects for you to tackle together:

☛ Separate seasonal clothing in closets, putting the current season's things where your child can reach them most easily. Wherever possible, use two rods, one above the other, and use the lower rod for the current season's clothing. Store out-of-season garments on the higher rod.

☛ Divide drawers into sections so that children can take their clothing out and put it away easily. There are many kinds of dividers on the market, but shoe boxes work well, too.

☛ Store shoes and bulky toys, such as dolls and stuffed animals, in open baskets or bins.

☛ Label shelves, drawers, and storage containers with words or pictures to make it easier for kids to put things away.

☛ If you have more than one child, use different-colored hangers for each one, and mark each kid's clothes with his or her initials or a distinctly colored dot. (Be sure to use a permanent marker that's intended for use on fabric.)

CHAPTER TWO

THE KITCHEN

I n most households, the kitchen is the most cluttered room of all. And that goes for whether it's a gathering place for a large family, or a small space that serves only one or two people. Regardless of which category your kitchen falls into, the basic recipe for a clutter-free environment is the same: Divide it into separate zones, and tackle them one at a time.

FREE UP THE FRIDGE AND FREEZER

With food constantly going in and out of these two appliances, getting—and keeping— them uncluttered can be a major challenge. The key to success is to develop a game plan that works for your family, and make sure that everyone in the household plays by the rules.

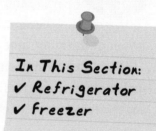

In This Section:
✔ Refrigerator
✔ Freezer

SORT

Your first step on the road to clutter-free cooling compartments couldn't be simpler: Empty out the refrigerator and freezer, and separate the food you *do* want to keep from the food you *don't* want to keep. Follow the tips below to make this job a snap.

GATHER YOUR GEAR. Start your sorting by rounding up two ice-filled coolers, some big trash bags, and a bucket or large pot. Then, as you pull each item out of its cool quarters, put it into one of those containers according to the guidelines that follow.

THE BUCKET BRIGADE. Use your bucket or pot for anything you can compost, including fresh produce that's over the hill—or will be by the time you'll have a chance to use it. But don't stop there. Leftover salads and cooked vegetables, rice, and pasta are also prime ingredients for "black gold" as long as they aren't swimming in dressings or sauces. The same goes for opened packages of frozen fruits or vegetables that you know you're not going to use.

LIQUID ASSETS. Past-its-prime produce isn't the only soil-building superstar that may be living in your freezer or fridge. Just about any kind of beverage you can think of contains important plant nutrients and valuable organic matter. So set aside any liquids or semiliquids that are flat, sour, moldy, or simply too old to be tasty. Then, when you're through with your sorting project, take them outside and pour the contents onto the soil. These are some of the "cocktails" plants love best:

✔ Beer

✔ Fruit or vegetable juices

✔ Iced tea or iced coffee

✔ Milk, cream, half-and-half, or buttermilk

✔ Soda pop

✔ Sour cream or yogurt

✔ Wine

BUT I DON'T *HAVE* A COMPOST PILE! In that case, simply dig a hole in your garden or in a flower bed, and drop in your

Ask Jerry

Q. *I am confused by the expiration dates that are printed on food packages. What do they mean?*

A. Here's the rundown:

Sell by: The store should move the product off its shelves by this date, but you still have time to consume it before the quality goes down. Take milk, for example. If the date says, "Sell by July 25," you have a good week to use it before it will be unsafe.

Best if used by: This suggests how long the product will be good to eat or drink, but is only a guide. It doesn't mean that your potato chips will become inedible at midnight of that day, but they'll begin to decline in flavor and crispness.

Use by or Expires on: If you don't use the product by this date, you're likely to see a marked deterioration in quality and safety.

cast-off organic matter. You can even bury it in the middle of your lawn, as long as you dig the hole carefully, so the piece of turf on top stays intact. Then empty the bucket into the hole, and replace your "divot."

INTO THE TRASH. It goes without saying (I hope!) that you'll toss out any spoiled or moldy foods. But also get rid of meats or packaged foods—opened or otherwise—that are more than a week past their printed sell-by dates, or that appear to be harboring other life forms. The trash (or the garbage disposal) is the place for these, too:

- Any leftovers that are more than three days old—or that you know you won't eat, even if they're left from last night's dinner

- Half-empty bottles of sauces, condiments, or dressings that no one is ever going to use (even if they're still good)

- Anything in the freezer that's over six months old, is suffering from freezer burn, or has turned into an unidentifiable, icy lump

- Things that you bought for one-time use in a recipe and haven't opened since then

COOL IT. As for the two coolers I mentioned earlier, they are both meant to be temporary "holding tanks" for food that is still fresh and good to eat. But even those edibles fall into two different categories:

MAKING SPACE

While you're sorting through the stuff that's inside your refrigerator, take a good look at the outside, too. Is the door covered with snapshots, your grandchildren's artwork, to-do notes, shopping lists, and magnetic business cards galore? If so, take 'em all off and find someplace else to keep them. (You'll find some great ideas in the "Organize" section on page 48.) Simply by putting a clean face on the fridge, you'll take a giant step toward de-cluttering the whole kitchen. In fact, you may be astonished at how much visual space you'll gain!

1. Anything you know that you and your family will eat, drink, or use in a recipe. This stash will go back into the fridge or freezer when you're through with your sorting campaign. Put them in Cooler Number One.

2. Things that no one in the house will eat—at least not before the food goes bad. For instance, maybe the supermarket was running a special on a new kind of frozen dinner, so you bought three of them. But when you served up the first one, everyone in the family hated it. They're not likely to change their minds anytime soon, so toss the two hangers-on into Cooler Number Two.

FIND 'EM A HOME. So what do you do with the stuff in Cooler Number Two? It's simple: Give it to a friend, relative, or neighbor who can use it. You could also offer it to your local food bank, but don't be surprised if they say, "Thanks, but no thanks." Very few of them will accept perishable foods of any kind.

WASH IT DOWN. Once your refrigerator and freezer are as bare as Old Mother Hubbard's cupboard, remove the meat and produce bins, and give them a good soak in warm, soapy water. (Unless you've got an extra-roomy kitchen sink, use a bathtub for this job.) While the bins are bathing, wash the inside of the fridge with warm, soapy water and a sponge. Then rinse it using a fresh sponge and cool,

OUT OF THE BOX

Would you believe that a castoff from your fridge can help ease your stress load? Well, it's true! Just rinse out a small glass jar with a tight lid (a fancy mustard or jelly jar is perfect). Fill it with baby oil or mineral oil to within roughly $1/4$ inch of the top, and add 15 to 20 beads (either glass or plastic will do). Brush or squeeze superglue onto the inside rim of the lid, and screw it onto the jar. If you like, paint the lid your favorite color. Then, anytime daily life begins to feel like an out-of-control roller coaster, sit down in a comfortable chair, and turn the jar end over end. The beads gliding through the oil will serve as a visual mantra, letting your mind relax and—for a few minutes, at least—ease you out of the fast lane.

clear water. Finally, fish the bins out of the tub, and wipe them clean. Rinse them under the tap, dry them with a towel, and return them to their rightful places in the refrigerator.

KEEP IT UP. Fridge and freezer sorting is not a once-in-a-lifetime—or even a once-a-month adventure. In fact, it's a good idea to take a quick inventory at least every week, and toss out anything that's not fresh (or that you know won't be eaten or drunk anytime soon). In particular:

- Look in the crisper drawers, and compost limp or spoiled fruits and vegetables.

- Peek inside opened containers of cottage cheese, yogurt, sour cream, and ice cream.

- Sniff the milk and half-and-half.

- Open up any mystery containers, and examine the contents.

BEHIND CLOSED SHELLS.
Rats! The last time you bought eggs, you took them out of their original carton. Without a sell-by date to guide you, how do know whether to keep the eggs or pitch them? It's simple: Set one of them into a bowl of cold, salty water. If it sinks, hang on to the eggs (but use them as soon as you can). If the "guinea pig" rises to the surface, toss 'em all out.

EGG OVERLOAD. If you find that you have more fresh eggs than you can use before they go bad, do what my neighbor does when her pet chickens are extra generous. One by one, break each egg into a bowl, beat it lightly, and pour it into a greased ice

MAKING SPACE

Unless you have a big family—or you only shop for groceries once a month—don't buy giant-size containers of ketchup, mustard, mayo, and salad dressings, no matter how low the price per ounce may be. Instead, opt for smaller sizes, and restock your supply as needed. Besides freeing up space in your refrigerator, you'll always know that your condiments are at their freshest, tastiest best.

cube tray compartment. When the tray is full, pop it in the freezer. Once the contents are frozen, pop them out of the tray, and store them in a plastic freezer bag. To use them, thaw out as many as you need for a recipe, and proceed as usual. They'll taste as fresh as they did the day you tucked them away.

When you reach into your fridge and pull out a bunch of celery that's beginning to wilt, don't toss it out. Instead, soak it in a bowl of ice water for 45 minutes. It'll be crisp, crunchy, and ready to munch on!

PLENTIFUL PEPPERS. If your sorting session turns up bell peppers that are about to head downhill—or simply more of them than you can use anytime soon—don't toss them out. Instead, seed, chop, and freeze them in plastic containers. (Unlike most vegetables, peppers don't need any fancy pretreatment.) The next time you need a chopped pepper, it'll be right at your fingertips.

IN A PICKLE. After you've used up a jar of pickles, the juice may look like nothing but fridge-clogging clutter. Not so! That elixir can jazz up all sorts of foods. Instead of pouring it down the drain, try a few of these tricks:

• Make a basting sauce for ham. Just stir cloves and mustard into the juice, and dribble some of the mixture over the ham every 30 minutes or so until the meat's done.

• Dress your macaroni salad with pickle juice and relish instead of mayonnaise. You'll give that ol' pasta a zesty tang—with zero grams of fat.

• Combine pickle juice with cream cheese for a chip or veggie dip that'll make your guests sit up and say "Yum!"

• Make pickled eggs by adding hard-boiled eggs (still in their shells) to boiling pickle juice. Boil for about five minutes, then cool, and serve.

• Make cucumber salad. Combine pickle juice, sour cream, and a pinch of sugar. Pour the creamy mixture over paper-thin cucumber slices, and toss lightly.

ORGANIZE

A well-organized refrigerator and freezer can save you time, hassle—and money. After all, what good is freezing last night's lasagna if it's only going to get lost in leftover land? By the time you rediscover it, it'll be flavored with freezer burn and ready for the trash. Fortunately, it's easy to make your fridge a no-waste zone. All it takes is logic, common sense, and a few simple tricks like the ones below.

TAKE THEIR TEMPERATURE. Food goes downhill fast when it's not kept cool enough. So after you've cleared out the clutter, take a few minutes to check the temperature in both the refrigerator and freezer compartments. In order to slow the growth of mold and bacteria, the fridge should stay below 40°F, and the freezer should be chillin' along at a frosty 0°F.

THAT'S IT EGG-ZACTLY! If your refrigerator is an older model, it probably has a compartment on the inside of the door that's designed especially for eggs—complete with little egg-shaped cubbyholes to nestle the hen fruit in. Well, ignore that space. Your eggs will stay fresher if you keep them in their original carton, and set it on a shelf inside the fridge.

MORE INSIDE OPERATORS. Eggs aren't the only edibles that fare better on your refrigerator shelves. Milk also deteriorates faster when you put it in the door. So does refrigerated cookie dough, as well as ready-to-bake biscuits, rolls, and pastries.

SO WHAT *CAN* YOU PUT IN THE DOOR? Your refrigerator door shelves are the perfect places to park soft drinks, beer, bottled water, and other beverages that don't spoil quickly.

MAKING SPACE

If you have a refrigerator with a wide-open freezer compartment on top, this organizing tip is just for you: Buy some freestanding wire shelves at a hardware or house-wares store, and put them inside the freezer. This way, you can use *all* of the available space—not just the bottom half of the unit.

They also work just fine for condiments like mustard, mayo, pickles, and ketchup.

LET SUSAN HELP. Lazy Susan, that is. Just put one of these handy turntables in your refrigerator, and arrange all your bottles, jars, and cartons on top. When everything is just a spin away, nothing will get lost and go bad behind your back.

A GROUP EFFORT. Whether you opt for a lazy Susan or set your food containers directly on the shelves, organize them the way photographers organize people for group photos: Put the shortest bottles, jars, and packages in front, and the tallest in back. This way, you can see at a glance exactly what you've got.

TOGETHERNESS IS GOOD. You can save a load of time and money simply by keeping like items together in both the fridge and freezer. For example, put all the salad dressings in one place, the condiments in another, and so on. In the freezer, keep the vegetables, baked goods, and meats in separate areas. This way, you'll know right where to find everything—and never again will you buy a bag of frozen peas because you didn't remember that you already had two or three of them.

TIMING COUNTS, TOO. In both your fridge and freezer, try to keep the oldest items

PACK RAT ALERT!

Problem: Food that's past its prime builds up in your fridge because you never remember when you put it in there.

Solution: Whenever you put leftovers or just-opened jars or food packages into your refrigerator, write two dates on the container: the date you put them in, and the date by which you should pitch them. (If the container is one you want to keep, use an adhesive label or sticky note.) But how do you know how long to keep your food if there's no use-by date on the package? Simple: Just do an Internet search for "food storage chart." You'll find a passel of sites filled with expert advice on storing food safely, including how long you can keep everything, from hard cheese to hot dogs and eggplant to egg yolks.

up front, so they'll get used up before they go bad. (I know: Unless you live alone, this—and many of the previous tips, for that matter—may sound like nothing more than a pipe dream. Well, don't fret about it. Just do the best you can and eventually, your brood will start following your example!)

OFF OF THE DOOR... And then where? As I mentioned earlier, you can eliminate a lot of visual clutter in your kitchen simply by making your refrigerator door a no-posting zone (see the Making Space box on page 44). But what about all the stuff you've removed from that all-too-handy metallic bulletin board? Well, for starters, throw out all the junk—for instance, a postcard announcing last month's garden club meeting, a delivery menu for a pizza place that's gone out of business, and magnetic business cards for places you never call. As for the things that you want or need to keep, consider these clever possibilities:

- To display photographs or kids' art—whether current work or classic favorites—designate a spot in your home as a special art gallery. A hallway, a wall in your bedroom or powder room—or even a solid-panel door—will work just fine. Buy some plastic box frames that allow you to pop the pictures in and out. Then you can change the show whenever the mood strikes.

- As for any artwork or photos that don't rank in the extra-special category—or that you simply don't have enough wall space for—

Ask Jerry

Q. *I've heard that a freezer works best when it's filled to capacity. Is this true? And if so, does the same thing apply to the refrigerator, as well?*

A. Yes, it is true that a *freezer* operates most efficiently—and keeps your food fresher, longer—when it's fully loaded. So anytime you find yourself with empty freezer space, fill it immediately. (My favorite filler-uppers are milk cartons or jugs filled with water.)

On the other hand, a *refrigerator* does its best work when air can circulate freely around the contents. That means you don't want to fill up any more than three-quarters of the inside space. And keep beverages and moist foods tightly covered, so moisture can't escape into the unit. The more humid the air is, the harder the refrigerator has to work to keep it cool.

tuck them into scrapbooks, photo albums, or acid-free storage boxes (you can find all of them in photo-supply stores, catalogs, and online).

- Attach a magnetic board to the inside of a cabinet door, and use it to hold magnetic business cards, and anything else you can hold with a magnet, like meeting notices, your shopping list, or a wall calendar.

 ## STORE

In the last section, we talked about *where* to keep all the things in your fridge and freezer. Now let's look at *how* to store your food to make the most of the space at hand—and to make sure that bounty lasts long enough for you to enjoy it.

AS YOUR LEFTOVERS SHRINK…

Shrink the containers, too. For instance, instead of leaving leftover lasagna in the huge pan you baked it in, transfer it to a smaller container. Yes, this does require a little more work on your part, but it gives you two big benefits: First, you gain space in the fridge or freezer, and second, because there's less air in the container, your food will last longer.

STAND 'EM ON THEIR HEADS.

Cottage cheese, sour cream, and yogurt will keep longer if you store them upside down. Just make sure the lids are on good and tight. To be extra safe—especially if a container has been opened—put it in a plastic bag before sticking it in the fridge.

MESS-MAKER ALERT!

Problem: You want to clear the clutter off your refrigerator door, but there are a lot of papers that you need to keep in plain sight.

Solution: Make an attractive, no-tacks-needed bulletin board. Just find fabric that blends with your kitchen decor, and wrap it around a 1-foot-square piece of $1/2$-inch-thick wood or corkboard. Then stretch color-coordinated, extra-long rubber bands around the board in both directions to form a grid pattern. The bands will hold notes and papers securely—and you won't have to clutter your kitchen with thumbtacks or pushpins.

SAY CHEESE! To keep your favorite hard cheese from going moldy before its time, wrap the block in a paper towel that's been dampened with vinegar. Then slide it into a ziplock plastic bag, and put it in the fridge.

TIMELY TOMATO TIPS. The tomato may be the crown jewel of the garden, but when it comes to storage, it's a temperamental little bugger. This handful of hints will help you give it the TLC it needs:

1. Tomatoes retain the most flavor when you keep them at room temperature (55°F or above). If they're fully ripe and fresh from the garden (or farm stand), they'll keep for a day or two.

2. Whatever you do, keep tomatoes away from direct sunlight. They'll overheat and ripen unevenly, or spoil more quickly.

3. To bring unripe tomatoes to the eating stage faster, tuck them into a brown paper bag with an apple or a banana. Both fruits give off ethylene gas that speeds the ripening process.

4. If you have to store ripe tomatoes for more than two days, you'll need to put them in the fridge. For best results, stash them in the butter compartment—it's the warmest place.

5. Never refrigerate a tomato that's not fully ripe. The cold will destroy the flavor and stop the ripening process in its tracks!

LET 'EM FREEZE. Although tomatoes don't fare too well in the refrigerator (see "Timely Tomato Tips" above), they do just fine in the freezer. What's more, they don't need any fancy treatment before

It's no secret that leaf lettuces wilt or rot more quickly than the firmer types. To give these softies the longest possible life span, put the entire bunch into a jar full of water, just as you'd do with cut flowers. Then put a big plastic bag over the whole thing and carefully set it in the fridge. *Note:* If you grow your own leaf lettuce, pull up the whole plant and put it, roots and all, into the jar of water.

you freeze them. Just wash them, cut out any bad spots, put them on baking sheets, and slide the sheets into the freezer. Once the tomatoes have frozen, store them in plastic bags or freezer containers. (The skins will crack during the freezing process, making the fruits easier to peel after they've thawed out.)

HANG YOUR ONIONS. And garlic, too. These pungent bulbs should never be stored in the fridge. Instead, keep them in a cool, dry place using this method: Drop a bulb into a panty hose leg, tie a knot, drop in another one, and so on. Then hang the bulging pouch from a wall hook in your pantry—or from the ceiling, if it's low enough. When you want to use one of the bulbs, cut just below the knot that's above it.

WONDERFUL WINTER SQUASH. Most varieties of whole winter squash should be stored unwashed in a warm, dry place with good air circulation. Given these conditions, all types will keep for up to three months, with two exceptions:

- Spaghetti squash lasts for only about two months.

- Hubbard squash keeps well for as long as six months.

THE ONE ODDBALL. The rugged individualist in the squash family is acorn squash, which needs a cool, moist environment. Under those conditions, it'll stay fresh and tasty for up to three months.

Ask Jerry

Q. *Do you have any good advice for storing wine after it's been opened?*

A. I sure do! If your leftover wine is white or rosé, just shove the cork into the bottle as far as possible, and pop it into the refrigerator. It will stay drinkable for three to five days. And if you opened a bottle of red wine, put the cork back in, and set the bottle in a dark place (like a kitchen cabinet). It'll keep for two to three days.

If you know you won't have time to drink your wine—red or white—before it goes south, pour it into ice cube trays and put them in the freezer. Then use the cubes to perk up soups, stews, marinades, and casseroles.

PAPER, PLEASE. The next time you buy a package of mushrooms, remove 'em from the plastic package and keep them in a paper bag in your refrigerator. That way, they'll stay fresh twice as long.

HERBS ON ICE. If you like to use fresh herbs in your cooking, you know that when you put them in the fridge, they can turn into a wilted mess almost before your very eyes. On the other hand, when you freeze them, they retain their fresh-picked flavor and aroma for months. So wash 'em up, and use any of these three methods:

MAKING SPACE Instead of freezing sauces and soups in bulky containers, try this space-saving trick: Pour the liquid into tight-sealing freezer bags, and lay them flat. Once the contents have frozen solid, stand the slim, trim packages straight up like file folders.

1. Wrap bunches of herb sprigs (one kind per bunch) in aluminum foil, and stash the bunches in the freezer.

2. Chop fresh herbs and freeze them in plastic containers.

3. Puree chopped herbs with water, butter, or olive oil. Then pour the mixture into ice cube trays. When the cubes are frozen, pop them out of the trays, and store them in plastic containers.

POTATO POINTERS. Never store spuds in the refrigerator, or anyplace else where the temperature gets below 40°F. If you do, they'll develop a sweet taste and turn brown when you cook them. On the other hand, they'll stay fresh and tasty for a month or more when you follow these simple guidelines:

✔ Handle potatoes with care. If they get bruised, they'll quickly turn dark and begin to rot.

✔ Store your spuds in a cool (45° to 50°F), humid (not wet), dark place with good ventilation. Whatever you do, avoid warm places, such as under the sink or in a cupboard that's close to a sunny window. At best, the potatoes will sprout and shrivel up. At worst, they'll attract bugs and rodents.

✔ If potatoes are exposed to light during storage, they'll turn green and produce a bitter, toxic substance called solanine. Throw away any potatoes that are mostly green, but if there are just a few colorful patches, slice them off, and you're good to go.

Timing Isn't Everything

No matter what the experts say about the storage life of fresh produce, you need to give each kind of fruit or vegetable the particular conditions it needs. Otherwise, it'll go downhill faster than an Olympic skier (well, almost). Read on for a roundup of tips that will help you keep your vitamin-packed produce fresh.

FRUIT	CARE
Apples	Store uncovered and unwashed in the refrigerator, away from onions and other odor-producing foods. Will stay fresh for up to two weeks.
Citrus fruits	Keep uncovered (washed or unwashed) at room temperature for up to three days, or refrigerate uncovered for up to two weeks.
Peaches	Store ripe peaches uncovered and unwashed in the refrigerator. Will stay fresh for up to one week.
Strawberries	Best eaten upon purchase. Otherwise store unwashed in the coolest part of the refrigerator for up to three days.

VEGETABLE	CARE
Broccoli	Store unwashed in a loose plastic bag in the refrigerator crisper. Will stay fresh for up to five days.
Cabbage	Store unwashed in a loose plastic bag in the refrigerator crisper. Will stay fresh for up to two weeks.
Peppers	Store unwashed in the refrigerator crisper. Will stay fresh for up to two weeks.
Summer squash	Store unwashed in a plastic bag in the refrigerator for up to one week.

BE THERE AND BE SQUARE. Or maybe rectangular. When you're freezing leftovers or made-ahead meals, store them in straight-sided containers with flat lids. They'll stack neatly, and unlike round containers, they'll nestle right into the corners of your freezer. (Beware of any storage containers that have a raised circle on top of the lid. This feature is designed to make the lids fit neatly together in your cabinet—which they do. Unfortunately, it makes for unstable stacking when you fill up the containers and pop 'em in the freezer.)

BOX THE BAGS. If you want to go all out to maximize space, put any bags of frozen food into square or rectangular containers. (Don't open the bags. The contents will stay fresh longer if you leave them in their original packaging.) Besides making the most of your freezer space, you'll make it easier to put your finger on exactly what you want. Just be sure to either label each container, or arrange the inner bag so that the label shows through the outer box.

CONQUER CABINET CLUTTER

In This Section:
✔ Cabinets
✔ Drawers

Have you ever met anyone who thinks they have enough kitchen cabinet space? Neither have I. But take it from me: You have all the space you need. Just put our SOS plan to work, and you'll feel like you've got a brand-new kitchen—without the hassle and expense of a remodeling job.

SORT

If you're still harboring all your wedding presents in your kitchen, it's all but guaranteed that you're short on space. And I'll bet there are plenty of other things hanging around that don't need to be hogging valuable real estate in your cabinets and drawers, either. So don't just stand there—get the show on the road!

GET READY, GET SET... Step one on the path to clutter-free cabinets and drawers is to rustle up some sturdy cardboard boxes. On the side of one of them, write Up Front. Set this one aside for now. On another, write Take Elsewhere. On a third, write Donate or Sell. On a fourth, write Recycle. Leave several more boxes blank. (I'll tell you why in a minute.)

GO! Take all of the nonedibles out of your cabinets and drawers, and use this five-part plan to sort them out:

1. As you come across things you know you'll never use—three extra bottle openers, for instance, or a duplicate salad spinner—toss them into either the Donate or Sell box or the Recycle box.

2. Everything that you do use—but not normally in the kitchen—goes into the Take Elsewhere box (your dog's ball, your hammer, and those tins of shoe polish, for instance). Then take the box elsewhere. Pronto.

3. Fill the unlabeled boxes with all your "necessary" kitchen gear, and keep them close at hand. Then, as the need arises, grab a gadget. Making tacos? Pull out the cheese grater. Toasting your team's victory? Go for the corkscrew. Scrambling eggs? Out come a skillet and a wire whisk. When you've finished using whatever tool it was, move it to the Up Front box. (You'll probably need several of these boxes by the time you're finished.)

4. After a few weeks, examine the boxes. I'd bet my last pot holder that you've been pulling things from the Up Front boxes over and over again—and that there's a fair amount of stuff in the other cartons that you haven't even glanced at.

MESS-MAKER ALERT!

Problem: Food that gets lost and forgotten among your kitchen gear.

Solution: This should be a no-brainer but, in many homes, it isn't: No matter how small your kitchen is, be sure to keep the edibles and the equipment in separate places.

5. Organize the Up Front contents in whatever way works best in your kitchen, and get the other boxes out of the way for now—but not too far out of the way. As weeks or even months go by, you'll no doubt be reaching for some of those pots, pans, dishes, and utensils. Whatever you do, don't toss out anything that's in those boxes until a full year has passed. Why? Because you don't want to give your punch bowl away in June and then, come December, end up buying a new one for your New Year's Eve party!

MAKING SPACE If you save the paper napkins, plastic utensils, and tiny packets of mustard, ketchup, and seasonings that come with take-out food, you can free up a fair amount of drawer space simply by getting rid of that junk. Just gather it all up and dump it into the trash.

OUT OF THE KITCHEN AND INTO... Just about any other room in the house. I'm talking about the contents of your Recycle box. Those extra odds and ends may be causing chaos in your cabinets and drawers, but they just might help you conquer clutter in other areas. This rundown will give you some clever ideas for putting your kitchen helpers to work around the house—and outdoors, too.

✔ Canisters. Bring decorative containers into the bathroom and use them to hold cotton balls, bath beads, wrapped guest soaps, extra toothbrushes, and the like.

✔ Cookie cutters. Move them to your workshop or hobby room, and use them as stencils to make patterns for wall decor, homemade wrapping paper, hand-painted fabric, or other craft projects.

✔ Muffin tin. Put it in a desk drawer, and fill the compartments with tiny supplies like pushpins, paper clips, and mini sticky-note pads.

✔ Pot-lid rack. Use it to hold mail in your entryway or office, or seed catalogs in your garden shed.

✔ **Spice rack.** Hang it on a wall and fill the shelves with any tiny trinkets you may collect, such as souvenir shot glasses, fancy thimbles, or small porcelain figurines.

✔ **Turkey baster.** It's perfect for draining excess water from plant saucers—especially any that are sitting under heavy pots that are too cumbersome to move.

✔ **Wine rack.** Just the thing for holding rolled-up towels and washcloths in a guest bathroom.

DOUBLE UP. Kitchen gadgets are like any other kind of tool: There's one for every purpose under the sun. The good news is that you can probably gain a lot of storage space simply by getting rid of specialized gizmos that you don't really need—or keep the space available by not buying them in the first place. As you check your inventory, keep these facts in mind:

A garlic press is a perfect addition to a young artist's supply kit (or your own, for that matter). It's just the ticket for making "hair" out of clay or play dough. All you do is put a lump of the material in the bowl of the press, squeeze the handles together, and out come the makings of, say, Santa's beard or a lion's shaggy mane.

• A food processor does just about every chopping and grinding job there is—so if you have one, there's no need to hang on to drawer-cluttering gadgets like meat grinders and cheese shredders.

• Any sharp knife will slice pizza every bit as well as a fancy pizza cutter will.

• A good old-fashioned potato peeler will pit cherries, hull strawberries, shave chocolate, and even peel oranges and apples—so why waste space storing specialty tools that do those jobs?

• A colander set on top of a saucepan will get your broccoli and cauliflower just as tender-crisp as any vegetable steamer would.

CLANG GOES THE TREASURE!

To you, extra pieces of kitchen gear may just add up to clutter, but to a small child, those gadgets and gizmos can mean hours of good old-fashioned fun. Here are a dozen castoffs that'd make dandy additions to your favorite youngster's collection of bathtub, sandbox, and wading-pool toys. (And you can probably think of a lot more on your own.)

✔ Colanders

✔ Funnels

✔ Ice cream scoops

✔ Measuring cups

✔ Measuring spoons

✔ Mixing spoons

✔ Plastic food-storage containers

✔ Plastic ice cube trays

✔ Pots and pans

✔ Soup ladles

✔ Strainers

✔ Turkey basters

A PLACE AT THE TABLE. As you pull dishes out of your cabinets, consider how many plates, bowls, glasses, and mugs your family uses regularly. Keep those on hand, along with a few extras for unexpected guests. Put the rest into your

MESS-MAKER ALERT!

Problem: Piles of plastic and paper grocery bags crammed into drawers and cabinets.

Solution: Haul them out and reuse them as garbage or dog-cleanup bags. Then, to keep the mess from building up again, buy some sturdy, flat-bottomed canvas shopping bags and take them with you whenever you go grocery shopping. When the clerk at the checkout counter says "Paper or plastic?" say "Neither, thanks. I brought my own." Many supermarkets now sell canvas bags—and even special, insulated versions that you can use to tote perishable foods. You can also find both types on a multitude of Web sites. Just search for "canvas shopping bags" or "reusable shopping bags."

Take Elsewhere box, and store them in the basement or attic. That way, they won't clutter up the kitchen, but you can still pull them out of hiding if you have an overflow crowd to feed.

BUT THEY'RE BEAUTIFUL! What do you do with things you don't use but can't bear to part with? I'm thinking of things like your grandma's ancient potato masher, or your mother's collection of souvenir teaspoons or copper cookie cutters. Display them on the wall—that's what! How you do that depends on how much space you have and the objects in question. Here are two good options:

• If you have a number of rustic, old implements, like huge wooden spoons, potato mashers, butter paddles, and so on, simply arrange them on the wall in an attractive grouping.

• Show off smaller treasures, like cookie cutters and silver spoons, in a shadow-box display case with a hinged opening. You can find such cases at picture-framing and art-supply stores, and on the Internet. Simply attach your treasure to the case's backing using a T-shaped craft pin, and hang the case on the wall. Then, if you ever decide to use your works of art, just open the door, and take them out.

PLASTIC CONTAINERS 101.

If you're like a lot of folks I know, you probably have cabinets that are filled to the brim with plastic containers—both the ones that are designed for food storage, and others that once held edibles like yogurt, cottage cheese, and spreads of one kind or another. There's

MAKING SPACE | While you're sorting through the contents of your kitchen cabinets, be sure to tackle the hutch or sideboard in your dining room—or wherever else you keep dishes, silverware, table linens, and so forth. Decide what to keep, recycle, donate, or sell, following the same criteria you use for the things in your cabinets. Most likely, you'll wind up with a lot of free space that you can use to store the kitchen "dwellers" that you want to keep, but don't need for everyday cooking.

a lot of space a-wastin' in those cabinets. To discover it, here's your plan of action:

1. Weed out any smelly, stained, or damaged food containers, and any that are not meant for food storage. (These would be the yogurt cups, margarine tubs, and cottage cheese cartons.) They're all fodder for the recycling bin.

2. Figure out how many containers you usually have on duty in the freezer and fridge at any one time, and how many you send out in lunch boxes each day.

3. If you don't have enough good ones left over, write down how many you need, and in what shapes and sizes. Then buy high-quality replacements. It's okay to buy a few extras to have on hand, but don't go overboard!

PACK RAT ALERT!

Problem: Grocery coupons piled up in your drawers.

Solution: Fasten the coupons together with a binder clip, and hang it on your kitchen bulletin board, or on the rack where you keep your car keys. Then, as you head for the supermarket, grab the clip and its contents, and tuck in your shopping list. When you get to the store, attach the whole shebang to your shopping cart.

4. If you have more good containers than you can possibly use in the kitchen, put the extras in your Take Elsewhere box. They're just the ticket for corralling all kinds of tiny doodads, ranging from nails in the workshop to tubes of lipstick in the bathroom.

MAKE YOUR MARK. Once you've identified all the containers that are worth keeping, make sure each bottom has a matching top, and vice versa. Then use an indelible marker to identify the pieces that fit together. For instance, write a 1 on all the tops and bottoms that are one size and shape, a 2 on another matched group, and so on. This way, anytime you need a container, you can instantly grab two matching pieces.

NIX THE DULL KNIVES. Don't get me wrong—I don't mean that you should get rid of high-quality knives that simply need to be sharpened! I'm talking about the cheap ones that you may have bought when you first started cooking, or when you needed something to slice cheese for a last-minute picnic. If you're not using them, they're nothing but drawer-clogging clutter. And if you are using them, chintzy, dull knives are not only dangerous, but also make you work harder for inferior results! So do yourself a favor: Pitch 'em, pronto.

PROCRASTINATORS, TAKE NOTE. If you have good knives that just need a little sharpening, either do it yourself or take them to a professional sharpener—*now*. Otherwise, sell them at your next yard sale, or give them to a thrift shop and take a tax deduction.

KEEP TABS ON YOUR JUNK DRAWER. The things inside a junk drawer are a lot like wire coat hangers in a closet: You turn your back for a few hours, and they multiply like rabbits… or at least that's the way it seems at my house. For that reason, de-cluttering a junk drawer is not a one-shot operation.

> ## MAKING SPACE
>
>
>
> With all the tools they keep in their drawers, some folks I know could practically remodel their whole kitchen. If that description hits home for you, take all that stuff out to the workshop where it belongs, and replace it with a multipurpose gadget that combines as many as 12 different tools in one handy "package." You can buy these gadgets at home-improvement and camping-supply stores and (of course) over the Internet.

It's an ongoing process. Once a month or so, take a few minutes to give that clutter catchall a good going-over by following this routine:

• Toss out what you can, like expired grocery coupons, extra pocket calendars from your insurance agent, and the lone picture hook with no matching nail.

• Grab the things that have strayed in there by accident, and toss them into your Take Elsewhere box—for instance, golf balls, spools of thread, and leftover seed packets—and (you guessed it) move 'em to their rightful places.

• Tidy up the stuff that's left, so you can find what you need, when you need it. (You'll find some good ideas on that score in the Store section on page 73.)

FOUR STEPS TO RECIPE RATIONALITY. Do you have a drawer that's crammed full of recipes that you've clipped from newspapers, magazines, butter cartons, cereal boxes, and sugar sacks? If so, then gather them all up and go at 'em using this technique:

1. Sort the recipes into three piles: the ones you've whipped up and like, the ones you've made that turned out to be duds, and the ones you haven't even tried yet.

2. Toss out the duds.

3. Take a cold, hard look at the "haven't tried" pile, and throw out the ones you know you'll never make—like the chèvre-stuffed lamb burgers with raspberry-mint sauce.

4. Organize the rest in whatever way works best for you (see "Round up the Recipes" on page 78).

UNDER THE SINK. Is the thought of even *looking* inside your under-sink cabinet—much less cleaning it out—enough to send chills down your spine? If so, you're not alone. But it's got to be done, so grit your teeth, open the doors, and dredge out anything that doesn't belong there, including:

✔ Bars of soap that are brown and cracked

✔ Dishcloths and cleaning rags that have turned as stiff as boards

PACK RAT ALERT!

Problem: Recipes that you think you might like to try someday.

Solution: Record the name of each recipe in a notebook or on your computer, and throw the recipe itself away. If you really do wind up wanting to make that casserole, cake, soup, or stew, you'll be able to find a suitable replacement recipe online or in a cookbook.

✔ Grungy sponges, rusty scouring pads, and worn-out brushes

✔ Rusting cans of solidified powdered cleansers

✔ Spray cleansers with just a squirt of solution left

The hygiene experts say that kitchen sponges should be replaced weekly, but that doesn't mean you have to throw them out—at least not right away. Instead, move them to the garage or workshop, and use them for messy cleanup chores in those rooms until they're finally too far gone to keep.

ALL SPRAY BOTTLES ARE NOT CREATED EQUAL. They should be, but they're not—as you well know if you've ever bought a glass cleaner at the supermarket, brought it home, and had it dribble liquid down your arm every time you squeezed the handle. If you find any of these less-than-perfectly-packaged products under your sink, you have two good de-cluttering options:

1. If only a little bit of cleaner is left in the bottle—or if you don't care for the product no matter how efficiently it flows out of its container—pitch it (see "Discard with Care" below).

2. If you like the product just fine, and there's a fair amount remaining, trot off to your local hardware or housewares store, buy a sturdy spray bottle, and transfer the contents. The new version won't set you back by more than a buck or two, and you can use it again and again. But before you even think of combining the contents of a few faulty bottles, make absolutely sure that the brands and formulas are identical. If they aren't, don't ever, *ever* do it!

DISCARD WITH CARE. When it comes to tossing chemical cleaning products, proceed with caution. Otherwise, you could create an environmental problem that's far worse than clutter under your sink.

And don't even think of just pouring the stuff down the drain! Instead, follow these guidelines:

- Unless the label says not to, it's okay to pour water-soluble products down the drain. Most municipal sewage treatment and household septic systems can handle them just fine. Prime pouring candidates include all-purpose cleaners, dishwashing liquid, and bleach. But before you pour anything, always read the label just to be safe! You also need to rinse the discarded liquid down with plenty of water, and don't ever drain two products at once — no matter how harmless you think they are. They could combine to form a nasty chemical reaction.

- *Never* pour any solvent-based product down the drain. Nor should you dump it into a storm drain, flush it down the toilet, or throw it out with your household trash. This no-no policy includes any product that's labeled as flammable, and anything that contains turpentine. Many metal and furniture polishes also fall into this category. The bottom line: Before you toss any of this nasty stuff, call your local sanitation department, and find out how to deal with it properly.

- Check before you recycle. Some communities will not accept containers that once held caustic substances like bleach or oven cleaner. So find out whether you need to send these containers to a hazardous waste collection site before you add them to your recycling bin.

TAKE OUT TOXIC STUFF. Insecticides, flea sprays, poison baits, and other toxic pest-control products do not belong in the kitchen — period. If you feel that you absolutely must use these nasty things, keep

MAKING SPACE While you're pulling all sorts of things out of your under-sink cabinet, take the time to make space for one useful tool—namely, a small flashlight. Keep it on the inside of the door, either hanging from a hook or tucked into a wire bin. It'll help you see all the way to the back of the cabinet, so you can always find what you're looking for—before it turns into yucky, useless clutter.

them under lock and key in your garage or garden shed.

TAKE OUT TOXIC STUFF, PART TWO. If you have small children or inquisitive pets in the house, beware of any caustic chemical products, like bleach, liquid or powdered cleansers, and drain de-cloggers. Either move them to a locked cabinet in your laundry room, or if that's not possible, install a lock on your under-sink cabinet.

A GREENER WAY TO DE-CLUTTER. Believe it or not, you can clear a whole lot of clutter from under your sink and go a little greener (and safer) at the same time. What's more, the process couldn't be simpler: Just get rid of all the commercial cleansers that are hogging up valuable real estate in your kitchen, and replace them with a couple of household superstars. What are they? None other than white vinegar and baking soda. We'll get to the vinegar in a minute, but here's a Baker's half-dozen common cleaning problems that the powerful powder in the bright orange box can help you solve:

1. Grease and grime on your appliances or stovetop. Dampen a sponge with hot water and sprinkle some baking soda on the sponge. Scrub lightly, then rinse.

2. Grout between ceramic tiles. Wet down the grout with a cloth or sponge, then dip a toothbrush in baking soda, and scrub.

Ask Jerry

Q. *I've always kept a bottle or two of commercial drain cleaner under my sink because the drain seems to clog up at the least opportune moment—like when dinner guests are due in five minutes. I know these products are terribly caustic, but they really do work! Do you know of any safer way to clean a clogged drain?*

A. I sure do! Just pour ½ cup of baking soda into the drain, and follow up with ½ cup of either white vinegar or lemon juice. Let the mixture sit for about 15 minutes. (The acid-alkaline combo will make a *lot* of noise, but don't be alarmed.) Rinse with hot tap water, and you're good to go! Just one word of caution: Do *not* use this method if you've already tried a commercial de-clogger. The vinegar or juice can react with the drain cleaner to create dangerous fumes.

3. Grungy oven. Sprinkle the surface with $^1/_2$ cup of baking soda (more if needed) and spray it with water. Let it sit overnight, then use a plastic scraper to slide the stains and burned-on food away. Rinse thoroughly with clear water.

4. Painted-wood surfaces. Make a solution of 1 teaspoon of baking soda per gallon of hot water. Apply it with either a mop or a sponge, then wipe the surface dry with a soft cloth. (To dry a wooden floor, use a dust mop with a soft cloth wrapped around the business end.)

5. Scuffed floors. To remove black shoe-scuff marks from any kind of bare floor, rub the spots with a paste made from 3 parts baking soda to 1 part water.

6. Small appliances. Pour a teaspoon or so of baking soda onto a clean, cotton flannel cloth that's slightly damp, and rub it onto your dirty blender, food processor, or other pint-size kitchen helper. (Believe it or not, this trick will even remove a bread wrapper that's burned onto your toaster.)

7. Stubborn stains on a porcelain sink. Make a paste of baking soda and water, and cover the marks with it. Let it sit for an hour or two, then rinse.

ACT WITH VIM AND VINEGAR.

If you store a jug of white distilled vinegar under your sink, you can clear that cabinet of a whole lot of specialized cleaning and deodorizing products. Plus, if a pet or toddler manages to take a sip from the bottle, the only consequence will be an unpleasant jolt to his taste buds! Just take a gander at the feats this tangy liquid can perform around your house:

OUT OF THE BOX

Nowadays a lot of folks are concerned about pesticide residue on the fruits and vegetables they get at the supermarket. You can buy special products to wash the nasty stuff off, but there's no reason to add one more bottle to your crowded cabinets. Instead, just mix a pinch or two of baking soda in a sink full of water, swish your produce in it, and rub the fruits and vegetables gently with a soft brush. Any clinging pesticide will come right off.

✔ Clean your kitchen floor. Mop or scrub it with a solution made from $^1/_2$ cup of vinegar per gallon of warm water. This stuff will cut right through the toughest grease and dirt, and it works on just about any kind of floor, including linoleum, vinyl, ceramic tile, and cork.

✔ Clean your garbage disposal. Be forewarned: This technique is noisy, but it works like a dream. Fill several of the ice cube trays with vinegar and freeze them. Run several of the cubes through the disposal, and let the cold water flow for a minute or so. The grinding of the blades will remove any clinging food particles, and the vinegar will eliminate odors.

✔ Clear the air. Chemical air fresheners cover up unpleasant aromas while interfering with your sense of smell, so you don't notice offensive odors. But vinegar can actually banish unwanted smells—and fast. Just pour a little into a few bowls, set them around the problem areas, and breathe easier.

MESS-MAKER ALERT!

Problem: Food grime that's built up in your microwave.

Solution: Pour 2 cups of water and $^1/_2$ cup of vinegar into a microwave-safe bowl, and put it in the microwave. Nuke the liquid on high for three to four minutes, or until it starts to boil. Let it sit for another three to four minutes, with the door closed, so the steam can loosen the food gunk. Then open the door, remove the bowl, and wipe the compartment clean with a damp sponge.

✔ Disinfect and clean wooden cutting boards by rubbing the surface with vinegar. If the board has deep knife grooves in it, soak it in vinegar for 5 to 10 minutes.

✔ Remove rust from knives and cast-iron pans. Soak your "stricken" pieces overnight in full-strength vinegar. The rust will dissolve, then wash away like magic.

ORGANIZE

Cooking is no fun when you have to rummage through crowded shelves and drawers to find the utensils you need. The tips on these pages will help you put your cabinets in apple-pie order—so you can spend less time preparing your meals and have more time to enjoy them.

WHAT GOES ON HERE? Before you start restocking your freshly emptied cabinets, consider not only what you can fit into them, but also what activities will occur around them. For example, store pots and pans within easy reach of the stove. Keep the microwave supplies close to the contraption. Put the glasses (at least some of them) in a cabinet or on a shelf near the refrigerator. And stash cups or mugs by the coffeemaker or close to the stove, where you boil water for tea. This way, you'll save steps—and a lot more time than you might think.

ALL IN THE FAMILY. When you fill your cabinets, try to organize the contents according to use. For instance, keep the mixing bowls and beaters close to the measuring cups and spoons. Put the coffee grinder and scoop with the filters—and keep all of them as close to the coffeemaker as you can.

TAME THE UTENSILS. Don't let chopsticks, shish kebab skewers, and fondue forks go every which way in your drawers. Instead of just dropping them back in, use

If your kitchen reorganizing plan calls for actually replacing your cabinets, don't get rid of them. Instead, put them to work de-cluttering other parts of the house. If they're still in good shape, paint them, and add new handles if you like. Then use them to store stationery supplies in your home office, towels and toiletries in a bathroom, soaps and stain removers in the laundry, or toys and books in a child's bedroom. Even if the cabinets are not much to look at—or if you have all the storage cupboards you need in the rest of your house—you can still put those castoffs to good use. Just haul them out to your garage or workshop, and fill 'em up with tools, hardware, or gardening supplies.

rubber bands to wrap 'em all into bundles (one kind of utensil per bundle, please). They'll stay neatly together.

LOW LIFE. If you have children or grandchildren in the house, keep plastic cups, bowls, and plates on a low shelf where the youngsters can reach them easily.

A MATTER OF TIMING. Take the time to decide which supplies you need to have close at hand, and which can be tucked away on high shelves—or even moved to the attic or a closet in another room. If, for example, you only use your giant-size stockpot to make hearty soups and stews in the winter, don't let it take up prime real estate near the stove all year round. And, if the only baking you ever do is at Christmastime, keep your cookie sheets and cutters, flour sifter, frosting tubes, and so forth with the Christmas decorations.

ON THE OTHER HAND... If you love making and decorating fancy cakes and cookies, designate one of your drawers as a storage space for your baking supplies. Stash your cookie cutters and cake pans in it, along with your containers of dots, jimmies, colored sugars, and other decorative materials.

INSIDE OPERATIONS. Standard kitchen cabinets come with a set number of shelves, which can leave you with a lot of wasted space above the things you store on them. Of course, you can take advantage of some of that space by stacking up your mugs, bowls, and plates—but if the tower topples, you can wind up

MAKING SPACE

When you're organizing your cabinets, try to leave easily accessible spots for any small appliances that you use frequently but don't have room for on your countertop. This way, you can have the toaster and coffeemaker front and center on the counter in the morning. Then when it's time to make dinner, you can tuck them away and pull out the food processor.

with a lot of pottery shards on your hands. A safer option is to add more shelves. You have four good choices:

1. Solid shelves, like the ones that came with your cabinets. Whether you make them yourself, or buy extras from a local cabinet supplier, these provide good, stable storage space. Bear in mind, though, that each shelf will take up close to an inch of space itself, and the less room there is between shelves, the harder it is to reach to the back. Also, the more likely it is that when you take something out, you'll bump it on the shelf above—possibly with unfortunate results.

2. Wire stacking shelves. These are lightweight, inexpensive, and easy to arrange in just about any configuration. Most of them are a little shallower than standard kitchen cabinets, so you can wind up with a little room to spare at the front or back, but that's a small price to pay for the extra vertical storage space they give you. You can find wire shelves in large hardware stores, housewares stores, and online.

MESS-MAKER ALERT!

Problem: A jumbled assortment of soaps and spray bottles in the cabinet under the sink.

Solution: To make use of all the space inside the cabinet, install an under-sink organizer that's specially designed to fit around the pipes. You can buy sturdy plastic versions that snap together easily without tools. What's more, they have adjustable shelves, so you can space them in whatever way works best for you. Look for them in your local housewares store, or in organizing catalogs and on Web sites.

3. Wire shelves that slide onto the shelves above them. They hang down anywhere from 4 to 6 inches, giving you a perfect place to store flat, lightweight drawer cloggers like napkins and boxes of plastic wrap, aluminum foil, and wax paper.

4. Wire-mesh shelves that run on rollers. If you need something from the middle or back, you just pull on the handle until your target is easy to reach. Their rectangular shape makes the most efficient use of the available space, and raised sides keep the contents from

falling off of the shelves when you slide the unit out. You can find these dandy devices at home-improvement or organizing stores and in catalogs—both print and online versions. *Note:* In most cases, you will have to remove the shelves that are now inside your cabinets to make room for the roll-out unit.

STORE

So you've cleared the clutter out of your cabinets and drawers, and organized the space in the way that works best for you—great job, but we're not done yet! With a few simple tricks and some highly helpful storage aids, you can make that freed-up space work even harder.

MATERIAL MATTERS. Either stainless or galvanized steel will work just as well for your pot rack (see Making Space at right) as copper tubing will—it's all a matter of your taste and budget. Galvanized steel is the least expensive of the three (and you can spray-paint it any color you like), stainless is the highest-priced, and copper's in the middle. (Whichever you choose, just make sure you get it at a plumbing-supply shop—the stuff will cost at least three times as much at a hardware or home-improvement store.)

DANGLE THE GADGETS. How many times have you reached into a drawer for the tongs and pulled out a tangled mess of kitchen gadgets? Well, say good-bye to gadget gridlock: Hang your oddly shaped tools on the same kind of rack you use for your pots

---

MAKING SPACE

Hanging pots and pans on the wall is a great way to free up space in your cabinets. You can buy pot racks of all kinds in kitchen-supply and housewares stores. But it's a snap to make your own in exactly the size you need. (It's also a lot less expensive than pretty much any store-bought rack you'll find.) Just buy some $3/4$-inch-diameter copper tubing, cut it to the size you need (or have the folks at the store do it), and fasten it to the wall with screw-in hooks. Then get some S-hooks that are big enough to go over the pipe and hold your pots. Presto—you're in business!

and pans. It's the perfect way to store cheese graters, measuring cups, potato mashers, tongs, and anything else that'll slide over an S-hook.

STORAGE ON HIGH. In most kitchens, there's a fair amount of space between the tops of the cabinets and the ceiling. And that's the perfect place to store your picnic supplies, coasters, cocktail napkins, swizzle sticks, and other lightweight gear that you don't need very often. Put it all in attractive, covered baskets or tins, and bingo—you'll free up space in your cabinets, and add a decorative touch to your kitchen at the same time.

LOOK OUT BELOW. The bottoms of your over-the-counter cabinets are also valuable real estate. Consider these clever storage options:

COLLECTOR ALERT!

Problem: Bakeware in all shapes and sizes cluttering your cabinets.

Solution: Buy an adjustable organizer that's specially designed to store baking gear. These contraptions easily accommodate cake pans, cookie sheets, muffin pans—even casserole dishes and pot lids. Look for them in catalogs, or on the Internet.

✔ Install wire or wooden racks that are specially made to hold stemware, like wine and martini glasses. (You can buy them at housewares stores and from catalogs and Web sites.)

✔ Screw large cup hooks into the underside of a cabinet, and use them to store your everyday coffee mugs.

HAVING SAID THAT... Although hanging stemware and mugs from the bottom of your upper cabinets *will* help de-clutter the insides of those hold-alls, you do need to follow two basic guidelines:

1. Only hang glasses and mugs that you use at least once a week. Otherwise, they'll just collect dust and add to your workload.

2. Don't hang them—or any other breakables—over your primary workspace, or anywhere else they're likely to be bumped.

SWING TIME. An in-drawer knife tray can be a great place to keep knives organized and within easy reach. But if your drawer space is at a premium, and you don't want a knife block cluttering your counter, here's a better idea: Buy a wooden knife holder that mounts on the underside of an over-the-counter cabinet. It stores knives horizontally in a trim wooden block that swings out when you want to retrieve a knife, then swings back into hiding. And because the knives are held in place by magnets, there's no danger that they'll drop out onto the counter. You can find swing-out knife blocks in housewares stores and catalogs (both print and online versions).

DOOR TO DOOR. The inside of your cabinet doors provides some of the most efficient storage space you could ever ask for. Consider some of these clever ideas:

- Hang a clipboard on the door, and use the clip to hold your placemats. They'll stay wrinkle-free and ready to snatch at a moment's notice.

- Screw cup hooks to the door, and hang pot holders, oven mitts, or even lightweight cutting boards from them.

- Attach wire baskets on the inside of the door below your sink. (You can buy them at housewares stores, hardware stores, and even some supermarkets.) They're tailor-made for holding dishwashing liquid, sponges, and other kitchen cleaning supplies.

- Screw on a rack that has vertical slots to store boxes of foil, plastic wrap, and sandwich bags.

OUT OF THE BOX

Here's another clever way to use the space on the inside of a cabinet door. You'll need a three-holed, transparent plastic sleeve (available in office-supply stores), an old key ring, and a cup hook. Screw the hook into the inside of the door, attach the key ring to one of the holes in the sleeve, and hang it on the hook. Then slide in whatever information you need to keep close at hand—say a list of emergency phone numbers, a favorite recipe, or an ingredient-substitution chart (see "Accept Substitutions" on page 88).

DON'T OVERLOOK THE OUTSIDE. Buy a stainless steel towel bar that fits over the top of a cabinet door (no tools needed), and use it to hold your dish towels. Or, choose an over-the-door rack that has hooks for pot holders or oven mitts. You can find both versions in housewares stores and in catalogs.

SURE DOESN'T LOOK LIKE A FORK! Cutlery trays are good for a lot more than holding flatware in a drawer. If you ask me, they're tailor-made for your junk drawer. Those little compartments are just the right size to hold screwdrivers, box cutters, twist ties, and other small doodads that you like to keep handy. And while you're at it, stash another tray in the drawer that's closest to the telephone, and use it to hold pens, pencils, and a notepad.

MORE OPTIONS FOR THE JUNK DRAWER. Cutlery trays aren't the only devices that can keep tiny stuff from turning into big-time clutter. Any of these work well, too:

✔ Egg cartons

✔ Glass baby-food or spice jars

✔ Ice cube trays

✔ Mini cardboard boxes like the ones jewelry comes in

✔ Small plastic storage containers (with or without lids)

✔ Small, shallow baskets

✔ Tins or plastic boxes that once held candy, breath mints, or cough drops

MESS-MAKER ALERT!

Problem: By nesting bowls and stacking plates and platters, you've freed up space in your cabinets, but the things on top leave ugly scratches on the ones that are below.

Solution: To keep your china pieces scratch-free, put paper plates, coffee filters, or bubble wrap between stacked bowls, plates, and platters.

IN A BIND(ER). When you were sorting through your drawers, you probably pulled out the owner's manuals and warranties for your kitchen appliances (large and small). Well, don't you dare put those important papers back into a drawer! Instead, put them into a three-ring binder, and keep it in a cabinet or on the bookshelf with your cookbooks. If any of the booklets are too thick for your hole-puncher to penetrate, you have two excellent options that you can find in office-supply stores and catalogs.

1. Put them into paper or plastic sleeves that have prepunched holes.

2. Use magazine holders. These are plastic strips, each one with a vertical slit and prepunched holes. You just slide your booklet into the holder, and insert it into any standard-size binder.

HANG AROUND. If you have a tiny kitchen, a pegboard could be the answer to your storage dreams. A friend of mine, whose kitchen is smaller than some people's closets, covered a whole wall with pegboard. She hangs everything she uses regularly, including pots, lids, colanders, oven mitts, cooling racks, measuring cups, and even utensils that have holes in the handles.

USE YOUR COLLECTIBLES.
Instead of having one collection of beautiful kitchenware that you keep on display, and another assortment of less-special versions that you actually use, take another tip from my pal with the tiny kitchen: Get rid of the so-so stuff, and use the bowls, plates, glasses, and so on that you really love. You'll cut clutter in your kitchen, and add some pizzazz to your daily life at the same time!

OUT OF THE BOX

If you'd like to go entirely paperless with your recipe collection, check out the Web. A number of good cooking sites, including www.epicurious.com, www.allrecipes.com, and www.cookingvillage.com, all offer a "recipe box" function. This allows you to choose certain recipes from a huge database, and store them in your own file on the site. Whenever you want a certain one, just pull the recipe up and follow the directions. How easy is that?

ROUND UP THE RECIPES. Recipe collectors, take note! Once you've sorted through your stash and pulled out the keepers, use one of these storage methods to make sure they're always on hand:

• Buy a photo album that has plastic sleeves, and use it to store your recipes. They'll stay neat and orderly, and if you try a recipe but don't like the results, you can just pull the piece of paper out of the sleeve, and toss it into the recycling bin.

• Tape or glue each recipe onto a 5- by 8-inch index card, and file it in either a special recipe box or an old-fashioned file box.

• Scan the recipes into your computer. Then save them as your own electronic recipe collection.

• If you prefer paper copies, print the recipes onto $8^1/_2$- by 11-inch paper, and put them in a three-ring binder.

CLEAR THE DECKS!

Or rather, the countertops. Nothing makes a kitchen look—and feel—more spacious than neat, uncluttered work surfaces. Read on to learn how you can have counters that make mincemeat out of meal prep—and can do the same for cleaning, too.

In This Section:
✔ Countertops
✔ Kitchen island

SORT

If you can't remember the last time you could make dinner without having to move mountains of stuff out of the way, it's time for action. (Unless your counters are so cluttered that you can't even see the surface, you shouldn't need designated boxes for this sorting project.)

NO NEWS IS GOOD NEWS. At least not when it's hogging space on your kitchen counter. Pick up any newspapers and magazines that are waiting to be read, and take them to the living room, family room, or wherever you and your family do your reading. As for the others, toss them into the recycling bin.

PASS 'EM ON. Don't be too quick to dump your magazines, because there's a good chance someone else would love to have them. Hospitals, nursing homes, doctors' and dentists' offices, and even many thrift shops usually welcome recent issues. Magazines that focus on cooking, decorating, fashion, travel, and sports are especially popular.

SCHOOL'S OUT! And the school books and papers are piled high on your island or countertops. So get 'em off—and keep 'em off! Exactly how you do that depends on the available space in the rest of your house, and where your kids do their homework, but consider these options:

1. Issue an order that the youngsters take books, backpacks, and other school-related gear to their rooms as soon as they come home.

2. Designate a drop zone, and insist that it be used consistently. This could be a table, shelf, or dresser near the entryway that the kids use most often. If there's no space for furniture, hang a shelf on the wall, or simply assign a large basket to each child.

EDIT YOUR APPLIANCES.
Take a quick look around your kitchen. Are appliances sitting out that you don't use every day—or at least every couple of days? If so, then clear them

MAKING SPACE

Just as uncluttered countertops make your whole kitchen look neater, cleaner, and bigger, so does a clutter-free floor. So, unless you have a lot of room to spare, get rid of your big garbage can and replace it with a smaller version that will fit under the sink—or even hang on the inside of the door. Of course, you will need to make more trips to the garage, or wherever you keep your large trash cans, but that's a small price to pay for more space in the kitchen. Plus, the more often you empty the can, the less time there'll be for odors to build up.

off the island or countertops, and move them into a cabinet. Or, if there are things you never use, such as the slow cooker that you bought because it seemed like a good idea at the time, send them off to a thrift shop or set them aside for your next garage sale.

SINK YOUR DISH DRAINER. If you have a double sink and you keep a dish drainer sitting on your countertop beside it, this tip should be music to your ears: With a quick trip to a housewares store or your local hardware store, you can free up close to 2 feet of counter space. How? Simply buy a dish drainer that fits right into the sink. Besides gaining more room, having your dishware inside the sink will reduce visual clutter on the counter.

DON'T DITCH YOUR OLD DISH DRAINER. Instead, take it out to your garden shed. It's just the ticket for rinsing off vegetables before you bring them into the house. Just put the veggies in the rack, give 'em a gentle shower from the hose, and let the water and dirt run right off.

COLLECTIBLE CLUTTER. A cookie jar can be a useful item to have on your kitchen counter. But having a dozen of them adds up to major clutter. The same goes for teapots, salt and pepper shakers, and other kitchen-related collectibles. Now, don't get

Ask Jerry

Q. *My husband recently bought a bread box. He insists that our bread will stay fresher longer in there than it does in the drawer where we've been keeping it. I don't think it will make any difference at all, and that box is just cluttering up our countertop. Who's right?*

A. You are! At room temperature, bread stays fresh and tasty for about three days, whether it's in a drawer, cabinet, or bread box—no matter how expensive or high-tech the box is. If you really want to keep that bread at its peak, stash it in the freezer, where it will keep for three months or so. When you're ready to eat it, just thaw it out. It'll taste as fresh as it was the day you bought it.

me wrong—I'm not suggesting that you get rid of your beloved (and possibly valuable) collection! But simply find another place to display your treasures, and you'll free up a whole lot of space in your kitchen. Consider these possibilities:

- Cookie jars. Take those colorful containers to another room—or several rooms—and use them. Fill one with soap and toiletries in a bathroom, another with small supplies in your home office, and a third with all sorts of odds and ends in your craft room.

- Salt and pepper shakers. Arrange them on shallow, wall-hung shelves in any room where you have the space. You can buy special display units in catalogs (both paper and online versions), but for more offbeat options, scout antique shops and flea markets. Old wooden soda pop cases, post office boxes, brick-making molds, and shallow, glass-doored cabinets are just a few of the treasures you may find.

- Teapots. Move them to a hutch in the dining room. Or if you have a kitchen wall that's free of cabinets, hang a shelf near the ceiling, and use that. Besides adding a decorative touch to the room, your fragile collection will be well out of harm's way.

- Mugs. Use them in your home office or hobby room to hold things like pens, pencils, paintbrushes, or knitting needles. Or take them to a bathroom to corral toothbrushes, toothpaste, combs, and brushes. And if you need a small plant pot for starting seedlings or growing windowsill herbs, a mug fits the bill and adds a decorative touch.

COLLECTOR ALERT!

Problem: Too many cookbooks and not enough space in the kitchen.

Solution: Pull out the ones you use most often, and make space for them in a cabinet or on a shelf in the kitchen. Move the rest to a bookcase that's nearby. This way, you'll still be able to grab them quickly when you need them, but they won't be taking up space that you need for other things.

ORGANIZE

Even in a kitchen with oodles of cabinets, there are things that you need to have on your countertops. Arranging them efficiently and logically will ensure that those things can do their job without turning into clutter.

CORNER IT. The ideal place for any countertop appliance is in a corner, where two walls meet. There, it takes up a minimum amount of work surface.

CLIMB THE WALLS. One of the simplest ways to keep your countertops organized is to mount as much stuff on the walls as you possibly can. Replace the telephone that's sitting on your counter with a hanging version. Ditto for the answering machine.

GO UNDERGROUND. Or rather, under the cabinets. If you feel the need to have a radio, television, CD player, or computer monitor in your kitchen, look for a model that can be mounted on the underside of a cabinet—thereby freeing up space on your countertop. You can even buy an under-cabinet "charger station" that comes complete with a concealed, six-outlet extension cord. You just plug your cell phone, MP3 player, or other rechargeable gadgets into the outlet, and you're good to go. You can find these in catalogs and on Web sites that specialize in kitchen gear.

MORE UNDERCOVER OPERATIONS. Electronics are not the only things that you can move off your countertops. When it's time to

> ## MAKING
> ### S P A C E
>
> If you're in the market for a new kitchen table, look for one that's counter height (about 36 inches) so it can easily double as extra work space. And if it provides storage in the base, that's even better. This could be anything from a single closed compartment to a wine rack to—in at least one case—a large shelf, four open cubes, and cubbies for 10 bottles of wine. You can also order matching barstools, so you and your family can belly right up to the table. Counter-height tables are easy to find in furniture stores, in catalogs, and online.

buy any of these essentials, look for versions that you can mount under your cabinets:

- ✔ Can opener

- ✔ Coffeemaker

- ✔ Microwave

- ✔ Paper towel holder

- ✔ Wine rack

HELP FROM THE KITCHEN SINK. To gain more counter space instantly, buy a cutting board that's big enough to fit across your sink. Then anytime you need a little more room to work, put it in place, and chop away.

INTO THE GARAGE. As you know if you've glanced at a home-improvement magazine or watched Home & Garden TV lately, appliance garages are all the rage in space-conscious kitchens. And it's no wonder. These countertop conveniences hide toasters, coffeemakers, and other small appliances while keeping them within easy reach. The garages can be recessed into a wall, or simply nestled under a wall-hung cabinet. To find the right make and model for you, search the Internet or visit a home-improvement store near you.

OVER AND OUT. One of the niftiest countertop organizing aids I've seen is an over-the-sink shelf about 6 inches deep and roughly 36 inches long (long enough to span a double-bowl sink). It stands on legs that are anywhere from 9 to 12 inches high, and rests securely on the counter behind your sink. You can use it to organize all kinds of stuff,

COLLECTOR ALERT!

Problem: A bulky wine rack that's taking up too much space on the countertop.

Solution: Buy a wine tower from a housewares store or catalog. These marvels of efficiency take up very little floor space (some as little as 16 square inches) but store up to 18 or 20 bottles of wine. Plus, some models come equipped with a drawer, a couple of shelves, and a convenient hanging rack on top for your wine glasses.

like dishwashing liquid, hand soap, sponges, paper towels, and vegetable brushes. Models are available in housewares stores and catalogs and (as usual) on many Web sites.

STORE

Once you've cleared your countertops of nonessentials, you need to find places to put them. And, of course, you also need to find the best way to arrange the things that do need to remain at your fingertips. The storage solutions in this section will help you do just that.

REACH FOR THE SKY! Or rather, reach for the wooden spoon…or the spatula, whisk, or pastry brush. Any utensils that you use frequently should be kept close at hand. So find a couple of attractive containers to hold your utensils, and keep them on the counter near the stove so you can quickly grab what you need. Crocks, pitchers, or new flowerpots are just a few good options.

ROLLING RIGHT ALONG. If you've got the floor space, consider buying a microwave cart on wheels. Look for a model that has shelves underneath, so it can not only free up counter space, but also provide more storage—and roll out of the way when you're done using it.

OUT OF THE BOX

If you use plastic cutting boards, you know that they tend to retain the odors of the foods that you cut on them. But there's a simple way to keep the aromas from mixing and mingling: Just color-code your boards. Use one color for bread, a second for meat, a third for strong-smelling vegetables like onions and garlic, and a fourth for less aromatic fruits and veggies. Problem solved!

KEEP ON ROLLING. If you have a kitchen island where you can store stuff that might otherwise clutter your counters, count your lucky stars! If you don't have such a treasure, don't fret. Just go out and buy the next-best thing: a wheeled kitchen cart with storage space below and a work surface on top. When it's time to prepare a meal, just roll the cart to your work site, then roll it away when you're through. You can find kitchen carts in just about any housewares store, in kitchen-gear catalogs, or on Web sites, and they come in many materials, sizes, and price ranges.

THE QUESTION OF CUTTING BOARDS.

What's the best way to clear cutting boards off the countertop, but still keep them close at hand? The answer is, it all depends. Consider these de-cluttering options:

- If you have attractive wooden boards, hang them above the counter where you use them.

- Hang plastic cutting boards, or worn wooden versions, on the inside of a lower cabinet door. (Again, use the cabinet that's closest to the place where you do your slicing, dicing, and chopping.)

- Stand plastic cutting boards upright in a wire file organizer. You can find one in any store that sells office supplies.

WHAT NOT TO STORE ON YOUR KITCHEN COUNTER.

If you pick up just about any kitchen-gadget or garden-supply catalog these days, you'll see fancy ceramic or stainless steel compost containers that are designed to sit out on your kitchen counter. They even come with disposable filters that keep unpleasant aromas from escaping. The basic idea is great: As you're preparing a meal or cleaning up afterwards, you just toss all your produce peelings, scraps, and suitable leftovers into the

MESS-MAKER ALERT!

Problem: A kitchen trash can that's brimming with table scraps and leftovers, and no compost bin to toss them in.

Solution: Don't throw that stuff in the garbage! Instead, collect it in a plastic container, and then dump the contents into your compost pile, or simply dig a hole and bury it in your yard or garden. Besides produce peelings and scraps, you can also compost coffee grounds and filters, used tea bags, over-the-hill flowers, and even breakfast cereal, complete with the milk, this way. (For more tips on how to compost kitchen style, see "The Bucket Brigade" on page 42.)

container. When it gets full, you take it outside and dump the contents into your compost bin. But do you *really* want garbage sitting out on your kitchen counter? I know I don't—no matter how it's packaged!

So what's the alternative? Do what I do: Put your compostable scraps and such in a lidded plastic container, like a big yogurt or ice cream tub, and keep it in a plastic bucket under the sink. When it's full—or preferably sooner—take it outside and add the stuff to your bin or pile.

PARE DOWN THE PANTRY

Maybe you're lucky enough to have an actual built-in pantry where you store your nonperishable foods. Or maybe you have to keep the whole stash in your kitchen cabinets. Either way, that "warehouse" can turn into a cluttered mess in the blink of an eye—or at least it seems that way. The secret to conquering chaos is, you guessed it, putting our SOS plan to work.

In This Section:
✔ *Pantry*
✔ *Food cupboards*

SORT

For some folks, the job of cleaning out the food cupboards ranks right up (or down) there with scrubbing the siding on the house. If you haven't looked at the back of those shelves since the last time you bought grape jelly in a Howdy Doody glass, you may feel that way, too. Well, relax. Whatever's lurking back there can't hurt you. Just grit your teeth and grab some trash bags and boxes. Then open a door— any door—and start sorting.

INTO THE FRAY. As you pull each item off a shelf, assign it to one of the following categories:

• Trash. All bulging cans, any jar that's leaking or on which the warning button on the lid has popped up, anything that's more than a week or so past its printed sell-by date—and (of course) all those half-filled bags of limp snacks left over from last year's Super Bowl party.

- Food bank. Anything that's still good but you *know* you won't use—such as the canned crabmeat that you've just learned you're allergic to, or the bean soup that you've been meaning to eat for the past three months. (Be sure that you get a receipt: Most likely, your donation will be tax deductible.)

- Use soon. Any food that you routinely use, and is still good, but has gotten lost in the crush of clutter.

- Get creative—*now*. Goodies that you bought on impulse, such as marinated artichoke hearts or pickled peppers, because you thought they'd be a great new taste treat. Well, they will be—*if* you eat them or work them into a recipe. Otherwise, they're just cupboard-clogging clutter.

TO THE RESCUE! Some foods that seem like prime candidates for the trash may simply need a little first aid. Take these, for instance:

PACK RAT ALERT!

Problem: Shelves that are crammed with outdated cans and boxes of food that you bought in large quantities at unbelievably low prices.

Solution: When you shop for food, don't buy any more than you can consume before the expiration date rolls around—no matter how low the price tag may be. Besides adding lots of needless clutter to your pantry, it's a good bet that in the end you will wind up spending far more money than you saved!

✔ Hard rolls that are too hard. To freshen them up, put them in a damp paper bag and heat in the oven for 10 minutes at 350°F.

✔ Raisins that have turned hard. As long as they're not showing signs of mold, put them in a pan and cover them with water. Bring it to a boil, and then remove the pan from the heat. Let it stand for five minutes. Then drain off the water, and gobble 'em up!

✔ Crackers that have gone soft. Spread them out on a baking sheet, and heat them in a 300°F oven for five minutes. Then cool completely, and bring on the cheese!

Accept Substitutions

It's a good bet that a number of items that are cluttering up your pantry are things you bought to use in a certain recipe—and then never glanced at again. So clear out all those partially filled containers of this and that. Then, the next time a recipe calls for an ingredient that you don't have on hand, don't rush out and buy it. Check this chart first, because there's a good chance you already have what you need.

IF YOU LACK THIS	USE THIS INSTEAD
1 tsp. of baking powder	$^1/_2$ tsp. of cream of tartar + $^1/_4$ tsp. of baking soda
1 cup of buttermilk	1 tsp. of vinegar or lemon juice + enough milk to measure 1 cup
1 cup of cake flour	$^7/_8$ cup of all-purpose flour
1 tbsp. of cornstarch	2 tbsp. of all-purpose flour
$^3/_4$ cup of cracker crumbs	1 cup of bread crumbs
1 cup of dark corn syrup	$^3/_4$ cup of light corn syrup + $^1/_4$ cup of molasses
1 cup of half-and-half	1 tbsp. of melted butter + enough whole milk to measure 1 cup
1 cup of honey	$1^1/_4$ cups of sugar + $^1/_4$ cup of liquid *
1 tsp. of lemon juice	$^1/_4$ tsp. of cider vinegar
1 cup of light corn syrup	1 cup of sugar + 1 cup of liquid *
1 cup of molasses	1 cup of honey
2 tsp. of tapioca	1 tbsp. of all-purpose flour
1 cup of tomato sauce	$^3/_4$ cup of tomato paste + 1 cup of water
1 unsweetened chocolate square (1 oz.)	3 tbsp. of cocoa + 1 tbsp. of vegetable oil or shortening

* Water or whatever other liquid your recipe calls for, such as milk, cream, or fruit juice.

WHEN YOUR BREAD GOES STALE... Don't toss it out. Instead, toast it, tear the slices into cubes, and freeze them in a ziplock plastic bag. Use them in stuffing or crush them up for any recipe that calls for bread crumbs. (This trick works with stale biscuits and bagels, too.)

DOES THE SODA STILL SIZZLE? Whether you use baking soda for its intended purpose or as a miracle cleanser, its powers are severely limited if it's not fresh. So when you pull that familiar orange box off a pantry shelf, make sure the stuff is still potent before you put it back. To make the call, simply add 1 tablespoon of baking soda to $1/4$ cup of vinegar. If it fizzes, you're good to go.

ORGANIZE

Before you start reloading your clean, empty pantry, take some time to plan the new arrangement. Remember, though: There's no right or wrong way to organize your food. All that matters is putting everything where *you* can put your hands on it quickly. So pick and choose from this smorgasbord of possibilities.

SEPARATE QUARTERS. In the best of all possible worlds, a pantry holds only food. But in real life, that's rarely possible. Still, no matter how small your storage area is, it will function much more efficiently if you keep edibles and nonedibles apart. So if you must keep things like aluminum foil, plastic wrap, and paper towels in your pantry, at least assign them to a shelf of their own.

LIGHT UP! If your pantry is a closet or deep cabinet, make sure there's enough light inside so you can find what you need quickly

OUT OF THE BOX

Your pantry doesn't have to be in your kitchen. If space is really tight, keep food and paper products to the bare minimum in your kitchen, and store the overflow on shelves or in a big cupboard elsewhere in the house. A laundry or utility room would work fine. So would the basement (as long as it's dry and insect-free) or the attic (as long as it doesn't get too hot).

and easily. Either have an electrician install a ceiling light, or buy cordless, battery-powered lights that you can hang on the wall yourself. They're inexpensive and come in versions that you attach with adhesive, nails, or screws. Look for them at your local hardware store, or in home-improvement stores and catalogs.

CLUTTER BUSTER PRO

Patrice Flynn is a professional organizer who specializes in coaching her clients in the fine art of de-cluttering their homes—and keeping them that way. She is the owner of House Call in Carver, Massachusetts (www.housecall-hq.com), and she offers these general tips for conquering clutter in the pantry:

☛ Allow 30 to 90 minutes for your reorganizing project.

☛ Plan to do the job at a time when you're alone, so you won't be distracted.

☛ Before you start, spend some time considering which arrangements work well for you and your family, and which ones cause hassle and chaos.

☛ Decide which foods need to be most accessible, and put them at eye level.

☛ Store everything where it's as easy to find and as easy to reach as possible, with the smallest items in front.

☛ Place small items or half-used bags together in containers.

☛ Group paper products, like paper plates and napkins, together on a lower shelf.

☛ Organize your pantry contents so that you can take a quick inventory of what you need, when you need it.

☛ Hang a pad of paper on a pantry door, and use it to keep a running shopping list as items are used up.

☛ If you have young children, keep snacks on a shelf they can reach easily.

☛ The key to maintaining an organized pantry is to follow this classic advice: Make a place for everything, and keep everything in its place.

SHELF LIFE. There's a good chance your pantry has shelves that are so deep that you're either wasting space or building towers of stuff that could topple over at any minute. The solution: Add more shelves. What kind you choose is up to you. You can use metal strips and brackets for wooden shelves, or simply set freestanding wire shelves on top of the existing ones. Either way, you'll gain valuable storage space and reduce the chance of a culinary avalanche.

ON THE STRAIGHT AND NARROW. No matter what kind of shelves you opt for, make sure they're as narrow as possible. Ideally, they should be only deep enough to hold one or, at most, two items. That's because if, let's say, cans of refried beans are lined up in rows that are three or four cans deep, you'll never see the stuff that's way in back. Then you'll wind up either going to the store to buy things you already have—or simply losing track of what you've got and letting it go bad.

MAKE ROOM FOR THE KIDS. Well, their stuff, anyway. If your children or grand-children use the kitchen table for homework and craft projects, keep their supplies in the pantry. Stow everything in transparent plastic storage boxes with lock-down lids and handles. Choose small containers that are easy to carry and put them on shelves that the youngsters can reach without climbing on a chair—or calling for help.

SNACKS FRONT AND CENTER. Save time and hassle by keeping crackers, chips, cookies, and other snacks where everyone in the family can see and reach them easily.

OUT OF THE BOX

If you routinely keep your household first-aid kit in the bathroom, I have a question for you: How many times have you ever gotten burned or cut in the bathroom? (Aside from razor nicks, that is.) That stash of ointments, bandages, and such belongs in your pantry. After all, the kitchen is the room in the house where people are most likely to get burned, cut, or scraped. Plus, your kitchen probably has a direct link to the great outdoors, which is the other major venue for minor injuries—and insect bites and stings, to boot.

ROUND AND ROUND. If you pay any attention to the sell-by dates in the grocery stores (and I sure hope you do!), you know that the folks who stock the shelves always slide the new supplies to the back and move the older ones up front. Well, you need to keep those cans and jars moving in just the same way in your pantry. If you buy chicken soup, let's say, and you already have some in the cupboard, tuck the new cans behind the old ones. Otherwise, one of these days, you're liable to dive into a bowl of chicken soup that tastes like the tin can it came from, and trust me, friends—that soup's not good for *anyone's* soul!

CATEGORICALLY SPEAKING. When it comes to simple ways to organize your food, you can't beat this old standby: Just arrange everything by category. For instance, group canned fruits and veggies on one shelf, canned fish and meats on another, and soups and stews on still another. Put all baking supplies together, all cereals, all snack treats, and so on.

Ask Jerry

Q. *I've always kept my herbs and spices on a pretty rack above my stove, but recently a friend told me that's not a good place for them. Is this true?*

A. Yep, it's true all right. When herbs and spices are exposed to heat and light, their volatile oils, which give them their fragrance and flavor, evaporate fast. So always keep them in a cool, dark place. The same goes for all your herbal vinegars and flavored oils, too.

WE'RE ALL IN THIS TOGETHER. If you like to put meals on the table ASAP, this system's for you: Group the foods that you tend to use together in the same place. Keep the pasta with your favorite sauce makings, put the refried beans and salsa next to the taco shells, and gather all the broth and canned veggies into one big huddle.

OVER THE RAINBOW. Frankly, I find this system a little kooky, but I know folks who swear by it: You color-code your food. First, label each shelf with a color (or two, depending on how many shelves you've got). Then, arrange the cans, jars, and boxes accordingly. For example:

- Green shelf—pickles, relish, green beans, green chilies, peas, spinach, artichokes, asparagus, and green olives

- Yellow shelf—corn, yellow mustard, squash, pineapple, chicken broth, lemonade, and apple juice

- Red shelf—ketchup, salsa, spaghetti and pizza sauces, red beans, chili, strawberry jam, cherry and strawberry gelatin, and canned tomatoes

- Orange shelf—carrots, yams, peaches, orange marmalade, orange-flavored drink mix, and Thousand Island salad dressing

- White shelf—pasta, popcorn, rice, sauerkraut, pears, white or light rye bread, saltine crackers, mayonnaise, canned tuna or chicken, oatmeal, sugar, and flour

- Brown/black shelf—dark mustard, nuts, canned sausages, cocoa, and black olives; wheat, dark rye, or pumpernickel bread; and barbecue, teriyaki, and soy sauce

Here's a food-storage option you may not have thought of: Try organizing your food alphabetically. Start with (let's say) applesauce, then proceed through baked beans, cashews, dog biscuits— you get the picture.

HIGHER AND HIGHER. Regardless of what pantry-organizing system you use, if you have small children, dogs, or cats around the house (even if they're only frequent visitors), put anything that you don't want little hands or paws dipping into or knocking over way up high, or even behind locked doors. After all, we all know that when the little rascals *really* want something, they'll use every trick in the book to get it!

STORE

Just like your bedroom closet, your pantry can hold a whole lot more than its size suggests. The tips coming up will help you almost double the storage space in your culinary warehouse. They'll also clue you in on how to store your food the right way, so it doesn't turn into annoying clutter.

TURN DOWN THE HEAT. Even "nonperishable" food can go bad when the temperature gets too high. To help it stay tasty, try to keep the temperature in your food-storage area no higher than 72°F.

IT'S ALL RELATIVE. Most dry foods keep best when the relative humidity is 15 percent or less, but unless you can look out your door and see a cactus or two, that level won't be easy to maintain. Keep the air as dry as you can, though. Running your air conditioner in the summer will help keep moisture at bay, and so will storing your dry goods in glass jars with tight lids (see "A Jarring Idea" below), or in plastic storage containers.

LIGHTS OUT! To ensure that your food stays at its healthy best, keep it behind closed doors—or at least away from direct light. Both artificial light and the sun's rays can make the nutrients fade fast.

A JARRING IDEA. When it comes to storing dry goods, for my money, you can't beat big glass jars with clamp-top lids. They're perfect for flour, sugar, pasta, rice—and even tea bags, cereal, crackers, and dog biscuits. Thanks to the tight seals on the jars, the food inside stays fresh

Restaurants and delicatessens buy pickles and other condiments in giant-size jars that make perfect now-you-see-it storage containers for everything from cornflakes to jelly beans. The next time you're having lunch at your favorite deli, ask whether they've got any empty jars to spare. Your host is all but guaranteed to say, "Sure do! We were just about to toss half a dozen of 'em in the recycling bin, but now they're all yours!"

longer than it ever would in its original bags and boxes. Plus, you can see at a glance when you're running low on something.

HONEY DO. Honey is the only food on earth that never goes bad. But it is important to store it in a dry place. Otherwise, it tends to absorb moisture and turn crumbly. If that happens to your supply, don't panic: Just sink the jar up to its neck in hot water. That honey'll be flowin' like liquid gold before you know it!

How Long Will It Last?

So just how long *can* you count on keeping your foods fresh and tasty in storage? It all depends. Here's a rundown on the life expectancies of some common, packaged edibles. (Bear in mind that these are approximate time frames. Also, the longevity of a particular product can vary from one brand to another, so always check the date on the box, can, or jar before you chow down!)

GOOD FOR UP TO 5 YEARS	GOOD FOR UP TO 2 YEARS	GOOD FOR 12 TO 18 MONTHS	GOOD FOR 6 MONTHS OR SO
Canned chili	Canned beef, chicken, and ham	Baby food	Baking powder
Canned tuna	Canned fruits and vegetables	Barbecue sauce	Crackers
Cocoa	Canned soup	Cake mix	Dried fruits
Gravy (jars or cans)	Catsup	Canned and bottled juices	Dried herbs and spices
Refried beans	Chocolate syrup	Cooking oils	Flour
Rice (long-grained white)	Mustard	Flavored gelatin	Hot cereal
Spices (whole)	Pasta	Instant tea	Instant potatoes
Tomato paste	Pasta sauce	Jams and jellies	Juice boxes
Unflavored gelatin	Peanut butter	Oatmeal	Mayonnaise
Vanilla	Peanuts	Quick-cook rice	Powdered coffee creamer
Vinegar	Popcorn	Salad dressing	Pudding Mix
	Powdered drink mix	Salsa	Rice mixes
		Sugar	

HERBAL REMEDIES. In the last section, I reminded you that in order to retain their full flavor and aroma, herbs and spices need to be kept in a cool, dark place. Easier said than done? Not at all! Here are three clever ways to keep those flavorings at their peak and make the most efficient use of your pantry space:

1. Instead of keeping your herbs and spices on a pantry shelf, assign them to a shallow drawer that isn't near the stove. You'll be amazed at how many jars you can fit into the space when you stand them shoulder to shoulder.

2. Buy little round tins to hold your herbs and spices. (They're available in storage and housewares stores and over the Internet.) Then attach a magnetic knife rack or a magnetic board to the wall or the side of a cabinet—again choose one that's not close to the stove—and pop the tins onto it. *Note:* Make sure the tins you buy have opaque lids, not transparent ones.

3. Use a spice rack that attaches to the bottom of an over-the-counter cabinet, and folds up flat when it's not in use. They're available from Web sites that specialize in storage supplies and kitchenware.

DON'T FORGET THE LABELS! Whether you choose jars or tins for your herbs, be sure to label the lid of each one to show the contents. You can buy fancy, preprinted versions on the Web and in houseware stores, or simply use stick-on dots from an office-supply store.

Ask Jerry

Q. I'd like to keep plenty of pasta, rice, beans, and other dried foods on hand, but I'm concerned about insects getting into them. How can I keep the invaders out?

A. The answer to this dilemma couldn't be simpler: Just scatter some bay leaves across the shelves. Wily weevils, beastly beetles, and other pesky pests will keep their safe distance.

USE THE DOOR. Even in a large pantry, the back of the door is useful storage space. But in a small one, it's priceless real estate! Here's a handy half-dozen ways you can put it to work:

✔ Install a long wire shelf unit on the door, and use it to hold lightweight boxes, jars, and tins. (You can find them at large hardware and home-improvement stores.)

✔ Attach hanging files, like the ones you see on the doors of the examining rooms in your doctor's office. Fill them with local restaurant and take-out menus, cooking magazines, catalogs, or even outgoing mail.

✔ Screw on clasping hooks to hang brooms, mops, and other cleaning tools.

✔ Hang up a bulletin board—either cork, magnetic, or elasticized (see the Mess-Maker Alert! on page 51).

✔ Paint on a chalkboard. Just pick up a can of chalkboard paint at the hardware store, and create a space for everyone's lists, messages, and doodles.

✔ Hang a clear plastic shoe bag on the door (either a screw-on or over-the-door model). Then stash your dried soup mixes, nuts, candy, and other small packaged foods in the pockets.

HELP FROM THE BATHROOM.
If you rely on a lot of spray cleaners to keep your kitchen shipshape, attach a towel rod to a wall in your pantry (or on one side of your under-sink cabinet). Then suspend your spray bottles from

MAKING SPACE When every inch of your pantry counts, buy a broom that has a collapsible handle. When it's not on active duty, you can fold it up to a tidy 36 inches long. You can find these space savers at hardware and housewares stores.

the rod by their triggers. You'll be able to grab what you want instantly. Plus, because everything will be out in plain sight, you'll be less likely to forget that you have one and accidentally buy another.

FLOORED! If you keep cleaning supplies in your pantry, assign them to the floor under the lowest shelf (or the shelf itself if your pantry is a tall cabinet). But if you have young children or pets in the house, limit the inventory to gear like buckets, tubs, and dustpans. Don't keep *any* cleansers in that easy-to-reach spot—liquids or powders. Even so-called "green" products can cause major damage if they wind up in the hands (or stomach) of a curious child or pet.

BUCKETS ON THE DOUBLE.

Whether you store your cleaning supplies in the pantry or under the kitchen sink, a plastic bucket is a handy thing to keep them in. But two buckets are even handier—and they don't have to take up double the space. Just slip a same-size pail under the one you have now, and you'll have one to work from and one to carry your gear in. This way, you won't have to take everything out of the bucket when you start your cleaning project, and put it all back once you've finished.

OUT OF THE BOX

Before you rush out to buy buckets, take a look around to see what substitutes you may have. One great option is to use the large plastic tubs that some cat litter and laundry detergent brands come in. For corralling small stuff like sponges and scrubbers for the kitchen sink, use plastic containers that once held deli salads or Chinese takeout.

CHAPTER THREE

THE LIVING ROOM

When it comes to general living areas, all homes and all families are *not* created equal. For instance, maybe your house has a "living room" for entertaining guests and a separate "family room" where you just hang out with the family. Or maybe you and your clan do all of your living and entertaining in one big (or not so big) "great room." Regardless of how many separate rooms you have, or how you use them, the basic formula for keeping them clutter-free and ready for action—or relaxation—is the same: sort, organize, and store.

THE BIG PICTURE

There's no doubt about it: Living areas tend to attract more than their fair share of small objects that can quickly turn into big-time clutter—everything from board games to baseball cards and magazines to marble collections. But before you even think about all that little stuff, tackle what could be your biggest clutter culprits of all—your furnishings and the way they're arranged.

In This Section:
✔ Furniture
✔ Accessories
✔ Lighting
✔ Traffic flow

SORT

The first step on the road to a clutter-free—and *livable*—living space is (you guessed it!) to weed out the stuff that doesn't need to be there. So don't just stand there—dive right in!

LOVE IT OR LOSE IT. If you're like a lot of folks I know, you have at least a few pieces of furniture that are just sitting around taking up space. Maybe you inherited your Aunt Ethel's mahogany writing desk, and you've never had the heart to get rid of it—even though everyone in your family hates it. Perhaps you're still hanging on to a recliner you bought years ago because you thought your hubby would love it—but he never sits in it. Then there's the plant stand you snapped up at a flea market because it fit perfectly in a corner where you "needed" something—but you don't have a single houseplant. Well, do yourself a big favor, and get rid of those hangers-on!

TAKE STOCK. Take a good, hard look at each piece of furniture in each of your living spaces, and ask yourself these questions:

1. Does it serve a purpose in this room?

2. Do I really like it or, better yet, love it?

3. Is it taking up space that I could really use for something else (like bookshelves or a cozy reading chair)?

FROM TIME TO TIME. As you examine your living and/or family room, consider whether they suit the way you and your family live now. For instance, does your family room look exactly the way it did when your children were toddlers—and your baby left for college two years ago? Is your living room set up for the formal entertaining you used to do—even though you've switched to more casual get-togethers? Did you downsize, and now you have a single room functioning as both a living room and dining room? If any of those scenarios hit home, it's a good bet that at least some of your furniture falls squarely into the clutter category.

MAKING SPACE

One instant way to add space to a room—and give your de-cluttering campaign some big-time momentum—is to get rid of one large object that you either don't use or don't like. Are you hanging on to a ratty couch with stains all over the cushions, or your Aunt Sally's old piano that simply will not stay in tune? Well, get it outta there! The room will instantly look like it's almost doubled in size.

LET THERE BE LAMPS. But not too many of them. A lot of small lamps scattered around a room can make it look like a cluttered junk shop. And the jumble of cords can pose hazards of their own. People can easily trip over them, or heaven forbid, a toddler or pet could decide to take a bite, with the results being tragic. So hang on to a few good floor or table lamps that suit your decor and give off good light in the places you need it, and send the rest packin'.

A ROOM OF THEIR OWN. So what can you do with furniture and lamps that you really don't want to part with, but that just aren't working in their current spots? Take them to other parts of the house! Maybe a chair that's crowding the living room would be perfect in the family room or even a guest room. The buffet you banished from the living/dining room could be just the ticket for holding a bunch of supplies in your home office. And a lamp that's one too many in the family room could provide the light you need in your bedroom.

In a combination living and dining room, a more conventional buffet, a.k.a. sideboard, takes up more space than its storage value is worth. So if you have other places to store things like table linens and serving platters, replace that monster with a narrow, wall-mounted shelf made of glass or wood. And if you find that you really do need the surface room that the buffet provided, pick up a wheeled serving cart that you can roll out of the way when the meal is over.

GIVE 'EM A NEW HOME. Sometimes it's hard to part with old hand-me-down furniture because of the happy memories associated with it. Well, you don't have to leave it at the curb. If you live in a college town, the week before school starts, advertise your free furniture in the school paper, or post notices on campus bulletin boards. Students who need to set up housekeeping on a shoestring budget will really appreciate your couch, and any other tables, chairs, or bookcases you have to offer. Their enthusiasm will remind you of the days when you really needed this furniture—and how far you've come since then!

GET A JUMP ON DOWNSIZING.
If you have family heirlooms that don't
fit the space you have now—much less
the smaller quarters you'll have when you
retire—start finding good homes for them
ASAP. After all, why keep them around for
another 5 or 10 years, cluttering up your
place, when someone else could be putting
them to good use? But to make sure this de-
cluttering strategy is a win-win situation for
everyone involved, you need to go about it
in just the right way. Here's your three-step
key to success:

1. Ask before you give. Decide on whom
you would like to give each piece to.
Then ask whether he or she would
indeed enjoy owning the item. Don't
request an immediate answer. Instead,
give the potential recipient a time limit
to reach a decision. In the meantime,
have a runner-up or two in mind, just
in case the answer is "Thanks, but no
thanks." This way, you'll have a willing
taker, instead of simply passing the clutter
"buck" to someone else.

2. Make deliveries. If you wait for the lucky recipients to come and
haul your furniture away, it could sit around for years, and that
would defeat the whole purpose of your mission. So, as soon as
you've found a new owner for everything you want to get rid of,
load the pieces into a truck and deliver them to their new owners.
Yes, this may mean springing for a DIY moving van, or even hiring
a delivery service, but take it from me: Freeing up all that space will
be worth every penny!

PACK RAT ALERT!

Problem: A lot of yard sale
and trash-day finds that
need just a few cosmetic
fix-ups—which you haven't
done yet.

Solution: Give those things
to someone who can
use them *now*, not when
they can find the time to
spruce 'em up. Call some
church groups, shelters,
or the closest Habitat for
Humanity office, and ask if
they know of any folks who
could use some decent
furniture. You'll find it a
lot easier to part with your
lucky finds when you know
they're going to someone
who really needs them.

3. Practice unconditional giving. Don't tell your daughter that she can have Grandma's piano only if she promises never to part with it. If you do, you'll put too much pressure on her—and she may feel as though she has to live with the thing even after it's become clutter in her own house.

HELP THE SHOW GO ON. How'd you like to de-clutter your living and family rooms and do your bit for the local theater at the same time? Just donate some of your castoffs to the props department of a nearby drama school, college drama department, or community theater. These places are often delighted to get furniture, lamps, rugs, curtains, and other accessories that are in good condition. But before you cart the stuff over, call and ask what—if anything—they could use. There's a good chance they'll even swing by and pick it up.

STEP ON THE GAS. If you can't imagine a fireplace without the crackle and aroma of real burning wood, then this tip is *not* for you. But if you'd like to have the warmth of a fire without all the clutter—tools, baskets of logs, and a lot of dust and grime—consider this cleaner option: Switch from wood to gas. If there's a natural gas line running to your house, all you need to do is have a contractor run the line to your fireplace and install a gas insert. And if natural gas isn't available, just have a contractor hook up a liquid propane tank for you. Both versions are a whole lot cleaner than wood-burning fires. And, unlike fake electric models, gas fires create real

If your windows are covered by heavy draperies, you have a golden opportunity to make your living spaces feel airier, more spacious, and less cluttered—in the blink of an eye. What is it? Replace the drapes with lightweight fabric shades or woven wooden shades (a.k.a. matchstick blinds). To get the biggest space-gaining bang for your buck, go with shades that match your paint or wallpaper. Matching colors or patterns will make the room seem even larger and less cluttered.

flames, so you'll get the classic hearthside experience, minus all of the soot, splinters, and flaking bark.

SPEAKING OF FIREPLACES...

In many homes, the mantel is a major source of clutter. Either it's crammed from end to end with knickknacks, plants, vases, picture frames, and who knows what else, or it's a prime dumping ground for an assortment of things like car keys, mail, and the dog's leash. Well, do yourself a favor: Clear all that stuff off. If you have an impressive picture hanging over the mantel, all you really need to accent it are a few candlesticks. (That is, except at Christmastime, when no mantel would be complete without some holiday greenery and—of course—a stocking for everyone in the family!)

COLLECTOR ALERT!

Problem: Your cherished collection is taking over your living room!

Solution: Do what museums and art galleries do: Rotate your treasures on a regular basis. Keep some of your paintings, vases, candlesticks—or whatever—on display, while the rest go into storage. Then, on a planned date, change the "show." Besides keeping your room less cluttered, you'll be able to appreciate each object more when there are fewer items to look at.

ORGANIZE

Even after you've cleared out all of your unnecessary furniture and accessories, your living spaces may still feel crowded—and even a little messy. Fortunately, all it takes to make those rooms truly clutter-free is a little savvy organizing—using the tricks you'll find in this section.

MAKE ROOM TO ROAM. The key to creating a feeling of uncluttered openness in any room is to make sure people can move through the space comfortably. This is a definite must, whether they're passing through with a basket of toys, or walking from the couch to the bookcase. How can you accomplish this? Simply by keeping these two guidelines in mind when you arrange your furniture:

1. If your floor plan has the furniture spread around the walls, be careful not to block doorways. Be sure to keep everything far enough away so that people don't bump into it as they come into the room. The exact distance depends on how far the piece of furniture juts out from the wall, so you'll have to experiment to find just the right spot.

2. If your furniture is grouped together into different clusters throughout the room, leave enough space for folks to walk easily around each cluster.

HOW MUCH SPACE IS ENOUGH? To see if you've really left enough distance between furniture groupings, or between, say, a table or couch and a doorway, try this trick: Picture your dog or a couple of small children running through the room. Could they do it without bumping into anything? If the answer is "yes," then you're home free. But if the answer is "no," then that means you've still got some furniture movin' to do.

MAKING SPACE

No law says that your dining table has to be in the center of the dining space. If quarters are tight, as they usually are in a living or dining room, consider moving the table to one side. Just find a firm-seated sofa or a comfortable bench (with a back, of course!), and put it up against a wall. Then move the table up to the bench, and bingo—the whole room will look bigger and less cluttered! By the way, this trick works just as well in a dining area that's part of a kitchen.

FOCUS IN. Think of all the serene, relaxing, uncluttered rooms you've ever seen, and I'll guarantee you that they all have one thing in common: a focal point. In designers' lingo, that's the spot you notice immediately when you enter a room. If nothing in particular stands out, your eye wanders all over the place. The effect can be confusing and unsettling. In other words, the

room *feels* cluttered, even though it isn't. A
fireplace or a wall of bookshelves provides
a natural focal point. If you have neither
of those, consider organizing your living,
dining, or family room around one of these
focal points:

✔ A large window with a beautiful view

✔ A chest or table with a dramatic piece of
   art above it

✔ A beautiful hutch or cabinet displaying
   your favorite china and/or glassware

✔ A large quilt or tapestry hung on a wall

A GLASS ACT. Here's another trick
of the trade that can make your living
room seem less cluttered: Choose glass
or Plexiglas™ tabletops instead of wood
or marble versions. Better yet, look for
tables that are made entirely of transparent
acrylic or Plexiglas. They'll provide the
illusion of more space, and these no-see-'em materials
are compatible with just about any furniture style.

MESS-MAKER ALERT!

Problem: Stuff that's
constantly straying from
other parts of the house
into the living room and
family room.

Solution: Keep a good-
looking basket in your
living area, and when you
spot any out-of-place
objects, toss them into
the basket. Then the next
time you go from room
to room, take the basket
with you and deposit
the "wanderers" in their
rightful places.

MIRROR, MIRROR ON THE WALL. In decorating magazines
and on home-and-garden TV shows, you often see mirrors used to make
rooms look more spacious. But the fact is that when it comes to visually
de-cluttering a living area, a looking glass (as my Grandma Putt used to
call it) can be your best friend…or your worst enemy. If you put it in the
right place, it will make the room look more open, spacious, and serene.
But in the wrong spot, it'll turn the scene into a cluttered jumble that
will set your teeth on edge. The simple reason, of course, is that a
mirror doubles everything—the good, the bad, *and* the ugly!

CLUTTER BUSTER PRO

Monica Premo, a professional organizer and owner of Practically Perfect (www.practicallyperfect.biz) in Bonaire, Georgia, says, "Use the library as your guide to taking good care of your books. Librarians recognize the value of treating books with care so they last for generations."

Here's Monica's checklist of the most important things to do to preserve the value of your books:

☛ Store books away from dirt, excessive dust, extreme temperatures, and extreme humidity or dryness. The temperature and humidity fluctuations in attics, basements, and garages are especially hard on books.

☛ Don't pack your books too tightly on the shelves, and leave some space between the tops of the books and the shelf above so that air can circulate around them.

☛ Never turn corners down to mark your place—you'll tear the pages that way. Instead, use bookmarks made of paper, ribbon, or leather. Don't use paper clips or metal bookmarks because they can leave permanent marks on pages, and may also rust in damp weather.

☛ Support your spines! If a row of books doesn't reach from one end of a bookshelf to the other, use bookends to hold the volumes upright and stable. If they're allowed to lean, the pressure on the spines will break them down.

☛ When you take a book off the shelf, always pull it from the side rather than the top of the spine.

☛ Whenever you handle books, make sure your hands are clean. You don't want any dirt and oils from your skin to mar the cover and pages.

☛ If you must make a note in a book, use a soft pencil, and make your marks as light as possible so that they can be easily erased. Whatever you do, never use a pen, marker, or highlighter. Besides being impossible to remove, markings from these implements can bleed and make a real mess of any book.

CONSIDER THE REFLECTION. Before hanging a mirror, think about what you'll be doubling. For example, a mirror that reflects a window with a beautiful view will bring in natural light and a sense of spaciousness. On the other hand, if the view you're doubling is that of your seating area, your living room could wind up looking about as homey and inviting as a hotel lobby. And if it faces a collection of small objects—even beautiful ones that are nicely arranged—all you'll see is a cluttered mess.

DOUBLE-DUTY DINING. If your family enjoys casual dinners in the family room, but space is tight, go with a coffee table that can double as a dining surface. You have two excellent choices:

1. A coffee table that sits at least 18 to 20 inches off the floor. Keep oversize pillows underneath, and pull 'em out when it's order-in Chinese or pizza night.

2. A table that adjusts from coffee- to dining-table height. You can find these handy furnishings in catalogs, on the Internet, and in some furniture stores.

 ## STORE

No, this section isn't about storing your furniture! Instead, it's chock-full of good advice on using furniture to solve storage problems, and tips on displaying your treasured art and collectibles in ways that don't make your living spaces look cluttered. So read on!

Attention do-it-yourselfers! You say you like the idea of an adjustable-height table, but you can't find one that suits your taste or budget? Don't despair—the solution to your problem is as close as your computer! Just search for "pop-up coffee-table mechanism," and you'll find a device that can turn any kind of table into one that can go from coffee- to dining-table height. You simply attach the bottom of the mechanism to a solid base (or the top of your current coffee table), and the top to your choice of tabletops. Then when it's time to ring the dinner bell, just pull the tabletop upward and toward you.

DROP IT RIGHT THERE. It's a fact of human nature: When people walk into a house, they set things down in the first spot they come to. So what do you do if the prime dumping ground in your house happens to be the living room coffee table or your favorite armchair? The answer is simple: You create a "parking spot" near each outdoor entrance that folks will come to *before* they reach the main living areas. Any of these will do the trick:

- A cabinet or armoire

- A table with attractive baskets or storage boxes underneath

- A bench with a lift-up seat

- A freestanding coat tree with a shelf on the bottom

- A wall-hung shelf and/or wall hooks

CORRAL YOUR COLLECTIBLES. Instead of spreading your collection of pottery vases, hand-carved wooden animals, or ship models all over the living room or great room, group them in display cabinets with glass doors. The room will look less cluttered, and your treasures will be protected from dust. *Note:* If small children are on the scene, take your protection plan one step further, and keep the doors locked!

CORRAL YOUR COLLECTIBLES, PART TWO. Take advantage of the wall space in your living room or family room by installing a shelf a foot or so down from

COLLECTOR ALERT!

Problem: A few large pottery vases that you want to show off—and a toddler grandchild who's getting into everything within reach.

Solution: Get a few small, ornamental display shelves—one for each vase—and hang them together on a wall up out of your grandchild's reach. Just be sure to place them away from any chairs or low tables the little rascal could climb onto to bring himself within grabbing range! (Look for individual display shelves in furniture stores and on the Internet.)

the ceiling, and displaying your prized possessions up there. Depending on the size of your collection, you can put the shelf on just one wall, or run it all the way around the room.

IT'S A GREAT IDEA, BUT... Using a flat-lidded trunk or blanket chest as a coffee table is a classic way to gain storage space in a living room or family room. Just make sure you fill it with things you don't use very often like Christmas decorations, your down comforter, or linens for the sofa bed. Otherwise, you'll have to spend a lot of time clearing off the top of the table to get at the stuff that's inside.

SOFT STORAGE. It's always nice to lean back in an easy chair and put your feet up on a big, comfy ottoman. And it's even nicer when the top of that ottoman lifts up to reveal a hidden storage compartment. Best of all, you can use that cubbyhole to stash things you use frequently—your dog's toys, for example—because you won't have to move anything off the top of it before you lift up the lid.

GO ONE STEP FURTHER. In really tight quarters, your storage ottoman can double as a coffee or end table. Just get an attractive tray that's the same size as the top, or make one by gluing molding around a piece of wood, and painting it to suit your decor. When you need a solid surface, set the tray on

Ask Jerry

Q. *I live in a tiny house that has very little closet space. I love the idea of using a trunk as a coffee table, but I need storage space for things that I use regularly. Are there other options?*

A. There sure are. Get yourself a flat file like the ones art galleries use to store unframed prints and photographs. They come in a variety of sizes, with several shallow drawers each, so you'll never have to remove the stuff on top to get at what you need. And though you can't store bulky things in these drawers (because they're only 2 to 3 inches deep), they're perfect for holding placemats, folded tablecloths, board games, road atlases, and anything else that's flat. You can buy these files in art-supply and office-furniture stores.

the ottoman. When it's time for feet-up relaxation, tuck your travelin' tabletop in a closet, or slide it under the nearest chair.

STORAGE ON END. Or maybe "ends" plural. If you have simple, open end tables beside your couch and chairs, consider replacing one or more of them with small chests of drawers. They'll give you perfect homes for everything from playing cards and coasters to flashlights, your reading glasses, and your TV remote.

PICTURE THIS. In one sense, how you display paintings and photographs is a matter of personal taste. However, unless you follow a few basic guidelines, you can wind up with a cluttered mess, no matter how beautiful (or valuable) your pieces may be. Anytime you're hanging pictures in a group, consider these tips from gallery owners and interior designers:

- Use frames that are as uniform as possible. If you don't want them to be identical, they should at least be approximately the same width and in the same family—for instance, all wood, all metallic, or all the same color.

- Avoid novelty frames like ones in the shape of logs, hearts, or dog bones. They'll detract from the other pieces in the group. Instead, stick with basic squares or rectangles.

- Keep mats simple and use the same color for all of them. Light neutral colors are best—preferably white or off-white. Stay away from strong colors, patterns, or borders, and too many textures.

MAKING SPACE

If you have a fireplace that you don't use during the warm-weather months, turn it into a storage space for items that you never need in the summertime—things like boots, mittens, and winter hats. Pack 'em all into a basket or box, and tuck it into the fireplace (after it's been swept out and cleaned, of course). Add a decorative fire screen or chimney board to hide your stash, and forget about it until Old Man Winter comes a-callin'.

• Space your pictures evenly, keeping the same distance between them, and make sure the top and sides of the grouping are level.

TAKE A TEST DRIVE. Even folks who have had a lot of practice hanging art find it tricky to get a grouping just right if they arrange it on the fly (so to speak). So to avoid cluttering up your wall with a lot of unnecessary nail holes, follow this three-step routine:

1. Lay your pictures out on the floor, and move them around until you've got a balance of colors, shapes, and sizes that appeal to you.

2. Measure the outline of the whole grouping, and then measure that space on the wall, so you can make sure that everything will fit.

3. Hang the pictures on the wall, beginning in one of the upper corners.

THE EYES HAVE IT. When you're hanging individual pictures, place them at eye level. If you hang them too high (which most people tend to do), you have to strain to view them, and that gives the whole room a chaotic feel. If you're hanging more than one painting or photograph in a room, make sure the center of each one is at the same height, regardless of the sizes of the individual pieces.

OUT OF THE BOX

When you're hanging a group of pictures on a wall, getting the right distance between the frames can be tricky—if you use a measuring tape or ruler, that is. But it's a piece of cake with this simple trick: Grab a hardcover book that's the same thickness as the space you want between the frames. Then use the book as a spacing guide. It'll save you a lot of hammering and remeasuring!

TUCK 'EM AWAY. The space under your sofa is perfect for storing your off-duty pictures or other long, flat items like board games or the leaves for your dining room table. Just one word of caution: If you have trouble bending over, use that space only for stuff you don't need very often.

CLUTTER BUSTER PRO

"We're not all born organizers, so we need to teach our children how to conquer clutter," says Risa R. Goldberg of Simply Marvelous Organizing in San Diego, California (www.marvelousorganizing.com). The keys to success are to designate a place for everything, keep the system simple—and above all else, teach by example. Here are a few tips from Risa to help your children keep your home's living areas clutter-free and well organized.

☛ The floor is not a receptacle for clothes, shoes, games, toys, or papers. Hang up coats and heavy sweaters in the hall closet; keep a small step stool handy so your child can reach the clothes rod. Dirty clothes go into bedroom hampers or straight to the laundry room.

☛ Set up a shoe cubby by the front door for frequently worn shoes, and put the rest away in bedroom closets. Install some hooks above the shoe cubby for school backpacks, and be sure that your children retrieve their belongings daily.

☛ Create a game and puzzle area in the living room. Store all family games on shelves, or in cabinets, closets, or a big, covered wicker basket. And issue a standing order: Last one to play puts the game away.

☛ Invest in a rolling plastic drawer unit on wheels. Give each child a drawer for his or her school papers and miscellaneous stuff, and designate one drawer for craft supplies and another for drawing paper. Any papers that you want to save should be stored somewhere else.

☛ If your home has two floors or more, buy each child a basket, and set it at the foot of the stairs. Then before bedtime, have the children empty their baskets and take the contents where they belong. This will eliminate much of the stuff that gets dumped on the family room floor because each child is responsible for carrying his or her possessions upstairs.

☛ Set a timer for 5 to 10 minutes before meals, and teach your children to put their things away before sitting down to eat. They'll need help at first, so don't simply say, "Go clean up the living room." Instead, take the time to work together. Eventually your kids will be able to do the job on their own.

VACATION QUARTERS. If you have more art than you have wall space for, and you rotate your collection, be *very* careful how and where you store the off-duty pictures. Never, ever put paintings, prints, drawings, or photographs in an attic or basement. High humidity levels and fluctuating temperatures can damage them in a hurry. Instead, keep them in a closet that has a relatively constant temperature and humidity level. Wrap framed pieces in bubble wrap or thick blankets. And, if there's any chance they could be bumped, put them in sturdy boxes for good measure.

LONGER-TERM STORAGE. When you need to store unframed artwork for longer periods of time, put each piece between sheets of acid-free paper, and tape a piece of foam board to each side. (Both materials are available at art-supply stores and on the Internet.) Write the title or a description of the picture on the foam board, so you'll remember what's in there. Or, if you'd prefer, take a snapshot and tape it on the outside. Then either stand your "sandwich" upright in a safe location, or slide it under your sofa.

THAT'S ENTERTAINMENT!

Your living room, family room, and/or great room are the places where you hang out as a family and entertain guests. But if those rooms are so cluttered that you can't find the TV remote, the snapshots from your last vacation, or the book you want to read, it's hard to enjoy 'em! Not to mention the fact that when visitors drop by, you're ready to die of embarrassment because of the mess. Well, those days are about to become history. Armed with some of the helpful hints in these pages, you can free your living areas from fun-blocking clutter, and keep them that way.

In This Section:
✔ Books
✔ CDs, DVDs,
   and records
✔ Games
✔ Party supplies
✔ Photographs

SORT

The road to clutter-free entertainment areas begins with (guess what?) getting rid of stuff that doesn't need to be there. Here's the easiest way to do it.

FUN FOR ALL. Having trouble getting motivated to sort through all of your books, music, and movies? Then tune in to some first-class entertainment while you de-clutter your entertainment center. Just schedule an evening or a weekend afternoon, load up the CD player with your favorite music, pop a good movie into the DVD slot, or turn to a ball game on TV, and sort while you listen or watch!

DONATE DUPLICATES. If you're like most folks I know, you may well have two or even three copies of the same books, music recordings, or DVDs in your closet. So get some instant gratification by weeding out the extras like these, for instance:

✔ Paperback books that you later bought—or were given—in hardcover versions

✔ Recordings that you have on both CD and LP (or even cassette tape)

✔ Books, records, or movies that you and your spouse each had copies of before you were married

✔ Any gifts that were duplicates of things you already had—but you never got around to exchanging

MESS-MAKER ALERT!

Problem: A bulky TV and stand that are taking up too much space—and look as ugly as sin, besides.

Solution: Depending on your budget and your available wall space, you have three excellent options: Simply get a hanging mount for your current, tube-type television; turn that clunky box in for a wall-mounted, flat-screen model; or opt for a home theater projector. A projector costs less than most new TVs, and you can mount it right to your ceiling. Then broadcast your favorite shows on a pull-down screen—or even a blank, white wall—for the ultimate in space-saving entertainment.

LOOK TO YOUR LOCAL LIBRARY. A classic piece of clutter-control advice is to only buy and keep books that you really need or really love, and borrow the rest from the library. But don't stop there: At most libraries, you'll also find a good selection of music CDs and movies on both DVD and even videocassettes—and sometimes video games, to boot. So it always pays to check before you run out and buy something you may not want to keep.

IF YOU CAN'T BORROW, RENT. Instead of buying DVDs or video games, rent them from a local retail outlet or, even easier, sign up for a by-mail rental service. For a small monthly fee, you get your choices of games, movies, or TV episodes delivered right to your door, and you get to keep them for as long as you like, with no late fees. A quick Internet search will bring up dozens of such companies.

> ### MAKING
> ### S P A C E
>
> Want to call a halt to movie and game clutter *and* save money at the same time? Then share a rental service membership with a friend or neighbor. You'll each get to watch or play for half the price—with no unwatched DVDs or games lingering around to take up space.

MORE MUSICAL MOMENTS. Toss out any sheet music that is torn beyond repair, missing pages, or so badly stained that you can't see all of the notes. If you come across pages with minor tears, patch them up now, before they get worse. (Use acid-free tape that's especially made for archival paper; you can find it at art-supply and stationery stores.)

BEEN THERE, DONE THAT. Once a book or recording—whether it's audio or video—comes into your home, it tends to get lost in the shuffle. So take the time to gather up and find new homes for any of these items:

• CDs or records that you bought, listened to once, and didn't care for

• Movies you've watched and know you won't watch again

- Books that you ordered by mail, or got as a book club selection, but weren't what you expected after all

- College textbooks you haven't glanced at since the last time you (or your kids) crammed for finals

- Books on any subjects that are no longer of interest to you

SPREAD THE LOVE OF READING.
I would never want you to part with hardcover books that your children treasure—especially the ones that they'll love just as much (or even more) when they're all grown up with youngsters of their own. (I'm thinking of classics like *Winnie the Pooh, Huckleberry Finn, Eloise,* and *Charlotte's Web.*) But if your kids have a few duplicate books they received as presents, paperbacks they no longer read, or board books that simply haven't held up well, that's another story altogether. Plenty of young readers would be thrilled to get their hands on those items. So pick up the phone, and call any of these places:

✔ After-school-care programs

✔ Church nurseries

✔ Day-care centers

✔ Foster parents (If you don't know any personally, call your local human services department.)

✔ Friends who homeschool their kids (If necessary, call the local home schooling association for names.)

Throughout this book, we've been taking a room-by-room approach to de-cluttering your home, sweet home. But in some cases, especially if you're having a hard time getting started in a particular room, it may be easier to focus on particular types of objects—the things that can show up anywhere. For instance, gather up all of the books in your house, and sort, organize, and store them in whatever way and in whatever room(s) work best for you. Then move on to photographs, baseball caps, cat toys, batteries, rubber bands, sports equipment—I'm sure you get the picture.

- ✔ Groups or churches that provide emergency food or shelter for families

- ✔ Reading-improvement programs run by elementary schools or other organizations

- ✔ Shelters for homeless families or battered women and children

MUSIC ON THE CUTTING EDGE.

Thanks to the wonders of modern technology, it is possible to have a humongous music library that takes up little or no space at all. If you'd like to free up room that your CDs now occupy, consider one of these two simple yet technologically savvy strategies:

1. Transfer your CDs to an electronic computer database, and load them onto an MP3 player. Then get rid of the discs, or store them in an out-of-the-way location.

2. Pack your MP3 with downloads from itunes.com, and give your CDs the boot.

HALFWAY MEASURES. Do you have multiple copies of your favorite CDs—one to listen to at home, one for the car, and maybe another one for your weekend getaway place? Well, if so, do yourself a clutter-cutting favor by loading those tunes onto a portable MP3 player. Then you can tote it along with you whenever you hit the road.

SPEAKING OF MUSIC... If you still think that it takes gigantic speakers to produce

Ask Jerry

Q. My friends keep telling me I should transfer all of my music to one of those MP3 players, and get rid of my CDs and LP records. They claim computerized music is the "wave of the future." But I love all my old LPs. They have a warmer sound than you get from digital music. I really enjoy putting them on the turntable, pouring a glass of wine, and sitting back to listen to my favorites, like Perry, Bing, and Ella.

A. So keep your records, and forget that high-tech stuff! Even though storing your music in electronic files will save space, MP3 players have their downsides, too. For one, their small size makes them very easy to lose. And for another, computers can crash, taking your treasured collection with them. So tell your pals (politely), "Thanks, but no thanks."

fabulous sound, I have great news for you: It just ain't so. In fact, some of the highest-quality sound comes from speakers that are tiny enough to tuck on top of a bookcase or into the corner of a shelf. Or, if you like, you can mount 'em on a wall or from the ceiling. So don't hang on to a pair of 1970's monsters that are hogging valuable floor space in your living room. Instead, trot down to your local electronics store and check out the mighty mini speakers in stock.

CUT CATALOG CHAOS. Depending on your point of view, mail-order catalogs are either a convenient shopping aid, a form of entertainment that ranks right up there with magazines and novels, or a first-class pain in the neck. But any way you look at it, they can add up to major clutter—fast. Fortunately, this four-part program will keep them from taking over your living quarters.

1. Gather up all of the catalogs that you have now. Recycle any that are outdated or that you're unlikely to order from.

2. Quickly thumb through the ones that have products you're interested in. If you spot something you'd like to buy, tear out the page along with the order form if you plan to order by mail. Otherwise, make sure the company's phone number or Web site address appears on the page.

3. Order the product now. If that's not possible, put the page in your To-Do file (for more on that, see Chapter Four).

4. Follow this same procedure for every catalog that comes to your house.

OUT OF THE BOX

For the ultimate in space-saving versatility, opt for wireless speakers. Because they don't even attach to your stereo receiver, you can place them anywhere in the room, or tuck them away in a closet or utility room when you're not using them. Just remember that the quality of wireless speakers varies greatly, so shop carefully, and don't try to pinch pennies. Because they even work through walls, you can also use them as auxiliary speakers in other rooms of your house—so you can enjoy the benefits of music throughout your house, without the clutter (or expense) of installing multiple stereo systems.

ONE-STOP NONSHOPPING. The Direct Marketing Association offers a service that lets you reduce many types of unwanted mail, including advertising flyers, prescreened credit offers, and catalogs. You can find the full details at www.dmachoice.org. Just two points to remember:

1. This service covers only companies that are members of the Direct Marketing Association, so it will not stop catalogs or other mail from local businesses.

2. You need to reregister for the service every three years, or whenever you move.

'TIS THE SEASON. Is your party closet (or wherever you keep your holiday entertaining supplies) overflowing with holiday-specific stuff? By that I mean things like glasses featuring Santa's picture, a platter with "Happy New Year!" sprawled across the surface, and placemats for every holiday from St. Patrick's Day to the Fourth of July. Well, if you want to clear out the clutter, you have two choices:

1. Sort it all by occasion, put each holiday's stash into a separate box, and label it accordingly. Then take the boxes to the basement, attic, or wherever else you keep things that you use only once a year.

2. Get rid of the goods that are appropriate only for specific occasions, and replace them with ones in seasonal colors that you can use for many months of the year. For instance,

MESS-MAKER ALERT!

Problem: Mail-order catalogs pouring in so fast you can hardly keep track of them—many for products you don't even use or want.

Solution: If you receive a catalog you don't want, pick up the phone and call the toll-free number that's listed on or just inside the cover. When you get through to a real person, ask politely, but firmly, to have your name removed from the mailing list. Because catalogs are printed and addressed far in advance, you may receive one or two more, but eventually, they'll stop coming. Yes, this process will take a few minutes of your time, but it will cut back on a lot of clutter in the long run.

instead of placemats and napkins with Easter bunnies and eggs all over them, get versions in a range of pastel colors. They'll look just as festive at your Easter brunch—and they'll go right on adding a touch of spring to your table till summertime. The same goes for coasters, cocktail napkins, and hors d'oeuvres plates. Take it from me: Your guests won't miss them, and you'll free up a lot of space in your party closet or buffet. Just remember that I'm talking about everyday holiday table- and partyware here—I'm *not* suggesting that you get rid of precious heirlooms, like your grandma's collection of Christmas china, or your own prized candleholders in the shapes of Santas, pilgrim hats, and shamrocks!

I'M GAME. If your family really loves to play games—either the board or computer type—the clutter can mount up fast. So go through your stash, and get rid of anything that falls into one of these four categories:

1. Games that have torn boards, or missing or broken pieces

2. Earlier versions of games that you've recently bought

3. Games your family doesn't play because they're too easy or too difficult

4. Games that are too violent or otherwise inappropriate

CONSIDER REPLACEMENT PARTS. Don't be too quick to throw away games that are just missing a playing token or two. Instead,

PACK RAT ALERT!

Problem: Belongings that you're keeping only because they hold fond memories of dear friends or family members who have passed on.

Solution: Donate them to charities or other organizations in memory of your loved one(s). A local sports hall of fame might be delighted to get your grandpa's collection of vintage baseball books. A hospital, senior center, or shelter may welcome a library table, a beautiful chess set, some good garden furniture, or a nice sturdy bookcase.

replace those pieces with small doodads that may be cluttering other parts of your house, like extra thimbles, large buttons, or even spools of thread.

WHAT A CANDLE CAN DO! You open a drawer in your living room end table and find a bunch of candles that have burned down too far to use in your candlesticks. Obvious candidates for the trash, right? Wrong! Just take those nubbins to other parts of the house, and put 'em to work in one of these ways:

• Turn white candle stubs into art supplies. Just draw a design with the candle on a sheet of white paper. Then paint over the paper with watercolors. When the paint dries, the wax will show through. *Note:* This process is fun for kids, but it's also a clever technique to use if you make your own Christmas cards.

• Pop a partially burned candle into your toolbox. Then the next time you want to make a zipper, window, drawer, or even your car's radio antenna glide more smoothly, just rub the candle along the (potentially) moving parts.

• Stash a candle or two in your workshop. Then anytime you're cutting plywood or other lumber, rub the cut edge with the side of a candle. The wax will keep the wood from absorbing moisture.

Ask Jerry

Q. *My family has gone on a real de-cluttering spree, and we've got boxes full of books, CDs, toys, and other stuff to donate to a charity. It's way too much to fit into our car, but I've called every thrift shop in town, and they all said the load is too small for them to pick up. I really don't want the hassle of having a garage sale. Do you have any suggestions?*

A. Actually, I have a terrific idea: Talk to your neighbors, and see if they have things to give away, too. Odds are they'll be more than happy to round up a few boxes of stuff. Then call those thrift stores back, and ask what their minimum load is. Many charities won't drive across town to pick up a few boxes—but they might beat a path to your doorstep if you have a whole truckload of goods.

IT'S A PHOTO FINISH. Even if you keep most of your current photographs on your computer, it's a good bet that you've got a lifetime's worth of snapshots and formal portrait photos stashed in the living or family room. If that's the case, getting them all sorted, organized, and stored is going to be a *big* project. So don't even try to tackle it all at once. Just start by pulling out the first box, envelope, or drawer that's filled with pictures, and toss (or pass on to family or friends) the ones that meet any of these descriptions:

✔ They're too dark, too light, or out of focus.

✔ The people or pets in the shot look bad. (For instance, their eyes are red, half their heads are cut off, or they're simply having a bad hair day.)

✔ You have several more exactly (or almost exactly) like it.

✔ You don't recognize any of the people or animals in the picture.

✔ You don't recognize the scenery in a scenic shot.

MESS-MAKER ALERT!

Problem: Your husband's souvenir shot glasses are lined up on the bookshelves in front of the books, and they make the whole room look cluttered!

Solution: Clear away those tiny glasses and give them a home of their own. Buy some wall-hung display shelves that are just deep enough to hold the glasses in a single line, and put the shelves in whatever space works best in your house. Just be careful not to choose a spot where people might bump into them and send the fragile souvenirs crashing to the floor!

EXCEPTIONS TO THE RULE. There are some photos that you shouldn't simply send off with the trash, even if they do meet some of the criteria above. For instance, if it's the only shot you have of your dad in his World War II uniform, keep it even if it is a tad fuzzy. Or if there's a chance the stranger in a very old photograph is your Great Aunt Martha, and you were named after her, try to get a positive ID before you drop the thing into the circular file.

DAY BY DAY. In rooms that see a lot of action every day, clutter can sneak up on you, bit by bit, and you won't even notice that it's happening. Then, before you know it, you're right back where you started. But don't worry—it's a lot easier to take care of creeping clutter than it is to deal with it when you're knee-deep in junk. All it takes is a few minutes a day—and some firm ground rules like these:

- After you've read a book, watched a DVD, or listened to a CD or record, put it back on the shelf where it belongs. And make sure everyone else in the family does the same.

- Tell your kids in no uncertain terms that when they've finished playing with a toy or game, they have to put it away immediately. Like now!

- Get rid of newspapers and magazines once everyone has read them. And if some people in the family take a *long* time to do that, set a time limit. For instance, keep the newspaper for only a day or two beyond its issue date, and send magazines packin' when the next issue arrives.

- Every evening before bedtime, take a quick look around your living spaces. If you spot anything that doesn't belong there—say, a pair of shoes on the floor, glasses or plates on the coffee table, or school books on the recliner—put 'em away immediately. Better yet, have the responsible parties deal with them.

MESS-MAKER ALERT!

Problem: Keeping the clutter from creeping back.

Solution: Once you've de-cluttered your entertainment area, keep the junk from piling up again by declaring an annual Clutter-Clearing Day. Write it in your calendar, and then every year on that date, set aside an afternoon or evening, and jump into the fray. Don't worry: If you've been keeping on top of potential clutter (see "Day by Day" at left), this project should be a snap. Pay special attention to things you've acquired since your last sorting spree. If you come across books, movies, or music that you bought, but don't really enjoy, get rid of 'em. Give them to a friend, donate them to a thrift shop, sell them to a used book or record store, or set them aside for your next garage sale.

ORGANIZE

There is no right or wrong way to organize your books, music, games, and other entertainment gear. The best system is the one that works for you. That's why, in this section, you'll find a whole smorgasbord of ideas to choose from.

BACK-TO-BACK. If you'd like to separate a large (or even not-so-large) living room into two or more distinct areas, your books can help. How? Just set two freestanding bookcases back-to-back to serve as a wall. You'll organize the space and create more room for your library at the same time! (Of course, your room divider can hold a lot more than books. Those shelves are also the perfect place to stash games, CDs, or decorative containers filled with playing cards, coasters, and other odds and ends.)

FINE-TUNE THE SYSTEM. For serious book lovers who have varied interests, organizing bookshelves can be a challenge. If that description fits you, then try to follow the example of a friend of mine, who divides her enormous library into more specific categories. Only you can decide how you want to divvy up your titles, but this list will give you an idea of how to proceed.

✔ Architecture and interior design

✔ Art

✔ Baseball

✔ History

✔ Irish literature

✔ Music

✔ Mysteries

✔ Nature and animals

✔ Pet care

✔ Politics and current events

MAKING SPACE

If you have a large collection of cookbooks or craft books, you probably don't have the space to house them all in your kitchen or hobby room. That's okay. Just put these categories of books in an easily accessible area of your larger library, so you can quickly pull out the book you need when you're looking for a recipe or starting a new craft project.

ORGANIZE BY GENRE. This is a great system if your book collection is fairly small. Simply assign separate shelves to different basic categories. For instance, put all general nonfiction titles on one shelf, fiction on another, and cookbooks on a third.

REMEMBER YOUR ABC'S. Whether or not you choose to organize your books by category, it's a good idea to arrange them alphabetically, either by the title or by the author's last name. This way, whenever you want a particular book, it'll take only a second to find it.

HEIGHT MATTERS. If you have small children or grandchildren, keep their books on low shelves that they can reach easily. And as soon as the youngsters are old enough to read, let them organize the books any way they like.

COLLECTOR ALERT!

Problem: A bookcase with no place to shelve any biographies and/or autobiographies.

Solution: Here, you have two choices: You can assign them their own separate categories, or just shelve them in each subject's area of interest. Got a biography of Bing Crosby? It belongs in the music section. Or one on Henri Matisse? That falls firmly into art. And James Joyce belongs in the Irish literature section.

AVOIDING MUSICAL MAYHEM.
There's no getting around it: If you have a sizable collection of CDs and/or LP records, getting—and keeping— them organized can be mighty tricky. As with books, the only right system is the one that works best for you. Here are a couple of methods:

1. Separate the recordings by type of music (jazz, classical, and so on), and then alphabetically within each section by either composer or performer.

2. Don't bother with categories. Simply alphabetize your records or CDs by either composer or performer. This arrangement works best for those folks who feel there are only two kinds of music: good and bad. (And if any bad music had found its way into your collection, you weeded it out during your sorting spree, right?)

THE MISFITS. No matter which organizing system you use, recordings like *Big Band Hits of the '40s*, *The Best of Broadway*, and *All-Time Christmas Favorites* are probably going to be tough to place. So be sure to set aside a separate area for compilations that feature more than one performer or composer. This way, they won't get lost in the shuffle, and you'll be able to put your finger on them instantly.

STORE

The way you store your books, music, and games is important for reasons that go beyond clutter control. Storing these items properly can also ensure that they'll stay in good shape so you can enjoy them longer, or get back their full value if you ever want to sell them.

Ask Jerry

Q. *New books that I buy tend to vanish into my collection before I have a chance to read them, then I forget all about them. Have any suggestions?*

A. Sure do: Instead of putting a new book on the shelf right when you bring it home, put it on the table next to your reading chair (or place it on your bedside table, if you do most of your reading in bed). Leave it there until you've read it, and then move it to its rightful place in the bookcase when you are done.

ENTERTAINMENT CENTRAL. Entertainment centers have become all the rage in recent years, and for good reason: They allow you to corral your television set, stereo equipment, and recordings all in one handy spot. The room looks less cluttered, and you can always put your hands on exactly the music or video you want, when you want it.

ROLL IT! If you don't have room for an "official" entertainment center—or you just don't want one—buy a rolling TV cart from any housewares store or catalog. Put the TV on top and your favorite DVDs on the shelves below, and store the whole shebang in an out-of-the-way corner of your room. Then whenever you want to watch a movie or your favorite TV show, roll the cart out and plug everything in. When you're done, simply push it back against the wall.

ROLL THE GAMES, TOO. A cart on wheels is also just the ticket for storing a video gaming system. Just put all of the components on the shelves, and tuck the "vehicle" in a closet or behind a decorative screen in a corner. Haul it out when you're ready to play, and then roll it back when you're done.

THE ART OF THE GAME. Calling all chess fanatics! Instead of putting your board and chessmen away and bringing them out every time you want to play, make your pastime part of your decor. Buy an attractive table that has a chessboard painted on the top (you can find them on the Internet and in some furniture stores). Then top the board with a nice-looking chess set, and you're good to go at a moment's notice. Of course, you can also use the board for cutthroat games of checkers with the grandkids!

BEYOND CHESS AND CHECKERS. For the ultimate in efficient game storage, look for a table that comes complete with four different game boards—Scrabble®, Monopoly®, chess/checkers, and backgammon—tucked neatly into a compartment in the top. Drawers in the table's sides hold the playing pieces, with room left over for decks of playing cards. These game tables come in many styles and sizes. For the best selection, check out www.game-table.com.

THE CD UNDERGROUND. Or rather, under a shelf. If space is tight, but you don't want to use a tiny MP3

MAKING SPACE

No room in your living room or family room for a video gaming system? That's no problem! Just put all of the components and a small TV set in a spare room or bedroom, and designate that as your video play space.

device instead of a CD player, this tip has your name on it: Buy a small CD player that attaches to the underside of a shelf in your bookcase, and store your CDs (or at least some of them) below it on the shelf. Put the small speakers on other shelves, and bingo — full-size sound in a small package!

MAKE IT A DOUBLE FEATURE. You can fit twice as many DVDs into a bookcase or media cabinet simply by shelving them two deep. Store the flicks that you watch only once in a while (like your collection of Christmas classics) in the back row. Use the up-front space for films you haven't seen yet, or favorites that you love to watch over and over again (maybe the *Green Acres* episodes that you put on every time you need a good belly laugh).

IF THE SHOE FITS... Store it (and its  mate) on a shoe rack or in a hanging shoe bag in your bedroom closet, and use the box to hold CDs in your living room or family room. Of course, shoe boxes are not the most decorative storage containers in the world, so even if you keep your CD collection behind closed doors, you'll probably want to dress the box up a little by covering it with fabric or wrapping paper, or painting it a color that matches your decor.

THE ART OF LITERATURE. As any interior designer will tell you, a bookcase full of colorful books has the same visual impact as a major work of art. So if you've got an impressive collection of books, give it prime real estate in your living room or family room. And to make sure all that color doesn't add up to clutter, paint your walls white or a neutral

COLLECTOR ALERT!

Problem: No place to put all of your CDs and DVDs.

Solution: Buy some binders with plastic sleeves that are specially designed to hold the discs and the booklets that go with them. You can find them, in many styles and price ranges, in catalogs and on the Internet. Some even look like leather-bound books, so they'll be right at home on your bookshelves.

shade. Whatever you do, steer clear of patterned wallpaper. It'll just make the room look like a jumbled mess!

BUILD 'EM IN. The ultimate in classy-looking storage is a whole wall of floor-to-ceiling, built-in bookshelves. To get the biggest visual and practical bang for your buck, follow these guidelines:

- Match the style of the shelves to your room's existing decor.

- Make the shelves deep enough to hold big books, LP records, and your stereo equipment. Sixteen to 18 inches should do the trick (but to play it safe, measure your items before you order the lumber).

- Don't use adjustable shelves that you space randomly. They can give the whole arrangement a cluttered look. Instead, go with fixed shelves that are the same height across the whole width of the bookcase. Some of the shelves can—and should—be taller than others to accommodate books of different heights, but again, just make sure all of the shelves across each row are the same height.

STOP THE STACKS. If you've been storing your collection of art and design magazines in baskets, you know how aggravating it is to plow through the stacks looking for a specific issue. Here's a better idea: Get some acrylic magazine cases from an organizing store or catalog. Each one holds a year's worth of magazines in an upright position so they can stand on a shelf just like a book. And you can see right through the clear plastic to read the titles and dates. But you'll still need to sort through your collection once a year or so, and weed out any issues that you no longer want and/or use.

MAKING SPACE

If you have more CDs and DVDs than you have shelf space for, make your collection disappear. Just build an open box that's the right size to fit under your coffee table and just deep enough to hold the plastic jewel cases on end. Paint the box to match your decor, and attach four wheels to the bottom. Add a decorative handle to one side, and you're ready to roll!

SWEATING THE SMALL STUFF. If you have children or even grandchildren who visit frequently, it's all but guaranteed that you're up to your ears in tiny toys and games that have a zillion separate pieces, like Lego® products, Tinkertoys®, and Lincoln Logs®. Of course, you could store them all in plastic bins, but if that's not the look you want in your living room, consider these more decorative options:

✔ An apothecary chest that's got lots of small drawers

✔ Decorative tins

✔ Hatboxes

✔ Wicker baskets with lids

✔ Wooden boxes (again with lids)

THEY'RE NOT JUST FOR KIDS' STUFF. Of course, the great-looking containers I mentioned above can hold a lot more than toys. They're also perfect for corralling all of the small odds and ends that can clutter up your living room or family room, like playing cards, coasters, cocktail napkins, matches, pens and notepads, and your current knitting project.

> **OUT OF THE BOX**
>
> In craft shops and catalogs you often see great-looking cabinets, complete with doors, that are specially made to store CDs. The only problem is that most of them don't hold more than a few dozen discs. So if you have a midsize or larger collection, they won't solve your music-storage problem. But they're just the ticket for storing all sorts of other pint-size stuff, like reading glasses, note cards, flashlights, candles, or anything else you want to keep close at hand, but out of sight, in your living areas.

REIN IN THE REMOTE(S). If the only remote-control device you have in the family room is the one for your television set, here's a supersimple way to make sure you can always find it when you want it: Use Velcro® to attach it to the side of the TV. On the other hand, maybe you've got a whole herd of remotes for video games, your sound system, and who knows what else. In that case, find a container that will keep them all in one place. Check out catalogs and the Internet to find special holders just for this purpose. But remember, a bowl, tray, basket, or decorative box will work every bit as well.

PRESERVE YOUR PICTURES.

Earlier in this section, I gave you some pointers for sorting through your collection of photographs. Once you've decided which ones you want to keep, you have plenty of choices for storing them in ways that will keep them safe and sound. For instance:

- Keep them in archival, acid-free photo boxes with dividers that separate them by date and/or topic. The categories can be as broad or specific as you choose (for instance, "Christmas 1998," "Road Trip to Yellowstone," or simply "Christmas" or "Vacations").

- Use special photo albums—but make sure they're made from archival materials.

- Incorporate them into scrapbooks.

- Buy special flip-through frames that let you store as many as 100 photos in each one.

- Frame extra-special photos and hang them on the wall or in a grouping.

MESS-MAKER ALERT!

Problem: Photographs in frames with no mats.

Solution: Whenever you frame photos, don't ever let them touch the glass! Over time, moisture can creep into the frame, and even the smallest bit can make the pictures stick. Always use an archival, acid-free mat, or if you've chosen a decorative, stand-up frame, insert spacers that keep the surface of the photo from coming into contact with the glass. Better yet, have a professional picture framer insert the spacers for you.

CHAPTER FOUR

THE HOME OFFICE

A "home office" can be anything from a section of kitchen counter where you sit down to pay your bills every month to a spacious, well-equipped room where you run a full-fledged, home-based business. But whether your home office falls into one of those extremes—or anywhere in between—one thing is certain: It's a prime target for clutter. So don't just sit there! Swing into action with our quick and easy pick-it-all-up plan.

DIG OUT THE DESK

Without a doubt, your desk is the star of the show in your home office. And just like any showbiz superstar, it seems to possess magical powers of attraction. But instead of fans, your desk unfortunately attracts lots and lots of stuff—everything from printers to paper clips and folders to fingernail files. What's more, what happens at the desk stays at the desk— long after it should have been stashed away. That is, unless you've got a plan.

In This Section:
✔ Desk
✔ Office equipment
✔ Office supplies

SORT

The first step to a smooth-running, clutter-free office is deciding what needs to be in your command post and what doesn't. So bite the bullet, and proceed as follows.

CLEAR YOUR DESKTOP. Start your sorting spree by removing anything that's on your desktop just because you love it—things like your dog's picture, your cherished autographed baseball from the 1960

World Series, your lucky peacock feather, or your collection of beach stones. But don't panic—I'm not suggesting that you get rid of your treasured keepsakes! And you don't have to move them out of your office entirely, either. Just hang them on the wall, or display them on a shelf where you can enjoy these items without their cutting into your valuable work space. If you declare your desktop strictly a business zone, it will always look and feel less cluttered.

MOVE THE TOOLS, TOO. You really don't need to clutter your desktop with things like staplers, hole punches, tape dispensers, and mugs filled with more pencils, pens, and markers than you'll use in a year. As for where you should keep them, we'll talk about that shortly. For now, just set them aside—and notice how much more work surface you've gained already.

SHIP THE SUPPLIES. There's no getting around it: Things like scissors, paper clips, rubber bands, and pads of sticky notes are home-office must-haves. But they don't necessarily belong on your desktop. So when you're not using them, keep them in a drawer, or in one of the other sensational storage options you'll find beginning on page 147.

CLEAR THE GEAR. If your main work surface is covered with equipment like a printer, fax machine, copier, or calculator, do yourself a favor and "stable" that stuff someplace else. It

MAKING SPACE

If you're like a lot of folks I know, you probably have an old computer or two sitting around, gathering dust on your desktop or other surface in your home office. Well, get it (or them) outta there now! If you don't know someone who could use them—or they don't work anymore—log on to www.earth911.org to find out where to recycle them. Just one word of caution: Before you get rid of any computer, be sure to remove or destroy your hard drive. If you don't know how to do that, and you don't have a computer-savvy teenager in your house, have a pro do the job. It will be worth every penny it costs you because if an unscrupulous operator gets hold of any of your sensitive data, it could easily result in fraud or identity theft.

doesn't matter if all you do at your desk is write checks for the monthly bills, or you're hard at work on the Great American Novel. The job will be a whole lot easier and much more pleasant if you have a free and clear space to do it on.

COMBINE FORCES. No matter where you keep your electronic equipment, you can save a whole lot of space by getting rid of all those separate machines. Replace them with a single unit that's a printer, scanner, copier, and fax machine all in one, and you'll gain that much more work space.

DITCH THE DESK PHONE. On a tiny desktop, even a telephone can hog too much valuable real estate. Fortunately, you now have two good de-cluttering options:

1. Use a cell phone in your office.

2. If you still prefer the feel and sound quality of a landline telephone, trade in your desktop version for a wall-mounted model.

DOWNSIZE YOUR COMPUTER. Unless you really want or need a full-size monitor, swap your standard desktop model for a laptop with wireless capability. Then when you're not using it, you can simply fold it up and stash it in a drawer, in a cupboard, or on a bookshelf—leaving your desktop free and clear. What's more, by installing a wireless router, you'll get rid of that tangled

MESS-MAKER ALERT!

Problem: Those cute, miniature versions of office tools seem ideal for saving space in your home office.

Solution: Avoid these like the plague! It's true that tiny staplers, scissors, paper cutters, hole punches, calculators, and so forth take up less space than their full-size counterparts—and they're adorable, too. But the fact is that almost nothing miniature ever really works well or lasts long. Plus, it's often very difficult for large adult fingers to handle small office things. (Have you ever actually tried to use a mini calculator, which is about the size of a business card?) So do yourself a favor: Go for the gusto and get full-size, good-quality office tools that will get the job done—and won't simply turn into clutter in the blink of an eye.

mass of cords and cables that's so darned unsightly.

SCRAP THE SCRAPS. Here's a dandy de-cluttering project for you: Gather up all the sticky notes, envelopes, and pieces of scrap paper that you've written reminders, ideas, or phone numbers on. Then copy all that information into a notebook, personal planner, calendar, or Rolodex®. This way, it will be easy to find when you need it—and you'll be much less likely to toss it into the wastebasket by mistake.

BEWARE OF GOING PAPERLESS. If you want to type your random notes into your computer or personal digital assistant, and program phone numbers into your cell phone, that's fine, but don't just leave it at that! Remember that gadgets— especially small ones—are famous for vanishing or crashing when you need them most. So play it safe: Always keep paper copies of any information you cannot retrieve easily (like unlisted phone numbers) if the electronic data somehow mysteriously disappears.

GO WIRELESS. If a wireless network (wi-fi) is available in your area, you have a super-simple way to get rid of a most unsightly form of home-office

MAKING SPACE

We're constantly being reminded to shred personal documents if we want to avoid financial fraud and identity theft. But the truth is that in most cases, you don't need to shred the entire document—only the parts that contain sensitive information, like your account numbers, Social Security number, and signature, and maybe your name, address, and phone number. So what, you may ask, has that got to do with de-cluttering? Just this: Unless you receive a steady stream of confidential documents, you can get rid of that bulky paper shredder that's sitting in the corner and replace it with a pair of shredder scissors (available in catalogs and on the Internet). They work like ordinary scissors, but they have five cutting blades instead of one, so they snip paper into ultraslender shreds quickly—and quietly. For more on conquering paper clutter (including what documents you should shred), see "The Paper Chase" on page 151.

clutter—namely, computer wires, cables, and modems. Just sign up for the service, and bid that tangled mess of spaghetti good-bye!

CLEAR THE CABINET AND DREDGE THE DRAWERS. Remember the box (or pile) system I told you to use for sorting the stuff in your bedroom dresser drawers? (See "Clear the Deck!" on page 2.) Well, the same system works like a charm for de-cluttering your office-supply cabinet, your desk drawers, or any other furniture that's in your home office. So gather up five boxes, or make space on the floor or your desktop for five piles. Then, as you pull each item out of the cabinet or a drawer, assign it to one of these categories:

1. Trash

2. Keep Here

3. Take Elsewhere

4. Donate or Sell

5. Recycle

THERE'S NO BUSINESS... Like outdated business cards—whether they're your own or somebody else's. They might seem like obvious candidates for the trash (or the recycling bin), but think twice before you throw them all out. I always keep a supply of old cards on hand because they make terrific bookmarks, and they're perfect to use as label inserts on hanging file folders or the spines

PACK RAT ALERT!

Problem: You've got mountains of paper on, in, and all around your desk and cabinets.

Solution: Paper poses the most daunting office-sorting challenge of all, and if you try to deal with it at the same time that you're sorting all of the other stuff in your office, you'll go nuts. (It's happened to me!) For the time being, as you come across any item that demands immediate attention, like a bill that's due soon or a permission slip your child needs for a field trip next week, take care of it now. Then place everything else in a separate stack or box, and set it aside. In the next section, I'll share my time-tested tips for corralling paper piles in your home office (see "The Paper Chase" on page 151).

of three-ring binders. (Depending on the size you need, either use the whole card, or cut it into strips.) They're also particularly handy for cleaning between the keys of your computer keyboard. Just slide a card along each row, and the pet hair, dust, and other gunk will come right out!

TOSS IT. It's all but guaranteed that you can free up a fair amount of space in your drawers and cabinets simply by trashing anything that's damaged or over the hill. Do any of these sound familiar? (I thought so!)

✔ Address labels from your previous residence(s)

✔ Bent paper clips

✔ Bottles of correction fluid with a thin layer of white crust on the bottom

✔ Broken rubber bands

✔ Dried-up marking pens

✔ Orphaned pen tops

SORT THE KEEPERS. As you go through your drawers and cabinets, you'll find all kinds of things that you want or need to keep in your office—everything from pushpins and postage stamps to rubber bands and Rolodex® cards. Well, do yourself a big favor: Group similar items together in mini piles in your Keep Here pile or box. This way, you won't have to sort through that stuff all

Ask Jerry

Q. *Every time I pick up a decorating magazine, I see an article about converting a closet into a home office. They look slick, but just the thought of working in a closet kicks off my claustrophobia. The problem is that I really need a place to work at home, and I have no space to spare in the kitchen or any other room—but I do have an extra closet. How can I put it to good use?*

A. It's fairly simple. First, add as many up-high shelves to your closet as you can to hold files and supplies, but leave room below them. Next, buy a file cart on wheels and roll it into one side of the closet. Then find a rolling desk or worktable that can hold your computer, and tuck it in beside the cart. When you're ready for action, just roll your gear out into the great wide open. And when you're finished, simply slide it back into the "garage."

over again. Plus, you'll be able to easily tell how many containers you'll need to hold all of your supplies, and what sizes they need to be.

ENOUGH IS ENOUGH. No matter what you do, certain office supplies seem to multiply in drawers and cabinets until you've got more of them than you'll ever need in a lifetime! Well, you could—and should—tuck most of them into plastic bags and toss them into your Donate or Sell box. But some excess office supplies are prime candidates for the Take Elsewhere box. Consider these for instance:

- Binder clips. Use them in the bathroom to squeeze the last drops out of tubes that hold medicinal ointments, toothpaste, or hair gel. They can also help de-clutter your toolshed. Just attach appropriate-size binder clips to gloves, floppy sun hats, seed packets, or anything else you want to hang, and slide the clip handles over wall or pegboard hooks.

- Erasers. A white eraser is perfect for removing dirt and scuff marks from walls, parchment lamp shades, suede shoes, gold or gold-plated jewelry—and even golf balls.

- Rubber bands. To prevent your clothes from slipping off hangers—whether they're made of wire, plastic, or wood—wrap two or three rubber bands around each end of the hanger.

Yikes! You've just discovered that you have enough paper clips to make a chain that could easily stretch from your house to your neighbor's and back again. What should you do? Well, if you have small children or grandchildren, you could take a page out of my Grandma Putt's book by helping the youngsters play a game called Gone Fishin'. First, cut fish shapes from cardboard, and write a different number on each one. Slide a metal paper clip onto the snout of each fish, and toss all the fish into a big, empty tub. To make a fishing pole, tack a string onto the end of a dowel or an old broomstick, and tie a large magnet on the loose end of the string. Then let the kids take turns casting the line into the bucket and "reeling in" a numbered fish. When the bucket's empty, tally up the numbers. The fisherman who hauls in the highest score wins!

CLUTTER BUSTER PRO

Kathi Burns is a professional organizer, the owner of Add Space to Your Life in San Diego, California (www.addspacetoyourlife.com), and the author of *How to Master Your Muck! Get Organized, Add Space to Your Life, Live Your Purpose!* Here are her general guidelines for how to conquer office-supply clutter:

☞ Begin by emptying out every closet, cupboard, and drawer in your office. Then gather up all of the office-related supplies that may be in other areas of your house, take them to your office, and spread them out on your floor or desktop. This way, you'll be able to take inventory of what you have and what items, if any, you need.

☞ Group like items together—paper clips, pens, glue sticks, and so on.

☞ Merge the groups into broader categories, each with a similar purpose. For instance, Kathi groups glue sticks, sticky tack, and rubber cement, as well as various kinds of tape together. And paper clips, binder clips, and staples fall into a single category because they all hold papers together.

☞ Get rid of any excess supplies. The definition of *excess* varies from one person to the next, but a good rule of thumb is to limit your inventory to a one-year supply of any one item. *Note:* Consider donating your extra supplies to a local school. Teachers often use their personal money to buy supplies for students who don't have the means to buy for themselves. Your contribution will be put to good use and will be greatly appreciated.

☞ Once you've sorted, grouped, categorized, and purged, then it's time to containerize. Plastic shoe boxes with lids make excellent storage containers for loose office supplies, and they stack neatly on shelves, too! Buy regular-size shoe boxes for pens and smaller supplies, and double-size shoe boxes for larger items. They're about the same height as regular shoe boxes, but approximately 12 inches wide to easily accommodate 8½- by 11-inch paper and tablets.

☞ Label one short and one long side of each box to show the contents. This way, you'll never have to search through stacks of containers to find exactly what you're looking for.

REASSIGN THE DUPLICATES. Got several pairs of scissors in your desk drawer? A couple of tape dispensers? Some extra three-ring binders? If so, before you toss the extras into your Donate or Sell box, consider whether you can use them someplace else around the old homestead. Scissors, for instance, come in mighty handy in just about any room, whether it's the bathroom, laundry room, or bedroom. The same goes for transparent tape and three-ring binders, which are just the ticket for holding recipes in the kitchen, gardening tips in your toolshed, or how-to instructions in your workshop.

SUPPORT YOUR SCHOLARS. While you're cleaning out your home office and gathering up the endless amounts of paper clips, rubber bands, pencils, and so on, keep in mind that your school-age children or grandkids could probably put a lot of your discarded supplies to good use. They won't mind getting a half-empty box of pencils or only a handful of binder clips—it'll save them (and their parents!) the hassle of purchasing new school supplies.

KEEP ON KEEPING ON. After you've got your home office shipshape, make darn sure that you never have to stage a major sorting spree again. How? Whenever you need a break from work, take a quick look at your desktop and the surrounding territory. Grab anything you haven't used lately—or that has strayed into your office from someplace else—and put it back where it belongs. If you take this simple inventory every few days, you'll never be buried by office clutter again!

 ## ORGANIZE

Once you've figured out what furniture, equipment, and supplies you need to keep in your home office, it's time for step two: organizing everything in a way that works best for you.

MAKE YOUR SPACE WORK HARDER. It's easy to gain space three ways with one simple maneuver: Just place a table at a right angle to your desk. Use one stretch of this L-shaped arrangement for your computer, monitor, and keyboard (or better yet, your laptop), and leave the other portion free for writing or spreading out papers. The corner of the L is the perfect place to park a small file rack or even a mini supply cabinet.

...AND MAYBE EVEN HARDER.

If you have enough floor space, and you really need a lot of room to spread out, then build yourself a U-shaped work/storage space. Use a long table for the flat "bottom" of the U or, better yet, set a flat door or a long piece of wood on top of two cupboards, filing cabinets, or dressers. Then put a table at a right angle to each end of the main desk.

MAKING SPACE No room at all for a permanent desk? Then try my "Now you see it, now you don't" approach. Get a sturdy folding table that you can use for office work, and stash it in a closet or under a bed when it's "off duty." For any downtime, reserve a space nearby for work-in-progress materials that you can't finish in one sitting. A good-looking trunk or wicker basket with a lid will fill the bill, as will a small cabinet or chest of drawers that goes with your decor.

A-SHOPPING WE WILL GO.

So you're setting out to organize a home office from scratch, and you want professional-quality furnishings. Well, you could go to an office-furniture store, pick out everything you need, and have it delivered right to your doorstep. The delivery folks may even do any assembling that's required, and each piece will carry a warranty. There's just one minor drawback: That furniture's gonna cost you a pretty penny. Fortunately, there are places where you can find a big selection of high-quality office furniture at rock-bottom prices. What are they? County surplus stores! They sell used government merchandise like desks, chairs, and filing cabinets for a fraction of what you'd pay in a regular, retail store. Granted, you will be buying your goods "as is," with no warranty. Plus, you'll have to cart the stuff home yourself, and you may need to perform some minor cosmetic fix-ups. But on the upside, all the cash you'll save will make it well worth the effort! Search the Internet to find your closest county surplus store. Just one word of warning: Before you head off to the store, make a list of all the pieces you need, along with measurements of the spaces they'll have to go in. (After all, even a bargain-basement desk won't help you much if it won't fit in your room!)

MORE BARGAIN-HUNTING HAUNTS. If you don't have a county surplus store nearby, don't fret. You can also get some good deals at stores that specialize in used office furniture. But for the biggest bang for your buck, try more offbeat sources. Check classified ads, both online and in your local newspaper, and also visit any or all of these low-cost shopping options:

✔ Antique and secondhand stores

✔ Estate sales

✔ Flea markets

✔ Garage and moving sales

✔ Going-out-of-business sales

✔ Thrift shops

MAKE IT A PERFECT FIT. If you're setting out to furnish an entire home office, start by measuring the room and making a sketch of the layout. Be sure to include doorways, windows, closets, and phone, cable, and electrical outlets. If the room is on an upper floor, measure the width of the staircase and any landings too, as well as the ceiling height if it's on the low side. After all, you don't want to find the desk of your dreams and haul it home— only to find out that you can't get it up the stairs!

MEASURE YOUR EQUIPMENT, TOO. If you're buying furniture specifically for your computer equipment, remember that

OUT OF THE BOX

No law says your office work surface has to be an actual desk. If you find a great-looking table that's priced just right and fits the space you have, go for it. Then, if you like, attach a rollout keyboard tray to the underside of the tabletop. You can find one, complete with mounting hardware, at office-supply and home-improvement stores, and on the Internet.

size is critical. Before you go shopping, get the precise measurements of your computer monitor, CPU, and any other gear. Also note the locations of any cord and wire connections. Then, when you get to the store, look at every piece of furniture that catches your eye, and make sure your equipment will fit into it, and its compartments and cubbies won't prevent cords and wires from reaching your power outlets.

ORGANIZE YOUR SUPPLIES. Remember the box of office supplies that's marked Keep Here? Well, before you start deciding how to store them, organize the supplies into two groups:

1. The things you use daily, or almost every day. You'll want to keep these at or very close to your work area, so you can grab them quickly.

2. Items you use less often. These can be stashed in other parts of your office or, if necessary, even in another room in your house.

PUT YOUR WALLS TO WORK.
Is floor space at a premium in your home office? Then take full advantage of your vertical space, and organize your room with hanging helpers like these:

• Kitchen cabinets. If you've recently remodeled your kitchen, or you're planning to do so, you've got some great office storage on your hands, and it's free! Simply move some or all of your old wall cabinets to your office. (Paint them and add new handles if you'd like.) Or, if you don't have any kitchen cabinets to spare, buy some brand-new versions at a housewares or home-improvement store.

• Open shelves. Either go with simple pine boards on brackets, have shelving

MESS-MAKER ALERT!

Problem: You've got a nightmarish tangle of equipment cables, cords, and wires.

Solution: Separate the cords, and straighten them out so they all run parallel to one another. Then fasten them together with wide twist ties or strips of Velcro®, so you make one nice neat bundle of wires.

built to fit your available space, or attach a small, ready-made bookcase to the wall.

- A medicine cabinet. Maybe you can reuse one that's left over from a bathroom redo. Or find a vintage, wooden version in a thrift store or antique shop.

- Pegboard. Whether you choose a small panel, or cover an entire wall with the stuff, you'll have an efficient, versatile—and instantly changeable—system. Depending upon the kinds of hooks and hangers you choose, you can attach shelves, bins, or baskets of all shapes and sizes. Plus, anything that has an opening in it (like a pair of scissors, a clipboard, or a ruler with a hole in the end) can hang from its own hook.

MAKING SPACE

If you only want to get your pens, pencils, stapler, and maybe a few pictures off your desktop, hang a single, shallow shelf on the wall above your desk, using decorative brackets. The shelf should be just deep enough to hold all your items in a single row (in other words, no more than 6 inches deep). Otherwise, the objects will tend to pile up behind one another, and before you know it, you'll be right back in Clutterville, USA!

MAKE YOUR CLOSET EARN ITS KEEP. A home office that was formerly a bedroom has a built-in advantage: a closet. But to get the most out of that storage space, you need to organize it in just the right way. Fortunately, you have a couple of excellent options. Which one is best for you depends upon how much time and effort you're willing to spend to get the job done:

1. Gut the current closet, removing all the hanging rods and built-in shelves. Then install wall-to-wall shelves that are 10 to 12 inches apart, from floor to ceiling. Either wood or vinyl-coated wire versions will work out fine.

2. Simply remove the hanging rod(s) and find a freestanding bookcase that fits under and/or beside the existing shelves.

FINE-TUNE THE SYSTEM. Whether you install shelves in your closet, or opt for a ready-made bookcase, you can wind up with a lot of wasted space when you set small items on the shelves. So consider dividing the available space into smaller niches, using wire shelves like the ones commonly used in kitchens. They come in two types, both of which you can find in large hardware stores, home-improvement stores, and online.

- Wire stacking shelves. These are lightweight, inexpensive, and easy to arrange in just about any configuration.

- Wire shelves that slide onto the shelves above them. They hang down anywhere from 4 to 6 inches, giving you a perfect place to store flat or shallow items like printer paper, envelopes, ink cartridges, or hole punches.

GATHERING THE GOODS. How you should arrange the supplies in your office closet depends upon the kinds of items you have, and that depends on the type and amount of work you do in your home office. But the three basic rules are the same as they are for organizing a kitchen pantry:

1. Try to use shelves that are shallow enough to hold only a single row of items.

2. If you must put some things behind others, keep the tallest objects in back and the shortest in front, so that nothing gets lost in the shuffle.

3. Keep the tools and supplies that you use most often in the spots that are easiest to reach.

PLAY POST OFFICE. For my money, no home office is complete without a mail station—a centralized place where you keep stamps,

OUT OF THE BOX

An antique jelly cupboard makes a great home-office organizer. If you can get your hands on one of these, it'll give you more room than you'll have in a medicine cabinet (see "Put Your Walls to Work" on page 144). Plus, it'll add real pizzazz to your home office decor.

pens, envelopes, paper, and greeting cards, along with a slotted rack to sort incoming and outgoing mail. When you have everything together in one spot, you'll never again have to search high and low for the things you need when it's time to pay a bill or send a birthday card.

TAKE A MESSAGE. How many times has this happened to you? You're on the phone and you need to write something down—a message for another member of the family, or directions to someone's house. But there's nothing to write with—or on. So the search for a pen and paper begins, while the caller waits patiently (you hope) on the line. Well, your scrounging days will be over with one simple organizing step: Set up a message station by the phone your family uses most often. Make sure it includes:

MESS-MAKER ALERT!

Problem: There's no ceiling fixture in your supply closet, and the dim light makes it hard to put your hands on the things you want—and to put them back where they belong.

Solution: Simply use cordless, battery-powered lamps (available online and in home-improvement stores), or have a licensed contractor install light fixtures on the walls or ceiling in the closet.

- ✔ A pen or pencil and notepad

- ✔ A wall-hung bulletin board or a standing, magnetic version where you can post messages

- ✔ A household address book or Rolodex® (with extra cards), so you can look up existing numbers and write down new ones

- ✔ A calendar so you can check dates and make appointments

 ## STORE
When it comes to storage solutions for your home office, one size— or shape or style—definitely does not fit all. In fact, your options are as wide as the big, blue sky. Read on for some of the best.

ARM YOURSELF WITH AN ARMOIRE. If you don't have a closet you can use for supplies—and you'd like to add a little character to your home office—scout antique stores, flea markets, and thrift shops for an old armoire. Add whatever shelves and hooks you want, and tuck in some file and document boxes (available at office-supply and housewares stores and, of course, on the Internet). When you open the doors, everything you need to work with will be right at your fingertips. Close the doors, and you'll have a beautiful focal point for your room.

ENTERTAIN ANOTHER POSSIBILITY. You say you'd love to stash your supplies in a piece of homey furniture, but there's no room for a big, old-fashioned armoire in your office? No problem! Just get a smaller, trimmer entertainment center that will keep your supplies and files behind closed doors (and drawers).

OUT WITH THE IN-BOX. If you keep traditional in- and out-boxes on your desk—either the single- or double-tiered kind—try replacing them with a desktop caddy. This is an upright box that holds hanging file folders, and it takes up only about as much surface space as a shoe box. The papers that you're actively dealing with will be easier to get to, and you'll have more working room, to boot!

THE DOCTOR ISN'T IN. But the door-hung organizer he or she uses to hold patients' charts can make a dandy stand-in for your desktop in- and out-boxes. So can the hanging plastic magazine holders in the waiting room. You can find both items at office-supply stores. Just remember to check the contents every day, so the papers tucked inside really do keep moving in and out!

OUT OF THE BOX

One of the handiest office-storage systems I know of was made for the kitchen. It's a rolling cart with a flat surface (often a cutting board) on top and slide-out wire baskets below. You can put things like your in-box, calendar, Rolodex®, and so forth on top, and your frequently used supplies and current works in progress in the bins.

WHAT'S COOKIN'? On the Internet and in office-supply and housewares stores, you can find a zillion and one containers that are specifically designed to hold office supplies. But before you spend your hard-earned dough, "shop" around in your kitchen. Here's a Baker's dozen contraptions that may be causing chaos in your kitchen cupboards—but can help you corral the stuff that's cluttering up your desk, worktables, and supply cupboards:

✔ Baking pans

✔ Berry baskets

✔ Bread boxes

✔ Canisters

✔ Cutlery organizers

✔ Dish drainers

✔ Glasses

✔ Mugs

✔ Napkin holders

✔ Pot-lid racks

✔ Spice racks

✔ Utensil crocks

✔ Wire-mesh produce baskets

CLOSE THE DOOR ON CLUTTER.
A hanging plastic shoe bag with transparent pockets is perfect for storing small supplies. Choose either a hook-mounted or over-the-door version, and use the pouches to corral ink cartridges, sticky pads, envelopes, rolls of address labels—or anything else that'll fit neatly into a space the size of a shoe.

COLLECTOR ALERT!

Problem: Your treasured collection of vintage pottery bowls, planters, and vases is cluttering up your living areas.

Solution: Put those pretty containers to work de-cluttering your home office. They're perfect for holding small supplies like pens, pencils, stamps, printer ink cartridges, and notepads. And remember: Pottery vessels aren't the only collectibles you can use to store office supplies. Baskets, hatboxes, lunch boxes, vintage suitcases, and even doll-size (not doll-*house*) bureaus and hutches make fine office-storage aids.

CLOSE THE DOOR ON CLUTTER, PART TWO. In large hardware and home-improvement stores, you can buy wire shelf units that are about 4 inches deep, and anywhere from 12 to 30 inches wide and 10 to 72 inches high. When mounted on a wall or the back of a door, they provide the perfect place to stash all types of containers filled with small supplies, or boxes of envelopes, business cards, or CDs.

TACKLE YOUR STORAGE PROBLEMS. Some of the tiniest office supplies can create the biggest—or at least the most annoying—kinds of clutter. So gather up all of your paper clips, pushpins, erasers, mini sticky pads, and extra file-label inserts, and put them in a container that's tailor-made to hold itty-bitty stuff: a fishing-tackle box!

REST YOUR WEARY FEET. And get small office supplies out of the way at the same time. How? Just get a sturdy, lidded plastic box that measures about 14 by 9 by 7 inches, and tuck paper, envelopes, or what have you inside it. Then slide the box under your desk, and use it as a footrest while you're working.

ROUND AND ROUND. A desktop carousel is a classic office accessory, and for good reason: It's perfect for storing pens, pencils, rulers, scissors, and other small cargo in one handy spot. Plus, anything you want is just a quick flick of the wrist away.

By now, you already know that I think apothecary chests make terrific storage solutions. And these beautiful old-timers work just as well in your home office as they do in your bedroom or living room. So what are you waiting for? Look for one at your favorite flea market, antique store, or secondhand shop. If you have no luck on the first try, keep searching. Eventually, you're sure to strike gold!

And while you're searching for an old apothecary chest, keep an eye out for other antique finds like sturdy wooden fruit crates and oversize ceramic sauerkraut crocks. Both make great additions to your home office—the crates are perfect for holding books, magazines, catalogs, or other papers; set the crock on the floor and use it to hide computer disks, DVDs, or other similarly sized items.

THE PAPER CHASE

I'm sure you've heard the old saying that work expands to fill the time available to do it in. Well, you could say a similar thing about paper: The stuff actually seems to propagate until it's filled every nook and cranny in your home office—at least it does at my house! Well, don't give up hope. Once again, our SOS strategy can charge to the rescue.

In This Section:
✔ Bills
✔ Magazines and journals
✔ Personal records
✔ Tax and financial papers
✔ Addresses and calendars
✔ Equipment manuals and warranties

SORT

In the last section, I told you to simply clear all the papers off your desk and out of your cabinets and drawers, and set the stack aside. Well, now it's time to come to terms with that pile. Here's how to do it:

PURGE THE PAPER. For starters, it's important to sort your papers into broad categories. You'll need a recycling bin or wastebasket and four file folders labeled To Do, Pending, To File, and To Read. Or, if you've got mountains of paper, label boxes or baskets and use them to hold it all. Take a quick look at each document, bill, receipt, or what have you, and assign it to a category as follows:

1. Recycling bin (or maybe shredder). This category should be self-explanatory. It includes ancient receipts and paid bills that you don't need for tax-deduction backup, outdated catalogs, advertising flyers, and articles or brochures you haven't glanced at in ages.

2. To-Do folder. Here's where you put bills that you need to pay, products you want to order, and the renewal notices for your magazine subscriptions.

3. Pending folder. This is the place to park things that you've acted on and are now waiting for a response. Confirmation numbers for products that you've ordered online, or from catalogs, but that

haven't arrived yet fall into this category.
So do lottery tickets, contest entries, and
invitations that require an RSVP.

4. To File folder. Any receipts, canceled
   checks, or bank statements that you need
   as backup for tax deductions fall into this
   category. So do medical records for your
   family and pets and any recipes or articles
   that you've clipped from magazines and
   want to keep.

5. To Read folder. Newsletters from
   organizations belong here, as do recent
   catalogs you like to order from, travel
   brochures you sent away for, and
   correspondence you just haven't gotten
   around to yet.

DOWNLOAD TO DOWNSIZE. If
you're *really* determined to cut down on
paper clutter, take one extra step during
your sorting spree: Set aside any brochures,
operating manuals, reference materials, or other publications that
may be available online. Then when you have some time to spare,
log on and check to see what's on the various Web sites. For example,
you can probably find the instruction manual for your printer on the
manufacturer's Web site under "support" or "customer service." If it's
there, download it, save it to your hard drive, and toss the paper copy
away. First, though, tear out and file any pages that contain warranty
forms or important information like serial numbers, registration codes,
or proof of ownership.

KEEP THE ARTICLES, NOT THE ADS. So what do you do if
you open a magazine and find a terrific article that's chock-full of rose-

MESS-MAKER ALERT!

Problem: You have so
many filing categories
that you have trouble
keeping track of which
papers go where.

Solution: Pre-label your
stacks. To do this, pull
the bottom sheet of each
stack about halfway out,
attach a sticky note to
it, and write a tentative
file name on it. This way,
you'll be able to see at a
glance where each of your
documents belongs.

growing tips? Or maybe fabulous ideas for decorating your house for Christmas, or a road trip route you'd love to take next summer? Well, don't hang on to the whole, ad-filled publication for the sake of one or two stories! Instead, clip out the articles you want to keep, and start a separate file folder or three-ring binder for each topic. The labels can be as broad or as specific as you like—for instance, Roses or Gardening; Holiday Decorating or Christmas; and Road Trips or Travel.

SHARE THE WEALTH. So what happens when you read a magazine and *don't* find any articles that you care to keep? Well, you could toss it into the recycling bin. Or you could do the neighborly thing, and take it—and all the other magazines that you've already read—to a place where other folks can enjoy them. Senior centers, shelters, hospital emergency rooms, and even dentists' offices welcome recent publications, especially those that cover topics like gardening, art, interior design, or history, where up-to-the-minute timeliness is not vital.

SORT YOUR SUBSCRIPTIONS. Do you find that the new issue of a magazine, journal, or newspaper often shows up before you've even opened up the previous edition? If so, then you should let the subscription lapse. Or better yet, pick up the phone and cancel it. You'll stop clutter in its tracks, and

When you get your new telephone directory, you could send your old one off to your town's recycling center. Or you could turn it into a booster seat for a very young diner. Just cover the book (or two or more, depending on the size of your book—and your tot) with fabric or textured wallpaper, and you've got an easy way to elevate a small visitor at your dinner table—or at a restaurant that doesn't happen to have a booster seat on hand.

may even get a refund for the remaining issues, to boot. Of course, you don't have to go cold turkey on the publication—you can always buy an individual issue here or there if it grabs your attention at the newsstand. And don't forget about the Web—most magazine sites feature some of their best articles online for free!

'Til We Don't Meet Again

How long you need to keep various records varies greatly, depending on the document. Here's a rundown of the most common, along with their "expiration dates."

TYPE OF DOCUMENT	KEEP THEM UNTIL...
ATM receipts	you verify them on your bank statement.
Credit card receipts	you verify them on your statement.
Leases of any kind	seven years after they expire.
Pay stubs	you verify them on your W-2 form.
Veterinary records	the animal is no longer part of your household.
Sales receipts	the warranty expires.
Vehicle records	you no longer own the vehicle.
Warranties and operating instructions	you no longer own the product.
W-2 and 1099 forms	you start receiving Social Security benefits.

"SNAIL" MAIL: GOOD OR BAD? We all know the old pessimism-optimism test: A pessimist sees a glass as half empty; an optimist sees it as half full. Well, you could look at advertising mail in much the same way. Some folks look at a desktop full of the stuff and see, well, not a whole lot. Others look at that same pile of papers and see a golden opportunity. No, make that opportunities, plural—like these, for example:

• Art material. If you don't care to cut the stuff up and make colorful collages from it, give it to a day-care center, senior center, art class, or creative youngster (or not-so-youngster) who'd love to have it.

• Entertainment, grandchild-style. Save your unopened ad mail in a box (or better yet, a genuine mailbox) and present it to your grandchildren when they come to visit. While they happily busy themselves with their important correspondence, the grown-ups can chat in peace.

- Moving assistance. If you're planning to move in the near future, hang on to any sturdy envelopes you receive in the mail. Then, when you disassemble a table, bookcase, or other piece of furniture, put all the nuts, bolts, and screws into one of the envelopes, and tape it to the back or underside of the piece. When you get to your final destination, you'll have the hardware right where you need it.

- Shopping aids. Write your shopping list on the back of an envelope, and tuck your coupons inside of it. When you pick up a product that you have a coupon for, attach the coupon to the outside of the envelope with a paper clip. At the end of your shopping trip, hand the coupons to the cashier. If there are some you haven't used (maybe because the product was out of stock, or you found a better bargain), take them back home in the envelope.

- Tax help. No, you can't deduct the cost of your time spent sifting through your mail! But you *can* use the big envelopes to organize receipts, bank statements, and other backup documents that you need to keep with your yearly tax returns. (After all, why pay good money for file folders to hold papers that are just going to stay in a closed box for umpteen years?)

WHAT SHOULD YOU SHRED?

According to the experts, to fend off fraud and identity theft, you should shred, or

PACK RAT ALERT!

Problem: Your grocery-store coupons are scattered all over the place—except where you look for them when it's time to go shopping.

Solution: When you clip coupons, keep them together in one spot where you're sure to see them as you leave for the store—maybe near your car keys or with your collection of canvas shopping bags if you use them. And if you still keep forgetting to take the coupons with you, stop clipping them because they're not worth the time it takes or the clutter they cause.

otherwise completely destroy, the following items once you no longer need them:

✔ Anything that contains your Social Security number

✔ ATM receipts and bank statements

✔ Canceled or voided checks

✔ Copies of birth certificates or citizenship papers

✔ Credit card bills and receipts

✔ Credit reports and histories

✔ Expired credit, insurance, or identification cards of all kinds, including driver's licenses and voter registration cards

✔ Investment, stock, and property transactions

✔ Legal and insurance documents

✔ Medical and dental records

✔ Pay stubs and employment records

✔ Preapproved credit card applications

✔ Résumés

✔ School transcripts and report cards

✔ Tax forms

We've all been there: You're wrapping a Christmas or birthday present, and you discover that you're fresh out of ribbon. Don't run out to the store—instead, get rid of a little paper clutter. Just shred a document you don't need that complements the color of your wrapping paper. Then wrap the shreds around a knitting needle, or large bamboo skewer, and spritz lightly with water from a handheld mist sprayer. Set the whole shebang in a warm place to dry, and bingo: You've got colorful curlicues for decorating your package!

PUT THOSE SHREDS TO GOOD USE. So just what can you do with all that shredded paper? Here are a half-dozen handy suggestions:

1. Use it as "grass" in Easter baskets or centerpieces.

2. Substitute it for tissue paper in gift bags (color-coordinating the paper and the bag, of course).

3. Pack breakables in it for mailing, moving, or storage.

4. Donate it to the local animal shelter. It's perfect for stuffing pillowcases to make pet beds, and puppies love to play in it.

5. Add it to your compost pile or bin. It's an excellent source of carbon. No pile or bin? Then just dig the shreds right into the soil.

6. Mulch your garden with it. It forms a dense weed barrier, while gradually breaking down and adding organic matter to the soil.

ORGANIZE

Even after you've carefully sorted through your papers and thrown out the ones you don't need to keep, your documents will still be a cluttered mess—until you organize them in the way that works best for you!

CREATE AN ARCHIVE. The first step on the road to successful paper organizing is to find a place to stash files that you rarely use but need to keep, at least for a while (see "'Til We Don't Meet Again" on page 154). Simply go through your files and pull out any documents that are not active, like three-year-old tax records, expired insurance policies, or old medical records. Put them in plastic or cardboard file boxes, or a filing cabinet, and move them to a safe, dry place in your house.

HIDE YOUR ARCHIVE IN PLAIN SIGHT. If you don't have a safe, dry place available to park your inactive files, simply tuck them into a filing cabinet, and cover it with a tablecloth that matches your decor. If the size or shape of the cabinet won't work with your furniture arrangement, have a piece of plywood cut into a circle, square, or rectangle of the proper dimensions, and

MESS-MAKER ALERT!

Problem: You're constantly misplacing files because you can't read your own handwriting on the labels.

Solution: Invest in a small label maker (they're very inexpensive), so you can make a positive ID at a glance—every time.

simply perch it on top before you add your fabric covering.

WORK IN PROGRESS. When it comes to organizing your active files, there is only one right way to do it: the way that works best for you. But if you have more than a few files, simply arranging them alphabetically by the first letter on the label can lead to major clutter—fast. So instead, set up a system of categories and subcategories. Your broad categories might include:

- Employment
- Finances
- Home Improvement and Maintenance
- Insurance
- Medical
- Personal Interest
- Pets
- School

DIVVY 'EM UP. Then within each broad group, come up with whatever subcategories you need, and arrange them in alphabetical order. For example, your Finances category might contain separate files for bills, investments, and various bank accounts. And your Personal Interest file might include things like cooking, gardening, interior design, and travel.

PACK RAT ALERT!

Problem: Travel files stuffed full of clippings from magazines and newspapers are taking over your filing cabinet.

Solution: Make it a point to go through your travel folders on a regular basis, and get rid of anything that's more than a year old. Remember that this kind of information goes out of date rather quickly. For example, in the space of 12 months, hotel and restaurant ratings can plummet, their prices can skyrocket, or they can even go out of business. A charming town square that was filled with art galleries and small shops just a few years ago could now have a bunch of cookie-cutter chain stores. By keeping your files current, you'll cut clutter and decrease the chances that you'll be disappointed in your next vacation getaway.

COLOR IT NEAT. After you've chosen your broad categories, assign each one a color—maybe green for Finances, blue for Home Improvement and Maintenance, red for Insurance, and so on. This way, when you open a drawer to file your current phone bill, your eye will go straight to the green section.

MAKE ROOM FOR MORE. It's a fact of home-office life that files multiply. So as you set up your categories and subcategories, tuck some spare folders into the back of each one. If you have to scrounge around for a green folder when you open a new bank account or tend to any new financial matter, then you're likely to wind up with a pile of papers on your desk, rather than a filing system that cuts through the clutter.

MAKE AN INDEX. Having trouble remembering exactly what files you have, and where they are? One easy solution is to make a list of all the files in each drawer, and tape it to the front. Just be sure to update it as the contents change.

CURRENT AMOUNT DUE. Don't you just love paying bills? I didn't think so. After all, who enjoys seeing good money fly out the window? But you don't have to compound your monthly misery by letting all of that financial paper clutter up your home office. These three ultrasimple techniques will de-clutter the bill-paying process—and make sure you don't get slapped with late fees because a bill got lost in your files:

1. Sign up for online billing and payment options. If you do it right, you may never see a paper bill again!

Ask Jerry

Q. *I'm inundated with mail, mail, and more mail. How can I keep all this paper under control?*

A. Minimize mail clutter by going through the daily haul right over your recycling bin. Don't even take a second glance at anything that's obvious trash, like a catalog you know you won't order from, or a postcard advertising a cable service you don't need. Instead, just drop it in the bin. And as you open other mail, let the envelopes, bill enclosures, and other non-keepers fall right in, too.

2. If any of your regular bills can be paid automatically, sign up for the service, and let your bank handle the money transfers. You'll avoid paper clutter and save time, to boot.

3. Stick with the traditional pay-by-check approach, but pay each and every bill the day you receive it. Then write the date and check number on your portion of the invoice and tuck it into the appropriate file folder.

CURTAIL THE CARDS. One surefire way to conquer bill-paying clutter is to keep your credit card collection to a minimum. So the next time you're buying something in a department store and the checkout clerk tries to talk you into signing up for a store card, say "Thanks, but no thanks." The "terrific deals" you'll get aren't worth the bills that come along later. Try to limit yourself to one or two major credit cards and maybe a separate gas card. Besides having less paperwork to bother with, you'll be better able to keep track of the money you're spending.

PUT IT ON THE BOARD. One of the best ways to organize your home-office papers—and make good use of wall space at the same time—is also one of the simplest: Just hang up a bulletin board. You can pick up a standard corkboard and a collection of thumbtacks or pushpins at any office-supply store. Or opt for a metal version that uses magnets to hold your papers in place. Whichever type you choose, just remember this golden rule of office organizing: Only keep active materials on your board, like appointment

MAKING SPACE

When your toilet springs a leak, you won't want to waste even five minutes scanning a bulletin board for your plumber's phone number. So make a "household helpers" sheet. Buy plastic business card sleeves from an office-supply store and use them to hold the cards of your plumber, electrician, etc., and hang the sheets on your bulletin board. During a household emergency, you can quickly find the pro you need without having to remember his or her name!

reminders, notes relating to current projects, business cards that you refer to frequently, and your daily to-do list. Check the inventory every day, and file, toss, or shred anything that you're not using right now. Otherwise, your organizing tool will turn into a giant clutter catcher!

BUILD A BETTER-LOOKING BOARD. Want something a little more decorative than a standard-issue bulletin board? Then get to work on this easy do-it-yourself project:

1. Have a piece of ³/₄-inch Homasote® (a type of wallboard made from recycled paper) cut to the size you want. Your local lumberyard can do this for you.

2. Cut a piece of sturdy, plain-colored fabric 2 inches larger than the board on all sides. (Denim, linen, burlap, and cotton canvas are all good choices.) Lay the fabric face down on a work surface, and set the Homasote board on top.

3. Pull the fabric taut around the board, and use a staple gun to fasten it to the back.

4. Lay a pattern of ribbons on the front. A simple grid or a diamond layout will work fine, but if you want to go all out, you could even copy a pattern from a favorite garden trellis. Use upholstery tacks to hold the ribbons in place.

5. Attach a picture hanger to the back, and hang the board on the wall.

6. Tuck your business cards, to-do notes, invitations, and ball game tickets behind the ribbons. You'll need few, if any, pushpins to hold the papers in place.

Everyone wants to keep papers that bring back cherished memories like greeting cards, children's drawings, extra-good report cards, or theater programs. But if you're not careful—and you've got a houseful of people collecting memories—you can wind up buried in mementos. Keep it all organized by giving each family member a decorative box, basket, or other attractive container to hold his or her special keepsakes. They only get one, so when it's full, it's up to him or her to make some tough choices about what to keep and what to pitch.

STORE

If you never want to be surrounded by mountains of paper again, then you need to take one more de-cluttering step: Store everything from bills to business cards in a way that lets you find exactly what you want—when you want it.

WHAT NOT TO STORE IN YOUR HOME OFFICE. All of your really important, life-or-death documents belong in a safe-deposit box at the bank or in a fireproof home safe. But before you tuck them away there, make photocopies for your own personal use, and keep them in a labeled folder in your filing cabinet. Then put the originals of these vital documents under lock and key:

✔ Adoption papers and birth certificates

✔ Copies of wills, living wills, and advance medical directives

✔ Divorce decrees

✔ Marriage certificates

✔ Medical records

✔ Military records

✔ Passports

✔ Property deeds, titles, and mortgage notes

✔ Savings bonds

✔ Social Security cards

✔ Stock certificates

Ask Jerry

Q. I've always heard that you need to keep income tax records for only three years, because that's how long the IRS has to go back to audit your return. But recently I've been told I should hang on to my records for seven years. Is that true, and if so, why?

A. Yes, it is true: You should keep your federal tax returns and all supporting documentation for seven years. The reason for the confusion is that the IRS has three years to audit your return if the agents think you've made a good-faith error on it. But if, for any reason, they suspect that you've underreported your income, they have a full six years to go after you. And if that happens, you want to have as much proof of your innocence as you can get!

FILING CABINET SHOPPING TIPS. When you set out to buy a filing cabinet, whether you go to an office-furniture store or a less traditional shopping venue (see "More Bargain-hunting Haunts" on page 143), take three things with you: measurements of your space, a measuring tape, and the heaviest book you can find. (A huge, unabridged dictionary is ideal.) At the store, perform this two-step test:

1. Measure the cabinet to make sure it will fit into your available space.

2. Test the unit for quality. To do that, put the book in a drawer, and open and close it. Follow the same procedure with each drawer. If any of them screech or don't open easily and smoothly, then it means the cabinet is too flimsy to support a full load of files for very long.

GO LATERAL. Instead of buying a traditional filing cabinet with deep drawers that hold files from front to back, consider getting a model with drawers that hold them from side to side. These lateral files have several advantages:

• When you pull out a drawer, the files are all there in plain sight, right at your fingertips. You don't have to reach way into the back to find what you want, possibly scraping your hand in the process.

• Lateral files look better, especially in a home-office setting, because they're shaped like bookcases and don't jut way out from the wall, like traditional filing cabinets do.

OUT OF THE BOX

If you decide to replace your traditional, two-drawer, metal filing cabinet with another file-storage option, don't just send the old thing away to a thrift shop—not, that is, if you have small children or curious pets on the scene. As long as that cabinet has at least one locking drawer (which most of them do), it's the perfect place to store cleaning potions or other no-no products safely away from little hands and paws. Just paint the cabinet in a color to suit your decor, and stash your off-limits substances inside. Then use the drawers that don't lock to hold your stash of nonhazardous cleanup supplies, such as cloths, dust rags, and sponges.

- With a lateral file, you get some nice shelf space on top, where you can keep containers of office supplies, frequently used reference books—or even that rock collection or those pictures of family and friends that you've moved off your desktop—or should move!

PLAY THE ACCORDION. Accordion file, that is. These multisection marvels, with labeled dividers, are just the ticket for storing all kinds of important papers in your home office. Consider these possibilities:

- Instead of putting your manuals and warranties in a three-ring binder, get an accordion file that has as many sections as you need, and use one pocket for each product's paperwork.

- Keep your children's school papers neat and orderly. Get one file for each child, and stash long-term assignment instructions in one section, Scout or 4-H handbooks in another, absentee blanks and permission slips in another, and so on.

- Use labeled, 12-pocket files for things you organize by month, like bills, receipts, or birthday cards.

- Transfer your To-Do file from a single, flat folder to a divided accordion version. Label the dividers by either the day of the week or the date of the month. Then assign each task a deadline, and drop it into the appropriate slot.

RINGS THAT BIND. When you were sorting through your drawers, you probably pulled out instruction manuals and warranties for your computer, printer, and other office equipment. Well, don't you dare

MESS-MAKER ALERT!

Problem: Groups of papers fastened with paper clips go astray or snag other papers that don't belong with them.

Solution: Never use paper clips in a file folder. Instead, staple related groups of papers together for easy in-and-out access.

put those important papers back into a drawer! If the publications are not available online (see "Download to Downsize" on page 152), or you simply prefer paper copies, put them all into a three-ring binder, and keep it in a cabinet or on a bookshelf. For booklets that are too thick for your hole punch to penetrate, you have two excellent options that you can find in office-supply stores and catalogs:

1. Put them into paper or plastic sleeves that have pre-punched holes.

2. Use magazine holders. These are plastic strips, each one with a vertical slit and pre-punched holes. You just slide your booklet into the holder, and insert it into any standard-size binder.

BANK ON A BINDER. Three-ring binders are good for corralling a lot more than manuals, warranties, and other product information. They also make terrific alternatives to those tiny check registers that come with your checkbooks. The full-size sheets you put inside will give you plenty of room to record your checks, deposits, and debit card transactions. Plus, you can keep your statements and any bank-related correspondence (hole-punched, of course) in the same binder.

RING AROUND THE OFFICE. If you really don't care to cope with a zillion separate file folders, or to have a massive filing cabinet in your home office, do what a friend of mine does: Keep all of your active files in three-ring binders, and line them up on shelves—either in an open bookcase or

MAKING SPACE If you've got file folders piling up on your desk because it's too much trouble to muscle them in and out of your jam-packed filing cabinet, your storage problems are only going to get worse. Get back to business by always leaving enough room in the drawers so that the stand-up folders lean a little, or hanging ones slide easily along the tracks. When a drawer starts getting cramped, purge some documents, archive some folders, or transfer some to an empty drawer. By the way, this tip also applies if you keep your files in a rolling cart, or in wicker baskets or boxes, rather than a traditional filing cabinet.

behind closed doors in a cabinet or armoire. As various documents move into the inactive category, put them in labeled envelopes, and store them in cardboard file boxes in an out-of-the-way closet or attic.

RING OUT COMPUTER CLUTTER.

Just like rubber bands and paper clips, computer disks seem to multiply right before your eyes—making a cluttered mess of your work surfaces. You can buy storage boxes that are specially designed to hold disks, but there's also another option: plastic sleeves that hold four disks each and are pre-punched to fit into three-ring binders.

A TISKET, A TASKET... Keep your

files in baskets. Housewares stores, catalogs, and Internet sites all have wicker file baskets (with lids) that hold about three dozen hanging folders. They're as sturdy as can be, but they're also lightweight enough so that you can carry them around if you need to. Best of all—especially if your "home office" is an alcove in your living room, kitchen, or guest room—they're so attractive, you can make them a permanent part of your decor.

MORE DECORATIVE FILING

OPTIONS. You say you like the idea of file baskets (see "A tisket, a tasket…" above), but you're not a big fan of wicker? No problem! The same kinds of places that sell the baskets

PACK RAT ALERT!

Problem: Stacks of business cards, held together with rubber bands, are scattered all over your home office.

Solution: First, get rid of any cards that are outdated, or that you know you'll never use. Then turn the keepers into your personal Yellow Pages. Organize the cards into categories, such as Antique Shops, Home Repairs, Insurance, Medical, and Pets. You have several good storage options. I keep mine in a Rolodex® that has 3- by 5-inch cards, each covered with a plastic sleeve. If you prefer, you could tape or glue your business cards to regular index cards, and file them in a box. And you can even arrange them in a photo album that has small picture pockets.

also carry lidded file boxes that are covered in fabric, decorative paper, and leather. Furniture stores even carry ottomans and coffee tables with tops that flip up to reveal hanging file storage.

THEY'RE NOT SO DECORATIVE, BUT... In office-supply stores and on the Internet, you can find scads of file-storage containers that are sturdy, inexpensive, and portable. Your best choices depend upon whether you want to store archived files in a closet or attic, or active files behind closed doors in your office. When looks don't matter, consider any one of these options:

- Classic cardboard file boxes with either removable or tie-down lids, available in both letter and legal sizes. The Bankers Box® brand is best known, but dozens of others are available in office-supply, home-improvement, and discount stores.

- Plastic versions of the standard file boxes with tight-fitting lids. These are good if you absolutely must store your files in a place where dampness could affect them.

- Open cardboard boxes that are about 8 inches deep—just the right size for holding a dozen or so files on a shelf.

- Plastic milk-crate look-alikes that feature rods for hanging files. You can keep these on a deeper shelf, or perhaps on a table in your office-supply closet.

- Rolling plastic file cabinets in both one- and two-drawer models. If you're into contemporary furniture and/or don't mind the look of plastic, these can stay in plain sight. But they're also a snap to roll back undercover when you're through using them.

MAKING SPACE If you have only a small collection of files, don't bother with space-hogging cabinets, boxes, or baskets. Instead, get a hanging unit that's designed to hold file folders, and mount it to a wall or the back of a door. You can find these handy space savers in catalogs, in office-supply stores, and (of course) on the Internet.

CHAPTER FIVE

THE BATHROOM AND LINEN CLOSET

I n most homes, these particular spaces are crammed to the gills with a zillion and one daily necessities and extra-special luxuries. And that, my friends, can add up to major—even nightmarish—clutter fast! But never fear; using our SOS strategy, you can save the day and clear the clutter in no time at all.

BATHROOM BRAINSTORMS

You know how it is with bathrooms: Most mornings, you just need to get in and out of there as fast as possible. But then there are days—or evenings—when you finally have the time for a nice, long, leisurely soak in the tub. By putting our de-cluttering tips and tricks to work, you can ensure that your bathroom is ready and waiting.

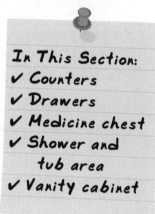

In This Section:
✔ Counters
✔ Drawers
✔ Medicine chest
✔ Shower and tub area
✔ Vanity cabinet

SORT

Bathrooms have one thing in common with home offices: They tend to attract a whole lot of small objects that can turn into big clutter. Well, don't despair. Just dive in and start (you guessed it!) sorting.

HAUL IT ALL OUT. As usual, step one in your de-cluttering mission is to take everything out of the drawers and cabinets and off the counters and other surfaces. Then spread it all out on your dining room table, your bed, your living room floor—or wherever else you can take a good, hard look at everything you've got.

BRING ON THE BAGS AND BOXES. You'll need one or more sturdy bags to hold all of the stuff you're going to pitch, and three boxes. Label them Keep Here, Take Elsewhere, and Donate.

NO "SELL" OPTION? Probably not. It's unlikely that you'll find any items in your bathroom that are worth selling, even for peanuts at a yard sale. But a shelter for homeless or battered women would probably be delighted to accept nice things that would give their residents a little bit of much-needed pampering. Any of these, for instance:

- Brand-new or next-to-new appliances like hair dryers and curling irons

- New and unopened bottles of shampoo, conditioner, or other grooming products that you bought on impulse and know you won't use

- Lotions, soaps, bath oils, or other fancy things you've received as gifts, but are just not your cup of tea

TOSS THE ANTIBIOTICS.
Remember that nasty flu that attacked you in 1999? I didn't think so. So how come you're still hanging on to the half-empty bottle of pills the doc prescribed? Because they might come in handy the next time a bug strikes? Well, forget that noise! Medications go downhill fast, so chances are they've completely lost their potency by now. And if there is still some oomph left in those meds, they could actually harm you.

MAKING SPACE

Donating your unwanted, unused, and still-fresh toiletries to a shelter will free up a whole lot of space in your bathroom and make some less fortunate folks happy at the same time. To find a shelter near you, check the government pages of your local phone book under "Social Service and Welfare Organizations" or "Health and Welfare Agencies." Any church will also be happy to put you in touch with a needy group or an individual who would welcome your castoffs with open arms.

So get rid of them now. If the container isn't childproof, put it into one that is. Then put that in another tightly sealed container, and toss it into the garbage can. (Never flush antibiotics down the toilet because they can be harmful to the water supply.)

HANG ON TO THE DETAILS! Even though an outdated medication is no good to you, the information on the label could be very helpful to you and your doctor the next time an illness strikes. So before you throw out any prescription medicines, remove the label if you can. Then tape it to a sheet of paper, and tuck it into the file folder that holds your medical records. If the label refuses to budge, copy down the essential information, and file that paper away. You should include:

✔ The name of the medication

✔ The prescription date

✔ Dosage and other instructions

✔ The condition it was prescribed for

✔ The doctor's name and phone number

✔ The pharmacy and prescription number

✔ The cost of the medication

✔ A note about how well it worked, including any side effects you experienced

CAN THE OLD COSMETICS. Unlike packaged foods and medications, cosmetics are not required by law to show expiration dates on their labels. But they do deteriorate over time. When you use a product that's past its prime, at best, you won't get the maximum benefits. At worst, you could pick up a nasty infection because bacteria start building up

When you take any current medications (both prescription and over-the-counter versions) out of your medicine cabinet, put them right into your Take Elsewhere box. That's because all medicinal products retain their potency longer when they're kept under cool, dry conditions—exactly the opposite of those found in most bathrooms. Those meds will fare much better if you keep them in your bedroom, linen closet, or pantry (safely protected from little hands or paws, of course).

the minute you open a new jar, bottle, or tube. So if you still have the tube of "Pretty in Pink" lipstick that you wore to your senior prom, or some glittery mascara that you keep on hand for your annual New Year's Eve party, do yourself a favor: Pitch that stuff now! Also discard any cosmetic, regardless of its age, that has changed in color, texture, or aroma.

When to Say When

Anytime you open a new personal-care product, it's a good idea to write the date on the package with a waterproof marker. Use it until it reaches the milestone noted below, then pitch it.

PRODUCT	HOW LONG IT LASTS	PRODUCT	HOW LONG IT LASTS
Blusher	3 months	Hair spray	2–3 years
Body wash	3 years	Lip gloss and lipstick	1 year
Concealer	6–8 months	Loose powder	1 year
Eye and lip pencils*	1 year or more	Mascara	3 months
Eye shadow	3 months	Moisturizer	1 year
Facial cleanser	6 months	Mouthwash	3 years
Facial toners	1 year	Nail polish	2 years
Foundation, cream	4–6 months	Pressed powders	3 months
Foundation, liquid**	3–6 months	Rubbing alcohol	2 years
Hair conditioner	2–3 years	Shampoo	2–3 years
Hair gel	2–3 years	Sunscreen	1 year

* Sharpen pencils at least once a week to prevent bacteria from being transferred to your eye and mouth areas. And if the product dries or crumbles, that means it's gone bad, so get rid of it pronto.

** This time frame applies to foundation in a bottle. Products that come in wide-mouthed jars, which expose them to more air, should be tossed sooner. You'll know it's time to buy a new supply when the ingredients begin to settle or separate, the texture thickens or thins, or the aroma changes.

MAKE 'EM LAST LONGER.

The experts differ on how long it's safe to keep various types of cosmetics. You'll find some general time frames in "When to Say When" on page 171. But the fact is that a product's life span can be greatly shortened if the cosmetic isn't used and stored properly. By following these six simple guidelines, you can help ensure that your cosmetics don't turn into useless—and possibly disease-causing—clutter before their time:

1. If at all possible, store your makeup someplace other than the bathroom. Just like medicines, foundations, powders, and other cosmetics last longer when they're kept under cool, dry conditions.

2. Before applying any makeup, wash your face and hands with soap and water.

3. Never reach into a container and touch makeup with your fingers. Instead, pour a little bit of it into the palm of your hand, or scoop it out with a tiny cosmetic spoon, applicator, or cotton swab.

4. Don't ever share your makeup with anyone else.

5. Keep all cosmetic containers tightly closed and stored upright when you're not using the product.

6. Don't moisten makeup with water—and certainly not with saliva. Either liquid could introduce bacteria that could quickly grow (and spread) out of control.

PACK RAT ALERT!

Problem: Piles of tiny containers of shampoo, hair conditioner, hand lotions, and even shower caps and mini sewing kits that you've collected over the years during your stays at various hotels.

Solution: Stash a set of the things in your overnight bag for short visits to family or friends. Keep two or three more sets on hand for houseguests who forget to bring their own toiletries. (Just remember to replace the products with new ones when they pass their prime.) Toss all the rest, or if they're still fresh, donate them to a shelter or church group.

MAKING SENSE OF SCENTS. Most fragrances, like colognes, aftershave lotions, and perfumes, stay at their peak of aromatic performance for about a year. After that, they start to oxidize, and their aroma heads downhill. How long it takes before the smell actually becomes unpleasant varies from one product to another, but your best bet is to get rid of any bottle that's been open for more than 12 months.

NATURAL IS NICE, BUT... Just like natural and organic foods, natural cosmetics are showing up in more and more drugstores and supermarkets—and for good reason: Many people find harsh, synthetic chemicals irritating to their skin. Others simply prefer the gentle feel and more subtle aromas of plant-based shampoos, soaps, body washes, and other personal-care products. If you're among that growing legion of purists, there's just one thing you need to remember: Products that are made from plant-derived ingredients and contain no chemical preservatives have a shorter shelf life than their synthetic counterparts. As a general rule, you should keep "all-natural" cosmetics and toiletries for no longer than six months after you open them.

IF YOU DON'T USE IT, LOSE IT. Get rid of any toiletries that you haven't used in several months, even if they are still fresh. After all, if they've just sat around all that time, they can't be very important to you. Either toss them in the trash, or tuck them into your Take Elsewhere box, and give them new careers in other parts of your house or around the yard. Consider these nine nifty examples:

1. Aerosol hair spray. It kills flying insects on contact—indoors or out. It's also perfect for keeping wooden tool handles smooth and splinter-free. (Just spray a thin coat onto the wood, and let it dry.)

Ask Jerry

Q. *The cords for my hair dryer, curling iron, and electric razor and toothbrush chargers get all tangled up in my bathroom vanity drawer. Any suggestion for sorting them out?*

A. Yep—and it's a really easy one, too. Simply fold up the cords, stuff them into empty toilet paper tubes, and presto—end of mess!

2. Antiseptic mouthwash. Maybe you don't care for the taste of the stuff, but cut flowers love it! To make their glorious show last longer, simply add ¹/₂ teaspoon of the tangy germ fighter to each quart of water in the vase.

3. Hair conditioner. This stuff is one of the best lubricants you can find. It can keep drawers, windows, and sliding doors from sticking; make refrigerator racks glide smoothly; or silence squeaky hinges and screeching faucets.

4. Lip balm. Turn that tube into a handy helper in your garage or workshop. Rub it on your car battery terminals to keep them from corroding, and coat nails and screws with it so they'll go into wood more easily. And if you have tiny rust specks on your tools, you can keep them from turning into big ones by washing and drying the tools, then dabbing them with lip balm.

PACK RAT ALERT!

Problem: A colorful nest of hair scrunchies that your daughter left behind when she went off to college three years ago.

Solution: Take those stretchy ponytail holders to your toolshed and use them to keep tabs on your garden gear. Just slip them onto the handles of your trowels, hand rakes, and anything else that tends to vanish among the green, green grass of home.

5. Perfumed bath powders and soaps. These are classic deer-chasing weapons. Just put the powder or soap into pouches made from old panty hose feet, and hang them from the branches of trees and shrubs that the deer are gunnin' for.

6. Shampoo. Use up what's left in the bottle to do your laundry; it works especially well on delicate clothes. Less than half a cup will usually do a full load. Shampoo is great for washing dishes, too, because it cuts right through grease and oil.

7. Shaving cream. Take it to your workshop, and use it to clean your grimy or paint-spattered hands. Just squirt the foam on, and wipe it off with a paper towel—no water needed!

8. Talcum powder. Add it to your pest-control arsenal because it's perfect for fending off ants, indoors and out. Just sprinkle a line of it anyplace you don't want the tiny troublemakers to roam.

9. Toothpaste. This belongs in your household cleaning kit. A dab of white toothpaste (not the gel kind) on a soft, cotton cloth is just the ticket for getting crayon marks off walls, polishing silver, cleaning gold jewelry, or removing light scratches from windows, mirrors, or glass tabletops.

SAVE THOSE BRUSHES! Cosmetics are not the only bathroom residents that can go bad before their time. Oil, dirt, and bacteria also get trapped in the bristles of your hairbrushes, turning these tools into nothing but germ-spreading clutter. To head off trouble before it starts, you should wash natural-bristle brushes once a month, and synthetic brushes three or four times a month with my homemade cleaner below.

WAYS AND MEANS. You can buy commercial hairbrush cleansers, but why clutter up your bathroom with another bottle or jar? Instead, clean your brushes (and combs, too) by soaking them overnight in a solution of 4 tablespoons of baking soda per quart of water. Then to keep the bristles from breaking as they dry, lay flat brushes on their backs, and stand round ones, heads up, on their handles in a drinking glass or other container. (For more ways to cut clutter by putting baking soda and vinegar to work in your bathroom, see "The Dynamic Duo" on page 181.)

Have tent caterpillars set up camp in your trees? Well, if you have an old round hairbrush that's cluttering up a bathroom drawer, you can get rid of the culprits fast. Just fasten the brush to a long pole, and twirl the brush around inside of the tent until the gauzy stuff clings to the bristles. Then scrape it off into a fire, or a bucket of soapy water. Any worms that escape the brush-off will be fair game for birds and other predators.

GIVE OLD HAIRBRUSHES THE BRUSH-OFF. When your hairbrushes get too ragged to use on your hair, get 'em out of your bathroom—but don't throw them away. Instead, move them to the laundry or broom closet. Then put them to good use cleaning the inside of your bagless vacuum cleaner, your dryer's lint trap, and any other hard-to-get-at places.

IF IT'S BROKE, DON'T FIX IT. Instead, kiss it good-bye. Your trash bag is the place to park anything that's broken or malfunctioning and can't be repaired. Obvious candidates include:

✔ Balding hairbrushes

✔ Barrettes with missing clasps

✔ Combs with missing teeth

✔ Electric toothbrushes with dead (and non-rechargeable) batteries

✔ Hair bands with stretched, twisted, or broken elastic

✔ Razors for which you can no longer buy replacement blades

✔ Scratched or chipped mirrors

✔ Sprung bobby pins

✔ Torn or dried-out cosmetic sponges

MAKING SPACE

Your bathtub is intended to be used for bathing—not for storing your toiletries. So take all of the bottles, jars, brushes, and sponges off the ledge, and put them in a cabinet or inexpensive shower caddy. In the minute or two it takes you to move that clutter, you'll create visual space and a more relaxing atmosphere where you can enjoy nice long, leisurely soaks.

OUT AT THE COUNT OF THREE. As your dentist has always said, you should replace your toothbrush with a fresh, new one every three months. If you can't remember how long you and your family have been using your current brushes, don't try to guess. Just assume that they're over the hill, and drop 'em all into your Take Elsewhere box. Then take them to your utility room, your toolshed, or anyplace else where you keep cleaning supplies. Those compact, bristly brush heads are the best tools you'll ever find for getting dirt out of hard-to-reach places like the crevices in garden tools, your lawn mower's engine, heating vents—and even the treads in work shoes, hiking boots, and sneakers!

FIND NEW JOBS FOR THE EXTRAS. If you and your family have switched from regular, handheld toothbrushes to new electric models that fight bacteria with sonic technology, then you've probably still got a few brand-new brushes lying around. What do you do with them? Count your lucky stars and move those cleaning tools to the kitchen—that's what! Use them to scrub cheese graters, can openers, strainers, waffle irons, and other gadgets that have got tiny nooks and crannies. To keep the brushes themselves spic and span, just run them through the dishwasher with your regular load. Or you can simply dunk the bristles in boiling water after every use.

REASSIGN THE DUPLICATE DRYER.
Got an extra hair dryer that's hogging space in a bathroom drawer? Then put it in your Take Elsewhere box, and add it to your household cleaning and maintenance kit. That hot-air blower can do a whole lot more than dry hair. For starters, consider these nine nifty ways you can put it to work around the old homestead:

A toothbrush makes a fine substitute for the mushroom-cleaning brushes sold in fancy housewares stores. And at corn-shucking time, a toothbrush is the perfect tool for getting all of those final, clingy strands of silk off the ears. After you've removed the husks, just run the brush vertically down each ear. Any reluctant silks will slide right off.

1. Clean jewelry. Fill a bowl—*not* a sink—with lukewarm water and stir in a few squirts of mild dishwashing liquid. Put the jewelry in the bowl, let it soak for a few minutes, and scrub each piece very gently with a soft toothbrush. (One made for baby's first teeth is perfect.) Rinse with clear water, lay the pieces on a towel, and dry them with the dryer set on low. *Caution:* Don't use this trick on soft stones such as opals, pearls, turquoise, or jade. And when in doubt, check with a jeweler before you proceed.

2. Defrost your freezer. Blast the ice with a hair dryer, and it'll melt away before your very eyes. Just be sure you never lay the thing down inside the freezer or refrigerator—even if the dryer's turned off!

3. Defrost frozen pipes. Set the dryer on warm and hold it close to the frozen section. But use caution with plastic pipes—if you get too close, the pipe may melt along with the ice!

4. Dust your stuff. Use the coolest setting, take aim, and blow the dust away. This trick is just the ticket for lamp shades, fabric hangings, artificial flowers, and anything else with intricate carving or relief work—like wooden furniture or ceramic pieces. You can even blow the dust out from behind radiators, bookcases, and refrigerators!

5. Get crayon marks off wallpaper. Set the dryer on high, and hold it on the marks until the wax softens. Then wipe it off with a few drops of Murphy® Oil Soap on a damp cloth.

6. Reshape stretched sweater cuffs. Just dip them in hot water, turn the dryer on high, and let 'em have it.

7. Remove contact paper from shelves and drawers. Use the warm setting, and heat up one small section at a time, gently lifting up the edges and cutting off the paper as you go.

Ask Jerry

Q. *I often change my nail polish color, which leaves me with half-empty bottles of colors I no longer use. I hate to throw them away. Is there a way I can put them to good use?*

A. Sure is: Put 'em to work elsewhere in your house. Keep a bottle of clear nail polish with your panty hose, so you can grab it quickly to fix a run or snag. Use colored polish to label cosmetic containers. Or mark your golf, tennis, or squash balls with a tiny drop of polish, so your playing partners don't walk off with them by mistake.

8. Remove wax from candlesticks. First, leave the holders in the freezer for half an hour or so. Chip off as much wax as possible with your fingers, then set your dryer on low and blow air over the drips until the wax melts. Follow up by wiping away the wax with a paper towel or soft, dry cloth.

9. Shrink-wrap windows. If you seal out Old Man Winter by taping plastic sheeting to the inside of your windows, a hair dryer can increase its protective powers. After you've attached the plastic, just turn the dryer setting to high and blast away, starting at the center and moving out toward the edges of the windows. The covering will shrink to fit the glass, providing a nice tight seal.

CLEAR THE AIR... But get rid of those big cans of chemical deodorizers. The fact is that just about all they do is clutter up your bathroom counters and cabinets. You may think they make the air cleaner and fresher when, actually, they only fill it with chemicals that cover up the unpleasant aromas. They also interfere with your sense of smell, causing you not to notice the odors as much. So can the cans and try one of these natural alternatives:

• Pour some white vinegar into decorative bowls, and set them around the bathroom. The acidic liquid will banish the unwanted smells pronto.

COLLECTOR ALERT!

Problem: You have a treasured collection of big seashells that you'd like to display on a shelf in your bathroom.

Solution: Don't even think about it! Shells, beach stones, pottery, and other collectibles may look fabulous in the bathrooms you see in the glossy decorating magazines. But in real life, all they do is attract dust, which quickly turns gummy and yucky in the humid air of a bathroom. Unless you really enjoy heavy-duty dusting, either find another place to show off your collection, or keep it under cover. If you have the room for a glass-doored display case, put your big shells and pottery pieces in that. Items like small shells, beach stones, and fancy marbles will look great in clear glass jars or bowls with lids.

- Light a candle. Better yet, light several. But don't bother with the fancy, scented kind. Like air-freshener spray, they'll add odor-masking chemicals to the air. On the other hand, a pure candle flame will simply burn the odors away—even those foul-smelling swamp gases that occur in bathrooms every now and then.

...AND KEEP IT CLEAR. To make sure the air in your bathroom stays fresh and clean, adopt a houseplant or two. Green plants naturally absorb and neutralize air pollutants. What's more, they do an especially good job in small, enclosed spaces like bathrooms, where the air quality is usually bad. Any kind of plant can perform this feat, but according to the scientists at NASA (who certainly know about tight spaces), these are the air-cleaning superstars:

> **Aloe vera**
> **Chrysanthemums**
> **English ivy** (*Hedera helix*)
> **Fig tree** (*Ficus benjamina*)
> **Spider plants** (*Chlorophytum*)

FIRST THINGS FIRST. As you sort through your drawers and medicine cabinet, set aside anything that belongs in a first-aid kit, like antibiotic ointment, adhesive bandages, small scissors, tweezers, and rubbing alcohol. Then when you've finished your sorting mission, stash all those supplies in a plastic storage container or an old lunch

MESS-MAKER ALERT!

Problem: Cabinets and drawers stuffed with products you bought in large quantities at discount prices.

Solution: Beware of warehouse stores and other bargain outlets that offer low prices on multipacks of bathroom supplies. Yes, you may save some money, but you pay the price in a jumbled, cluttered bathroom. Plus, you may not even get to use it all before it goes bad. Sure, it makes sense to buy 12-packs of toilet paper—if you have the space to store them. But can you really go through four tubes of antibiotic ointment or six bottles of aspirin before the expiration date rolls around? If you want to take advantage of those low prices, play it smart and go in on the purchase with several friends.

box. Label it First-Aid Kit, and take it to the kitchen. Why the kitchen? Because that's the room in your house where you're most likely to cut or burn yourself. Chances are it's also the room you'll come to first if you rush in from the yard with a fresh scrape, splinter, insect bite, or other injury requiring quick first-aid.

TRASH THE TOXIC STUFF. If you have small children or inquisitive pets in the house, and you keep chemical cleansers, drain de-cloggers, or other caustic products under your sink, get 'em outta there *now*. Either move them to a locked cabinet in your laundry room, or install a lock on your vanity cabinet. In fact, you should do that even if you use natural, earth-safe cleaning products. Although "green" commercial products may pose no danger to our air, water, or soil, many of them could cause serious harm if they fall into the hands (or mouth) of a curious child or pet.

THE DYNAMIC DUO. You can cut a lot of clutter from your bathroom—and make it a much safer place, to boot—if you replace your collection of commercial cleansers and cleaners with two basic kitchen staples: a bottle of vinegar and a box of baking soda. Stash them wherever you keep your bathroom cleaning supplies, whether that's under the sink, or in your linen closet or utility room. Performing together, or in solo roles, these two superstars can keep your bathroom spic and span. Here's a sampling of what this dynamic duo can do:

✔ Clean grout between ceramic tiles. Wet down the grout with a cloth or sponge, then dip a toothbrush in baking soda, and scrub the dirt away.

✔ Wash the floor. Make a solution from $1/2$ cup of vinegar per gallon of warm water, grab your mop, and go to town.

✔ Unclog the drain in your tub or sink. Pour $1/2$ cup of baking soda into the drain, and follow up with $1/2$ cup of white vinegar. Let it sit for about 15 minutes, and rinse with hot tap water. Just one word of caution: Do *not* use this method if you've already tried a commercial de-clogger. The vinegar can react with the drain cleaner to create dangerous fumes. (To prevent future buildups, pour a cup of white vinegar down the drain every month or so.)

✔ Clean the toilet bowl. Sprinkle $^1/_4$ cup of baking soda into the bowl and drizzle $^1/_4$ cup of vinegar over the soda. Then grab a long-handled brush and scrub-a-dub-dub!

✔ Prevent mold and mildew in the shower. Pour vinegar onto a damp sponge or cloth, and wipe the surface. (This technique works on both ceramic tile and plastic laminate shower walls.)

✔ Unclog the showerhead. Remove the head, put it in a pot, and add enough vinegar to cover it completely. Heat the vinegar to just below boiling, then remove the pot from the burner. Let it sit overnight, or for at least six hours. Rinse the head with clear water, and you're good to go.

Soft-scrubbing cleansers are great for cleaning bathroom fixtures, but why add clutter to your cabinets? Instead of buying a commercial product, just mix $^1/_8$ cup of baking soda with enough pure liquid soap (available at the supermarket) to get a creamy consistency. Apply the mixture with a sponge or soft brush, and rinse with clear water.

WEED OUT VISUAL CLUTTER. Even if you have a fairly good-size bathroom, it's almost guaranteed to be the smallest room in your house. Here are a few simple tricks that will make it look and feel more spacious:

• Follow the one-mat policy. We've all been in bathrooms where there was a bath mat or a little rug in front of the tub, another in front of the sink, and yet another wrapping around the toilet—with maybe a matching, fuzzy cover on top of the flush tank, to boot. Not only do those multiple mats make the room look cluttered, but they also create tripping hazards, provide cozy hiding places for germs, and add to your laundry load. So get rid of the piddly little things, and replace them with a single larger rug or mat that covers more of the floor.

- Use a simple shower curtain. Nix the striped, polka-dot, or plaid curtain, and replace it with a solid version in a pale or neutral color. Instantly, the whole room will appear bigger and less cluttered. Oh, and while you're at it, get rid of the fancy curtain hooks with shells, flowers, or animals on them, too. Those elaborate designs might be fun in a child's bathroom, but in a room that grown-ups use, they just provide one more busy element.

- Close the curtain. And keep it (and the liner) fully drawn across your tub or shower stall. It will look like a neat, uncluttered wall. Plus, a curtain that's extended to its full width will dry out faster, which will help fend off mold, mildew, and germs, *and* lessen your cleaning chores.

MAKING SPACE

The space-expanding tricks that apply to your shower curtain (see "Weed Out Visual Clutter" at left) also go for your bathroom window curtains or shades, and your sink skirt, if you have one. For the biggest visual de-cluttering impact, use the same fabric for the shower curtain, window treatments, and the sink skirt. Or, if you prefer, opt for wooden or bamboo blinds in a single light color that blends with the shower curtain. Don't use blinds with a tortoiseshell or splotched pattern because just like patterned fabric, they'll make the room look more cluttered than it really is.

ONE MORE TIME. When the time comes to retire your old shower curtain, don't throw it away. Here's a tub full of good uses for that fabric or vinyl sheet:

✔ Temporary window covering. Just thread a spring-tension rod through the holes in the top of a fabric curtain, and pop it into place in the window frame—no rings or brackets needed!

✔ Packing "blanket." Wrap a fabric curtain around furniture to protect it in the moving van (or the back of your minivan).

✔ Painting drop cloth. Spread vinyl curtains on floors and furniture to catch drips. Rinse 'em off when you're done.

✔ Child-size "construction material." Give fabric curtains to the youngsters, and they'll have a field day building forts, castles, and stage sets.

✔ Pest-control aid. Lay a fabric curtain on the ground under plants plagued by beetles or weevils, and shake the branches gently. When the bugs come tumbling down, gather up the trap, and dump the contents into a tub of water laced with a cup of soap or alcohol.

✔ Plant protectors. Toss fabric curtains over plants when late or early frosts threaten. Or make a cold frame by draping a clear vinyl curtain over stakes that you've pounded into the ground.

ORGANIZE

Okay. You've gotten rid of all the unwanted stuff that's been cluttering up your bathroom. Now it's time to organize the space in the way that works best for you and the things you've set aside in your Keep Here box.

DRESS(ER) FOR SUCCESS. If your bathroom-organizing plan calls for replacing some or all of the fixtures, consider turning an antique or vintage dresser into a vanity. (Just coat the wood with polyurethane to

The same under-sink organizers that add heaps of storage space in your kitchen work just as well for organizing the space in your bathroom vanity cabinet. Just choose components that fit the space, and slide them right in. But what if you have a simple wall-hung sink? No problem! Tuck in whatever organizers you have room for, and conceal them with a sink skirt. (For the details on under-sink organizers, see the Mess-Maker Alert! on page 72.) As for what to keep under your sink and how to organize it, that all depends on what other storage options you have in your bathroom, and what kinds of things you keep there. There is just one golden rule you should keep in mind: If you keep cleaning products under the sink, store your cosmetics and toiletries elsewhere—and vice versa.

protect it from possible water damage.) Besides adding a personal touch to your bathroom, it will give you more storage space than you'd get with most standard bathroom vanities. And it could cost a lot less, too. Here are three simple tricks to help you maximize your storage space:

1. Choose a vessel-type sink bowl that sits on top of the dresser, rather than one that must be recessed into the surface.

2. Have your plumber recess the pipes into the wall.

3. Use a wall-mounted faucet and spigots.

CONTROLLING THE COST. Notice I said that a sink-topped dresser *could* cost less than a standard bathroom vanity. It could also cost a whole lot more if you buy an elegant antique dresser from an upscale shop, and top it with a fancy vessel sink from a retail bathroom- or plumbing-supply store. But you can get the same look—and the same expanded storage space—by following a few classic bargain-hunting guidelines:

• Shop first in your attic or basement. You just might find an old dresser that'll fill the bill perfectly, and you could find a great sink, too. That's because any good-sized, nonporous bowl or planting pot will serve the purpose. You (or your plumber) can easily drill a hole in the bottom to accommodate the drain and pipe.

• Scout out local yard sales, flea markets, and thrift shops for both dressers and bowls.

• Check top-notch plumbing-supply and bathroom-fixture shops for vessel sinks. If you get lucky, you could find a steal of a

MESS-MAKER ALERT!

Problem: A bathroom scale that's sitting out in the open, taking up precious floor space.

Solution: Besides making the room look more cluttered, a bathroom scale can be downright dangerous—as you know if you've ever stubbed your toe on it or, worse, tripped over it as you've wandered groggily into the bathroom in the middle of the night. So get that thing outta the way! Either put it into the bathroom closet if you've got one, slide it under the vanity, or if necessary, take it to your bedroom. End of problem!

deal on a discontinued or very slightly dinged model. Consider this inspirational (and true) story: A friend of mine, who was rehabbing an old house, spotted a drop-dead gorgeous, bronze vessel sink at her local plumbing supply shop. When she learned the price was $1,500, she said "Thanks, but no thanks." A couple of days later, the saleswoman she'd spoken with called her and said the boss had decided to redecorate the showroom. The bronze sink was on the "must-go-*now*" list, and if my friend still wanted it, she could have it for $100. Needless to say, she hightailed it over there and quickly snatched up her prize!

A LITTLE MORE COUNTER SPACE, PLEASE. Pedestal and wall-mounted sinks are great space savers in small bathrooms, but when you're trying to organize the place, they have one glaring fault: They have barely enough room to set a water glass and a soap dish on, let alone a hairbrush and dryer, your makeup, and all the other stuff you need at your side as you prepare for the day (or evening). So what do you do? Put a nightstand or end table next to the sink. If you can't find either piece in your or a relative's attic, get one at a local flea market or thrift shop, and paint it to match your bathroom's decor.

EVEN MORE COUNTER SPACE. Got extra room beside that counter-less sink? Then jot down the dimensions of the area (including the height of the sink), and go on the prowl for a dresser, cupboard, or table that'll fit into the space without making the room look cluttered.

GOING UP. You say your counters are plenty roomy, but you're short on drawers, shelves—and floor space?

MAKING SPACE

Looking for a quick way to add a lot of storage in a narrow space? Just put a bookcase in your bathroom! Either get one that reaches from the floor to the ceiling, or go with a lower, two-shelf model, and use the top as a counter. Bingo— you've just doubled or even tripled your storage area while taking up only a foot's worth of floor space!

Then think vertically. The fastest and easiest way to organize the space above your counter is to simply perch a freestanding cabinet or bookcase on top of it.

GOING WAY UP. Simply by installing a shelf a foot or so below the ceiling, you'll gain oodles of space to store things like extra soap and guest-kit toiletries that you need only once in a while. (Just make sure you put everything in attractive baskets or other containers, so they don't turn into dust-catching clutter!)

LOOK TO THE TANK. And don't forget the space above your toilet's flush tank. Home-improvement and housewares stores, as well as Web sites, sell organizers that are especially designed to fit over the flush tank, with open shelves or doored cupboards above. If you don't care for the way those units look (and lots of folks don't), then mount a cabinet, medicine chest, or open shelves to the wall. Just make sure to leave enough room so you can easily remove the lid of the flush tank without banging it into the shelf or cabinet that's above it!

CUT CORNERS. Don't let corner space go to waste. Depending on the size of the area, you can either install a wall-hung corner cabinet or move in a tall, freestanding model. (Look for these at flea markets and thrift shops.) You can even pick up a tall pot rack at a housewares store, and use the shelves to hold stacks of rolled-up towels, or bowls or baskets filled with supplies and toiletries.

PLAN FOR ACTION. Before you start reloading your cleaned-out cabinets and shelves, organize the contents according to their use. Keep your hair-care products in one spot, your oral hygiene gear in

To make room for a whole lot of storage without losing any space in your bathroom, build shelves recessed into the walls between the studs—or have a carpenter do the job for you. The opening will be just deep enough for 6-inch shelves made of either glass or wood—the perfect size for most bathroom storage needs.

another, your shaving supplies in yet another, and so on. Your morning routine will roll along much more smoothly when you don't have to scrounge through a drawer full of stuff in order to find your toothpaste and toothbrush.

ORGANIZE THE SMALL STUFF.

Loose things like tweezers, clippers, eyelash curlers, and hair clips can add up to a big mess if you just toss them in a drawer. So don't do it! Instead, buy an adjustable drawer organizer—or a few if you have a whole lot of small tools and accessories. You can find these handy and inexpensive inserts at home-improvement and housewares stores and (of course) on the Internet. Just make sure you get the kind with sections that you can adjust for width and/or length. If you opt for a version that has fixed compartments, the things you need to store may not fit in the available space.

ORGANIZE THE BOTTLES, TOO.

When they're kept in a drawer, small bottles of nail polish and makeup tend to go sliding all over the place every time you open or close the drawer. Fortunately, it's a snap to stop them in their tracks. How? Just tack a strip of elastic to the inside front of the drawer at whatever height suits your needs. Then slip the bottles into their homemade "seat belt." They'll stay put until you pull them out.

SUSAN TO THE RESCUE! The same lazy Susan that does such a good job of organizing the space in your kitchen cabinets can help keep

PACK RAT ALERT!

Problem: You've sorted through all of your toiletries and cosmetics, tossed the oldies, and donated the ones you don't care for, but you're still holding on to some extras that you just can't bear to part with.

Solution: Put 'em in your suitcase. You'll free up space in the bathroom—and when it's time to pack for your next trip, you won't be scrambling around trying to find everything; those supplies will be right where you need them!

things under control in your bathroom, too. Tuck a two- or three-tiered model into your vanity cabinet, load it up with toiletries or cleaning supplies (but not both!), and you're good to go.

CLEANING SUPPLIES TO GO. If you have more than one bathroom, you could keep a set of cleansers, sponges, and so on in each closet or vanity cabinet. Or you could save space (and money) with this simple trick: Keep all of your cleaning gear in a single movable container, and carry it to whichever bathroom needs sprucing up. A simple bucket will work fine, or check a home-improvement or hardware store for an inexpensive plastic tote that's specially designed to hold a bunch of cleaning supplies.

DON'T TRASH THE WASTEBASKET! Believe it or not, I've known folks who have gotten so carried away with clutter control that they actually got rid of their bathroom wastebasket. If you're tempted to do that—perhaps because you don't like the plastic models that are normally sold for bathroom use—think again. You have plenty of better-looking options, including these winners:

Would you believe that you can lose a little kitchen clutter and gain a one-of-a-kind wastebasket for your bathroom at the same time? It's true! Just grab a brown paper grocery bag and paint designs on it, or cover it with pictures cut from magazines or wrapping paper. Give it a couple coats of clear acrylic enamel, inside and out, and presto: a piece of functional art!

✔ A wicker basket or hamper. Put a plastic wastebasket inside of it to keep the fibers from getting wet and yucky.

✔ A big ceramic or terra-cotta flowerpot. Just be sure that it has no drainage hole in the bottom of it.

✔ A bucket. Pick up a sleek stainless steel version at a pet-supply shop or housewares store, or use a colorful, enameled-metal sand bucket that supermarkets and toy stores carry in the summertime.

BAG BASICS. If you use a plastic trash bag to line your bathroom wastebasket, take a tip from the folks who clean hotel rooms: Keep a few extra folded-up bags in the bottom of it, underneath the one that's currently in use. Then when you remove the one that's full, a fresh, new bag will be right at your fingertips.

PREPARE FOR BATHROOM BRAINSTORMS. This may sound strange, but always keep a notepad and pen in your bathroom. That way, when you're brushing your teeth in the morning, and you think of a question you want to bring up at today's staff meeting, you can jot it down before you forget it. Or maybe you notice that you're running low on facial tissue. Just write yourself a note to pick some more up on the way home. This time-saving trick works no matter how good or bad your memory is.

MESS-MAKER ALERT!

Problem: Ugly rust rings that are left on counter-tops and bathtubs by metal cans of shaving cream and hair spray.

Solution: When you first bring the cans home, coat the bottoms with clear nail polish, and the problem disappears. Don't have clear nail polish? No problem! Wrap the bottom of the can with a piece of plastic wrap and hold it in place with a rubber band. The beauty of this solution is that you can use the wrap over and over.

STORE

Now that you've got all your bathroom gear organized, it's time to put everything back into your neat, well-organized bathroom. So go to it!

PUT YOUR DOOR TO WORK. The back of the door is some of the most valuable real estate in your bathroom. Just think of all the wonderful ways you can use it!

• Add an organizing unit that has cubbies for storing things like slippers, towels, and bath brushes. (They're available, in both over-the-door and screw-on versions, at home-improvement and housewares stores and on the Internet.)

- Attach a full-length mirror.

- Screw on hooks or a rack to hold bathrobes or wet towels.

- Hang one or more flat-sided baskets on the door, and use them to hold toiletries or rolled-up towels.

LOOK OUT BELOW. If small children use your bathroom (even if they're only infrequent visitors), attach a peg-type rack or hooks with round eye-safe, ceramic knobs lower down, within the youngsters' reach. Use the hooks to hang the kids' towels, bathrobes, or a mesh bag or basket filled with tub toys.

RACK 'EM UP. Hanging wine racks are perfect for storing bath and hand towels. Just mount two or three on a wall, roll up the towels, and stick each one into a bottle cubby.

Do your hand towels end up in a damp heap on the floor after children use the bathroom? Chances are, the kids are tugging on the towels in an attempt to reach them in order to dry their hands. Here's a simple solution: Drape the top quarter of each towel over the bar, and pin it at both sides, just under the bar, with clip-type clothespins. The youngsters will get their hands dry with no trouble, and the towel will stay put where it belongs.

HOOKED ONE! In a small bathroom, or one that's shared by several people, traditional towel bars can be major contributors to clutter. But you already know that if you've ever walked into the bathroom and found a bunch of wet towels scrunched up on the bar(s). The simple solution: Replace those bars with big, decorative hooks, and assign one to each member of the family. (You can find an assortment of hooks at home-improvement stores and on the Internet.) That way, there will be no damp mess and no confusion about which towel belongs to whom.

TAKE A STAND. If your bathroom is short on towel-hanging space, pick up a couple of freestanding towel racks. Home-improvement stores, catalogs, and Web sites carry them in both large versions and smaller models that you can set on a vanity top or shelf to hold small guest towels. (They're just the ticket when company's coming.)

RISE UP. Just like kitchen and bathroom cabinets, standard medicine cabinets usually have too few shelves. As a result, when you put jars or other short items on them, you wind up with a lot of wasted space. The answer: Add more shelves. There are several simple ways to do this. The best method for you depends on the age and style of your cabinet. Here are your options:

1. If you have a new medicine cabinet that came with adjustable shelves, you can probably buy extra shelves and brackets. To find out, ask the dealer you bought it from, or check out the manufacturer's Web site.

2. Have a glass dealer or your local hardware store cut some shelves to fit, and then buy the appropriate number of brackets to rest them on.

3. Buy acrylic risers that are specially made for medicine cabinets, and set them on the existing shelves. These are available in catalogs and on the Internet.

MAKING SPACE

To keep tweezers, nail clippers, and other metal gadgets close at hand, attach a magnetic strip to the back of your medicine cabinet or the back of a cupboard door. Then attach your teeny tools to the strip. That way, you'll never have to search for them again!

WHAT GOES THERE? As for what you should keep in your medicine cabinet, that's entirely up to you. Use that space to hold anything that fits and that you like to have close at hand in your bathroom. There is only one no-no—medications of any kind—and one try-not-to: cosmetics. Both of these products should ideally be kept under cooler, drier conditions than you probably have in your bathroom.

IT'S A SHOE-IN. Two types of devices that are intended for shoes can provide you with super storage in your bathroom:

• Plastic shoe holders (the kind with separate, boxlike compartments) will add oodles of storage to the vanity cabinet under the sink. Just tuck one in (or use more if the space is big enough), and stash small jars, bottles, and tubes in the cubbyholes.

- Hanging shoe bags (either the screw-mounted or over-the-door type) are perfect for storing cosmetics, toiletries, and grooming tools of all kinds. Just hang it on the back of the bathroom door, linen closet door, or even on the wall beside the sink.

HANG YOUR DRYER. No drawer space for your hair dryer? No problem! Just screw a hook onto the back of your vanity door, and hang the appliance from that. Or, if you'd prefer, hang it on the wall next to the sink, using either a hook or a special caddy that's designed just for blow dryers. (You can find these in home-improvement and housewares stores and on the Internet.)

FISH FOR YOUR MAKEUP. As unlikely as it may sound, a fishing-tackle box is a terrific place to store cosmetics. The little compartments are just the right size for lipstick, eye shadow, and small brushes, and the larger ones can hold hair accessories or tubes of moisturizer and foundation. Best of all, when it's time to hit the road, you can just grab the box and go! (If you'd prefer a more girly look, paint a design on the outside of the box, or decorate it with attractive stickers or decals of your choice.)

Ask Jerry

Q. *I've heard that perfume will retain its fragrance longer if you store it in the refrigerator. Is this true?*

A. In a word, no. While perfume should be kept in a cool place, the refrigerator is too cold. Some of the oils in the perfume might congeal, which would change the scent. What's more, if the bottle isn't tightly sealed, the odor could be absorbed by fatty foods, like cheese and butter—and you could wind up with a grilled-cheese sandwich that gives off the distinct aroma of Chanel No. 5!

The best place to store perfume is in a drawer or cupboard, away from light and high humidity. Normal room temperature is fine, but during hot weather, try to make sure that the room is air-conditioned.

OUT OF THE KITCHEN... And into the bathroom. Some of the most useful, and often attractive, bathroom storage containers are objects more commonly used in kitchens. Try any of these, for instance:

- Clamp-lid canning jars. Use them to hold stuff that's pretty to look at, like cotton balls, bars of fancy soap, bath oil beads, and bath powders. As a bonus, the airtight lids keep the contents dry and free of dust.

- Cookie jars. They can hold the same types of items you'd keep in canning jars, but because you can't see into them, they're a better choice for supplies you don't really want to keep on display. Makeup containers, tissue pocket packs, and extra toothbrushes and tubes of toothpaste are some prime examples.

- Cutlery organizers. Slip them into drawers, and fill the compartments with cosmetics, razors, brushes, and what have you.

- Glasses and mugs. Set them right on the counter to store toothbrushes, or put them in the medicine cabinet for holding your makeup brushes, tweezers, combs, or anything else that can stand on end. *Note:* If you have youngsters using your bathroom, stick with plastic cups and mugs for safety's sake.

- Spice racks. Whether you screw them to a wall or a cabinet door, or stand them on a counter or shelf, they're just the ticket for holding lots of small bottles and jars.

MATERIAL MATTERS. We've all seen glossy magazines with pictures of bathrooms that are chock-full of storage containers made of unprotected metal, or cardboard covered with decorative paper or

COLLECTOR ALERT!

Problem: A big collection of eye and lip pencils, mascara tubes, and skinny makeup brushes.

Solution: Stash them in a toothbrush holder (or two or three of them if your collection is *really* big). The slots are just the right size to keep all that slim stuff in place.

fabric. And there are all shapes and sizes of canisters with fancy, preprinted paper labels identifying their contents. Well, take my advice: Unless you have a guest bathroom that's used only once in a blue moon, or a half-bath with no tub or shower, forget those fragile things. If you put them in a bathroom that sees everyday use—even by only one person—you're asking for a lot of rust, rot, or mildew. Instead, look for containers that are made of materials that can stand up and say "Boo!" to high humidity and splashing water. Any of these will work just fine:

✔ Breathable basketry

✔ Ceramic

✔ Glass

✔ Plastic

✔ Stainless steel

✔ Wood

GET SET TO SOAK. It's been a long, stressful day, and you can't wait to settle back into a nice relaxing bubble bath. But first, you have to scrounge through the bottles and jars under your sink to find your bubble stuff. Well, I know an easy way to avoid that treasure hunt: Just put all of your bath and body products in an attractive basket, and set it close to your tub. Then the next time you have a day from you-know-where, relief will be close at hand. In fact, you'll probably use your pampering potions more often when they're out in plain sight.

Ask Jerry

Q. *We have only one full bath in our house, but we are a family of four. There's not enough room to store everyone's shampoos, conditioners, shaving cream, etc. Help!*

A. Eliminate bathroom storage woes by giving every family member a portable container to hold their toiletries. The owner can keep the tote in his or her bedroom and take it to the bathroom as needed. Your choice of containers is almost unlimited. Lunch boxes, baskets, nylon or canvas tote bags, and toolboxes will all work like a dream. So will a vintage train case that was specifically designed for carrying cosmetics from one place to another.

CLUTTER BUSTER PRO

Do the words, "May I use your powder room?" or "Company's coming!" evoke feelings of terror? If they do, fear not! Linda Durham, professional organizer and owner of Organizing Matters (www.organizingmatters.com) in Houston, Texas, says that guest baths and powder rooms are a snap to reclaim. Here's how:

☛ First, list all of the ways you need to use your guest bath and/or powder room. It's very common for them to have secondary purposes such as linen closet, yard and pool toy closet, or pets' dining room.

☛ Remove anything you do not need, do not use, or do not love, along with anything that is not related to the purpose(s) of the room(s).

☛ Use drawers or cupboards for storing as many items as possible. Fill attractive baskets or boxes with things that can't be put away.

☛ Because guest baths and powder rooms are "public" rooms, look for wall and door solutions that are attractive and can accommodate nice containers or baskets. If you use a clear vinyl or mesh shoe bag on the back of the door, be sure the contents are discrete and not embarrassing.

☛ Use containers with lids or shelves in the cupboards that would allow you to utilize all of the upward space.

☛ Remember that the primary purpose of your guest bath and powder room is to make your guests feel welcome—so be sure that it looks and feels guest-ready at all times.

☛ Towel racks are often in short supply, especially when guests come. So be prepared with collapsible drying racks that can accommodate guest towels.

☛ Keep a couple sets of bath towels back from regular use so they are still fresh and new-feeling for company.

☛ Have an extra roll of toilet paper on hand that's easy to find. Most guests feel intrusive if they have to look in drawers or cupboards when it runs out.

☛ Keep a supply of baby wipes or cleaning wipes on hand and easy to find.

CORRAL THE LIBRARY. If you and your family read in the bathroom, you know that the reading material tends to get out of control. So contain it by mounting a magazine rack next to the tub or toilet (depending on whether you read more while soaking or sitting). Your books, magazines, and other publications will stay dry and within easy reach when you want them.

DISPLAY THE TOILET PAPER. No, I don't mean that you should keep your bargain-priced 12-packs stacked up on the counter! But do keep a few rolls out in the open so that guests won't have to fish through your cabinets to retrieve one if they need it. You have plenty of easy and attractive options for storing your supply:

- Heap the rolls in a basket, big bowl, or ceramic planter.

- Stack them, one on top of another, in a cylindrical glass vase.

- Slide them over the post of a vertical paper-towel holder.

- Prop a stuffed bear or other animal toy in a corner and have it "hug" an extra roll.

BEHIND CLOSED DOORS

Whether you have an actual linen closet, or you store your table, bath, and bed linens in a freestanding cabinet—or even in scattered locations throughout your house—the guidelines in this section will help you keep everything shipshape. And you guessed it: The secret to success is our SOS strategy.

In This Section:
✔ Towels
✔ Bed linens
✔ Table linens
✔ Paper goods
   and toiletries

SORT
Start your linen closet sorting spree by pulling everything off the shelves and spreading it out where you can see it. Then grab a trash bag and three boxes, and once again label these Keep Here, Take Elsewhere, and Donate or Sell.

INTO THE TRASH. Anything that falls into the to-be-tossed category should announce itself loud and clear. Prime candidates include:

✔ Outdated medications or cosmetics that have found their way into the linen closet

✔ A few wrinkled paper cocktail napkins

✔ The hair dryer that vanished five years ago—and that no longer works anyway

✔ Cleaning products with half an inch of liquid left in the bottom

✔ A box of solidified turtle food (Where on earth did *that* come from?)

MAKING SPACE

If the linen closet is the only place you have to store extra toilet paper, bags of cotton balls, and other bulky bathroom overflow, so be it. But get your toiletries out of there. If there's simply no place for them in the bathroom, keep them in your bedroom closet.

AND AWAY IT GOES! Your Take Elsewhere box is the place to park what you want to keep—but not in the linen closet. Your dog's Frisbee® would fall into this category. So would tins of shoe polish, small tools, or the crumpled-up string of Christmas tree lights that you stuffed in there because you forgot to pack it up with the others. Just get it all out of there!

NEW, BUT NOT NICE. As you pull towels out of your linen closet, are you finding some that you received as gifts or bought on impulse, and have never used—and are not likely to use anytime soon? Maybe they don't go with your bathroom's color scheme. Or maybe they're decked out with appliquéd snowmen, Easter bunnies, or flags, but when the appropriate holiday rolls around, you never remember to pull them out. Whatever the reason is that they've remained shelf bound, get rid of them. Either donate them to a shelter or thrift shop, or set them aside to sell at your next garage sale.

DON'T TOSS THE OLD TOWELS! It's always a treat to replace old towels with soft, fluffy new ones. But those sturdy veterans still have plenty of life left in them. They're perfect for drying your dog after his bath or after a walk in the rain; for mopping up water when your plumbing pipes spring a leak; or for tossing over garden plants when Jack Frost pays an early visit. So hang on to them! Whether you should take them elsewhere (say, to your toolshed or utility room), or keep them in a separate spot in your linen closet depends on how and where you intend to use them—and, of course, how much space you have to spare on your closet shelves.

HOLEY TOWEL! So what do you do with towels that are frayed, torn, or riddled with holes? Cut 'em into pieces and use them as cleaning rags—that's what! The nubby texture of all-cotton terry cloth gives it a tough yet gentle power that few other fabrics can equal. Or, if you already have more rags than you need—and you're sure that your old towels are made of 100 percent cotton—toss them into your compost bin, or simply bury them in your yard or garden beds. They'll break down and add valuable organic matter to the soil.

BLANKET AND SHEET SMARTS. When it comes to sorting your bed linens, the criteria are the same as they are for towels: Keep the ones you love and use, and donate or sell those that are still in fine shape, but don't fit your taste or the size of your beds.

NEW LIVES FOR OLD SHEETS. When you cut up old 100 percent cotton sheets, you wind up with some of the finest

MESS-MAKER ALERT!

Problem: Your linen closet is crammed with old bath towels, sheets, blankets, quilts, and comforters that are stained, or a little too worn to sell or give to a thrift store, but they are too good to use as rags.

Solution: Donate them to an animal shelter, veterinary hospital, or the local zoo. The caring folks who work long and hard in these places are always in need of linens to use for comfy animal bedding.

dust rags you could ever hope to find. But that's not the only thing you can do with your retired bedding. Consider these possibilities:

- Make a smock to wear when you give yourself home beauty treatments, or have a sloppy job to do. Just cut a head hole in the center of the sheet and a slit on each side for your arms, and you're good to go.

- Give them to someone who makes rag rugs—either the woven, braided, or hooked kind. If you don't know a rug maker personally, check with a local weaving shop or fiber art gallery, or call the closest art or craft school.

- When the time comes to un-trim your Christmas tree, spread an old sheet around the base. That way, any loose needles will fall onto the fabric. When you've removed all of the ornaments, wrap the sheet around the tree, and haul it outside for your neighborhood recycling pickup. Or, better yet, deck it out with edible treats for the neighborhood birds (they love pinecones stuffed with peanut butter).

- When you hit the road with children or pets, drape a king-size sheet over your car's backseat and floor. Then when you come to a rest stop, pull it out and shake off all of the hair, cookie crumbs, bits of paper and plastic, and whatever else fell to the floor.

- Tear the fabric into strips, and use them to tie tomato vines or other floppy plants to stakes in your garden.

PACK OFF, PESTS!... And into the great outdoors. Whenever any of my Grandma Putt's bedsheets got too old to use for their intended

PACK RAT ALERT!

Problem: You have some brand-new sheets that you bought because you loved the pattern—and you still do—but the colors just don't work with your bedroom decor.

Solution: Use the fabric in some other room of your house. It might be perfect for curtains in the kitchen, family room, or guest room. Or use it to make a slipcover for a small chair or ottoman. You could even sew yourself a pretty summer dress or skirt.

purpose, she gave them new careers as pest-control workers. I still do the same thing—and you should, too. Here's a trio of tricks for using your not-so-nice sheets to battle the bad-bug brigade, without resorting to toxic chemicals:

1. Remove a bug-infested plant. When only one or two plants in your garden are smothered by destructive insects, throw an old sheet over the plant(s), pull it up by the roots, and dump it into a tub of water laced with 2 cups or so of dishwashing liquid or rubbing alcohol. Leave it for a minute or two, then drop it in the trash. (If any stragglers have found their way to nearby plants, don't panic—you just need to handpick them off.)

2. Get chinch bugs out of your lawn. Make a solution of 2 tablespoons of dishwashing liquid mixed in 1 gallon of water, and pour it on the trouble spot, using a sprinkling can to ensure even coverage. Put an old white flannel sheet on top of the grass. Wait 15 or 20 minutes, then peek under the fabric. It should be teeming with chinch bugs that have crawled toward the surface to escape the soap. Gather up the bug-infested cloth, and dunk it into a bucket filled with soapy water. Then get out the hose, and spray your lawn thoroughly to remove the soap residue.

3. Banish beetles and weevils. Lay an old (but hole-less) sheet on the ground under your plagued plants, and shake the branches gently. When the bugs come tumbling down, gather up the trap, and dump the contents into a tub of water to which a cup of dishwashing liquid or rubbing alcohol has been added.

OUT OF THE BOX

If you're planning to move within the next year or so and you'll be doing your own packing, hang on to your old towels, sheets, blankets, and comforters. In fact, you might even want to send a notice to family and friends saying that you'll take any and all of their castoffs. When you wrap these soft linens around your belongings, they'll do a fabulous cushioning job, whether the treasures are packed in boxes or simply tucked away in the truck.

CLUTTER BUSTER PRO

Does having a clutter-free, well-organized linen closet seem like an impossible dream? It's not! And Julie Bestry, professional organizer and owner of Best Results Organizing (www.JulieBestry.com) in Chattanooga, Tennessee, is here to prove it. Here are her simple tips for creating the linen closet of your dreams:

☛ Minimize clutter and maximize space by keeping only what you need. Try to limit the linen closet to towels and bedding. If possible, move cleaning rags and other supplies to the laundry room, bathroom cabinets, or other more accommodating spaces.

☛ Most households can make do with two complete sets of sheets per bed and two pillowcases for each pillow: one set for "wash" and one for "wear," with an emergency set for kids' beds.

☛ Think of the closet in terms of zones, then sort by shelf—sheets on one level, towels on the next, and so on, with short, tidy stacks for each item type. (Tall stacks tumble; tightly packed fibers don't breathe!) If you have multiple bed sizes, make separate stacks for sheets and blankets for twin-, full-, queen- and/or king-sized beds.

☛ Keep matched sheet sets together. After laundering, fold matching fitted and flat sheets together and store them inside the matching pillowcase. For guest bedding, tie the entire set together with inexpensive grosgrain ribbon, like a pretty package.

☛ Eliminate random extras like pillowcases that don't match any sheets or fitted sheets without flat mates. If you have more bedding than you will actually use, donate the extras to charity, or keep a lidded plastic tub in storage for future college or camp use.

☛ If your closet has some depth to it, keep off-season (e.g., flannel) sheets behind your everyday bedding. Then when the seasons change, rotate the front and back stacks.

☛ Sort and store towels by type (bath sheets, bath towels, hand towels, washcloths); subdivide by color only if you have the patience. If you have an abundance of towels, store freshly laundered ones at the back, and move the back stacks forward. Rotating ensures even wear and tear. In winter, store beach towels at the back of the closet.

☛ Fold bath sheets and towels in half and then in thirds, hand towels in thirds and then in half, and washcloths in quarters—then stack like items together. Always match edges, and store with the folded side out for a tidy look. If space is at a premium, roll your towels and lay them horizontally, spa-style.

☛ If you must store non-linens in the linen closet, sort by categories (e.g., cosmetics, toiletries, gadgets, cleaning supplies, first aid) and store everything in plastic dishpans; they'll easily slide forward like drawers, but keep the clutter from spreading. If you lack space to store these items out of the reach of children, consider a childproof lock for the closet door.

☛ Keep lightweight, but cumbersome or infrequently used items (like extra comforters, quilts, and pillows) on the highest shelves, preferably in zippered bags to protect them from humidity and allergens. (Label opaque bags so you don't forget what's inside.)

☛ Store heavy, but lesser-used items like vaporizers, as well as bulk supplies of bathroom and facial tissue, on the closet floor (in pet hair-free homes).

☛ If you're short on space, don't feel obligated to keep all of your bedding in the linen closet. Blankets that are only used for forts and playtime can be stored in lidded tubs in the playroom; extra pillows can be piled on the guest room bed, or on shelves in bedroom closets.

☛ Tightly roll sleeping bags and tie them up with extra-long shoelaces so that you can store them vertically or horizontally on high shelves or the closet floor.

☛ Label all shelves so everyone in the house knows how (and where) to put things away properly.

DOWN AND OUT. So what do you do with blankets, bedspreads, and comforters that are stained or too worn to use on your beds? Use them to keep your plants warm—that's what! I always keep a supply of these warmer-uppers on hand to throw over cold-sensitive shrubs and large perennials, or to wrap around my cold frames when the temperature plummets unexpectedly.

GARAGE IT. Plants aren't the only things that an old blanket can protect. It also comes in handy when you need to load or unload the trunk and your car's exterior is, shall we say, less than spotless. Just drape the blanket over the back of the trunk and the bumper, and proceed with your task—confident that you won't mess up your clothes in the process.

READY TO ROLL. If you've got an extra blanket that's just taking up space in your linen closet, get it out of there and into your car's trunk. That way, you'll be prepared if you stop for an impromptu picnic, get stranded in the cold, or come across an accident victim who needs help.

COLLECTOR ALERT!

Problem: You have a few fringed, patterned tablecloths that don't match your decor, but they're so beautiful and colorful that you can't bear to part with them.

Solution: Hang on to them if any small children live at your house, or even come to visit periodically. Then when the kids need a magic carpet ride (as every youngster does now and then), one of your pretty tablecloths can provide their imaginary "transportation."

TABLE IT. Sort your tablecloths, runners, placemats, and napkins using the same decision-making process that you used for your bed and bath linens (see page 197). Get rid of them if:

✔ They're stained, frayed, torn, or have holes in them.

✔ They don't go with your kitchen or dining room color scheme.

✔ They don't fit the size of any table that you own.

ORGANIZE

Now that everything is out of your linen closet, stand back and take a good long look at the space. If it's still laid out exactly as the builder left it, then a little remodeling is probably in order.

THE CHOICE IS YOURS. If your house is like most, it's a safe bet that your linen closet has too few shelves, and they're a lot deeper than they should be. That leaves you with three reorganizing choices:

1. Gut the closet, and build a system of shelves that suits you and the things you need to store—or have a contractor do the job. Depending on the size of the closet, this could cost you a sizable sum, but you'll get exactly the storage arrangement you want.

2. Gut the closet, and install a premade organizing system, like the ones marketed for bedroom closets. You can find them at home-improvement centers and many local hardware stores. Just choose the combination of vinyl-coated wire shelves, brackets, hooks, hangers, and racks that you need. Then attach them to the walls and to each other in whatever arrangement you like. If you're handy with tools, the installation process is simple. The price will vary considerably, depending on the size of your closet and the components you choose—but it's guaranteed that you'll pay a lot less than you would for a custom-built system.

3. Leave the shelves as they are, and add whatever dividers, baskets, bins,

> ## MAKING
> ### S P A C E
>
> No matter how you choose to reorganize your linen closet, don't overlook the back of the door. Either attach a shallow wire shelf unit; install hooks for hanging baskets; or hang up a shoe bag (either a hook-mount or over-the-door model). Any of these options gives you great space to store small items like rolled-up guest towels, napkins, napkin rings, placemats, or candles—plus your medications, which really don't belong in your bathroom medicine cabinet because of moisture and temperature fluctuations.

boxes, and racks that you like. You may not wind up with a linen closet that's worthy of a fancy magazine spread, but with a little creativity, you can get one that meets all of your needs without spending a lot of money.

MEASURE UP. Before you call in a contractor to reorganize your gutted closet—or head off to the local lumberyard or hardware store to buy shelves for a do-it-yourself job— you need to sketch your closet and take two sets of measurements. First, draw a sketch of your closet. Then measure the space in the closet, writing the numbers down as you go (don't forget to include the height of the walls!). Then count and measure the items you intend to store there.

In lots of decorating books and magazines, you see instructions on the "right way" to fold towels and sheets. Well, forget that noise! The only right way to organize your bed and bath linens is to fold, stack, or roll everything so it fits the space you've got.

GIVE 'EM ROOM. When you plan your shelf arrangement, remember these general spacing guidelines:

• Leave 10 to 12 inches between shelves for sheets, tablecloths, and other thin linens.

• Give towels 12 to 15 inches of clear headspace.

• Keep the top shelf at least 18 inches away from the ceiling to hold large but light items like blankets, comforters, and sleeping bags.

WE'RE ON A ROLL. If you must keep extra bathroom supplies in your linen closet, tuck a wheeled cart under the bottom shelf and use it to hold cleaning products, toilet paper, or maybe the collection of bathtub toys that you keep on hand for visiting grandchildren. Most of the time, the stash stays out of the way, but when it's time to use the items, you can roll out the cart and take whatever you need. And when you return from a shopping trip, you can even take it into the kitchen, or wherever you unload your groceries. Then just fill 'er up, and roll 'er back "home"!

KEEP YOUR PRIORITIES STRAIGHT. When you assign your linens to their various shelves, remember the golden rule for organizing any storage space: The things you use the most often should be front and center—in the easiest-to-reach places. And that prime real estate consists of shelves that are located from shoulder height to mid-thigh.

IMPROVISE. What's that? You say you don't even have a linen closet in your house? Not to worry! Just find an attractive armoire or freestanding cabinet, and add whatever shelves you may need. Look for one in the usual hunting grounds: flea markets, thrift shops, garage sales, and antique stores.

OTHER CLOSET ALTERNATIVES. If you don't have room for a single, large piece of furniture, keep your linens in the rooms where they're used—table linens in the kitchen or dining room, towels in the bathroom(s), and sheets and other bedding in the bedrooms.

MESS-MAKER ALERT!

Problem: More blankets, comforters, and quilts than your closet can possibly hold.

Solution: Vacuum-pack those bulky bed linens! You can spend lots of money buying commercial bags that are specially made for that purpose at housewares stores and on the Internet. But it's easy to make your own. Just tuck each item into a plastic trash bag, suck out the air using your vacuum cleaner hose, and close the bag with rubber bands. Either way, you'll be able to fit three times as much stuff in the same available space.

MATCH BEFORE YOU STORE. No matter where you keep your linens, organize them into sets before you store them away. If you have certain napkins that you always use with a particular tablecloth, stack them up and tie a ribbon around them, so they'll stay together. Fold up each set of sheets, and put it inside one of the matching pillowcases. Or simply stack and tie each set with a colorful ribbon.

WHAT ABOUT TOWELS? When it comes to organizing bath linens, there are two schools of thought. Choose the one that works better for you:

1. Organize them in individual sets: bath towel, hand towel, and washcloth.

2. Arrange them by type with all bath towels, all hand towels, and all washcloths grouped together.

 STORE
Once you've gotten rid of all your linen closet clutter and organized the space just the way you want it, it's time to stash the stuff you need to keep in there.

COLLECTOR ALERT!

Problem: You've got such a big collection of table linens that it's hard to find what you need, when you need it.

Solution: Simply organize them by style (formal versus casual), season (spring, summer, fall, and winter), or color. Keep it simple, and you'll never again have to play hide-and-seek when it's time to set the table.

HANG 'EM UP. Instead of folding tablecloths and runners, get some special door racks (available in housewares and home-improvement stores and on the Internet), and put 'em in there. Or hang them on large, heavy-duty wooden or plastic hangers. Just remember to lay a thick towel over the hanger first to minimize creasing. And whatever you do, don't ever use wire hangers to store linens—they'll make knife-sharp creases in the fabric. Plus, they could even rust, leaving behind ugly brown stains on the material.

BE MY GUEST. If you like to set out extra-pretty hand towels and fancy soaps when folks come to visit, it pays to be prepared. Tuck those special-occasion staples into a basket, so you can pull them out at a moment's notice and whisk them to your guest bathroom or powder room when unexpected guests drop by.

BE MY GUEST, PART TWO. As long as there's enough room in your linen closet, be prepared by filling another box, bin, or basket with entertaining accessories like place cards, napkin rings, candles, candleholders, and cocktail napkins. And don't forget a book of matches or a lighter for the candles!

MAKE A LINEN SANDWICH. To store fine linen placemats and napkins, press them (after they've been laundered, of course!), and sandwich each set between sheets of white, acid-free mat board. It's available at frame shops and art-supply stores. Have the store cut the board to fit easily on your shelves and to fully enclose the linens. If you like, tie each set together with a ribbon to hold the pieces securely in place.

WRITE ALL ABOUT IT. To make sure everyone in the family (and guests, too) can find things easily, label the shelves in your closet. This is an especially helpful step if you keep several different sizes of sheets on hand. After all, it's a major hassle to grab a set of sheets and unfurl them on your bed—only to discover that they're full size, when you needed queen.

KEEP 'EM MOVING. When you put freshly washed sheets, towels, or table linens into your linen closet, rotate your stock by putting them at the bottom of the stack. And issue orders that everyone in your household should only pull linens from the top of the

MAKING SPACE

Do you have special linens that you only use for Christmas, Thanksgiving, or other holidays? If so, then free up space in your linen closet by storing those special-occasion items with your other holiday-specific decorations. Long, flat, clear plastic bins make good storage choices because you can easily see the contents. Just be sure your storage location is dry and dark, and to play it safe, tuck a bag or two of herbal moth repellent into each bin.

pile. This simple measure will help ensure that the items wear evenly, and last longer.

HOW NEAT! Smooth, wrinkle-free sheets look neater on your shelves—and feel better when you sleep on them, too. To keep wrinkles to a minimum, always pull your sheets out of the dryer and fold them while they're still warm. If they've cooled down before you can get to them, just toss a damp washcloth into the dryer, and turn it back on for another 10 minutes or so.

MAKE SURE THEY'RE DRY! Don't ever put towels or sheets away unless they're completely dry. Even a tiny bit of moisture could cause them to mildew or start to smell—and you sure don't want that in your closet!

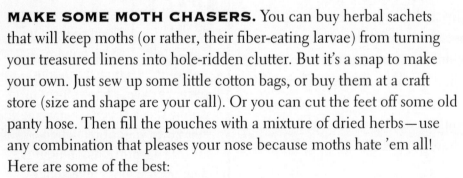

MAKE SOME MOTH CHASERS. You can buy herbal sachets that will keep moths (or rather, their fiber-eating larvae) from turning your treasured linens into hole-ridden clutter. But it's a snap to make your own. Just sew up some little cotton bags, or buy them at a craft store (size and shape are your call). Or you can cut the feet off some old panty hose. Then fill the pouches with a mixture of dried herbs—use any combination that pleases your nose because moths hate 'em all! Here are some of the best:

> **Lavender** (*Lavandula*)
> **Santolina**
> **Southernwood** (*Artemisia abrotanum*)
> **Tansy** (*Tanacetum*)
> **Thyme** (*Thymus*)
> **Wormwood** (*Artemisia absinthium*)

MESS-MAKER ALERT!

Problem: Moths can make a holey mess of your tablecloths and bed linens.

Solution: Always keep some cedar blocks, bags of cedar chips, or sacks of moth-repellent herbs in your linen closet.

CHAPTER SIX

THE LAUNDRY ROOM

Whoever said "Nothing is certain but death and taxes" obviously did not have to deal with the family laundry. For most of us, though, that chore is an inescapable fact of life. I don't know any way to make washing a mountain of clothes a barrel of laughs. But having a work space that's well organized and clutter-free can make it a whole lot more pleasant.

ACTION CENTRAL

If it seems like you have an awful lot of laundry to do, there's a good reason: The folks who study such things tell us that the average person generates more than 500 pounds of dirty clothes each year. Multiply that by the number of people in your household, and you've got a recipe for one messy laundry room! By using our strategy, you can get that clutter under control in a snap.

In This Section:
- ✔ *Washing*
- ✔ *Drying*
- ✔ *Folding*
- ✔ *Ironing*

SORT

The first step to making and keeping your laundry room shipshape is (surprise!) deciding which things can stay and which ones need to go. Here's the routine to follow.

WHAT'S THE USE? The road to a clutter-free laundry room begins with a single question: What do you use the space for? Is it simply the place where you wash, dry, and perhaps iron your family's clothes? Or does it also need to serve as a coat closet, mudroom, pantry, doggy dining room, or general storage area?

PURE AND SIMPLE. You say your laundry room is *supposed* to be reserved for the sole purpose of doing your laundry, but your family has gotten into the habit of using it as a catchall for everything from flowerpots to golf clubs? In that case, you'll need to undertake a full-scale sorting spree. Depending upon the size and quantity of the invading items, you may or may not need boxes for this project. But your modus operandi should be the same as it is for de-cluttering any other room in your house. In other words:

- Throw away or recycle obvious trash like chewing gum wrappers, empty detergent boxes, and old magazines. Also, get rid of anything that's broken and cannot be repaired, like that iron that refuses to get any hotter than lukewarm.

MESS-MAKER ALERT!

Problem: Mail piles up in your laundry/entrance area because that's where you open it when you come into the house.

Solution: Keep a recycling bin in the laundry area, and toss the envelopes, advertisements, and any unwanted mail into it. Then immediately take the rest—bills, magazines, and whatever else you want to keep—to its proper place.

- Donate or sell things that are in good shape but you don't use, don't like, or don't need—maybe your daughter's outgrown ice skates, a Chinese vase you got as a present but don't care for, or a cage for the hamster your son had six years ago.

- Relocate any items that you want or need to keep, but not in the laundry room—like sports equipment, dog toys, or garden tools.

- Set aside the stuff that does belong in the laundry room—including the sports equipment, dog toys, or garden tools mentioned above, if this is where you need to keep them. (I'll tell you how to deal with them in the Organize and Store sections later in this chapter.)

IT'S ALL RELATIVE. All too often, things that are laundry-related find their way into the laundry room—and then just sit there. If you've got a basket filled with an ever-growing mountain of mismatched socks, fraying underwear, or old towels, now's the time to plow through it. Set the towels aside to use for cleaning chores. Pitch the underwear. See if you can find new uses for some of the socks (see "Sock 'Em To It" on page 4), and then get rid of the rest.

SPOTS BEFORE YOUR EYES. Does this sound familiar? You've got a pile of stained clothes lying in your laundry room, and you can't bear to get rid of them because you're sure you'll eventually find the right way to get those spots out. But you've already tried commercial stain removers, bleach, and scads of tricks from household tips books. So give up already! Either toss those uncleanables into the ragbag, donate them to a thrift shop, or give them to an artist or craftsman who works with small pieces of fabric (see "Think Before You Trash" on page 3). You can also tear the cloth into strips that are about 8 inches long by $1/2$-inch wide, and set them out for songbirds to use as nesting material. Beginning in early spring, drape 5 to 10 strips at a time over shrubs, or lay them on the ground near your bird feeder, and watch the little guys and gals go to town!

You say you can't start sorting the stuff that doesn't belong in your laundry room because it's crammed full of dirty clothes? Then pack up those duds, and take them to your local Laundromat. If you go on a weekday morning or early afternoon, there should be plenty of machines available. You'll be able to do 5 or 10 loads—or even more—in the time it would take you to do a single load at home. That way, you can start your de-cluttering campaign with a clean slate.

SEW WHAT? Very often, you first notice minor clothing "injuries" like loose buttons, undone hems, or snagged threads just as you're loading the washing machine. And it's all too easy to set the garments aside, thinking that you'll make the repairs later. Then before you know it, you have a pile of impaired clothes cluttering up the laundry room. The simple solution: Keep a small basic sewing kit on hand, right by the washing machine, so you can perform fabric first aid on the spot. Here's what you'll need:

✔ A small pair of scissors

✔ Needles and a needle threader

✔ A variety of buttons

✔ Spools of black and white thread

✔ A little kit that contains small quantities of thread in many colors (If you don't have one that you got as a freebie at a hotel, you can buy one at a supermarket or drugstore.)

SNAGS NO MORE. If you've got a pile of clothes that have snags, but are otherwise in fine shape, you can give them a second life in no time flat. All you need is a snag repair tool—one of the handiest things to come along in ages. There are a couple of versions: One is a pointed metal loop on the end of a plastic handle, and the other is a sort of mini crochet hook. Both work the same way: You shove the loop or the curved end of the tool through the material from the back of the garment, hook the snag in the loop, and gently pull it through to the back. Then you remove the tool, and you're done. You can find these miracle workers in fabric and quilting-supply shops and (of course) on the Internet.

SAVE THAT WASHER! It's one thing to get rid of an iron that stops working, but a washing machine is a whole different kettle of fish. Believe it or not, the way you handle your laundry can spell the difference between a washing machine that gives you years of trouble-

MAKING
SPACE

Do you have a laundry room sink that's not usable because your family keeps throwing their dirty clothes into it? Then get yourself a Tub Top™ to solve the problem. This plastic shelf is designed to sit on top of a utility sink. Besides discouraging your loved ones from tossing their dirty duds into the sink, it will give you a surface for pre-treating stains and folding clothes. Plus, it has a carrying handle and attached hooks, so when you need to use the sink, you can remove the Tub Top and hang it over the side. This handy gadget is available in catalogs and online.

free service and one that turns into a worthless pile of junk before its time. Whether you're laundering bedsheets, heavy-duty work clothes, or delicate lingerie, always follow these four important guidelines when using a top-loading machine:

1. Whenever possible, wash full loads. Not only will you avoid wasting water and energy, but you'll also help your washing machine last longer. That's because it's designed to run most efficiently when it's set for its highest water level and filled to the maximum. Check your owner's manual to determine your washer's load capacity in pounds; depending on the model, it could be anywhere from 10 to 20 pounds. Then weigh a few loads to see how heavy the pile is. (It will vary considerably, of course, depending on whether you're washing, let's say, bath towels and blankets, or summer dresses and T-shirts.) In a very short time, you'll know just by looking when you've got the right amount to maximize your load.

2. Don't overload the machine because it strains the motor and therefore shortens your washer's life span. Regardless of the weight of your load, it should never be above the top of the agitator axle; don't pack it down to fit more in. The fabric needs room to spin around freely inside the drum in order to get clean.

3. Even when you must do a partial or tiny load (like a blouse you need to wear tonight), set the water level on high—or at least at a higher level than you think you need. If there's not enough water in the tub, the clothes can't circulate freely, and they'll get wrapped around the agitator. That'll cause wear and tear on the agitator seal—not to mention the damage all of that twisting and turning will do to your clothes. The extra pennies you might save on your water bill will be nothing compared to the cost of new clothes or a new washing machine!

4. One of the simplest ways to prolong the life of your washing machine is to make sure that it stays on a level footing. Otherwise, it may literally start to "walk" around the room with your clothes, which will not only ruin your floor, but can also wreak havoc on the inner

workings of the machine. To raise the legs of your washer, turn them clockwise. To lower them, turn them counterclockwise. It's that easy!

LET GO OF LINT. Lint is a dryer's worst enemy, and it could be yours, too. Lint builds up in the screens, filters, and vents, where it can foul up the appliance's mechanism and shorten its life span. What's even worse, it can cause a fire. To keep your dryer on the job—and a roof over your head—attend to these routine chores:

✔ Clean out the lint screen after each load of laundry.

✔ Every month or so, wash the lint screen in warm, soapy water. Let it air-dry overnight, and come morning, it'll be ready for action.

✔ About every four months, scrape built-up lint from in and around the outdoor vent using a stiff-bristled brush.

✔ Twice a year, remove the exhaust duct from the back of the dryer and have at it with a vacuum cleaner.

Ask Jerry

Q. I've put out handfuls of dryer lint near my bird feeder, but the birds don't pay any attention to it. Could it be because of the dryer sheets I use?

A. Nope. Truth is, birds rarely bother with dryer lint, maybe because the individual pieces are so small that they can't be woven or otherwise secured into place. And when the rains come, your ignored offering will get soggy, fall to the ground, and then dry into a stiff film that looks like slime mold. So save your yard from all that mess. Toss your unwanted lint into the trash, or put it to use in one of the innovative ways described below (see "Put Lint To Work").

PUT LINT TO WORK. When it's clogging up your dryer's screen, lint may be nothing but hazardous clutter. But elsewhere around the old homestead, it can be mighty useful stuff. Here's a trio of excellent examples:

1. Soil-building material. As long as the lint came from 100 percent cotton or linen fabric, toss it into your compost pile, or bury it in your garden or flower beds. In no time at all, it'll break down into valuable humus.

2. Fire-starter nuggets. First, cut a cardboard egg carton into 12 sections, and fill each one with dryer lint (but *only* from 100 percent cotton or linen fabric). Then melt down old candle stubs or paraffin sealers from homemade jelly, and pour a layer of melted wax on top of the lint. When it's time to light your fireplace or charcoal grill, set one of the nuggets in the kindling or briquettes, and hold a match to the cardboard edge.

3. Deer-tick eliminators. Lint from any kind of fabric will work for this trick. Simply soak it in a pet shampoo that contains a flea and tick killer called permethrin. Then pull off a small wad, and push it into an empty toilet-paper tube. When you've filled a half-dozen tubes or so, set them out in brushy areas or other sheltered spots where deer mice (the carriers of deer ticks) are likely to find them. The mice will take the fuzzy stuff home to line their nests, and the disease-spreading ticks will be history!

DON'T TOSS THE IRON! I know folks who have actually gotten rid of their steam irons because their entire wardrobes are made of fabric that's either cotton knit, permanent press, or dry-clean-only. Well, don't you do it! For one thing, even the most wrinkle-resistant fabrics may need a little pressing every now and then. For another thing, a common, everyday steam iron can help you with

Now here's a use for lint that you may not have heard of—making clay! Yep, that's right, you can create some fancy artwork out of yesterday's dryer lint. Here's how:

Start by gathering about 3 cupfuls of dryer lint. Tear it into small pieces and place in a medium saucepan. Cover with about 2 cups of water. Then slowly stir in 1 cup of flour. Add a few drops of vegetable oil and stir constantly over low heat until the mixture is smooth and binds together. Pour onto sheets of newspaper, parchment paper, or wax paper to cool. Then use the clay to sculpt models, cover forms, or pack into molds. Allow it to dry completely, which can take anywhere from three to seven days, depending on size. Enjoy your creation as is, or paint and decorate to finish it up.

chores that have nothing to do with your clothes. Like these, for instance:

- Getting grease marks off wallpaper. Just put a piece of brown paper over the spot, and hold a warm (not hot) dry iron on it for a minute or so. Then shift the paper, so that a clean portion covers the stain, and press it again. Keep repeating the process until all of the grease has been absorbed by the paper.

- Keeping your carpet safe from moths. Contrary to their name, clothes moths don't confine their egg-laying activity to clothing. Any natural-fiber object in your house—including your carpets and area rugs—can be a moth maternity ward. If you suspect that larvae may be lingering in your floor covering, saturate a bath towel with water, wring it out, and spread it out on the rug. Then grab your iron, set it on high, and press the towel until it's dry. No need to push down hard—it's the steamy heat, not the pressure, that kills the pesky little pests.

MAKING SPACE

Remember that stacks of clean laundry can add up to just as much clutter as piles of the dirty version do. So the minute the "done" buzzer goes off, whisk the load out of the dryer, and fold or hang up each garment immediately. Then deliver the goods to each family member's room or their designated collection spots (see "That's The Spot!" on page 221). Whatever you do, don't let those duds stay in the dryer for even 5 or 10 minutes because you'll have a wrinkled mess on your hands!

- Removing furniture dents from carpet. First, comb the indentation to loosen the fibers. Then soften them up by holding a steaming iron over the spot for a few seconds. Unless you know for sure that the carpet is pure wool or cotton, don't touch it with the iron—if the fibers are synthetic, they'll melt. Finish up by brushing with a clean, stiff brush. With a little TLC, you'll never even know that a piece of furniture used to stand on the spot.

SORT ON THE FLY. If you have enough space in your laundry room, get three baskets or attractive storage boxes, and use them as temporary holding tanks for things that should not be taken back to your family's closets when they come out of the dryer. Clearly label each basket with one of these categories:

1. Clothes that need repairs

2. Clothes or linens that are out of season and need to be put into storage

3. Clothes to be donated to charity, or sold at your next yard sale

ORGANIZE

You sort, you wash, you fold, you iron, and put your family's clothes away—then you blink, and there's another mountain of dirty duds staring you in the face. Short of sending everything out to a laundry or hiring someone to do the wash, nothing will make the task go away. But approaching laundry duty in an organized way can make it a lot more manageable.

SEPARATE QUARTERS. If your laundry "room" is in your basement, or if it also serves as a general storage area, organize the space by function. As much as you can, keep laundry and non-laundry equipment and supplies separate from each other. The business of getting your clothes clean generates enough clutter on its own—you don't need "help" from the stuff that springs up around other activities!

MULTIPLY AND DIVIDE. Your washing chores will go a lot more quickly—and your

Just because you've worn a garment doesn't necessarily mean that it's dirty. When you undress at the end of a long, hard day, take a good look at your clothes—and your children's clothes, too. If they still look just fine, fold them neatly or hang them up, and wear them another time or two before you toss them into the hamper. Besides cutting clutter in the laundry room, you'll save yourself a lot of work and extend the life of your wardrobe, too!

laundry room will be a lot less cluttered—if you sort your soiled clothes as you take them off each night. A couple of organizing systems will work for this chore; choose the one that's right for you and your family.

1. Keep three hampers in your laundry room: one for white and light-colored clothes, one for bright and dark colors, and one for delicate items. Or use a single hamper that has three separate divisions. (You can find this type in organizing catalogs and on the Internet.) Use a separate hamper or laundry basket for dry-clean-only clothes and linens, and make sure everyone in the family uses it for those nonwashables.

2. Put three hampers in each bedroom, and have your family sort their laundry according to those same light, bright, and delicate guidelines.

SHORT DIVISION. No room for multiple hampers? Then use one of these less space-consuming options:

• Put several standard laundry baskets on a shelf above your washer and dryer, and label them so that everyone knows which clothes go where.

• Get special fabric bags that hang from a rod above your washer and dryer. You can find them in organizing catalogs and on the Internet.

MESS-MAKER ALERT!

Problem: Your laundry room hampers are now overflowing with everyone's whites, colors, and delicates (see "Multiply and Divide" on page 219), and the laundry room's more cluttered than ever!

Solution: To save space in the laundry—and time on wash day—give each family member three extra-large mesh bags: one for whites, one for darks, and one for delicate washables. Then when it's time to do the wash, just toss the filled bags right into the machine. Just remember two important things: Don't stuff the bags too full because the clothes need room to move around. And take the clothes out of the bags before you put them in the dryer because they need even more room to flop around in there. If they don't get it, you'll end up with wrinkled clothing.

THE SOLO-SOCK PREVENTION PLAN. Tired of spending time trying to find mates that go missing in action—and even more tired of single socks hogging space in your laundry room while you wait for their mates to reappear? If so, then I have just the idea for you: Give each family member a zippered, mesh bag (or two if you like to keep light colors separate from dark ones). Then issue orders that all socks go into those sacks. On wash day, collect the bags, and zip 'em up. Toss 'em into the washing machine, and then right into the dryer. When they're done, return each bag to the owner's bedroom, or to his or her designated laundry-collection spot (see "That's The Spot!" below). *Tip:* To avoid confusion, give each person a different-colored bag, or write everyone's initials on the mesh with a waterproof marker.

THAT'S THE SPOT! If you want to keep clean laundry from cluttering up your laundry room, you *could* deliver it to the owners' rooms as soon as you've removed the clothes from the dryer and folded them. But if you've got better things to do with your time than run a delivery service (and who doesn't?), try this simple trick: Hang a shelf on the laundry room wall, or move a table into the room. Designate space for each family member, and post their names on the edge of the shelf or table. Then stack the folded clothes in the appropriate places. Just be sure to issue a standing order that everyone must pick up his or her laundry by a certain deadline—say, right after dinner or before bedtime.

MAKING SPACE

You've got no room for even a folding rack to hang your clean clothes on? Then get a retractable outdoor clothesline, which you can still find in hardware stores and catalogs. The line is wound around a reel inside a case, which you can attach to your laundry room wall. When it's time to hang up your clothes, just pull out the line and hook it to another wall, a cabinet, or any other vertical surface. When your family has collected their duds, retract the line. (Of course, you can use the line to air-dry delicate clothes as well as organize their machine-dried counterparts.)

HANG IT ALL. Take your clean-laundry organizing one step further and make a place to hang clothes as you take them out of the dryer. To avoid any chance of confusion at collection time, use a different-colored hanger for each person in the household. Then hang the articles from any one of these options (all available in housewares and hardware stores, in home-organizing catalogs, and on the Internet).

✔ A conventional, rolling clothes rack

✔ A rolling rack that folds up, so you can stash it away when it's not in use

✔ An over-the-door rack

✔ Conventional, screw-in wall hooks

✔ A closet rod or spring-tension shower curtain rod that you can install between two wall-mounted cabinets

✔ A wall-mounted, hinged rod that swings out when you need to use it, then folds up flat against the wall when you're through

✔ Wall-mounted wire shelves (like the ones made for bedroom closets) that do double duty as hanging rods and storage space

FRONT AND CENTER. If your laundry room organizing plan calls for new appliances, consider investing in a front-loading washing machine (of course, all dryers are front-loading, so you won't have to make a choice there). Yes, it's true that a front-loading washer will cost you more than a traditional

MESS-MAKER ALERT!

Problem: Your laundry room is very small, with no floor space for a table or cabinet where you can fold clothes. So you end up folding them on the dining room table. It works, all right, but it sure looks like a cluttered mess.

Solution: If you've got even a little bit of wall space in your laundry room, install a fold-down counter that hangs on the wall. You can find them at home-improvement stores and on the Internet, or you can make your own using fold-down brackets (available from those same places) and your choice of surface materials. Either painted plywood or a piece of plastic laminate counter-top works well.

top-loading model, but it will pay you back in three big ways:

1. When the tops of your washer and dryer are both free and clear, you gain a nice roomy surface you can use for folding clothes or treating stains. In fact, many home-improvement stores sell countertops that are especially made to fit over side-by-side, front-loading machines.

2. Today's state-of-the-art washers consume 50 to 65 percent less electricity than conventional, top-loading types, and they use about 50 percent less water. So besides gaining space, you'll save money on your utility bills.

3. Front-loading washers treat their contents more gently than top-loaders do, and that adds up to longer life spans for your clothes and everything else in your laundry hamper.

PUT IT ON A PEDESTAL. Here's another reason to consider a new front-loading washer-dryer combo: Many models come with optional pedestals that have drawers where you can stash detergent, fabric softener, and other supplies. (For more on supply storage, see "Supplies 'R' Us on page 228.)

STICK 'EM UP! Or rather, I should say *stack* 'em up! When you're shopping for a new washer and dryer, you can save a whole lot of space by opting for stackable models. If your laundry "room" is actually part of your kitchen or bathroom, you may want (or need) to go with apartment-size versions. But full-size stackable ones are available, too.

Ask Jerry

Q. My washer and dryer are in the bathroom of my condo. Sometimes I need to wash things by hand, but there's no place to keep even a stool and a basin. I hate keeping the bathroom sink full of soaking clothes! Can you think of any other alternatives?

A. How about this: Just get a sturdy, wooden TV tray and a plastic dishpan. When you're through using the setup, stash the dishpan under the bathroom or kitchen sink (or wherever else you have room for it). Then fold up the TV tray and tuck it into the nearest closet.

CALLING ALL CARTS. If you'd like to find an organizational superstar for your laundry area, type in "laundry cart" on your favorite search engine. Your computer screen will fill up with dozens of

CLUTTER BUSTER PRO

Does your laundry room double as an entryway or general storage area? If so, you're not alone. For Deb Vande Loo, a professional organizer in Roswell, Georgia (www.organizerdeb.com), dual—or even multipurpose—laundry areas pose a common challenge for her clients. Here are a few of Deb's top tips for making every inch of space count:

☛ Use attractive baskets, boxes, or bins on shelves to hold laundry supplies and any other small items you keep in the room. Label each container to make it easy for everyone in the house to put things back where they belong.

☛ When your laundry room is a designated parking place for coats, hats, umbrellas, and other things people bring in from outdoors, install wall hooks with a lift-top bench or locker-like cubbies below. Assign a section to each family member, and issue orders that only gear that's currently being used can stay in the room. (No snow boots in July, or sandals in December!)

☛ If the area is close to the exterior door that you use most often, make it a launching pad for your day. Each night, set out the things you'll need in the morning like your briefcase, school books, or dry cleaning that needs to be dropped off. That way, you can simply grab your stuff and go.

☛ Take advantage of vertical space by adding a shelf or two near the ceiling to store supplies you buy in bulk, such as paper towels and toilet paper, or things you don't need very often like Christmas decorations. (Just make sure that whatever you stow up there is lightweight.)

☛ Keep a step stool or ladder handy so you can reach your high-up storage area. Home-improvement and hardware stores carry full-size, lightweight stepladders that, when folded up, measure only a little over 2 inches deep—which makes them perfect for hanging on the back of a door.

wheeled helpers, ranging from simple hampers to a folding mobile laundry center that comes complete with a zip-up canvas "slipcover." When you open up the unit, you've got three stacked metal baskets, a roomy canvas hamper, and a full-size ironing board to work with. When you're done, you can fold up the hamper and ironing board, put on the cover, and you've got a traveling "package" that measures just 23 inches high by 34 inches wide by 15 inches deep.

SINK SOLUTIONS. Do you have a nice, roomy utility sink in your laundry area, where you can pretreat stained or extra-dirty clothes, or tackle a zillion and one sloppy household chores? If so, then count your lucky stars! Many folks who have downsized or have always lived in small quarters are stuck with just a teeny-tiny sliver of a sink. But whether your sink is large or small, these three organizing tools will help you make the most of that valuable piece of equipment. (You can find them all in home-improvement stores, in catalogs, and on the Internet.)

1. A wall-mounted, telescoping drying rack. Hang it above the sink, and use it to drip-dry clothes that can't go into the dryer.

2. A mesh drying rack that fits over the sink opening. This is just the ticket for sweaters and other items that need to lie flat as they dry. You can even buy stackable racks to double your drying area.

3. A wire or plastic-mesh bin. Set it inside the sink, and use it for garments that need to drain before you hang them up or put them in the dryer. This way, you'll gain valuable work space and still have access to the sink.

NO SINK TO CALL YOUR OWN? And no drain or water hookup, either? No problem! Just get yourself a washtub, basin, or plastic dishpan. Then find a cabinet, table, or even a stool to set it on (your best choice depends upon how much space you have). Put your sink facsimile on top, and keep big bottles of water handy. Then when you need to soak a pair of grass-stained shorts or pretreat some mystery spots, you're good to go!

STORE

Once you've weeded out the things that don't need to be in your laundry room and organized the space, it's time to store everything that's left.

ACROSS THE BOARD. Trying to figure out how to keep your ironing board out of the way, yet still easily accessible? Well, figure no more! You have three terrific options:

1. A small, hanging unit that's specially designed to hold both an iron and ironing board on either a wall or the back of a door. You can find this item at just about any hardware store, in both over-the-door and screw-mount versions.

2. A fold-down ironing board that attaches to a wall or door. This, too, comes in over-the-door and screw-mount versions. Look for it in home-organizing catalogs and on the Internet.

3. An attractive, wall-hung, doored cabinet that opens to reveal a fold-down ironing board. Some models also have a holder for an iron and shelves for laundry supplies. You can find these units on the Internet in a wide variety of colors, sizes, and prices.

BIN THERE. Keeping a few small bins, baskets, or boxes on a shelf in your laundry room can help you head off a lot of wash-day clutter. They can be made of any material you like; metal, plastic, wicker, and cardboard will

Ask Jerry

Q. My laundry area is in the entryway that my family and guests use all the time. The washer and dryer are tucked into what used to be the coat closet. Do you have any ideas for storing all the other things that need to be there—like coats, backpacks, and laundry supplies?

A. I sure do! If you have enough space, get a good-looking armoire. Install a rod for hanging coats, and shelves below and/or above for things like books, backpacks, and laundry supplies. If the area is less roomy, hang big, decorative hooks on the wall, and put a lift-top bench below them. You can keep detergent, fabric softener, and other laundry and cleaning supplies inside, and use the top for things people bring in from outside—and take with them when they leave.

all work fine. Use one container to hold money, keys, and other stuff that's gone through the washer in pants or jacket pockets. Another can corral socks that have temporarily strayed from their mates. Put dryer lint in a third container—but don't keep it there long because that stuff is a potent fire hazard. As soon as you can, toss it into your outdoor trash can, or use it in one of the ways described on page 216 (see "Put Lint To Work").

STORE 'EM IN PLAIN SIGHT.

Here's a simple trick that's perfect for a kitchen, bathroom, entryway, or even a wide hallway. Buy a front-loading washer and dryer, and set them side by side. Attach a countertop to the wall behind them so that it hangs out about 2 inches over the appliance tops on all sides. Fasten curtain rods onto the underside of the counter, and hang curtains from them using clip-on rings. When it's time to do your laundry, pull the curtains aside. When you're done, simply close up shop. To hide your washer and dryer without the bother of installing a countertop over them, find a table that's the right size to fit over them. Slide your appliances under it, and hang up your curtain rods.

DRESS 'EM UP.

Of course, if your hide-and-seek appliances are in an entryway or hallway, you will probably want to use a countertop material that disguises their true identity. Choose something like marble, or an attractive piece of wood. A salvaged antique table- or countertop would be perfect if you can find one—and you can if you search in architectural salvage and junk shops.

MAKING SPACE

If space is tight—as it may be if you've downsized to a condo, apartment, mobile home, or smaller house—your washer and dryer themselves may be clutter. Luckily, at least one major manufacturer makes a washer-dryer combo that's tailor-made to fit inside a closet. It takes up half the space of a conventional washer and dryer team, but the washer has a tub capacity that's 20 percent *larger* than that of a full-size machine. You'll need to have the necessary plumbing and electrical connections installed in the closet, but the extra living space you gain far outweighs any labor cost.

SUPPLIES 'R' US

Just as your laundry itself—dirty and clean—can cause major clutter in the area where you do your wash, so can the supplies you do it with. But using our surefire SOS strategy, you can whip that laundry space into shape in no time flat.

In This Section:
✔ Laundry supplies
✔ Cleaning supplies
✔ Clothespins
   and hangers

SORT

I know this is starting to sound like a broken record, but the very same guidelines you used to sort the supplies in your kitchen and bathroom apply just as well to your laundry room. So roll up your sleeves and dive right in!

TWO FOR THE SHOW. For this mission, you should need only a trash can (or trash bags) for your discards, and one or more boxes for items and cleaning supplies that you don't need in the laundry room, but could be useful elsewhere.

OUT IT GOES! As you come across any of the following items, toss them into the trash without giving them a second thought:

✔ Bent or broken hangers

✔ Broken or grungy clothespins

✔ Boxes with just a thin layer of solidified detergent or powdered bleach on the bottom

✔ Spray stain removers with just a thin layer of solution left in the bottom of the bottle

✔ Stick-type stain removers that you've tried and don't care for

✔ Any over-the-hill household cleaners that you keep in the laundry room (like rusting cans of scouring powder, or near-empty bottles of spray cleaners)

✔ Ancient cleaning rags that have turned as stiff as boards

✔ Ragged brooms, broken mops, and tangled, stringy mop heads

✔ Anything else that's torn, broken, outdated, or otherwise unusable

FABRIC SOFTENER TO GO. You've just tried a new brand of fabric softener, and you don't like the results one bit. An obvious candidate for the trash, right? Wrong! Just remove the stuff from laundry duty and put it to work in one of these ways:

• Loosen crusted-on food from baking pans. Pour a teaspoon or two of fabric softener into the pan, fill it with warm water, and let it sit overnight. The next morning, wipe the gunk away.

• Remove hard-water spots from freshly washed windows. Just wipe fabric softener onto the marks, wait about 10 minutes, and wipe again with a damp cloth (no need to dry). Presto—spotless glass!

• Eliminate static shock from carpets. Mix a capful of fabric softener with 2 cups of water in a handheld sprayer bottle, and lightly spritz the rug.

• Clean paint-covered brushes. Simply soak them for 10 seconds in a mixture of $\frac{1}{2}$ cup of fabric softener per gallon of water. They'll come out as soft and spotless as new. *Note:* This method works only on water-based paints, not oil-based products.

OUT OF THE BOX

When you're sorting the cleaning supplies in your laundry room and realize that it's time to toss out some old mops and brooms, hang on to the handles. Those sturdy posts make first-class tomato stakes. A handle also makes a fine stand-in for a Wiffle™ ball bat. (Just cut it down to about 36 inches long, and wrap duct or electrical tape around one end for a grip.) And if you have sliding glass doors, a retired handle can even help you protect your home, sweet home. Cut the stick so that it's just long enough to fit inside the slider track and keep the door from opening. You'll be able to remove it easily, but would-be burglars will have a much tougher time getting the door open.

DON'T DITCH THE LAUNDRY DETERGENT. You say you thought you were getting a bargain on a generic store-brand dry laundry detergent, but it just doesn't get your clothes clean? Don't toss it—instead, move it to the kitchen and use it to clean your broiler pan. While it's still hot, cover the surface of the pan with a thick layer of detergent and top that with a dampened paper towel. Let it sit for 20 minutes or so, and wipe it clean. That's all there is to it!

WHEN TRASH IS TREASURE. Empty plastic bottles that once held laundry detergent, bleach, and fabric softener are nothing but useless clutter in your laundry room. But elsewhere, they're some of the handiest household helpers you could ask for. So turn them into these terrific tools—after you've washed them thoroughly, of course:

- Boat bailer. Slice off the bottom of a large bottle, leaving the cap and handle in place. Then stash the bottle in your boat to scoop up excess water and toss it overboard.

- Buoy. Glue the cap on with waterproof adhesive, and tie a rope to the handle. Tie a weight to the other end of the rope, and drop the weight at your mooring site, or at a navigational trouble spot.

- Clothespin holder. Cut a large hole in the side opposite the handle, so you can pop in the pins. Punch small holes in the bottom for drainage, and hang it on the clothesline. (Either run the line through the handle, or dangle the bottle from a waterproof hook.)

MAKING SPACE

Got more laundry baskets than you need? If so, you can free up space in your laundry room and make shopping a little easier at the same time. How? Just put a basket or two in the trunk of your car. Then when you're out buying groceries or whatever, put all of your packages in the basket. That way, the goods don't get tossed about in your trunk, and when you get home, you can tote the whole load into the house in one quick trip.

- Drip irrigation system. Poke small holes in the bottoms and sides of a whole bunch of bottles, bury them in the soil at strategic spots in your garden, and fill them with water. The moisture will flow out at a slow, steady rate, and go directly to your plants' roots.

- Dumbbells. Pour equal amounts of sand into two bottles until they're heavy enough for your exercise program. When you're ready to handle more weight, simply add more sand.

- Funnel. Just remove the cap from a bleach bottle, and cut off the bottom half of the jug. Repeat the process with several more bottles, and keep them in your car, boat, garden shed, or anywhere else you might need a funnel for motor oil, antifreeze, water, or liquid fertilizer.

- Garden tool caddy. Make a big hole in a giant-size bottle on the side opposite the handle. Then insert your trowel, pruning shears, dibble, and other small hand tools into the bottle through this hole.

- Plant labels. Cut the sides of white or yellow bottles into long strips, write on them with a waterproof marker, and shove the strips into the soil next to the appropriate plants.

- Scoop. Slice diagonally across the bottom of a bottle, screw the top back on, and use it to scoop up cat litter, fertilizer, compost, potting soil, sand, or just about any other nonedible substance.

- Watering can. Drill a dozen or more holes in the cap of a giant-size bottle, fill the bottle with water, and screw the top back on. To water your plants, flip the bottle upside down, and let the H_2O flow!

OUT OF THE BOX

The big, sturdy, colorful lids on laundry detergent and fabric-softener bottles are every bit as useful as the bottles themselves. In fact, they can help you organize and de-clutter every room in the house. So when you turn the container bottoms into household helpers, use the tops to corral tweezers and makeup brushes in the bathroom, pushpins and paper clips in your home office, or tiny pieces of hardware in your garage workshop.

- Winter-weather aids. Detergent bottles are perfect for storing and dispensing cat litter, sand, or wood ashes onto ice-covered sidewalks. Keep a few filled jugs in your car, too. Then if you get stuck on ice or snow, simply pull out a bottle and spread the contents under your wheels for instant traction.

SOFTLY DOES IT. If you use fabric-softener (a.k.a. dryer) sheets, you know that the has-beens can be a major source of clutter in your laundry room. So throw them away—but only after you've used them to perform some essential chores around the house. Any of these, for instance:

✔ Clean your shower door. Wipe the glass with a used dryer sheet, and soap scum will disappear.

✔ De-hair your furniture (and clothes, too). Fido and Fluffy can't help leaving clumps of fur behind, so don't scold them—but don't put up with the mess, either. Just rub a dryer sheet over the fabric, and the offending hairs will vanish like magic.

✔ Dust your computer. And all of the other dust magnets around your house like television screens and metal mini blinds. Gently rub a dryer sheet over the surface, and dirt particles will leap onto the fabric.

✔ Freshen the air. Tuck a dryer sheet into the bag compartment of your vacuum cleaner. As you clean the floor, the aroma will spread around the room.

COLLECTOR ALERT!

Problem: You've got a big collection of ceramic figurines, and dusting them takes a lot of time— and the dirty dust cloths add to your laundry load.

Solution: The next time you use the last of a liquid cleaner that comes in a trigger-type spray bottle, hang on to the empty bottle. Wash it and let it dry thoroughly. Then use it to blow the dust off your figurines (just take aim, and pull the "trigger"). *Note:* This trick works just as well on fancy picture frames, carved furniture, or anything else that's got hard-to-get-at nooks and crannies.

✔ Keep your luggage ready to ramble. Between trips, store a dryer sheet or two inside each suitcase. When it's time to hit the road, you'll have a sweet-smelling home for your travelin' clothes.

✔ Pick up sawdust. When you're sanding or drilling wood, use a dryer sheet as a tack cloth to pick up the dust.

✔ Prevent odor buildup in garbage cans. Put a dryer sheet or two in the bottom of each trash can—indoors and out.

✔ Repel mosquitoes. Just tie a scented dryer sheet through a belt loop, and the bloodthirsty skeeters will keep their distance.

ENOUGH IS ENOUGH. Even if you put most of your laundry in the dryer, it's a good idea to keep some clothespins on hand for things that you need to drip-dry. But if you've got more than you need, get rid of the extras. If they're grungy, toss them into the trash. If they're in good shape, either give them to someone who still dries her laundry on an old-fashioned clothesline, or bag them up and send them off to a thrift shop. But hang on to some of them because clip-type clothespins can be mighty useful in a pinch. Consider these half-dozen ways you can put these problem-solvers to use, both indoors and out:

1. Reseal food packages, and hold phone messages and office papers together.

2. Use them as clamps when you're repairing broken china or gluing small pieces of wood together.

3. When you light the candles on a birthday cake, hold the match in a clothespin so you don't wind up with singed fingertips.

4. On the golf course, attach your scorecard to your golf bag with a clothespin. That

OUT OF THE BOX

After you wash wool gloves, make sure they don't turn into shapeless lumps that you'll never wear again (a.k.a. clutter). How? By simply shoving a rounded, wooden clothespin into each damp finger! They'll keep their shape as they dry.

way, you won't accidentally leave the card behind, and you'll always know what your score is (even when you'd rather not).

5. When you're cutting roses to take inside, protect your fingers by holding each thorny stem with a clothespin.

6. Make a family message center by gluing clip-type clothespins to a strip of wood and attaching it to the wall by your telephone or in your entryway. If you want, you can add labels above the pins. For example, you could assign one to each member of the family, or identify the clips by category, such as "phone messages," "shopping list," and "weekend chores."

ORGANIZE

Let me take a stab in the dark and guess that you'd like to cut back on the amount of time you spend doing laundry. Well, one of the surest ways to accomplish this is to organize your supplies so that you always have what you need—and know where to put your hands on it instantly.

TO EACH ITS OWN. If your laundry area is part of a room that has another purpose like the kitchen, bathroom, or bedroom, give each set of supplies its own quarters—even if it's only separate shelves in the same cabinet. This way, you won't be constantly reaching for the spot remover and grabbing a bottle of shampoo instead!

COVER YOUR BASES. How many times has this happened to you? You've just lugged a big load of dirty clothes into the laundry room, started to pour detergent into the washer—and discovered that the

OUT OF THE BOX

Are you one of those super-organized souls who pins socks together to keep them from being separated in the washer? If so, then go one step further and corral those wash-day pins in a magnetic paper-clip holder in your laundry room. That way, when you need them, they'll be right at your fingertips. (You can find these handy helpers in just about any office-supply or stationery store.)

bottle is almost empty. So you drop everything and run off to the store. Or you just let the pile of laundry sit there, cluttering up the room. Well, I know an ultrasimple way to avoid that kind of unpleasant surprise: Make it a habit to always keep an extra bottle of detergent, fabric softener, spot remover, and whatever else you use regularly on hand, so you never run out.

DON'T GET ME WRONG! I'm not suggesting that you clutter up your laundry room with multiple boxes, bottles, sticks, and tubes of stuff! Just keep one fresh, unopened extra of each product. As soon as you open a new bottle of detergent, for example, write "detergent" on your shopping list, and pick up a bottle the next time you're at the supermarket.

MAKING SPACE

If you have as little as 8 inches of space between your washer and dryer, you're in luck: You've got all the room you need to keep most, if not all, of your laundry supplies nearby. Just trot off to your local home-improvement store, or crank up your favorite Internet search engine, and look for a slim-line laundry cart. There are two versions, and both of them are only 7½ inches wide and have wheels, so you can roll them into and out of the little niche between your machines. One type has three shelves that are about 20 inches long; the other has 10-inch shelves on one side and a fabric laundry hamper on the other.

SPAN THE DISTANCE. If your laundry area is like most, there's a gap of anywhere from 10 inches to a foot between the wall and the backs of your washer and dryer. Well, don't let that space go to waste! You can buy an over-the-washer/dryer shelf that mounts on top of the appliance and covers the opening between it and the wall. These shelves are made of the same vinyl-coated wire as the ones that are commonly installed in closets. Get one for the washer and one for the dryer, and you're good to go!

PUT THE DOOR TO WORK. The space on the back of your laundry room door is just as useful as its counterpart in your bedroom, bathroom, linen closet, or pantry. You have your choice of ways to take advantage of that precious real estate:

1. Install hooks for hanging cleaning tools like mops, brooms, and even handheld vacuum cleaners.

2. Attach a wire shelf unit that's about 4 inches deep—exactly the right depth for holding laundry supplies of all kinds. You can find these units in large hardware and home-improvement stores, in sizes ranging from 12 to 30 inches wide and 10 to 72 inches high.

3. Hang a shoe bag—either a screw-mount or over-the-door version. Use the pockets to corral cleaning supplies, used dryer sheets, or small laundry aids like clothespins, spot removers, and old toothbrushes that you use for stain removal.

When you were busy de-cluttering your living or dining room, did you evict a buffet or other sizable storage piece? If so, move it into the laundry room—provided you have the space, of course. You can stash supplies in the bottom, and use the top to fold your clean clothes on.

TAKE A POLE. Home-improvement stores sell spring-tension poles that work just like spring-tension shower and curtain rods, but they stand straight up, and have adjustable organizer baskets or shelves attached to them. They're meant to be used in bathtubs and showers, but they're just the ticket for laundry rooms that are short on space. Just tuck one into a corner, and put your soaps, detergents, and other supplies in the baskets. In this case, there is no right or wrong way to arrange them; use whatever system works best for you.

PICK A PANTRY. If you store paper towels, facial tissue, and other household staples in your laundry room, consider getting one of the tall cabinets that are sold as kitchen pantries. Unless you keep more stuff on hand than anybody I know, it'll hold all of the supplies you have, with room to spare (say, for a couple of stacked laundry baskets).

PRIME REAL ESTATE. Whether you have a built-in closet in your laundry room or you use a freestanding cabinet, the golden rule of smart organizing is the same: Keep the things you use most often in the places where they're easiest to get at. And that easy-grab, easy-replace territory consists of shelves that are located from shoulder height to about midthigh. Save the higher shelves for storing items you have only occasional use for.

SURROUND THEM. If you have a side-by-side washer and dryer, you probably already know that hanging cabinets or open shelves above them is an obvious—and excellent—way to make use of otherwise wasted space. But here's an even better idea: You can buy wire organizing systems that actually surround the washer and dryer, providing enough shelves and cubbies on top and along the sides to hold all of your wash-day essentials, and then some. They come in both stainless steel and white versions, and (as usual) you can find them in home-improvement stores and on the Internet.

MESS-MAKER ALERT!

Problem: Old washer hoses that can burst, spewing water all over the laundry room, turning your supplies into soggy, useless clutter—and making a royal (and possibly expensive) mess of everything.

Solution: Before trouble strikes, replace those old hoses with flexible, steel-wrapped versions that are guaranteed never to burst. (They're available at home-improvement and plumbing-supply stores, or from your local plumber.) Take it from me: The peace of mind you gain will be worth every penny you spend!

LAY DOWN THE LAW. No matter how well you sort and organize the supplies in your laundry room, the place will become a cluttered mess in no time at all unless you issue one universal order: Anyone who uses anything must put it back exactly where it belongs—or else. (Only you can decide what "else" is, but you'd better make it a lesson they won't soon forget!)

STORE

Once you've organized the space in your laundry room and know generally where you want to keep your supplies, it's time to focus on actually storing them. Here's the gist of it.

OUT OF REACH, OUT OF MOUTH. If you have young children or pets in the house, store all laundry and cleaning products well out of their reach—and under lock and key if necessary. Even the greenest of the "green" concoctions can cause trouble if they wind up in the hand (or stomach) of a curious child or pet.

MAGNETIC ATTRACTION. Home-improvement stores and home-organizing catalogs (both online and print versions) sell magnetic storage bins that attach right to your washer and dryer. They're perfect for holding stain removers, dryer sheets, and anything else that's smaller (and lighter) than giant-size containers of laundry detergent.

MAGNETIC ATTRACTION, PART TWO. When it's time to wash clothes that need special treatment, do you have to scramble to find the instructions that came with the garments? If so, then store those tags right at the scene of the action. Just get a magnetic rack that's designed to hold files or other papers (available in office-supply stores), and attach it to your washer or dryer. This is also the place to keep a stain-removal guide—either the conventional type or my kitchen-counter version (see "Out, Out, Darned Spot!" on page 240).

Ask Jerry

Q. *I live in a tiny condo, and my washer and dryer are in a closet in the kitchen. A basket filled with dirty clothes looks unspeakably messy. Even a conventional laundry hamper looks out of place. Can you think of any more attractive alternatives?*

A. Here's one—just buy a big, round stainless steel trash can (the kind that you open by stepping on a pedal at the bottom). The container will look right at home. In fact, in a modern kitchen, these cans look downright classy!

THIS BULLETIN JUST IN. A bulletin board can be just as useful in your laundry room as it is in your home office. Hang one near your washing machine, and pin up your stain-removal chart and care tags for clothes that need special treatment. But don't stop there! Hang pre-threaded needles, iron-on patches, and even buttons. Just slide them onto an extra-long safety pin, and attach it to the board with a pushpin.

PUT UP A PEGBOARD. Use hooks to hold the same wash-day aids that you might hang from a bulletin board. Just attach binder clips to iron-on patches, stain-removal charts, and other hole-less items, and slide the tops of the clips over the hooks. Then get some flat-backed metal baskets, hang them from the hooks, and fill 'em up with detergent, fabric softener, dryer sheets, and other supplies. Of course, you can't put giant-sized bottles or boxes in the baskets, but they are roomy and sturdy enough to hold small to midsize containers.

WHEN LOOKS MATTER. If your laundry area is part of your kitchen, entryway, or other public space, and there's not much room for hidden supply storage, look for containers that are as attractive as they are practical. These winners are good-looking enough to sit out on open shelves (or on the floor, depending on their size), and they can hold everything from laundry detergent to old toothbrushes that you use to scrub spots away:

✔ Clamp-lid canning jars

✔ Cookie jars

✔ Kitchen canisters

✔ Lidded baskets

✔ Steamer trunks

✔ Vintage suitcases

OUT OF THE BOX

If your washer and dryer are in a room where you don't want unattractive laundry baskets on display, add a bench to the area that has space for three baskets below and a couple of cushions on top. Sort laundry into the baskets, and get comfy on the cushions whenever you need a break!

STORAGE STRATEGIES FOR BARGAIN HUNTERS. It's no secret that you can save a lot of your hard-earned cash when you buy laundry detergent in supersize boxes or buckets. But what do you do if you don't have the space to store those humongous containers? Just divvy up the contents among several smaller containers! They'll be easier to store, and a lot easier on your back when you have to move them around. One-gallon plastic bottles that formerly held water or milk are perfect. Just make sure they're completely dry and, in the case of milk jugs, super clean before you fill 'em up with detergent. Otherwise, you'll end up with a gooey, soapy mess on your hands.

Out, Out, Darned Spot!

If your washer and dryer live in your kitchen, chances are you don't have much space for storing laundry supplies. So here's some good news: You can get rid of all those spot-removing sprays, sticks, and gels that are taking up valuable room. That's right—some of the most powerful stain removers you'll ever find are in your kitchen cupboards. Here's a rundown of kitchen-counter laundry aids.

STAIN	MATERIAL	HOW TO GET IT OUT
Blood	Any fabric	Blot, then pour on cold club soda. Repeat if necessary.
Fruit or juice	Any washable fabric	Pour salt on the spots, and soak the article in milk until the stains are gone.
Grass	Any washable fabric	Rub the spots with molasses, let the garment sit overnight, and wash with mild soap (not detergent).
Grease or oil	Knit fabrics	Pour club soda (cold or room-temperature) on the spot, and scrub gently.
Grease or oil	Any smooth fabric	Cover the spot with cornstarch, wait 12 hours, and brush it off.
Ink (ballpoint)	Any washable fabric	Dampen a sponge with milk and dab the stain until it's gone. (Be patient; it may take a while to get all of the ink out.) Then launder as usual.

Ink (still wet)	Any fabric	Pour salt on the spot and dab it gently, taking care not to spread the ink around. Let it sit for 2 to 3 minutes, and brush off the salt. Repeat if necessary.
Mildew	Any washable fabric	Moisten the spots with a half-and-half mixture of salt and lemon juice, and then lay the item out in the sun until the marks disappear.
Mustard	Any washable fabric	Soak the soiled area in a half-and-half solution of white vinegar and water until the spot disappears. Blot with a soft cloth, and launder as usual.
Organic, protein-based substances like milk, egg, and blood	Any washable fabric	Make a paste of meat tenderizer mixed with a few drops of water, work it into the stain, and launder immediately.
Perspiration	Any washable fabric	Mix 4 tablespoons of salt with 1 quart of water, and sponge the stains with the solution until they're gone. Launder as usual.
Rust	Any washable fabric	Mix equal parts of salt and vinegar. Rub the paste into the stain, wait 30 minutes, and launder as usual.
Tar	Any fabric	Slather mayonnaise onto the spot, and let it soak into the fabric. Launder or dry-clean as usual.
Vomit	Any fabric	Remove the residue using a plastic scraper or paper towels. Then cover the spot with baking soda, let it dry, and brush it off. Launder as usual, or send the garment to the dry cleaner.
Wine	Any fabric	Blot up any excess moisture, and saturate the stain with club soda. Rub lightly, and blot dry. Repeat if necessary. Then dry-clean or launder as usual.

CHAPTER SEVEN

THE BASEMENT AND ATTIC

What do you do with those things you don't use very often? If you're like most folks, you stash them in your basement or attic. After all, they are the perfect places to park stuff that's cluttering up your everyday living space, right? Well, yes and no. If you're not careful, those out-of-sight, out-of-mind areas can quickly turn into black holes. On the other hand, if you put our advice to work, they can be your keys to truly clutter-free (and enjoyable) living.

DIG IN DOWNSTAIRS

Professional de-clutterers tell us that 95 percent of the stuff found in the average basement is useless junk. If that statistic even comes close to hitting home with you, take heart: You can clear out the clutter, organize the space, and turn it into whatever your heart desires, whether that's a playroom for the kids, a family room for everyone to enjoy—or simply a smoother-running, all-purpose storage area. Here's how.

In This Section:
✔ Liquids
✔ Appliances
✔ Furniture
✔ Recreational
   gear

SORT

In many homes, the basement is where everyone in the family routinely dumps anything that's too big to fit in the kitchen junk drawer. If that description sounds like your household, then the mere thought of sorting through all that stuff probably sends chills down your spine. Well, just ignore them. Round up some sturdy trash bags and boxes, and charge full speed ahead.

CATEGORICALLY SPEAKING. Of course, some of the items in your basement are bound to be way too big to fit into boxes—or in some cases they may already be in boxes (either their original containers, or ones that you've filled up with who knows what). So, in addition to labeling your boxes, lay down old sheets, drop cloths, or tarpaulins to create different zones within the basement. Then allot a section to each of these categories: Trash, Keep Here, Take Elsewhere, and Donate or Sell. (Either make signs on sheets of cardboard, or use a marking pen to label each floor covering.)

STEP ON IT. When you're sorting the contents of most rooms, it's fine to start anyplace you like. But in the basement, there is only one right place to begin: the stairs leading down to it. If there is anything on the steps, take it off—and don't put anything in its place. Leaving any objects on a stairway is downright hazardous to say the least. (Of course, what you should do with the items you remove depends on what they are; we'll get to that in a minute.)

CLEAR THE WALLS, TOO. Many people hang things on the walls on one or both sides of the basement stairs. I've even seen some de-cluttering books that actually recommend installing shelves or pegboard there. Well, take my advice, friends: Don't do it! You could easily brush against that stuff on

You say your basement is so small or so jam-packed with stuff that there's no room to spread everything out? Then make your sorting spree an outdoor project. Wait until the weather forecast guarantees a day or two of good weather. Then divide your lawn into zones (see "Categorically Speaking" above), and go to town. As you haul everything up from the depths, set it in the appropriate spot. If night falls before you finish, move anything that's especially fragile or valuable indoors or onto a covered porch, and toss some old sheets or plastic drop cloths over the rest.

your way down the steps, or bump into it with a box or laundry basket that you're carrying. If that happens—and you're lucky—the mop, coat, bottle, or what have you will go flying down the stairs. If you're not so lucky, *you* could go flying down the stairs!

DON'T PLAY WITH FIRE. Once you've cleared the stairway, tackle the next biggest danger zone in your basement: potential fire hazards. Gather up any containers of gasoline, kerosene, and motor oil, as well as oil-based paint, turpentine, and other solvents. Get rid of any almost-empty containers, dried-up paint, or products that you know you won't use (like kerosene for a lantern you no longer own). Then take the still-usable stuff elsewhere—preferably to a locked, metal storage unit in your garage, shed, or workshop.

CALL BEFORE YOU TOSS. When you need to get rid of hazardous substances or the empty containers that once held them, call your local sanitation department, and ask how it wants you to deal with them. Regulations vary from one community to another. Whatever you do, *never* pour any oil- or solvent-based product down the drain. Nor should you dump it into a storm drain, flush it down the toilet, or throw it out with your household trash. This no-no policy includes any product that's labeled flammable, and anything that contains turpentine.

BASEMENT BONANZA. Do you have a ratty, threadbare couch that you stashed in the basement "temporarily" when you got a new

MESS-MAKER ALERT!

Problem: Your basement is so dark and dirty that there's no telling what you'll find down there.

Solution: Arm yourself for battle with rubber gloves, a broom, wet/dry vac, and dust mask, along with insect spray (maybe a can of unwanted aerosol hair spray that you've weeded out of your bathroom). Then to shed light on the scene, gather up some hanging, battery-powered lanterns or flashlights, and have at it!

one for your living room? Well, send it to the local dump—now! Is there a chest of drawers or an old armoire that could provide needed storage space elsewhere in your house? Then move it upstairs—pronto! You'll free up space to use for sorting your other stuff and kick your de-cluttering mission into high gear at the same time.

PURGE THE PAPERS. A big stack of newspapers sitting in the basement is a potential fire hazard. But elsewhere around the old homestead, yesterday's news can be today's treasure. Here are 10 terrific ways to put that paper to work for you, indoors and out:

1. Get grease or moisture out of metal garbage cans. Just burn crumpled-up newspaper inside them. (Be sure to leave the lid off!)

Don't Moan over Mildew

It's all but guaranteed that your basement sorting spree will uncover some treasures that you'd completely forgotten about. Perhaps you'd like to use them elsewhere in your house, but they've picked up some mildew in that damp cellar. Don't fret—just go after the foul stuff using one of these techniques.

MILDEW VICTIM	RECOMMENDED TREATMENT
Book covers	Sponge alcohol on the spots, and set the books in sunlight until the splotches disappear.
Book interiors	Sprinkle cornstarch throughout the pages. Wait several hours until the moisture has been absorbed, and then brush out the starch. *Note:* Do this job outdoors, so the mildew spores don't invade your house.
Fabric (washable)	Brush off the mildew spores outdoors. Soak the item overnight in buttermilk, then wash and dry it as usual.
Leather	Wipe the mildew away with a solution of equal parts of rubbing alcohol and water. Follow up with a good leather conditioner.
Small wooden objects	Soak them for about 10 minutes in a bucket of warm water with $1/2$ cup of bleach and 1 tablespoon of laundry detergent added. Then set them out in the sun to dry.

2. Deodorize a smelly plastic bucket or garbage pail. Fill the container with black-and-white newspaper, cover it, and let it sit overnight. By morning, the odor will be gone.

3. Save your sopping wet footgear. The next time you get caught in a storm, stuff your wet shoes with newspaper, and lay them on their sides to dry away from any heat source.

4. Make fake logs for your fireplace. Roll two or three papers tightly together, and wrap them with wire or twine. Then light your fire, baby!

5. Wrap gifts. Spray the newspaper comics section with hair spray to make it smudge-free, and use it to wrap a present for a child (or a young-at-heart grown-up).

6. Spruce up storage containers. Use hair-sprayed comics to cover lidded cardboard boxes (like the ones that photocopy paper comes in), and put a child's toys or your home-office supplies in them.

7. Protect off-duty tools. Give them a light coat of oil (any kind will do), and wrap them in newspaper to keep them clean and rust-free.

MAKING SPACE

Donating your unwanted, but still functioning, appliances to a charity will deliver a win-win payoff in three ways: You'll do a good turn for a worthy cause, earn a deduction on your income tax, and free up valuable space in your basement. The Salvation Army, St. Vincent de Paul, and Goodwill Industries, as well as many independent thrift shops, accept small appliances like toasters, mixers, and microwave ovens. Their policies on large appliances vary, though, so call your local branch. Also check with nearby churches about shelters or group homes in your area. They may welcome washers, dryers, freezers, or refrigerators that are in good working order.

8. Water your houseplants while you're away. Line the bottom of your bathtub with newspapers and soak them with water. Set the plants on top, and they'll stay moist and happy for at least two weeks.

9. Make seed-starting pots. Cut strips of paper about 1 foot long and

6 inches wide. Wrap each strip lengthwise around a beer or soft-drink can, leaving 2 inches hanging over the bottom. Fold the extra piece over, press it in place with your fingers, and remove the can.

10. Feed your soil. Toss torn, shredded, or chopped-up newspaper onto your compost pile, or simply bury the paper in your garden or flower beds. It'll quickly break down into plant-pleasing humus.

DON'T THINK, JUST THROW. When you find items in your basement that fall into any of these categories, toss 'em right into the trash or the recycling bin:

• Anything that's broken and cannot be repaired

• Cardboard boxes that are damp, dirty, or damaged in any way

• Dry food (for humans or pets) you've stored that's gotten damp or buggy, or that's beyond its expiration date

• Over-the-hill cleaning supplies, including grungy sponges, worn-out mops and brooms, and spray cleansers with just a thin layer of solution left in the bottom (For tips on disposing of household cleansers safely—and legally—see "Discard with Care" on page 65.)

• Any fabric, leather, wood, or paper items that have suffered mouse damage, or that

Ask Jerry

Q. *Help! Mice have invaded my basement, but I have two young children and a very curious dog—so I definitely don't want to use poisons or traps. How can I get rid of the destructive little rodents?*

A. I have a simple solution: Just set out shallow containers of instant mashed potato flakes, with a dish of water close at hand. The mice will eat the taters, drink the water, swell up, and die. But if your youngsters or dog should manage to get into the basement and take a taste, it won't harm them one little bit. Just one word of warning, though: You certainly don't want your loved ones anywhere near dead mice, so if possible, keep the basement door locked. Check frequently for little furry bodies, and when you find any, get rid of them immediately.

are moldy or too badly mildewed to rejuvenate (see "Don't Moan over Mildew" on page 245).

- Parts that once belonged to appliances, games, toys, or other things that you no longer own

DEALING WITH DEAD APPLIANCES. It's one thing to toss out a nonfunctioning flashlight or a worn-out dog collar. But it's a whole different ball game when you need to get rid of an old washing machine, dryer, or freezer that no longer works. Here, you can choose among three practical approaches:

1. Call your town's sanitation department and ask what its policy is for disposing of large appliances. It may have scheduled pickup times for large items, or it may require you to deliver your castoffs to the local dump or other collection site (or hire someone to do it).

2. Contact local art schools, craft galleries, or the fine art departments of nearby colleges. Ask if they know of artists who work with recycled metal and mechanical gadgetry. It's a good bet that someone who does found-object sculpture, a.k.a. assemblage art, would love to have your deceased washer, dryer, toaster oven—or even water heater. Most likely, he or she will even come by to pick it up.

3. Check with the Steel Recycling Institute to find a steel-recycling

MAKING SPACE

If your appliances, large or small, are still in good shape and you'd like to get them out of the house, here's a way to also get some cash for them—advertise them for sale in local papers, list them on Web sites, or add them to your next garage sale. On the other hand, if you just want to get the things out of your basement *right now*, then haul them out to the curb and attach a sign saying "Works well—free to a good home." Before you know it, they'll be whisked away. Just one word of caution: If you set out a refrigerator or freezer, make sure you remove the door before it goes out to the curb to keep curious kids and pets safe from becoming trapped inside.

center near you. You can visit its Web site at www.recycle-steel.org, or call 800-876-7274, extension 201.

DON'T ASK FOR TROUBLE. If your basement is home to your gardening tools, lawn furniture, camping gear, or anything else that spends a lot of time in the great outdoors, do yourself a favor: Take that stuff elsewhere—ideally, to a detached garage or shed, or a storage cabinet under your deck. That way, you won't have to worry about bringing dirt and bugs indoors, and you won't have to clean everything ultra-thoroughly after each use. Remember that fungal spores are invisible to the naked eye, and many kinds of insect eggs are almost as small. So even if your things look clean, they could be harboring a potential pain in the neck.

MOVE 'EM OUT. The basement is no place for anything that could suffer harm from dampness, dirt, or pests (not to mention plumbing leaks or full-scale floods). The roster of items includes:

✔ Antiques, art, or photographs

✔ Birdseed, grass or garden seeds, dry pet food, and any other potential rodent fodder

✔ Books

✔ Boxed food

✔ Carpets or rugs

✔ Clothes, quilts, and other fragile textiles

✔ Functioning electronics

PACK RAT ALERT!

Problem: Stuff just keeps piling up in your basement.

Solution: Schedule a yearly tour, and get rid of anything that you don't like, don't use, or don't need, as well as the obvious toss-outs that we've already talked about. And no matter how well you've packed your storage containers, peek into each one to make sure things aren't becoming mildewed. This way, if you do notice any problems, you'll be able to move your things to safer territory before major damage is done (see "Don't Moan over Mildew" on page 245 for mildew-removal tips).

- ✔ Fur or leather

- ✔ Important papers

- ✔ Luggage

- ✔ Musical instruments

- ✔ Videotapes or audiotapes

- ✔ Vinyl records

- ✔ Anything that would cause you heartbreak or financial woe if you lost it

YOUR FUNDAMENTAL FREEZER.
If you're lucky enough to have a freezer in your basement—either the upright or chest type—make it part of your sorting agenda. Take out every package and inspect it. If you can't remember how long it's been in there—or even what's inside—get rid of it. And from now on:

- Only freeze foods you and your family like, which you know will be eaten before they turn into rock-solid, frost-covered blocks. If a friend gives you something you don't care for, don't toss it in the freezer; toss it in the garbage can. Or give it to someone who will eat it soon.

- Ditto leftovers. If you try a new recipe, and your hubby and kids give it two thumbs down, toss the extra portions.

- Every time you put something in the freezer, label it clearly with the contents and the date.

Ask Jerry

Q. *My basement is dry and I haven't seen more than an occasional spider lurking about. So I can store just about anything down there, right?*

A. Yep, anything your little heart desires—as long as it isn't hazardous, does not attract pests, and will not be easily damaged by dampness (see "Move 'Em Out" on page 249). In particular, the basement is the perfect place to store nonperishable foods and beverages in cans, bottles, or jars (no cardboard boxes!). It's also acceptable for things like sports equipment and outdoor Christmas decorations. In short, anything that's made of plastic, rubber, or rustproof metal will fare just fine down there.

- Conduct periodic inspections, and weed out anything that's been there beyond its ideal serve-by date (see "How Long Will It Last?" below).

How Long Will It Last?

The staying power of frozen foods varies greatly from one product to another. Here's how to tell, at a glance, how long you can expect some of the most common freezer residents to remain fresh and good to eat.

TYPE OF FOOD	HOW LONG TO KEEP IT
Lean fish (cod, flounder, haddock, sole, etc.)	6 months
Fatty fish (salmon, bluefish, mackerel, etc.)	2–3 months
Chicken, turkey, or duck (whole), uncooked	1 year
Poultry casseroles, cooked	4–6 months
Lasagna	3–6 months
Macaroni and cheese	3–6 months
Cooked meat & meat casseroles	2–3 months
Ground meat (beef, turkey, veal, pork, lamb, or combinations)	3–4 months
Roasts (beef, lamb, pork, veal)	4–12 months
Cakes, angel food & sponge	4–6 months
Cakes, layer	2–4 months
Cheesecake	4–6 months
Cookies, baked	4–6 months
Cookies, unbaked dough	6 months
Fruitcake	1 year
Ice cream and sherbet	1–2 months
Muffins and quick breads	1–2 months

ORGANIZE

Before you start restocking your newly cleared-out basement, spend some time organizing the space so you can take full advantage of this storage gold mine.

DIVIDE AND CONQUER. Because all basements are not created equal, there is no right or wrong way to divvy up the space. But when you're deciding what to store down there and where to put it, you need to consider three major factors:

1. Physical conditions. Is your basement finished or unfinished? How damp does it get? Is standing water (or worse, flooding) ever a problem? And are mice or other troublemaking critters frequent visitors?

2. How you use the area. Except for housing your furnace and water heater, is your basement devoted strictly to storage? Or does it also function as a children's playroom, laundry room, workshop, home office, or other kind of action center?

3. Your other storage options. Do you have a garage, attic, and/or shed? Or does your basement have to accommodate things that you would otherwise stash in one or all of those spaces?

> ## MAKING SPACE
>
> If your basement is simply too wet to store even fairly sturdy things like lawn furniture and sports equipment, and there's no room for them elsewhere, don't despair—and don't throw money out the window for a rented self-storage locker. Instead, invest in a plastic shed, and set it up in your yard. They're available in a variety of shapes and sizes at hardware and home-improvement stores and on the Internet. Of course, the bigger the shed, the more it'll cost you. But unless you're parking a few things for only a couple of months, you'll end up paying a whole lot less than you would for rented space.

FOLLOW THE GOLDEN RULES. Depending on how much of your basement is devoted to storage, you may or may not need to make an actual map (see "Make a Map" on page 273). But no matter how much stuff you store down there, remember these two crucial guidelines: Clearly label each and every container, and always keep the things you use most often in the places you can get to most easily.

DEAL WITH THE DAMPNESS.

Many basements will never be bone-dry, but these simple devices can help lower the moisture level:

- A dehumidifier. For mild to moderate dampness, this should be all you need. Look for a model that turns itself on and off automatically in response to the humidity in the air. Depending on your climate, you may have to use it only in the summer, or you may end up needing it year-round. *Note*: When you empty the water in the unit, don't pour it down the drain. Give it to your plants instead— they'll love it!

- A sump pump. If you ever get standing water in your basement, whether it comes from heavy rains or a naturally high water table, you need one of these babies in addition to a dehumidifier. A plumber or contractor can recommend the right model and install it for you.

MESS-MAKER ALERT!

Problem: Water, water—everywhere!

Solution: Even the driest basement can suddenly become a soggy mess if a pipe or washing machine hose bursts, a clogged drain overflows, or a window gets broken during a big rainstorm. The simple solution: Buy an inexpensive water alarm (available at plumbing-supply and hardware stores and on the Internet). These dandy devices detect even the tiniest amounts of moisture and send out a loud signal, so you can rush into action before any serious damage is done.

CONTAIN CONCRETE DUST. If you've got dust from your poured-concrete floor dirtying up everything in your basement and getting tracked all through your house, there's a solution. After you've cleared all the stuff out of your basement, give the floor a thorough cleaning with a wet/dry vacuum cleaner. Then apply a coat or two of concrete sealer (available at your local hardware store). It'll hold the dust in check and also inhibit moisture, which naturally seeps from any concrete surface. To keep it clean, just vacuum the floor frequently, and damp mop it periodically.

WAYS WITH WALLS. If your basement walls are actually leaking or have wet patches, the problem—and therefore the solution—goes far beyond the scope of a book on de-cluttering. But if you simply want to make them a little drier and cleaner, apply the same concrete sealer that I recommended for the floor (see "Contain Concrete Dust" on page 253). Then for good measure, paint them a nice shade of white to brighten up the place and make all of your stored belongings easier to see.

BE PREPARED. The first step in your organizing plan should be one that could potentially save your life: Set aside an easily accessible place to store emergency supplies in waterproof plastic bins with snap-on lids. Then if the need arises, you can either retrieve them from their designated storage area, or hustle the whole family downstairs to ride out the storm. Here's the basic inventory:

✔ At minimum, a three-day supply of food and water for each family member (pets, too)

✔ Basic kitchenware, including a hand-operated can opener, cups, plates, and utensils

✔ Candles and waterproof matches

✔ Flashlights and extra batteries

✔ Portable radio and extra batteries

✔ Sleeping bags

If you have the room, consider including a folding card table and folding chairs in your basement emergency kit, along with a deck of cards and any board games that your family enjoys. After all, if you find yourselves stuck down in the boring basement for several days, staring at the walls and listening to the radio could get mighty old—fast!

- ✔ Plastic sheeting

- ✔ Duct tape

- ✔ Plastic trash bags

- ✔ Antibacterial wipes or liquid hand cleaners, toothpaste, toilet paper, and paper towels

- ✔ First-aid kit and manual (including versions for pets)

HIGH AND DRY. Keep your emergency supplies in the driest spot you can find that's also as far away as possible from any windows. That way, if you need to hunker down for a while, you and your family will be safe from flying glass and as comfortable as the circumstances allow.

SAFE AT HOME. It goes without saying (I hope!) that you have at least one smoke detector and one carbon monoxide detector in your basement. If not, get them at a local hardware store and install them today. Also make sure you have a working fire extinguisher that's in a spot where you can grab it instantly.

AND FOR GOOD MEASURE... Leave plenty of space around the furnace, water heater, fuse box, and drain(s) so you can reach them quickly if you need to. And don't hang anything from overhead pipes—it will weaken them and also make it harder to detect leaks.

GET OFF THE GROUND. Keep everything off your basement's concrete floor, even if it's been painted with sealer. Even plastic storage bins fare better when they're raised up off the ground because they'll

Ask Jerry

Q. *I know my emergency supplies should include enough water for three days for each person and pet, but how much is that, exactly?*

A. Everyone's water needs differ, depending on age, physical condition, diet, climate, and activity level. A rule of thumb is to figure on 1 gallon per day for each person and each large- to giant-size dog, and one quart a day for cats and smaller dogs.

stay cleaner (sealed concrete gets dusty, too), and tiny bugs won't be able to crawl under them. You have several simple options for keeping your belongings high and dry:

1. Bring in some wire shelves. Attach screw-mounted versions to the wall studs, or use freestanding units (available in home-improvement and hardware stores). Either way, the things you put on them will benefit from good airflow, and you'll be able to see at a glance what you've got.

2. Use pallets. These are ideal for protecting things like furniture and lamps that are too big to fit into plastic storage containers. You can buy plastic pallets on Web sites and at some lumberyards. To find low- or no-cost wooden versions, check local supermarkets (they often give them away), or search the Internet for "pallet recyclers" in your area.

MAKING SPACE | If your laundry room is in the basement and you plan to sell your home in the next few years, consider moving your washer and dryer up to the first or second floor. Or get rid of them and replace them with new models in an upstairs laundry area. Not only will the location be far more convenient for you on wash day but, according to the National Board of Realtors, it will also add to the value of your property. Conversely, a laundry area that's in the basement can actually decrease the value of your home, sweet home.

3. Hang 'em high. Screw sturdy hooks into wall or ceiling studs, and use them to hold large bulky gear like bicycles, golf bags, and motorcycle helmets.

HANG TOUGH. In many—if not most—basements, the walls are made of concrete block. And hanging anything from that surface is not as simple as screwing hooks into wooden beams. But you can still put those hard walls to work for you. Just mount sheets of plywood to the blocks, using special masonry anchors. Then fasten shelves, racks, hooks, or pegboard to the plywood, and you're good to go!

STORE

Of all the storage areas in your home, the basement presents the most—and biggest—challenges. But using the tricks in this section can help conquer all of them, including dampness, beastly bugs, and rampaging rodents.

CAN THE CARDBOARD. The golden rule of basement storage is don't put anything in a cardboard box—not even things that are totally waterproof like beach or swimming pool toys. And if at all possible, don't keep empty boxes down there, either. Cardboard tends to harbor mildew spores, bugs, and even mice, all of which can easily spread to other parts of your house.

MAKE MINE PLASTIC. You can buy plastic storage cabinets that are waterproof and all but indestructible in home-improvement stores and on the Internet. They even have lockable doors, so you can keep the contents safely away from children and pets (or any uninvited visitors who are up to no good). These cabinets come in several sizes, and they're priced low enough so that you could easily line a whole wall with them if you want to.

A SPORTING CHANCE. Attention, jocks (or the parents of jocks)! The same company (Rubbermaid®) that makes the most popular brand of basement-ready cabinets also sells a storage unit called a Sports Station Organizer. It features hooks

MESS-MAKER ALERT!

Problem: Dampness, dampness, and more dampness.

Solution: No matter what kind of storage containers you use in your basement, it pays to take extra precautions. So make sure you put a drying agent into each bin, box, or cabinet. Web-based catalogs and hardware stores sell reusable desiccant products in both canister and cloth-pouch form. They contain a chemical that attracts, condenses, and stores water vapor. Every few months (or more often if necessary) you just pull them out, dry them in the oven, and put them back to work.

Valerie L. Walker is a professional organizer and owner of Destination Organized® in suburban Baltimore, Maryland (www.DestinationOrganized.com). Like her fellow Clutter Buster Pros, Valerie sings the praises of plastic storage containers with snap-on lids. Here are her tips for making the most of these modern marvels—in your basement or anyplace else in your house:

☛ Choose clear plastic bins when you're storing something that you may need to spot instantly, like emergency supplies or snow boots.

☛ When you're stashing things that you don't want others to notice (like Christmas presents), or items that could be damaged by light (such as photographs or fabric), opt for opaque plastic.

☛ Color-code your bins according to the contents. Either buy containers in different colors, or stick with a single color for the bins and use a different-colored label for each category. To make the most efficient use of this system, choose shades that will remind you of what's inside. Maybe use red for Christmas decorations, blue for beach gear, and your favorite color for personal keepsakes.

☛ Label each bin clearly, using specific wording that you will instantly recognize. For children's keepsakes, use the child's name or first initial with the year, grade, or sub-category. For instance, "Tommy—4th grade" or "Mary—4H Club."

☛ When you stack or shelve your bins, think about which ones you need to get into most often, and put them in the places that are easiest to reach.

and compartments that can hold bats, gloves, hockey sticks, skates, and just about any other kind of sports equipment you can name.

BIN THERE, DOING THAT. Plastic bins with snap-on lids are the darlings of folks who de-clutter houses for a living, and for good reason: These containers are sturdy, waterproof, and inexpensive. They come in a wide variety of sizes, shapes, and colors, and you can buy them at just about any store that sells home products—including your local supermarket. What more could you ask for? How about terrific tips on how to make the

most of these versatile helpers? You'll find them in the
Clutter Buster Pro box at left.

RACK IT UP. If you store 5-gallon water
bottles in your basement (either for your
upstairs drinking supply or as part of your
emergency stash), keep them in a special,
three-tier plastic water-bottle rack. They're
available in home-improvement stores
and catalogs, and they're just the ticket for
keeping those big jugs up off the floor.

SHELVE IT. In any room of your house,
shelves—either freestanding or wall-
mounted—are just about the most versatile
storage helpers you could ask for. And your
basement is no exception. Plastic or metal
shelves will work fine, and you can find
them at almost any home-improvement or
hardware store. What about wood shelves?
My advice is to use them only if your
basement is on the dry side, and even then,
raise them up on pallets so they're not resting directly on the concrete
floor (see "Get Off the Ground" on page 255).

OUT OF THE BOX

To keep your basement
windows clear, spotless,
and free of grime, clean
them regularly using a
spray made from $1/2$ cup
of white vinegar, $1/4$ cup of
rubbing alcohol, and
$1/2$ cup of water. Mix all
of the ingredients in a
handheld sprayer bottle,
apply the cleaner to the
glass, and wipe it away
with paper towels or
crumpled-up newspaper.
That's all there is to it! (Of
course, this formula works
just as well on any other
windows, mirrors, or glass
tabletops in your house.)

LET THE SUN SHINE IN. If you have windows in your basement,
congratulations! The heat and light that come through them can
help fend off the chill and dampness that can damage your stored
belongings. These simple maneuvers will help you make the most of
Ol' Sol's warming power, even in the coldest weather:

• Prune all of your foundation shrubs back so they don't cover the windows.

• If the windows are operable, open them during warm, dry weather
  (using screens, of course), so that fresh air can flow in.

- At the end of open-window season, remove the screens, so that the full intensity of the sunlight can reach the far corners of your basement.

- Keep the glass sparkly clean, inside and out. Even a thin film of dirt will block out a whole lot of light (see Out of the Box on page 259).

A STEP IN THE RIGHT DIRECTION. If you're lucky enough to have roomy, closed-in steps leading down to your basement, turn the bottom one into a mini storage chest. Just hinge the top of that step so you can raise and lower it. Set a small plastic storage bin inside to keep things from coming in direct contact with the concrete floor below. Use it to store small odds and ends that you may need in a pinch, like extra extension cords, a flashlight, batteries, or spare bulbs for basement light fixtures.

MAKING SPACE

Is the space under your stairway open? If so, count your lucky stars—you have a great place for storing all kinds of things. Tuck a cabinet or freestanding shelves under there, or install the kind of wall-mounted, wire shelves that are often used in bedroom closets (see "Reorganizing Options" on page 35). You'll be surprised at how much stuff you can fit in this nifty nook.

SKI-DO. Need a place to store your skis? Mount two shelf brackets on a wall high up near the ceiling, about 3 feet apart, and lay your skis and poles across them. They'll be out of the way, but easy to retrieve when you need them. This is also a great spot for canoe and kayak paddles, fishing rods, and anything else that's long, narrow, and light. *Note:* This trick works just as well in the attic as it does in the basement.

I'LL DRINK TO THAT! Take full advantage of the cool, dark conditions of your basement by storing—or starting—your wine collection down there. If you follow these three simple guidelines, your vino will age well and be ready to join the party for victory toasts, holiday celebrations, or nice relaxing dinners:

1. Claim the darkest corner of the basement for your wine cellar. You want a spot where lights won't shine directly onto the bottles. *Tip:* Keep a flashlight close by, so you can quickly find the bottle you want.

2. Make sure the spot you choose is as far away as possible from sources of vibration. That includes your washer and dryer, as well as the space under the stairway. Vibration can cause air bubbles to form in the wine, and that sends the quality downhill on a fast track. In fact, too much movement of any kind can make the quality deteriorate. So once you've found the right location for your bottles, try not to move them until it's time to uncork 'em.

3. Pick up as many inexpensive wooden wine racks as you need (you can find them in housewares, hardware, and home-improvement stores). Set them on a table or shelf—not on the floor—and insert each bottle into one of the cubbies, so that it's lying on its side.

ROOT CELLAR STORAGE TIPS. In addition to choosing the right spot (or creating the right conditions) for various types of produce (see "The Root of the Matter" on page 262), following some basic guidelines will ensure that your edibles stay fresh, tasty, and nutritious during their time in the basement. So before you stash your fruits and vegetables for the winter, keep this handful of tips in mind:

• Leave root crops in the ground for as long as possible before you store them. Or, if you buy them from a farmers' market or roadside stand, make your purchases as late in the season as you can. The cold weather causes these vegetables to produce more sugars and starches, but less water, which allows them to stay fresher longer.

MESS-MAKER ALERT!

Problem: Many common fruits like apples, pears, peaches, and tomatoes release ethylene gas, which speeds up their aging process. In addition, vegetables stored close to the fruit can go bad, and many develop a bitter, unpleasant taste.

Solution: Always store fruits and vegetables separately, keeping them as far apart from each other as you possibly can.

- Pick fruits and above-ground vegetables (like cabbage and broccoli) before the first frost if you intend to store them.

- Store only the best produce—not anything that's too ripe, not fully ripe, or damaged in any way. If you have apples, peaches, or other fruits that are bruised or a little past their prime, cut them up and use

The Root of the Matter

Do you need a place to store long-keeping produce that you grow in your garden or buy in bulk at roadside stands and farmers' markets? If so, then turn part of your basement into an old-fashioned root cellar. Which crops you can successfully store depends on the current climatic conditions that exist in your basement—or what you can manage to provide down there. Here's a rundown of preferences.

CONDITIONS	GOOD PRODUCE TO STORE
Cold and very moist (32–40°F, 90–95 percent relative humidity)	Beets Carrots Celery Horseradish Leeks Turnips Winter radishes
Cold and moist (32–40°F, 80–90 percent relative humidity)	Cabbage Endive and escarole Fruits (including apples, grapes, peaches, pears, and plums) Potatoes
Cool and moist (40–50°F, 85–90 percent relative humidity)	Cantaloupe Cucumbers Ripe tomatoes Watermelon
Cool and dry (32–50°F, 60–70 percent relative humidity)	Garlic Onions
Fairly warm and dry (50–60°F, 60–70 percent relative humidity)	Dry hot peppers Green tomatoes Pumpkins Sweet potatoes Winter squash

the pieces in fruit salad. Or stew 'em, can 'em, or turn 'em into sauces to use on ice cream and other desserts.

• Handle the produce very gently; bruised or dinged fruits and vegetables will quickly rot—and one bad apple (or anything else) will spoil the whole kit and caboodle.

• Never wash your produce before storing it in a root cellar because that can shorten its storage life dramatically.

PACK 'EM UP. Wrap each fruit or vegetable individually in newspaper or brown paper. Then carefully place each piece into a wooden box. To be extra safe, pack in dried leaves or crumpled newspaper between each layer of produce.

UNDER THE EAVES

The good thing about living in a house with an attic is that you have a great place to store things like a spare cot or two, the Christmas decorations, and all of those out-of-season clothes. Unfortunately, this wealth of storage space can quickly spiral out of control, becoming the final resting place for old grammar-school textbooks, board games with missing pieces, and table tennis sets with only one paddle. If that's happened at your house, then it's time to reclaim the space in those upper reaches.

In This Section:
✔ Seasonal decorations
✔ Off-season clothes
✔ Mementos

SORT

If your attic is like most, it's two storage spaces in one: It's the place where you stash seasonal things that you pull out every year. And it's also a three-dimensional scrapbook that holds generations' worth of cherished possessions. So be prepared for some powerful emotions to surface as you make your trip down memory lane. Take time to savor them—but don't let them stop you from getting the job done.

READY, SET, GO! Prepare for your attic sorting spree the same way you did in the basement: Gather up some trash bags and boxes, then section off the space into different areas labeled Trash, Keep Here, Take Elsewhere, and Donate or Sell. Either lay down old sheets or other fabric to create the zones, or simply make a sign to mark each spot.

NOW SEE HERE. Start by examining furniture and other large stuff that you can plainly see because it's not in boxes. First of all, ask yourself why it's there. Is it a set of lawn chairs or a croquet set that you use every summer? Haul 'em to the Keep Here zone. Or maybe it's your son's old high chair that you kept so you could pass it on to his baby—but the baby's mother got a brand-new one as a shower gift (and anyway, your grandson is now six years old). Put it in the Donate or Sell section. A balding artificial Christmas tree? Trash it. A beautiful cradle that's rocked six generations of family babies to sleep? Take it down to your living room and put it on display! I could go on and on, but you get the idea.

WHEEL OF FORTUNE. Got an old bicycle wheel lurking about in your attic? If so, use it to make your kids or grandkids a safe version of "lawn darts." (For my money, the commercial version deserves an award as the most dangerous toy of the century.)

PACK RAT ALERT!

Problem: You're hanging on to empty boxes that television sets, computers, and other electronics and small appliances came in because they might come in handy someday.

Solution: Well, they just might. But then again, they might not. Here's my rule of thumb: Save a box for about a month, just in case the product needs to be returned. After that, if you can't reuse the box, put it into the recycling bin. The exception would be if you were planning to move within the next couple of years. In that case, hang on to those boxes and all of the original packing material. The reason? When your fragile gear is cushioned the same way it was when it left the factory, it stands a much better chance of arriving safely at your new home.

Here's all you need to do in three easy steps:

1. Buy some dried corncobs at a farm-supply store, and some long feathers at a craft shop.

2. Poke holes in one end of each cob, then squirt a drop or two of glue into each hole, and shove in a feather.

3. Set the wheel on the ground and toss the feathered cobs at it from about 25 feet away. The players get points depending on what spokes the cobs landed between. (You can also play flying cobs using an old hula hoop or garbage can lid as the target.)

GO FOR IT, BABY! Even when you no longer need baby gear for its original purpose, it can still give you years of useful service. Consider these possible career changes:

• Baby bathtub. Fill it up with your favorite potion when you're treating athlete's foot, or maybe just soaking your dog-tired dogs.

• Baby gate (the kind made with plastic mesh). Take it to the bathroom or laundry room, and use it as a sweater dryer. Just lay the gate across a bathtub or laundry sink, and spread your fine washables on top of it.

• Baby toys, like rattles and teething rings. Give them to a parrot. The big baby will shake, rattle, and gnaw on those playthings for hours on end. (If you don't know any parrots personally, give the toys to a parrot rescue group or a veterinarian who treats birds.)

• Bassinet. Simply give it a new career as a laundry basket.

OUT OF THE BOX

Got an old wooden baby gate gathering dust in your attic? Turn it into a wall rack in the kitchen, entryway, or anyplace else you could use extra storage space. Paint the gate if you'd like, and attach a 1-inch-thick piece of wood to the back of each corner so the rack will stand out from the wall—thereby giving you enough depth to accommodate S-hooks. Fasten the whole thing to the wall by driving screws through the corners. Then add hooks, and hang up your gear.

- Playpen. Put it into service as a hamper at the bottom of your laundry chute.

TIME FOR TEA. Your child-size table and chairs saw a *lot* of tea parties in their day, but now that munchkin furniture is just sitting in the attic collecting dust. Well, it doesn't have to. For instance, it would make a perfect setting for displaying a grown-up's collection of teddy bears, dolls, or miniature china (or even all of the above).

MORE TIME FOR TEA. Not a collector? Then you could borrow this clever idea from a friend of mine who lives in a small apartment. She rechristened her old childhood tea table as a coffee table, and she uses the chairs to hold plants, books, and an eye-catching piece of folk-art sculpture.

WELCOME WAGON. Is the little red (or maybe wood-framed) wagon that you loved as a kid still lurking in your attic? Then why not give it a new career in the decorative storage business? You could use it to hold towels in a bathroom, magazines or CDs in the living room, or extra pillows in a bedroom.

WORKING WAGONS. If a wagon doesn't suit your taste in home decor, give that wheeled wonder a less visible job: Load it up with rags, sponges, sprays, and powders, and stash it in your broom closet. Then on cleaning day, instead of carrying all your gear

Ask Jerry

Q. *I've got a collection of old trunks and suitcases in my attic that I'd like to use for storage elsewhere in the house. Problem is, they smell musty inside. Can I salvage them?*

A. You sure can. Make 'em smell sweet again by putting half a dozen charcoal briquettes inside each case, and closing them up. (Put the briquettes on sheets of paper or plastic to keep the black powder from rubbing off onto the lining.) Then every few days, take out the charcoal and replace it with a new supply. Repeat the procedure until your vintage holdalls smell as clean and fresh as daisies. The deodorizing process could take anywhere from a couple of days to several weeks. Just remember to use plain, old-fashioned charcoal and not the kind that's been doused with lighter fluid.

from room to room, just roll it merrily along behind you.

BATTER UP! Even if your Little Leaguers have gone on to the Majors (or to nonsporting careers), there's good reason to keep at least one baseball bat that you may find in your attic: It makes a great defensive weapon against burglars and other invading bad guys. You need to wield it the right way, though. My friends on the force tell me that when someone is attacking you, you should not try to club the villain over the head, because his instinctive response will be to reach up with his hand and stop the bat in midair. Instead, swing your big stick as hard as you can in an upward motion. This will take him by surprise, and you'll stand a better chance of landing a stunning blow.

MAKING SPACE

It's not easy parting with your family's keepsakes. But if the trophies, uniforms, posters—you name it—are on the brink of taking over your attic, do yourself a favor: Take photographs of all those treasures and save them in albums marked "Athletic Endeavors," "High School Days," or whatever. The photos will take up a lot less room than the items themselves, and they'll give you almost as much pleasure as the genuine articles. To save even more space, use a digital camera, and either keep the shots on your computer's hard drive, or burn them to a disc.

USEFUL TREASURES. Some of the most useful—and decorative—storage containers were never designed for household storage at all. Just about every attic has at least a few of them, including vintage hatboxes, cigar boxes, military footlockers, or doll-size (not dollhouse) dressers and cupboards. Just take 'em downstairs and use 'em to corral out-of-season clothes, cosmetics, office supplies, magazines, or your TV remotes.

GO TO THE HEAD OF THE BED. How would you like to have a one-of-a-kind headboard for your bed? Chances are you can find a family heirloom (or an old flea market find) in your attic that's just the ticket. The way to transform it into part of the furniture depends on what it's made of. Here are your two options:

1. An old softie, like a hooked rug, tapestry, patchwork quilt, or vintage tablecloth: Stitch the top and bottom of a 2-inch-wide strip of muslin to the back of the fabric, along the top edge, leaving the ends open. If the piece is a valuable textile, make sure the stitches catch only the back of the material and don't show in the front. (Unless you're skilled at hand sewing, have a pro tackle this job.) Then push a curtain rod through the sleeve, and fasten it to the wall with curtain brackets.

2. More substantial stuff, like a decorative folding screen, doors from an antique cabinet, or fancy shutters: Simply bolt or screw the piece to the wall at the head of your bed—just be sure to use the proper hardware to support the weight of the item.

No law says that crystal decanters have to hold just liquor. If you've got some decanters hidden away in your attic, unpack them and take them downstairs. They'll make beautiful containers for mouthwash, bath oil, or cosmetic lotions in the bathroom or on your bedroom dressing table. (Just don't use them in a bathroom that you share with small children!)

THE HEAT OF THE MOMENT. Although the attic is a great place to store gear that you don't need to keep close at hand, remember that not everything can withstand an extended stay in temperatures that can reach as high as 150°F in the summer. If your attic is not temperature-controlled and you've stashed anything delicate or fragile up there, take it elsewhere—and do it *now*! The attic no-no list includes:

• Audiotapes and videotapes

• Candles or anything else that's made of wax

• Computer disks

- Cosmetics (including Halloween or theatrical makeup)

- Fireworks, firecrackers, or sparklers

- Flammable substances of any kind

- Food, including any in cans or jars

- Musical instruments

- Original artwork

- Photographs and photo albums

- Vinyl records and CDs

- Wool clothing

HARDIER STOCK. On the other hand, any of these things will be happy as clams up in the rafters, so feel free to put these in your Keep Here section: baby gear, books, camping gear (except for gas camp stoves and lanterns), Christmas decorations and gift wrap, financial records and other papers, furniture, memorabilia, outdoor furniture, outgrown toys, out-of-season clothes (except for wool), and sports equipment.

COME AND GET IT! If you have adult children who've left home, they could help you cut attic clutter fast. Just call 'em and tell them to come get the stuff they left behind when they flew the coop. Tell them if they don't reclaim their belongings by a certain date, you'll give them away or sell them at your next garage sale.

PACK RAT ALERT!

Problem: You used to buy panty hose that came in big plastic eggs, and you kept every one of them because you knew they'd come in handy one day.

Solution: Haul those things out of the attic, give them a good washing, and decorate them with paint, paper, fabric, or spangles. Then fill them with jelly beans, marshmallow bunnies, and other tiny treasures, and tuck them into Easter baskets. Or use them as clever small-gift boxes any time of the year. (No law says that eggs are *only* for Easter.)

These sturdy plastic shells can also help keep deer, groundhogs, and rabbits away from your plants. Just sink the open halves up to their rims in the soil, and fill with a mix of 1 part bloodmeal to 2 parts water, stopping about an inch from the top.

USE THE GOOD STUFF. If you stashed your grandma's heirloom china in the attic to keep it safe from your small children—who are now grown and gone—unpack it and start using it. After all, that's what it was made for. And you're old enough and careful enough to be trusted with it. Plus, you deserve the pleasure of the memories it will bring back.

OR MAYBE LOSE THE GOOD STUFF. On the other hand, maybe you never liked Grandma's china, and you only used your rambunctious kids as an excuse to get it out of the way. In that case, get rid of it. One of your adult offspring or another member of the clan might love to have it. If not, donate it to a thrift shop, or sell it on the Internet or through an antiques dealer who specializes in fine china.

THE ART OF MEMORY. When you start opening boxes in your attic, I guarantee that you'll find a whole lot of stuff that brings back floods of happy memories but isn't, well, terribly useful. This might sound strange in a book about de-cluttering, but don't be too quick to toss it out or even box it up again—at least not all of it. Instead, consider framing some of those mementos and using them to give a creative, personal touch to the rooms downstairs. To kick-start your imagination, here are dozens of my favorite hang-ups:

✔ Antique buttons

✔ Autograph collections

✔ Awards, certificates, and diplomas

✔ Baseball cards

MAKING SPACE

Are you hanging on to a box or two of retired ashtrays (maybe they're old wedding presents or cheap vacation souvenirs)? If so, free up some space in the attic by turning them into storage containers. They're perfect for holding small office supplies like paper clips, pushpins, tubes of glue, and rolls of tape. Or put them on the shelves of your medicine cabinet, and fill 'em up with pill bottles, tubes of antiseptic ointment, small quantities of bandages, and other tiny, health-giving odds and ends.

- ✔ Coin collections
- ✔ Collages made from vacation souvenirs
- ✔ Dust jackets from favorite books
- ✔ Foreign currency from your travels
- ✔ Front pages of newspapers from your kids' birthdays
- ✔ Letters from loved ones or VIPs
- ✔ Lock of hair from each of your kids' first haircuts
- ✔ Maps and nautical charts
- ✔ Matchbook covers
- ✔ Medals
- ✔ Menus from favorite restaurants or special occasions
- ✔ Needlepoint or cross-stitch creations
- ✔ Newspaper clippings featuring family or friends
- ✔ Old-time newspaper and magazine ads
- ✔ Political campaign buttons
- ✔ Postage stamps
- ✔ Records and album covers
- ✔ Ribbons that you or your pets have won
- ✔ School sports jerseys (yours or your kids')
- ✔ Stub from your first paycheck
- ✔ Ticket stubs from a memorable theatrical or sporting event
- ✔ Your mortgage (after it's paid, of course!)

OUT OF THE BOX

Is your grandpa's old collection of baseball memorabilia taking up half your attic, but you can't bring yourself to part with it? Well, get those boxes opened up and take a look at what's inside. Then go ahead and donate the collection to a sports museum or hall of fame. It will be easier to say good-bye to your grandpa's treasures if you know that generations of future baseball fans will be able to enjoy them. But do yourself a favor: Before you hand over the boxes to a local organization, have the contents appraised by a reputable dealer. There may be some things that the National Baseball Hall of Fame in Cooperstown would love to have—or that you might want to sell at auction or on eBay®.

ALL BOOKED UP. If you've got boxes and boxes of books piled up in your attic, here's good news and bad news: The good news is that they'll be fine for a few months, and maybe even a few years as long as the room is dry. The bad news is that too much paper of any kind creates a major fire hazard. Then, of course, there's the fact that if they're just sitting there, where you can't even see them—much less read them—what good are they? So go through those boxes and divide the volumes into these three categories:

1. Shelve 'em. It might remind you that you've been wanting to reread your old favorites. You'll also discover books that you haven't read yet—and forgot that you even owned! Besides, nothing adds pizzazz to a room like well-stocked bookshelves. (Why do you think all those interior decorators buy 'em by the yard for their nonreading clients?) What's more, book-filled shelves provide some of the best insulation you can find anywhere. On exterior walls, they help keep heat in and cold out. On inside walls, they muffle sound between one room and the next. Either way, that's a first-class bargain in my book!

OUT OF THE BOX

If you have any books that you even suspect may be valuable (like first-edition novels by Ernest Hemingway, memoirs by early western pioneers, or bestsellers that have been autographed by the authors), have them appraised by a reputable book dealer before you give them away or sell them for peanuts at a yard sale. They may be worth next to nothing, but on the other hand, they could very well help to fund your early retirement!

2. Give 'em away. Hospitals, nursing homes, senior centers, charity tag sales, thrift shops, and literacy programs all welcome donations of good books (and recent magazines, too).

3. Sell 'em. Your options include setting them out on a table at your next yard sale, taking them to a bookstore that buys used books, or selling them over the Internet.

ORGANIZE

Just think about this: Your attic occupies as much space as the entire floor below it. That means it's at high risk for turning into a big, chaotic mess again. So before you start restashing your stuff, take the time to organize your attic space in a way that's going to work best for you and your family.

MAKE A MAP. Step one in your attic-organizing plan is to measure the area and draw a map to scale. Include the ceiling height in various parts, especially in any small nooks or places that have strange angles. This may sound like unnecessary work, but believe me, it'll allow you to take full advantage of every last bit of space.

CREATE ZONES. While you still have everything spread out for your photo shoot (see Making Space at right), group the items into categories. Then look at your map and figure out the best place to put each one, based on how much of it there is, whether it's freestanding or boxed up, and how often you need to get at it. Of course, you'll want to store the things you need most often, like sports equipment that you use throughout the year, in the most accessible places. Items that you need to get at only once a year, like holiday decorations or the water skis you take on your summer vacation, can be stored a little more out of the way. Reserve the most remote spots for old tax files and similar papers that you (hopefully!) won't have to look at for years. Then step back and take a good look at your newly organized, easy-to-navigate attic plan. You're on your way!

MAKING SPACE

Once you've gotten rid of all the attic stuff that you've decided to pitch, donate, sell, or use elsewhere, spread out all the keepers and photograph them. This way, you'll have a record if you ever need to file an insurance claim. Keep the photos in your safe-deposit box, along with any receipts and relevant information such as model and serial numbers, dates of purchase, and—in the case of antiques—appraisal reports.

CLUTTER BUSTER PRO

"Attics can be heartwarming treasure houses or nightmarish repositories," says Taffy Cannon, a professional organizer and owner of Blue Skies Clutter Control in Carlsbad, California. Her advice is to "tackle the attic when it isn't too hot or too cold, and allow yourself plenty of time." Her general guidelines for successful attic de-cluttering include:

☛ If something can be dealt with quickly, do it first. Clearing extra space right away is psychologically liberating and provides more room for you to maneuver and organize.

☛ Label, label, label! Every box should be labeled on top and on at least two adjacent sides in thick black marker. Include the date and be specific in your description of the items, such as Christmas Wreaths, not Holiday Stuff. For plastic storage bins, use 3- by 4-inch or larger labels from an office-supply store. Check the labels after a few days to make sure they're sticking properly in your climate conditions; if they're curling or falling off, you'll need to tape them down or replace them.

☛ Use good lighting. If there's one naked bulb with a pull cord, make sure it's bright enough to see everything clearly. If it isn't, bring up a movable lamp that's connected downstairs via extension cords. While you're at it, bring up a folding chair or stool, so you're more comfortable while you're working. And consider leaving a lamp and chair in the attic if there's enough room.

☛ When you come upon old business or financial records, apply the same record-keeping test you use for papers in your home office (see "The Paper Chase" on page 151). As you find materials that are past their need-to-keep dates, take them downstairs to be shredded.

☛ Inexpensive shelving units offer easy access to materials you're likely to need or want more often, such as out-of-season clothing, holiday decorations, and luggage. Try not to pile storage boxes in tall, inaccessible stacks, but if you must, then be sure to leave aisles that are wide enough so you can unstack the cartons easily.

- ☛ Attic temperature extremes can adversely affect some items, so be careful what you store in uninsulated areas.

- ☛ If creatures have been at something, get rid of it.

- ☛ Don't trust old labels, particularly if someone else did the labeling. Look inside every box to make sure that it's what it claims to be and is worth keeping. Add a new label if necessary, including the current date.

- ☛ Don't forget to check the back corners. That's where you'll find the boxes that have made three moves without being opened, the miscellany from Great Aunt Edna's place, and the stuff that was there when you moved in.

- ☛ If an object is bulky, deteriorating, or only of sentimental value, consider photographing it and then either donating or discarding it. Maybe a children's museum would like that giant ship model, or the high school drama club could use the vintage clothing.

- ☛ If you come across something you want to spend some time with—old photo albums or yearbooks, baby's first toys, Uncle Edgar's belt buckle collection—set it aside to take downstairs and look at later. Consider displaying part of a collection in your main living area.

- ☛ Avoid hurt feelings by consulting with relatives before discarding things that might be considered family heirlooms.

- ☛ Be sure to allow more time than you think you'll need. Attics are filled with lots of distractions, many of which are quite pleasurable. Don't let yourself get sidetracked too easily, but do take enough time to appreciate the memories you'll rekindle.

LOOK OUT BELOW. Unless your attic floor is finished, remember that it's actually the ceiling of the rooms down below. So before you tuck heavy furniture or boxes of books up there, lay sheets of 1-inch (or thicker) plywood or particleboard across the ceiling joists, and nail them in place. If you're covering a large area, stagger the seams to get a secure, stable surface. Remember that if your treasures come crashing through, it'll cause you a real headache—in more ways than one!

SHED A LITTLE LIGHT ON THE SUBJECT. Any attic needs to have enough light so that you can see well. Here are three simple ways to illuminate the scene without having to call an electrician to wire the space for electricity:

MAKING SPACE If the walls of your attic are unfinished, take advantage of the exposed studs by turning them into a great organizing opportunity. Build small shelves in the spaces between the uprights using pieces of scrap wood, and store whatever fits on the 6-inch-deep surfaces.

1. Get a few flashlights or battery-powered lanterns that are equipped with rings for hanging. Then screw cup hooks into the rafters, spaced throughout the attic. When you need light in a particular area, just hang the flashlight or lantern from the nearest hook.

2. Install battery-operated closet lights throughout the attic. You can buy these dandy devices for next to nothing at hardware stores and supermarkets.

3. Buy some rechargeable, cordless LED lights (available at hardware stores and on the Internet). They come in both screw-mount and hanging versions. Just beware: These trendy things are a lot more expensive than the first two options!

HARD HAT AREA. Is there a part of your attic where the ceiling is too low for you to stand up to your full height? If so, then do your head a favor and get a hard hat. If that sounds extreme, bear in mind that if you should forget you're in tight quarters and stand up too quickly, the results could range from a big bump to a nasty cut from an exposed roofing nail. (I've learned this the hard way, folks!) That's why I keep an old yellow construction hard hat hanging on a nail right inside the entrance to my attic. If you can't find one at a yard sale or flea market, and don't want to buy a new one, improvise. A souvenir batting helmet, a bicycle helmet, or even a cooking pot will work well. Just put it on whenever you enter your attic, and your head will thank you time and time again.

LOOK UP. Exposed ceiling joists may not be attractive, but they sure are useful. If you have enough headroom, screw hooks into the joists, and hang sturdy bars or poles from the hooks. Bingo—you've got instant rods for your out-of-season clothes!

THINK BEFORE YOU RENOVATE.

It may seem like a great idea to convert your attic to extra living space or to a more "finished" storage area. Well, before you rush off to your local lumberyard for supplies, consult with the folks at city hall about your town's building codes. If you try to cut corners, you could wind up compromising the safety and structural soundness of your home, sweet home. Here are some typical requirements the powers that be just might insist on:

✔ A window you can climb out of

✔ A minimum ceiling height (usually at least 7 ½ feet)

✔ Easy up-and-down access (crucial in case of a fire)

✔ Minimum stair height and tread width

✔ Sufficient ventilation

✔ Minimum wall thickness

Lots of people use old kitchen cabinets to organize the storage space in their basement. Well, guess what? They work just as well in the attic—even better, in fact, because up there you don't have to worry about dampness penetrating the wood or particleboard. If a kitchen-remodeling job is not on your agenda, look for used cabinets in junk shops and stores that sell salvaged building supplies, like Habitat for Humanity's Re-Stores. To find out if there's one near you, check out the group's Web site at www.habitat.org.

STORE

Once you've got your attic zoning strategy all worked out, then it's time to tuck each category of stuff into the right spots and—just as important—in the right way.

THE LAYERED LOOK. You know those traditional Russian dolls that open up to reveal another doll and then another and yet another inside? Use this same principle when storing things in your attic. For instance, your mittens and scarves will fit nicely inside your winter boots, and they in turn will snuggle right into an empty suitcase. Just tape a label on the outside of the largest package to help you remember what's stored within.

DON'T STUFF YOUR STUFF. If you follow the system of storing "like with like" items, remember that it's perfectly okay to have a half-empty container. In other words, don't feel that you need to cram every bin full to make efficient use of your space. A partially empty container will fill up eventually. And isn't it good to know that when the time comes to put something else away, it has a home to go to?

STACK WITH CARE. If you possibly can, store your boxes on shelves (freestanding wire versions are perfect for attics because they allow air to circulate around the cartons). But if you absolutely must stack all or some of your boxes, be sure to do it right. Either put boxes of similar size in one stack, so they won't wobble, or stack them pyramid style with the larger, heavier boxes on the bottom and the smaller, lighter ones on top.

WEIGHTY MATTERS. For the sake of stability, always put the heaviest

> ## MAKING
> ### S P A C E
>
>
> Do you have an old net hammock stashed away somewhere? If so, then don't let it go to waste. Hang the hammock from the ceiling in your attic, and use it to store lightweight, nonbreakable stuff like sleeping bags, pillows, and out-of-season clothes.

boxes on the lowest shelves, or on the bottom of a stack. Use the middle area for slightly lighter boxes, and place the featherweight champs on top.

BEWARE OF CARDBOARD. Although cardboard boxes won't pick up dampness in your attic as they will in your basement, the contents could be harmed, or even destroyed, if your roof should spring a leak. But even if your attic is bone-dry, trouble lurks in the cardboard itself. You see, the acid it contains will damage anything that's made of fabric, paper, or leather. And believe it or not, it can even discolor plastic. A friend of mine learned this the hard way when she stored a food processor in its original cardboard box for about a year after she made a temporary move. When she got to her permanent quarters and opened the box, she found that the appliance's white casing had turned an ugly shade of yellow.

YOUR PROTECTION STRATEGY.
My motto is "If an object is worth keeping, it's worth protecting." So whenever you store anything that's made of fabric, leather, or paper—in your attic or anyplace else—put it in an acid-free archival box. Or wrap the item in acid-free tissue paper, and tuck it into a container that's made of plastic, wood, or metal. Whatever you do, don't use newspaper, packing paper, or regular tissue paper because they also contain acid that will

COLLECTOR ALERT!

Problem: You need to store a baby's christening dress.

Solution: Before you put it (or anything else made of delicate white fabric) into long-term storage, give it extra-special treatment. Carefully fold white, acid-free tissue paper around the little garment to protect it from dust and dirt, and tuck in a lavender sachet to repel moths. Then wrap dark blue tissue paper—again, acid-free—around the package to block out light, which can turn the fabric yellow. Keep your treasure in a cedar-lined chest, or in a box that's specially designed for heirloom storage. You can find acid-free paper and archival boxes at art-supply stores and in catalogs that specialize in storage products.

damage your treasures. Likewise, avoid plastic bags or wrappings, which can trap moisture inside, causing mildew to form.

PROTECTING PLASTIC. If the items you want to store are made of plastic, like small appliances, vintage toys, or Christmas decorations, then it's fine to wrap them in plastic. Depending on how fragile the objects are, you can use bubble wrap, foam packing peanuts, or even plastic bags. And as long as the entire surface is covered, it's safe to store them in a regular cardboard box.

ASK THE EXPERTS. If you have original historic documents or other important, but fragile, pieces of history, consult with professional conservators about how you should store them. An antiques dealer or someone on staff at your local museum should be able to point you in the right direction.

DO NOT LAMINATE. You may think you're doing your loved ones a favor by having a special piece of paper laminated—maybe the front page of the newspaper from the day they were born. But according to the folks in charge of preserving documents at the Library of Congress, laminating is a big-time no-no because it damages the paper. Instead, they say that if you want to display the paper, you should make a photocopy, and store the original in a flat, custom-size box (available in stores and on Web sites that carry archival supplies). Keep the box in a place where it's safe from heat, moisture, pollutants, dust, and pests.

Ask Jerry

Q. *I picked up some old wooden trunks at a local flea market, thinking they'd be perfect to use for storing out-of-season clothes in my attic. Unfortunately, the trunks still have that awful mothball odor that the previous owner apparently loved. Is there any way to get rid of the smell?*

A. There sure is! Just sand the inside of each trunk, and then coat it with polyurethane. Your trunks will smell as fresh as daisies, and you can protect your clothes with herbal moth repellents, which have a much more pleasant scent than those stinky mothballs.

ONE ROOM'S CLUTTER IS ANOTHER ROOM'S STORAGE AID. I said back in Chapter One that you should never store your clothes on wire hangers. But they're terrific for hanging other things that you store in your attic. Just bend each hanger's wire into a sturdy hook, and use it for items like boots, plastic snow saucers, backpacks, sleeping bags, or just about anything else that's light enough to hang from the walls or rafters.

LABELING 101. A box without a label is a clutter nightmare come true—especially when it's at the bottom of a tall stack of other boxes. So save yourself a lot of aggravation and grief by following these simple guidelines:

- As soon as you pack a box, label it in lettering that's big enough to see from across the room.

- Mark the top and at least two sides—and preferably all four.

- For cardboard boxes, use a thick, black, permanent marker.

MAKING SPACE

If you're saving a chest of drawers, an armoire, or other piece of furniture for future generations, please don't let it sit up in the attic empty! Take advantage of all that bonus storage space by filling it with out-of-season clothes, off-duty Christmas decorations, linens, or whatever else will fit neatly inside.

- For any other kind of container, use either self-stick labels that measure at least 3 by 4 inches, or pieces of white paper or index cards that are the same size.

- If you go with paper or cards, attach the labels to the containers using heavy-duty strapping tape (the kind that has visible fibers running through it) so that they don't come off.

- Whatever you do, don't use plain old cellophane tape. In a hot attic (even one that has a fan), the tape will quickly come unstuck and the label will fall off—and you'll be right back where you started, which is confused!

CHAPTER EIGHT

THE GARAGE AND SHED

I n many homes, garages and sheds are the places to stash things that you use only once in a blue moon or that you no longer want, but don't have time to cart to the thrift store or local dump. Then there's all the stuff that you just *know* will come in handy someday. If that description sounds familiar, take heart: You can clear out the clutter and reclaim that territory for its rightful inhabitants—like your car, trash cans, and lawn mower—and we'll show you how.

AUTO MOTIVES

Does your car have to "camp out" in the driveway or on the street because your garage is filled with everything from off-duty lawn furniture to broken toaster ovens? If so, you're not alone: According to a recent edition of *The Old Farmer's Almanac*, 75 percent of home owners in Southern California cannot park their car(s) in the garage because it's too crammed with stuff. Well, stop running with the crowd—instead, shout "SOS!" and get to work.

> **In This Section:**
> ✔ Hazardous materials
> ✔ Toys and sports equipment
> ✔ Your vehicles

SORT

If you can't even remember the last time Old Betsy saw the inside of your garage, digging through the mountain of stuff may be a long, dirty job. But it's got to be done, so put on some grubby old clothes, grit your teeth, and dive right in.

WHY BOTHER? It's a fact: In any part of the country, a vehicle that's kept indoors will stay clean longer than one that spends its nonworking time in the driveway or on the street—thereby cutting back on the time, money, and effort you'll spend on car washing. And if you live in a cold-weather climate, keeping your buggy indoors is also a super-simple way to save gas (and, therefore, money at the pump). How is that so? Well, during the first 5 miles of driving, a car that's spent the night in a warm, cozy garage burns fuel twice as efficiently as one that's been left out in the cold. So even if you don't go whole hog with your garage de-cluttering mission, at least clear enough room to tuck your wheels into a snug "bed" at night.

TWO FOR THE SHOW. You can approach your garage sorting in one of two ways, depending on how big the space is, how much clutter it contains, how much time you have to spend on the chore, and how quickly you want—or need—to clear out the space. Here are your choices:

MAKING SPACE Before you launch your garage-sorting mission, take some time to decide how you want to use the space once it's free and clear of junk. Do you simply want to make room for your car(s) and some auto-related gear? Do you need an area where you can install a workshop and/or major storage units? Or do you have your heart set on turning your garage into a gym, rec room, or even guest quarters? Your answer will help determine how ruthless you need to be in getting rid of unnecessary stuff. It should also give you the incentive to get started *now* and keep at it until the job is done.

1. A one-shot deal. This is the way to go if you simply can't stand that jumbled mess for another minute, or you know that if you don't clear it out now, you never will. Or maybe you're about to put your house on the market, and you had to make the garage presentable *yesterday*.

2. One step at a time. If you lack the time, the patience, or the need to conquer the chaos in one fell swoop, tackle one piece of the "pie" at a

time. Start with whatever pile of stuff is most annoying, or must be cleared out for a particular reason (maybe the mound contains the tent posts that vanished last fall, and your Cub Scout is going camping this weekend). Make a de-cluttering date with yourself for one or two weekends each month—and then *keep* that date no matter what.

ON YOUR MARK… My advice is to opt for the single-shot approach if that's at all possible. For one thing, it's easier to cart your castoffs to the dump or thrift shop all at once, rather than making a trip here and a trip there. Plus, if you let the project drag on, there's a good chance that even more clutter will sneak in behind your back, and you might never have the neat, clean, car-worthy garage of your dreams. The secret to waging a nonstop de-cluttering mission without losing your mind—or giving up halfway through—lies in preparation. These simple guidelines will make a world of difference:

This may not seem important, but be sure to watch the weather report before cleaning out your garage. Choose a day or weekend when there's no rain in the forecast and the temperature is going to be mild. Remember that unlike sorting the contents of your bedroom or kitchen, de-cluttering the garage is an indoor/outdoor affair. If you're too hot, too cold, or sopping wet, you're not likely to get much work done.

• Let your fingers do some walking. If you have curbside trash pickup, call the sanitation department and find out what type of stuff the trucks will take and what form they'll take it in. If everything has to fit inside your rolling trash can, you want to know that *before* you start piling decrepit lawn chairs and old window screens at the end of your driveway. Likewise, make sure you know what your town dump will and will not accept and what its business hours are. You don't want to drive all the way out there with a truck full of stuff, only to discover that the gates are locked.

• Recruit help. The job will go faster and be a lot more pleasant if you have friends to share the load. To maximize efficiency, have one of your willing workers drive your unwanted belongings to the dump or thrift store while you keep sorting. That way, you can't renege on your decision to get rid of that rowing machine you haven't used in five years!

GET SET... Before your troops arrive on D-day, assemble all the gear you'll need for the job, including a broom, dustpan, and wet/dry vac, as well as trash bags, recycling bins, and (of course) plenty of boxes. Label these Trash, Keep Here, Take Elsewhere, and Donate or Sell. Of course, many of the items in your garage will be too big to fit in the boxes. So, in addition to labeling your containers, divide your driveway and/or lawn into different zones, allot a section to each of the above categories, and identify each one with a clearly marked sign.

> ## MAKING SPACE
>
> If you plan to get rid of things that are too big to fit into your or a helper's vehicle, or you have so many boxes that you'd have to make multiple trips to the thrift shop or dump, do yourself and your work crew a favor: Rent a truck and have it parked at the curb, rarin' to go on sorting day. The time it saves you (not to mention wear and tear on the family car) will be well worth the money it costs.

GO! Start your garage-clearing session by rounding up any and all hazardous materials. Get rid of oily or greasy rags, dried-up paint, stacks of newspapers and magazines, dead batteries, and bottles with thin layers of windshield wiper fluid or motor oil in the bottom. Then gather up any still-usable containers of paint, motor oil, gasoline, and solvents of any kind. Ideally, these substances belong in a shed or workshop that's detached from your house and away from any sources of heat (like your car). If you must keep them in the garage, they should be locked up in a metal storage unit.

OUST THE ANTIFREEZE. If you have pets and you're still using a traditional brand of antifreeze, do them and yourself a big favor: Get rid of that stuff *now*. Dogs and cats find the sweet-smelling liquid irresistible, but it's extremely toxic. Even a single slurp from a spill can be enough to cause fatal results. Fortunately, there are "pet-safe" brands available that are just as effective in your car, and they cost only about a dollar more per gallon than the conventional products. Just one word of caution: Although these new brands are not deadly poisons, you should still keep them well beyond the reach of pets and small children. And for advice on disposing of antifreeze and other hazardous substances, see "Call Before You Toss" on page 244.

BEWARE OF OTHER FLUIDS, TOO. Although antifreeze is the most common source of ethylene glycol poisoning in pets, you may have other products in your garage that contain this nasty chemical. It's also found in heat-exchange fluids (sometimes used in solar collectors) and in some brake and transmissions fluids. The bottom line: Keep all chemicals under lock and key, and clean up any spills *instantly*.

GIVE OLD BATTERIES THE BOOT. One garage throwaway that's a no-brainer (at least it should be!) is dead car batteries. Not only will leaking battery acid eat through just about anything it comes in contact with, but the things can also explode—and that would leave you with a *real* mess on your hands. Check with your mechanic or auto parts store for the best way to dispose of over-the-hill batteries.

ANSWER THESE. As you pull each of the objects out of your cluttered garage, take a good look at them with the old eagle

PACK RAT ALERT!

Problem: You change your car's oil yourself, but you hang on to the old oil because you don't know how to get rid of it safely (and legally).

Solution: If your community collects hazardous waste materials, set the jug out on the appointed day. (A quick call to city hall should give you all of the necessary details.) Otherwise, take the used oil to the closest collection site. Most service stations, auto repair shops, and auto parts stores will accept and recycle used motor oil, whether you bought it there or not.

eye and ask yourself the following questions:

- When was the last time you used it? The rule of thumb is that if you haven't used something in a year, you should get rid of it. But don't be too quick to pull the trigger. If you bought a pair of roller blades a year or two ago and haven't put them on even once, they're obvious candidates for the Donate or Sell zone. On the other hand, if the Christmas decorations stayed in their designated storage area for the past couple of years because you spent the holidays with your daughter in Arizona—but she'll be joining you at home this year—hang on to them.

- Does it work? If the answer is no, either send it packing or make arrangements to have it repaired—*now*.

- Do you still need it? Are you hanging on to a tire pump for a bicycle you no longer own? Toss it into the Donate or Sell zone.

- Does it belong here? Unless you have a climate-controlled garage, gather up anything that could be damaged by dampness or extreme temperature fluctuations. This category includes photographs, artwork, valuable furniture, and anything that's made of fabric or paper. (For a more complete list of what not to keep in your garage—or shed—see "Move 'Em Out" on page 249.)

Ask Jerry

Q. *I've got some leftover paint stored in my garage in case I need it for touch-ups. How long can I keep it before it goes bad?*

A. It all depends on the conditions in your garage. If the temperature inside goes below freezing in the winter and/or gets blistering hot in the summer, your paint could become unusable in less than a year. On the other hand, if your garage is well insulated, paint can last a long time. I recently touched up some spots in my house using latex paint that I've had for more than 10 years. I just gave it a good, thorough stirring and it worked as well as it did the day I bought it. Oil-based paint will store equally well, as long as you keep oxygen from reaching it. *Note:* For more about storing and discarding paint, see Chapter Nine.

- Do you have more than you need? If you bought a new croquet set last year, but you're still hanging on to the old one, get it outta there. If it's still in good shape, either give it to a friend or family member who might enjoy it, or move it to the Donate or Sell zone.

- Is it still in good shape? Ratty doormats and split trash containers have obviously outlived their usefulness. Clear them out and replace them with new ones.

SEND INTRUDERS PACKING.

If you have a separate garden shed, but your hedge clippers and wheelbarrow have somehow found their way into the garage, put them back where they belong. (You'll find the whole lowdown on shed de-cluttering beginning on page 305.) And find the proper homes for things like those beach towels still hanging around after last summer's pool party, or that book you took out of the car, but forgot to bring into the house.

THINK BIG. As you're sorting, take care of the biggest things first. Moving out the canoe you haven't used in 10 years or the broken-down motorcycle your son left behind when he went off to college will instantly give you a whole lot more space to work with. Plus, you'll feel as though you're really making progress, and that will spur you on to further action.

EXTERIOR KEEPERS. When you do your garage perimeter check (see the Mess-Maker Alert! above), don't be too quick to move

MESS-MAKER ALERT!

Problem: If you have a detached garage, the outside walls (especially any that are not in plain view) can become prime dumping grounds for everything from tools to pruned-off tree branches.

Solution: Make it a point to include this exterior space in your sorting session. Toss obvious trash into the garbage can or recycling bin, and set everything else in the appropriate zone: Keep Here, Take Elsewhere, or Donate or Sell. And from now on, stroll around the perimeter periodically to make sure clutter isn't creeping back in.

everything away. The outside walls can provide plenty of usable hanging room for weatherproof gear like ladders, hoses, and plastic utility carts.

SORT, DON'T SELL. At least not yet. It may seem like a great idea to hold a garage sale and sorting spree at the same time. After all, what could be more efficient than pulling things out and selling them on the spot? Take it from me, my friends: That's a recipe for failure. You'll be so busy greeting neighbors and haggling over prices that you'll never get the garage cleaned out! For now, just put all your still-good, but unwanted, things in the Donate or Sell zone and deal with them later.

MAKING SPACE

Even though it's all but impossible to sort the contents of your garage and hold a garage sale on the same day, you could still make some cash while you free up space in your car's home. If you have a bicycle, a chest of drawers, or other large item that you want to sell, set it out on the lawn with a for-sale sign and a no-dicker price tag. It's a good bet that some passerby will snatch it up before you close down shop for the day.

DON'T SWEAT THE SMALL STUFF. This is not the time to start sorting nuts, bolts, and nails into individual jars. If you go down that road, you'll never get the garage cleaned out! Instead, whenever you come across small tools and hardware odds and ends, toss them into big, sturdy boxes—either to keep here, or to move to your shed or workshop (even if the workshop is part of your garage). Then make a note to yourself to sort and organize the contents later.

END BACKSEAT CLUTTER. If your family vehicle doesn't have pockets on the back of the driver's and passenger's front seats, you know how the clutter can pile up quickly in the backseat. Corral the chaos with organizers that have pouches to store cups, snacks, small toys, books, and what have you. They easily attach with straps that go around the front seats' headrests and are available in auto parts stores, in catalogs, and on the Internet.

CLUTTER BUSTER PRO

Commuting, carpooling, and running errands can result in a cluttered mess of toys, water bottles, small electronics, clothing, and all kinds of other junk piling up in your vehicle. But here's good news from professional organizer Jacquie Ross, owner of CastAway the Clutter! in Ellicott City, Maryland (www.castawaytheclutter.com). By making just a few simple changes and incorporating a little maintenance into your routine, you can enjoy a clutter-free and organized set of wheels. And that will result in a less stressful—and therefore safer—ride for you and your passengers. Here's the routine Jacquie recommends:

☞ Whip the trunk into shape. Use a sturdy container with a secure lid to store emergency supplies, including a small first-aid kit, maps, window washing fluid, small plastic bags, and an umbrella.

☞ Tote your stuff—easily. Keep one or two collapsible crates in your trunk or cargo area to hold shopping items, library books, and dry cleaning. These handy holders fold flat when not in use, and pop up in just a few seconds when you need 'em.

☞ Secure and organize your important documents. Having your registration and proof-of-insurance documents readily available will save time and embarrassment if you're ever pulled over by the police. Simply pick up a document holder or small wallet to store these crucial pieces of paper, and you'll be able to retrieve them without a hitch.

☞ Be ready for trash. Carry empty grocery bags in your vehicle at all times. Store them in a door or seat pocket, if you have one, and encourage your passengers to take their discards with them every time they leave the vehicle.

☞ Be prepared for those unexpected spills and splatters. Always keep a container of wet wipes in your vehicle, so you can clean up accidents as they happen.

☞ Corral front-seat clutter. Use a front-seat organizer that's designed to store things like CDs, pens, sunglasses, maps, and cell phones so they won't fly off the seat when you hit a bump. You can find them in auto parts stores, in catalogs, and on the Internet.

FOR ROAD WARRIORS. Do you spend a lot of time on the road for work? Are you usually reaching through a pile of stuff on the passenger seat to find that file or folder you need? Then a mobile travel organizer is for you. These handy helpers come in a variety of styles and sizes and can store a laptop computer, paper files, notepads, calculator, and other supplies. Now you can be organized in your office on wheels!

A SPORTING CHANCE. In most homes, the garage tends to be a magnet for sports equipment and outdoor gear of all kinds. So unless your family consists entirely of nonjocks, these two simple tips can make your de-cluttering routine a whole lot easier:

1. Before you start sorting, make a list of all the sports you and your family participate in. And that means *currently*—not things you used to do or would like to do, but somehow haven't gotten around to doing. After all, there's not much sense in hanging on to a pair of ice skates that you haven't put on since your senior year in college, or scuba gear that you bought five years ago but, after a plunge or two, decided it wasn't your "thing."

2. As you sort through the equipment for activities that you and your clan take part in, group it into specific categories. Put the golf clubs, shoes, and balls in one place. Ditto the badminton net, birdies, and rackets. This way, it will be a whole lot easier to organize and store the stuff when you reach that stage of the de-cluttering game.

HAVE A BALL! Your old croquet set seems to have vanished— except for those beautiful wooden croquet balls that you've uncovered in the garage. Well, don't toss 'em out! Instead, drill holes in them and use them as colorful finials on a garden fence. Or, if you're handy with a plane, shave off and sand down one section of each ball to make a smooth bottom, and use it as a sturdy doorstop or paperweight.

CALLING ALL WEEKEND WARRIORS! Or former or would- be weekend warriors. Some of the over-the-hill sports equipment that's cluttering up your garage could make good, sturdy plant stakes for your vegetable garden or flower beds. Any of these winners will keep your floppy flowers or vegetable plants on the up-and-up:

✔ Golf clubs

✔ Hockey sticks (sink the blade end into the soil)

✔ Pool cues

✔ Posts from badminton or volleyball nets

✔ Ski poles

✔ Stakes from a croquet set (for holding up smaller plants)

✔ Walking sticks

THE NET RESULT. If you've got an old, unused badminton net tucked away in the garage, you've got a dandy instant trellis for annual flower vines or up-and-coming vegetables and fruits like cucumbers, peas, and small melons. Just sink a couple of posts in the ground, attach the net, and bingo— your garden just got sporty!

SLIDING RIGHT ALONG. Got an old plastic snow saucer that's taking up space in your garage? Take it out to the shed and use it as a substitute for a wheelbarrow on wet days when the ground is mucky and you've got compost, transplants, or yard debris to move. No matter how heavy the load is, that round-bottomed sled will glide along smoothly over the mud or wet grass, instead of sinking in, as a wheel would do.

You probably don't think of badminton rackets as pest-control tools, but if yours have seen better days and you're facing an invasion of flea beetles, a pair of birdie whackers can rush to your rescue. Just cover the face of each racket with a plastic bag, pull it tight, and fasten it with tape or a twist tie. Coat the plastic with petroleum jelly, or spray it with a commercial stickum like Tanglefoot®, until it's ultragooey. Then hold a racket on each side of a beetle-ridden plant, and gently jiggle the foliage with your knee. The beetles will leap off the leaves and onto your trap. Then all you have to do is pull off the bags and drop them into the trash.

MORE SOPHISTICATED
SUPPORT. I'll admit that although an old badminton net does a fine job of supporting lightweight vines, it's not the best-looking trellis that ever came down the pike. But it's a good bet that there's other would-be trash in your garage that will hold up your vining plants and add a decorative touch to your yard or garden. Consider these possibilities:

- Iron garden gates

- Iron window bars

- Multipaned window frames (minus the glass, of course!)

- Old doors

- Old wooden ladders

- Orphaned brass or iron headboards or footboards

- Shutters

EVERYBODY INTO THE POOL!
Your kids long ago outgrew their little wading pool. Or you've just installed a backyard swimming pool, so you might as well toss that shallow plastic relic, right? Wrong! Set it next to the big pool, and encourage grown-ups and kids alike to dunk their feet in it to leave the dirt and grass behind before they dive into the refreshing (and clean) water.

PACK RAT ALERT!

Problem: A big old pile of rusty nails.

Solution: You probably think the only place for those nails is the trash can. Surprise! Take them out to your garden shed and put them to work whenever you have a plant that's suffering from iron deficiency. (Plants that aren't getting enough iron tend to attract mildew or an overabundance of insect pests, or sometimes both.) To deliver a health-giving dose of iron, throw a handful of the nails around the roots of the malnourished victim. If your surplus nails aren't rusty, douse them with water, and bury them half an inch or so under the soil. They'll rust up and start "bleeding" their iron into the soil in no time.

ALL DRIED UP. You say you don't have a swimming pool? In that case, clean up that kiddie pool, take it inside, and slide it under a bed.

It's perfect for storing out-of-season clothes, extra linens, or anything else you want to keep in that handy spot.

ALL DRIED UP, PART TWO. A plastic wading pool, lined with a thick layer of newspapers, also makes a fine nursery for newborn puppies or kittens. The sides are high enough to keep the babies in (at least for a while), but low enough so that Mom can come and go easily. And because the pool is watertight, you can put it anywhere without risking damage to your wood floors or carpeting. If you don't have a four-legged expectant mother at your house, donate the pool to a local animal shelter, rescue group, or veterinary clinic, where they will definitely put it to good use.

Out of the Garage and into the Garden

Garden centers and catalogs sell a zillion kinds of planting pots. So if you find yourself unable to decide what kind to buy, don't panic! The fact is, when it comes to adding real pizzazz to a garden, nothing beats a few plants that are nestled into (shall we say) unconventional containers—such as these soil-worthy treasures that might be cluttering up your garage. Depending on the composition and value of your container, you may want to use it as an outer liner, and set a potted plant (or several) inside instead of planting directly into the container.

SMALL	MEDIUM	LARGE AND EXTRA-LARGE
Canister sets	Birdbaths	Bathtubs
Ceramic bowls	Bushel baskets	Battered rowboats or canoes
Children's sand pails	Drawers	Sandboxes
Chimney pots	Galvanized buckets	Wading pools
Coal scuttles	Iron kettles	Washtubs
Decorative tins	Sinks	Watering troughs
Rubber boots	Tool caddies	Wooden barrels
Watering cans	Wooden wine crates	Wooden farm wagons

RE-TIRED. If you've got some old tires cluttering up your garage, you could cart them off to a tire store that will recycle them for you. Or you could put them to use around the old homestead. Here are seven sensational suggestions for doing just that:

1. Cushion your arrival. Attach a tire to the end wall of your garage to soften the blow when you forget to stop your car in time.

2. Grow pest-free squash and cucumbers. Set tires on top of your prepared planting bed, fill the center openings with a half-and-half mix of good garden loam and compost, and tuck two or three seeds in each one. (Later, thin the seedlings to one per tire—choosing the strongest one, of course.) No one is quite sure why, but something in the rubber repels both squash bugs and cucumber beetles.

3. Grow terrific tomatoes. Stack up three tires per plant in a spot that gets at least eight hours of sun a day at the height of summer. Fill the inside of this mini tower with a half-and-half mixture of loam and compost. In the middle, insert a sturdy wooden stake or, better yet, a metal pole that rises at least 6 feet above soil level. Then plant your seedling (only one per planter). The beauty of this setup is that the black tires will collect and hold the sun's heat, thereby providing the cozy warmth tomatoes crave.

4. Make a sandbox for small children. Just set the tire on its side, fill up the center space with clean play sand, and turn the tykes loose.

PACK RAT ALERT!

Problem: You're hoarding a pile of chamois cloths, even though you haven't washed your car at home in years.

Solution: Take those soft leather marvels inside and add them to your household cleaning kit. They make perfect, scratchless dust cloths for delicate surfaces like telescope and camera lenses, or even photographs. They're also just the ticket for drying your dog when he gets caught in the rain. The chamois will absorb water faster than a towel does, and will feel nice and soft on Fido's coat.

5. Make a stand. Fill the center of the tire with cement and, while it's still wet, insert a pipe that's 3 to 4 inches in diameter. Then insert whatever you need to hold up—a flagpole, a post for a mailbox, a kid-size basketball hoop, a tetherball post, or a bird feeder. *Note:* If you want to make your stand easy to move, cut a piece of heavy-duty plastic to the size of the tire, and glue it to the bottom before you pour in the cement.

6. Make a swing. Swinging on a tire is just as much fun today as it was way back when. All you need to do is tie one end of a rope to the tire and the other end to a sturdy tree limb, and climb aboard!

7. Protect your boat. You have two choices here: Either hang whole tires from the sides of the dock, or cut strips of rubber from one or more tires and nail them to the edges of the dock.

SCRAPERS ON THE MOVE. If you live in a cold-winter climate, you need to keep an ice scraper in your car, and it's a good idea to have a spare on hand in the garage. But if you have three or four—or even more—toss the extras into your Take Elsewhere box. Then take one to your workshop. The nonscratching plastic blade is perfect for getting dried paint splatters off ceramic tile, wood, or other easily scarred surfaces.

SCRAPE IT CLEAN. Extra ice scrapers can also help you inside the house. Tuck one into your cleaning kit and use it to scrape dripped wax off tabletops, or ice from freezer walls. It's also perfect for picking up spilled food—like the casserole you dropped on the kitchen floor as you were taking it out of the oven.

COOLING IT. If you have a refrigerator in your garage, you know how handy it is for storing lots of cold drinks and for stashing party-size quantities of food that won't fit in your kitchen fridge. Unfortunately, that

A new, clean ice scraper is also a dandy addition to your kitchen utensil basket. How so? Well, that broad blade makes smooth work of removing sticky blobs of dough from a countertop or pastry board.

backup icebox (as my Grandma Putt called it) is every bit as prone to clutter buildup as the one inside your house is. So put it high on your sorting agenda, and deal with the contents according to the guidelines in Chapter Two (see "Free Up the Freezer and Fridge" on page 42).

ORGANIZE

Now that you've decided what you do and don't need to keep in your garage—and before you put any of the keepers back inside—take some time to organize the space in whatever way works best for you and your family.

DIVIDE AND CONQUER. While everything you plan to keep in your garage is still sitting outside, divide it all into categories, and assign each one its own space. Group all the sports equipment together, all the kids' outdoor toys, all the car-related supplies, and so on. If your workshop is part of your garage, set all of your tools and hardware in one place. (For the full scoop on de-cluttering your workshop, whether it has its own quarters or shares space with your car, see Chapter Nine.) Likewise, if you keep your lawn and garden gear in your garage, gather it all in one spot.

GRAB A PENCIL. Most likely, your garage is just a big (or maybe not-so-big) rectangular space, so drawing it to scale should be a snap. Measure the sides and draw the shape on graph paper, with each square equal to so many feet. Then decide

MESS-MAKER ALERT!

Problem: Just like basements, garages can flood—leaving you with a big, wet, expensive mess on your hands.

Solution: If you think there's even the slightest chance that your garage floor could wind up under water, keep everything raised up off the floor. Use wall-hung or freestanding shelves, wall or ceiling hooks, or pallets—or all of the above. You can often find wooden pallets for free at supermarkets, but if appearances matter, invest in sturdy, good-looking plastic versions. You can find them in home-improvement stores, at lumberyards, and (of course) on the Internet.

where each category of stuff should go, depending on how much of it there is and how often you need to get at it.

THINK UPWARD. When you're measuring your garage, don't forget to include the height of the walls. If you're going to build or buy shelves or wall cabinets, it's a good idea to take them all the way to the ceiling. You can use the top ones to hold out-of-season things like lawn toys in winter and Christmas decorations in summer. Just make sure that everything you store up there is lightweight and nonbreakable. Also make sure your shelves or cabinets don't take up so much floor space that you have trouble pulling in your car, and opening its doors so you can get out!

THINK OVERHEAD, TOO. Measure the dimensions of your ceiling to determine what you can hang up there. Hooks screwed into the rafters are perfect for storing big, bulky things like bikes, boats, and ladders.

MAKE A PLAN. If you're going to build or buy shelving units for your garage, it's a good idea to measure the articles you intend to keep on them. You need to allow enough room between some of the shelves to accommodate tall items, but if you plan to store smaller stuff, too, make sure some of the shelves are closer together. Otherwise, you'll wind up wasting a lot of precious vertical space.

OUT OF THE BOX

Even though it is easier to install shelves, cabinets, pegboards, and other storage systems when your garage is empty, you need to measure the space you have for those units while your vehicle is *in* the garage. Check to make sure you have plenty of room to open all of the doors, as well as the trunk and hood. Also, leave space to walk in front of and behind the car—for when you're carrying suitcases, bags of groceries, or cumbersome sports equipment.

MEASURE FREESTANDING STUFF, TOO. Take accurate measurements of your vehicle(s), as well as bicycles, scooters, garbage cans, and any equipment (like lawn mowers) that you keep in the garage. This may seem like overkill, but take it from me: It will help you take advantage of every square inch of space. It may even make you realize that you need to add a few more things to your Take Elsewhere zone—or even get rid of them entirely.

ORGANIZE A CLEAN SLATE. If it's at all possible, install shelves or other storage systems before you start carting your keepers back into the garage. It'll be a whole lot easier to do any necessary building, assembling, or adjusting if you don't have to maneuver around lots of boxes, bins, and bicycles.

LOCATION, LOCATION, LOCATION. The golden rule of garage organizing is the same as it is for any other room in your house: Put the things you use most often in the places that are easiest to reach. But here are some garage-specific location guidelines to keep in mind:

- If you store your recycling bins in the garage, station them near the door to the house. That'll make it easy for everyone in the family to pitch newspapers, bottles, cans, and so forth into the appropriate bins.

- Likewise, keep any household supplies you buy in bulk and store in the garage—like paper towels, beverages, or pet food—close to the house entrance.

- Things that you use outdoors on a regular basis, like the snow shovel, hose, or leaf rake (if you don't have a shed), belong near the garage door.

- When you put items of any kind on shelves, always put the heavier things on the bottom and lighter ones on top.

MESS-MAKER ALERT!

Problem: Your garage is so narrow that if you're not really careful when you open your car door, you bang it against the wall.

Solution: Give your car door a soft crash pad by attaching carpet scraps to the garage wall. Bingo—no more worries about ugly scratches and dings!

IF IT'S OUT OF SEASON, GET IT OUT OF SIGHT. In the winter, things like skis, snow shovels, and sleds should be front and center, where you can grab them at a moment's notice—and quickly put them back where they belong when you're done using them. On the other hand, in the summer, those cold-weather friends are nothing but clutter. So when warm weather arrives, tuck 'em up in the rafters, or hang 'em up high on a wall. Then move the water skis, inner tubes, and pool toys into prime-time territory.

GET IN A RUT. One sure way to help fend off creeping clutter is to always park large, bulky things like bicycles, scooters, wagons, garbage cans, and (of course) your car in the same spots. One simple maneuver will make it a snap to do that: Just outline a parking space on the floor for each one using fluorescent tape or spray paint.

SEPARATE YOUR TOOLS. As you organize your space, plan to keep your automotive tools as far away as possible from any other tools you keep in the garage. The reason: Car equipment tends to get greasy, and saws, shovels, and the like tend to get dusty. And grease + dust = a big mess.

STORE

Once you've organized the space in your garage, you could fork out a thousand dollars or more on a fancy, custom-made storage system. Or you could use recycled containers and build-it-yourself arrangements that will cost you next to nothing. I have a hunch which route you'd prefer to take, and if I'm right, the tips in this section will set you on the high road to success.

> ## MAKING SPACE
>
> No matter how cramped your garage is, try to make room for a workbench or table where you can take care of minor repairs, small paint jobs, and other chores. You say space is *really* tight in your car's home, sweet home? No problem! Get a foldaway workbench that clings tight to the wall when you're not using it. Then when you have a project to do, you can back your vehicle out into the driveway, pull your bench down, and get to work.

RESCUE RETIRED KITCHEN CABINETS. Getting ready to remodel your kitchen? Well then, don't you dare get rid of the old cupboards and countertops! Instead, move them to your garage. On the other hand, if a redo is not in your planning book, don't despair — there are plenty of ways to find practically perfect performers for peanuts. Try these, for instance:

- Spread the word. Tell your friends, relatives, and co-workers that you're in the market for used cabinets. Don't mention money at this point. Instead, wait for word from the supplier. He may name a price, or he may simply be so glad to get the things off his hands that he'll give them to you free of charge. (Of course, you may want to reward his generosity by delivering a few dozen home-baked cookies, or offering to babysit his dog the next time he goes on vacation.)

- Check out places that sell salvaged building supplies and fixtures. To find one near you, look under "building materials, used" in the Yellow Pages. You may also be just a stone's throw from one of Habitat for Humanity's Re-Stores. To find out for sure, log on to www.habitat.org.

- Visit your local dump. If it has a section for "adoptable" stuff that folks have dropped off, you just might find cabinets that are still in good shape.

OUT OF THE BOX

If you're a busy person (and who the heck isn't these days?), you may not have much time for hanging around in a hammock, but don't let that stop you from buying one. Hang it from the ceiling of your garage and use it to store lightweight articles that get used only occasionally, like spare life jackets or the extra cushions for your chaise lounge. Just be sure that when it's full, it doesn't hang so low that you can't drive your car underneath it!

PLASTIC IS PRACTICALLY PERFECT. If you plan to buy shelving units from a home-improvement center or hardware store, take my advice and go for the plastic kind. They're usually easier and faster to assemble than metal ones, and in most cases, no tools are required.

What's more, they won't dent, corrode, or rust, and they usually cost less than metal versions.

PLAN ON MORE PLASTIC. If you store anything in your garage that needs to be kept behind closed doors, buy one or more plastic storage cabinets (available in home-improvement stores and on the Internet). They're sturdy, waterproof, and inexpensive. Best of all, the doors are lockable, so you can keep the contents safely away from children and pets (or any uninvited visitors who are up to no good).

BINS ARE BEST. In the previous chapter, I sang the praises of sturdy plastic bins with snap-on lids as the be-all and end-all of efficient basement storage (that is, for anything small enough to fit inside them). Well, guess what? They're also ideal for keeping small things organized on your garage shelves. To make the most of these handy helpers, keep the following five in mind:

1. Confine the contents to one category per bin (for instance, one bin for paintbrushes, one for car-washing rags, and one for pet supplies).

2. Use clear plastic bins for things that you want to identify quickly, like extra batteries or lightbulbs.

3. Remember the golden rule of shelf stocking: Keep the things that you use most often on the shelves that are easiest to reach—the ones between midthigh and shoulder height.

4. Mark each bin clearly using self-stick labels and indelible markers.

5. Use the smallest containers that will hold the items. This is especially important if you need to stack bins

MAKING SPACE

Need a place to store small things that don't need to be in a covered container? Well, if you've got an extra plastic dishwashing basin taking up space in your kitchen, bring it out to the garage. Otherwise, run down to the local hardware store and buy one. Then put your little doodads inside of it, attach a label to the side of the basin, and slide it onto a shelf.

on shelves because smaller bins are easier to move around than larger ones are.

DON'T FOLLOW THE BOUNCING BALL. No matter how hard you try, you cannot train a baseball, basketball, or football to sit still on a shelf—at least not for very long. But they don't have to come tumbling down. Here are a couple of ways to keep them corralled in their place:

- Put the balls in a big mesh laundry bag or shopping bag, and hang it from a nail or hook on the wall.

- Fasten big, flat-sided metal baskets on the wall, and keep the balls in there. (You can find them in home-organizing catalogs and on the Internet.)

- Hang a shelf that's an inch or two higher in the front than it is in back. For good measure, fasten strips of wood along the front and side edges of the shelf to make sure the balls won't roll off.

MESS-MAKER ALERT!

Problem: Frisbees™, Wiffle™ ball sets, jump ropes, and other outdoor toys are scattered all over the place, making a royal mess of your garage.

Solution: Stash the toys in a wheeled bin that the kids can roll into the yard when they go out to play, and then haul back into the garage when they come in. Just be sure to issue firm orders that everything that goes out must go back into the bin and back inside at the end of playtime!

BAG YOUR BATS. And poles and paddles, too! If you've replaced your old golf bag—or found one at a garage sale for peanuts—hang it on the wall of your garage and use it to store baseball bats, fishing poles, canoe paddles, and other long, thin stuff.

CLEAR THE FLOOR. For my money, no garage should be without a big supply of those heavy-duty, rubber-coated hooks that you see in just about every hardware store. I screw them into the ceiling joists and use them to hang bicycles, ladders, folding lawn chairs, and anything else I don't want cluttering up the floor.

THAT'S SPECIAL! For the ultimate in efficient garage de-cluttering, check out one of the many Web sites that sell storage systems that are specially designed for garages. You can find cabinets, wall-mounted grids, shelves that hang from the ceiling, and brackets that are tailor-made for holding everything from hand tools to ladders, bikes, and wheelbarrows. There are many sites to choose from, but three of the most popular are www.tidygarage.com, www.premiergarage.com, and www.garagetek.com.

CLEAR THE FLOOR, KID-STYLE. If you have youngsters on the scene, you might think that things like jump ropes, scooters, skateboards, hula hoops, and bicycle helmets actually stake out territory on the floor, where they build nests and proceed to propagate. Fortunately, there's a simple way to solve that problem: Just attach rubber-coated hooks to the garage wall at a height the kids can reach easily, and have them hang up all of that proliferating equipment.

MAKING SPACE

If your garage has exposed rafters, lay boards or sheets of $1/2$-inch plywood across them. Almost instantly, you'll have an "attic" where you can stash all kinds of stuff.

STORED FOR ACTION. Are you or your kids involved in a whole lot of different outdoor activities? If so, then this tip is just for you: Sort all of the equipment into individual tote bags and hang them on the wall. Use a different color or style of bag for each activity. That way, you'll be able to grab the baseball, bowling, soccer, or tennis gear and rush off without missing a beat—or arriving at the bowling alley with your catcher's mitt and face mask.

PUT THE WALL STUDS TO WORK. If your garage (or shed) has exposed wall studs, you have a golden opportunity to increase your storage space—quickly, easily, and without spending big bucks. Here are a couple of ways to do it:

1. Nail 1- by 2-inch strips of wood horizontally to the studs at roughly waist height. Then set your rakes and other long-handled tools, business ends up, behind the strips and between the studs.

2. Attach cup hooks to the inside-facing surfaces of two studs. Insert skis, ski poles, oars, fishing rods, or other long, narrow items between the studs. Then stretch a bungee cord between the hooks to hold the skinny contents in place.

PUT THE WALL STUDS TO WORK, PART TWO. Build shallow shelves between the studs using pine two-by-fours. First, cut the wood to fit the space between the uprights (usually it's 14 to 18 inches). Nail it into place at the height you want, driving two nails through the stud and into each end of the shelf. Then use the shelves to store any kind of narrow stuff, from cans of car wax to cans of tennis balls.

DRESS(ER) FOR SUCCESS. Got an old chest of drawers that's cluttering up your basement or attic? If so, then move it out to the garage and fill the drawers with tools, outdoor toys, sports equipment, or whatever else you need to keep in the garage.

A PLACE FOR EVERYTHING

There's no doubt about it: Even if your yard is only a tad bigger than a postage stamp, a shed is a mighty handy thing to have. But if you're not careful, it can fill up with useless junk in the blink of an eye. If you have to wade through piles of life jackets, leaning towers of flowerpots, and jumbled heaps of seed catalogs just to find the lawn mower, take heart: Using our plan, you can turn that disaster area into a true lawn and garden helper.

In This Section:
✔ Lawn and garden
✔ Pool supplies
✔ Pets and livestock

SORT

By now you know the drill: Start restaking your claim to your shed by getting rid of the stuff that doesn't belong in there. And do it *now*!

ANOTHER OUTDOOR ADVENTURE. Just like garage de-cluttering, sorting the contents of your shed is a project you'll want to tackle on a mild, dry day. Chances are you won't need to round up a crew of willing workers (not unless your "shed" is actually a barn that hasn't been cleaned out since Uncle Jed divvied up the farm 30 years ago). So gather some trash bags, recycling bins, and boxes. Then designate areas on the lawn for the usual categories: Trash, Keep Here, Take Elsewhere, and Donate or Sell.

GARAGE OR SHED? When you have both a garage and a shed, deciding which things to keep where can be a little tricky. There are no hard-and-fast rules, but these guidelines will help you make the right call:

- The garage is the place for anything that you normally carry in or use on your vehicle, including automotive tools and car-washing gear. It's also the most convenient home for tools that you usually use indoors if you don't have a separate workshop. Bicycles, scooters, skateboards, and other vehicles— motorized or not—belong in the garage. And in most homes, it's also the handiest

COLLECTOR ALERT!

Problem: You don't know where to store the large collection of chemicals, cleaning supplies, and other equipment that your in-ground swimming pool requires.

Solution: Rotate your gear. In the summer, keep those things in the shed, where you can get to them quickly and easily, and where (most likely) they'll be closer to the pool. When the outdoor swimming season ends, tuck everything away in the garage, where it'll be out of the way, and you'll also free up shed space for ice-melting products and snow-removal equipment.

place to keep sports equipment and the kids' outdoor toys.

- The shed is tailor-made for tools and equipment that you use for the lawn and garden. It's also where you should store any motor oil, gasoline, and other flammable substances you keep on hand— but only in small quantities, please! This is especially important if your shed is close to your house and/or contains heat-producing appliances like washing machines, dryers, or water heaters.

If you've got more plant stands than you need to hold plants, take some of them out of the shed and into the house, and use them to corral clutter there. At my house, we use one to store extra towels in the guest bathroom and another one to hold keys, gloves, and dog leashes by the front door. (Before you put an iron plant stand in a bathroom, give it a coat of rustproof paint or clear sealer.)

OFF YOU GO! As you pull each current "resident" out of your shed, assign it to one of your boxes, or if it's too big for that, simply move it to the appropriate zone. Most of your choices should be a snap. A box of moldy grass seed? Toss it on the compost pile. The instruction manual for a lawn dethatcher that you no longer own? Chuck it into the recycling bin. Your son's catcher's mitt? Pitch it into the Take Elsewhere box. Your lawn mower? That belongs in the Keep Here zone. A second lawn mower? Unless cutting the grass is a two-person-at-a-time task at your place, roll it to the Donate or Sell zone. The hedge clippers you moved from your previous home—but you no longer have a hedge? Those trimmers *definitely* belong in your Donate or Sell box! The list could go on and on, but you get the idea.

TOO HARD TO SELL, TOO GOOD TO TOSS. As you de-clutter your shed and garage—or any other room in your house—you will probably come across a number of things that you don't need and don't want, but can't bear to send off to further clog up the local landfill. And these days, many thrift stores won't make home pickups unless you can offer them a full truckload, or close to it. Of course, you could hang up "free to a good home" notices at local supermarkets, or advertise in the local paper (many of them provide free space for ads that offer free or very low-cost merchandise). But here's a wider-reaching option: The Freecycle Network™ is a consortium of local groups throughout the country that match up people who have stuff to give away with people who'd like to have it. To use the service, simply log on to www.freecycle.org, and type the names of your city and state into the "Find a group near you" space.

THINK BEYOND PLANTS. Got more ceramic planters than you need in your shed? Then turn the extras into wastebaskets in your bedroom, bathroom, or office. (Better yet, make them paper-only recycling "bins," so their good looks won't be marred by messy garbage or an ugly plastic bag.) Big planters are also the perfect containers for storing kindling by your fireplace.

COLLECTOR ALERT!

Problem: You bought a beautiful old garden gate at a country auction three years ago—and it's been sitting in your shed ever since because you have no place in your yard to use it.

Solution: Turn it into a headboard for your bed. Just clean up the gate (if necessary), paint it if you'd like, and bolt it to the wall behind your bed. Then go to sleep and dream of hollyhocks and roses. For more creative headboard options, see "Go to the Head of the Bed" on page 267.

HANG ON TO YOUR HOSE HANGER. You've replaced your old wall-mounted hose hanger with a big rolling model, so it makes good sense to pitch the old relic, right? Wrong! Hang it on the wall of your shed, garage, or workshop and use it to corral heavy-duty extension cords. Never use nails or hooks to hang electrical cords, or you'll run the risk of puncturing their rubber coating. If you put them in a drawer, you'll wind up with

Extend Yourself

Or at least your reach. How? With a long tool handle (either one from a broken tool, or an extra new one that you've hung on to "just in case," or from an old broom). All you need to do is screw or tape the appropriate gizmo to the end. Here's a hardy trio of possibilities.

ATTACH THIS	AND DO THIS
Large cup hook	Reach down behind the dryer or radiator to retrieve a dropped sock, or up to a high shelf to grab a basket or pillow (but nothing heavy, please!).
Paintbrush	Get at all those narrow places your arm won't fit (for instance, behind appliances or radiators), or high spots where you want to use a brush, not a roller.
Squeegee	Wash high windows without a ladder.

a tangled mess. But on the broad, flat surface of a hose hanger, your cords will stay untangled and puncture-free.

PUT 'EM TO THE TEST. You've found some unopened packets of flower or vegetable seeds on a shelf, and you'd like to save them to plant this year. Should you do that, or simply toss 'em out? That's anybody's guess. Unfortunately, you can't tell whether seeds are still viable simply by looking at them, but you can find out by giving them my old sink-or-swim test: Just pour the seeds into a glass of water. The ones that float on the surface are nonstarters, so throw 'em on the old compost pile. The seeds that sink stand a good chance of growing just fine. You'll need to plant them soon, though (either in the garden or indoors, under lights) because they'll have soaked up water and will be sprouting before you can say "Everybody out of the pool!"

WHAT ABOUT THIS YEAR'S LEFTOVERS? When you don't use up all of the seeds in a packet, it's fine to save the remainder for next year. They should perform just as well because most annual flower and vegetable seeds remain viable for two to three years, as long as you store them properly. The secret is to keep them cool and dry. So put them in your Take Elsewhere box while you finish sorting the rest of the stuff in your shed. Then as soon as you can, take those seeds to the kitchen, and proceed as follows:

1. Get a container of powdered milk and some glass jars with tight-fitting lids (one jar per type of seed).

2. In each jar, put 1 part seed to 1 part powdered milk.

3. Seal the jars very tightly, and stash them in the refrigerator (not the freezer). The milk will keep the seeds dry and fresh all winter long. Then, come spring, they'll be rarin' to go!

ORGANIZE

When you've got your shed all cleared out, give it a good cleaning. Then—before you move anything back into it—figure out how you want to use the space.

WHAT DO YOU DO IN THERE? Is your shed simply a place to store your lawn mower, shovels, rakes, and other outdoor tools? Or do you also use it to start seeds, pot up container plants, and maybe even plan your garden each year? Does it need to house items other than lawn and garden accessories, like swimming pool gear and supplies, outdoor sports equipment, or food for pets and/or livestock?

PLAN TO PLANT. If you answered "yes" to that second question above, make it a point to include a table and chair in your shed-organizing plan, along with shelves for gardening books. You'll also want good light, so you can read planting instructions and (of course) all the descriptions in seed and plant catalogs—not to mention maintenance and repair manuals for your lawn mower and any other equipment you keep in your shed.

"ROOMS" OF THEIR OWN. As you did when you were organizing your garage, separate the contents of your shed according to function. Keep motorized tools and their accessories in one place, pots and potting soil in another, animal food and gear in yet another, and so on.

MAKE SURE YOU SEPARATE THESE. Gather all your garden fertilizers and pest-control products together in one place, and put them as far away as possible from pet food (or any human food snacks that you may keep on hand in your shed). Keep all fertilizers and pesticides—even "food-safe" organic products—in their original containers. In the case of homemade concoctions, label each container clearly with an indelible marker, and don't use that container for anything else! Store all of these things well out of reach of children and any animals (wild or domestic) that may wander into the shed. And if at all possible, toxic products should be kept in a locked cabinet.

MESS-MAKER ALERT!

Problem: Just like basements and garages, sheds can attract more than their fair share of dampness, dust, and marauding pests.

Solution: Organize the space in your shed so that, as much as possible, everything is raised up off the floor. Take full advantage of shelves, wall-mounted storage systems, and sturdy hooks that attach to wall studs and ceiling beams.

ACCIDENTS HAPPEN. And they happen frequently when you're working in the yard. So keep a first-aid kit in a prominent place in your shed, and make sure it's stocked with antibiotic ointment, bandages, and whatever product you use for treating insect bites. Include a pair of tweezers for pulling out ticks and bee stingers. And if you live in a place where poisonous snakes pose a threat, make sure you have a snake-bite kit close at hand.

I'VE SAID IT BEFORE... And I'll say it again: Keep the things you use most often in the spots where you can get at them most easily. And keep in mind that the criteria will change from one season to the next. In the spring and summer, you'll want the lawn mower, garden hose, and watering cans in prime territory. Come fall, leaf rakes and plant-protection gear need to move up front. Then when Old Man Winter arrives, just about everything you needed during the growing season can retire to the back to make room near the door for snow-removal gear, ice-melting substances, and plenty of seed for your bird feeders (if this is where you store it).

ORGANIZING THE GOODS. When it comes to keeping a shed neat and uncluttered, shelves are a godsend. But to take full advantage of that valuable storage space, it's essential to follow three basic organizing rules:

1. Try to use shelves that are shallow enough to hold only a single row of items because deeper shelves take up too much room. Plus, it's a royal pain in the neck when you have to move the items in front to reach the stuff in back.

2. If you absolutely must put some things behind others, keep the tallest objects in back and the shortest in front, so that nothing gets lost in the shuffle.

3. Keep the tools and supplies that you use most often in places that are easiest to reach.

PEG O' YOUR HEART. Whether you choose a small pegboard panel or cover an entire wall with the stuff, you'll have an efficient, versatile — and instantly changeable — system. Depending on the kinds of hooks and hangers you choose, you can attach shelves, bins, or baskets of all shapes and sizes. Plus, anything that has an

MAKING SPACE

If your shed has a pitched roof or a high ceiling, build a loft that's high enough off the floor to walk under. Depending on the height, you'll have a space that's a foot or two deep, where you can stash things like plant stakes, row covers, and rolls of chicken wire. You can find loft-building plans (for both sheds and garages) at most home-improvement stores and on the Internet.

opening in it, like scissors, small watering cans, or binder clips (see "Zip It Up" on page 316) can hang from its own hook.

STORE

Got the space in your shed organized just the way you want it? Great! Now move on to the final step in your de-cluttering mission: storing everything so that it's easy to find and protected from dirt, dampness, and pests.

CAN THE CARDBOARD, AND PASS ON PAPER. Instead, look for storage containers—large or small—that are made of metal, plastic, or wood. If you buy a product like grass seed, fertilizer, or bird seed that comes in a cardboard carton or paper bag, put it into a moisture-proof container immediately. That way, you won't start to fill the bird feeder, only to find that you've got a sack full of wet seed.

HELP FROM HOME. Before you rush out to buy storage containers for your lawn and garden supplies, shop around your house first. There's a good chance that a lot of things that are cluttering up your kitchen, attic, or home office can help de-clutter your shed. Consider these possibilities:

✔ Baby-wipe boxes

✔ Clamp-lid canning jars

✔ Cookie jars

✔ Decorative tins that held popcorn or other snack foods

✔ Plastic food-storage containers

✔ Plastic sweater and shoe boxes

COLLECTOR ALERT!

Problem: Your shovels, rakes, pruning shears, and other sharp tools are essential gardening aids—but they also pose real safety hazards if you don't store them properly.

Solution: Never prop up sharp tools against a wall. Instead, hang them up with the sharp edges toward the wall, away from high-traffic areas, and out of reach of children.

✔ Retired medicine cabinets

✔ Standing file holders (great for keeping seed catalogs and garden magazines close at hand)

✔ Umbrella stands (perfect for holding plant stakes)

ROLLING RIGHT ALONG. One of the most useful storage aids you could find for your shed may be cluttering up your attic or your garage. What is it? Your (or your kids') old wagon. Here are two ways I use my little red wagon:

1. Hardening off transplants (either seedlings that I've started indoors or young plants that I've brought home from my local garden center).

2. Displaying tender houseplants. Besides adding pizzazz to my garden, the pots can be whisked to a sheltered spot when a storm blows in, or an early (or late) frost is forecast.

OUT OF THE BOX

When you're raiding your kitchen for shed storage containers, don't overlook that extra magnetic knife rack that's lying unused in the back of a drawer. It's perfect for holding trowels, hand rakes, dibbles, and other small metallic tools on a wall of your shed.

SPEAKING OF ROLLING... One of my favorite garden "tools" is an old rolling golf bag that I rescued from my garage and took straight to the shed. I slide hoes, rakes, and shovels into the plastic tubes, and the zippered pockets hold hand tools, seed packets, and all kinds of odds and ends. Best of all, the big wheels make it a cinch to pull the whole kit and caboodle along right behind me.

OR MAYBE HANGING IN THERE. Even if your retired golf bag doesn't have wheels, it can still be a superstar in the world of tool storage. Just hang it securely to the shed wall, and use it to hold your long-handled gear.

According to Katherine Trezise, a professional organizer and president of Absolutely Organized® in Cockeysville, Maryland (www.absolutely-organized.com), the secret to having a well-organized yard and garden shed is simple: Just remember the old adage to "have a place for everything, and keep everything in its place." She offers these tips for doing just that:

☞ Sort your yard and garden gear and supplies by type—long-handled tools, hand tools, power tools, seeds, potting soil, fertilizers, and so on.

☞ Draw a rough sketch of the inside of your shed. Then assign an area of the shed for each category of items you intend to store there.

☞ Make every inch count by putting the walls (and ceiling) to work. To make the most of the available wall space, alternate hanging tools right side up and upside down.

☞ If a tool has no hole in the handle, simply hammer two long nails partway into the shed wall and hang the tool upside down between them.

☞ Use sturdy, plastic-coated hooks (available at your local hardware store) to hang heavy items. Just make sure you screw the end of the hook into a stud, so you've got plenty of support.

☞ Install shelves (either hanging or freestanding) on one wall of the shed to hold supplies that can't be hung up.

☞ Here's the ultimate secret for maintaining an organized shed: Get an electronic label maker (available at office-supply stores and on the Internet). Make a label for each hanging tool, and put it on the shed wall under the appropriate hook or nails. The "Rake" label, for example, will remind you to rehang the rake in its proper place after you've finished using it. Also, label the edges of each shelf with the appropriate category name, like Fertilizer, Seeds, Planting Pots, or whatever else you've got. This will ensure that all your tools and supplies will be in the right place every time you need them.

PERFECT POUCHES. A hanging shoe bag can come in just as handy in your shed as it does in your bedroom. Get the screw-mounted kind that has clear, plastic pockets. Hang it on a wall and fill the pouches with seed packets, twist ties, balls of twine, spray bottles, and all of the other small stuff that can quickly turn even the neatest shed into a cluttered mess.

ANOTHER SMALL-STUFF STORAGE WINNER. Large hardware and home-improvement stores sell wire shelf units that are about 4 inches deep and anywhere from 12 to 30 inches wide and 10 to 72 inches high. Mount one on a wall or the back of your shed door and use it to hold fertilizers, pest-control products, hand tools, or anything else that fits on the shallow shelves.

ZIP IT UP. Ready for another idea for storing tiny stuff? Okay, here it comes: Stash seed packets, plant labels, planting instructions, or what have you in ziplock plastic bags. Then you can simply hang the bags up in one of these ways:

✔ Thumbtack them to a bulletin board.

✔ Attach a binder clip to each bag, and slide the clips onto pegboard hooks, or onto cup hooks that you've screwed directly into the shed wall.

A DROP IN THE BUCKET. If you want to hang your garden hose on the wall rather than have a rolling caddy take up floor space, you could go out and buy a special hanger—or you could try this simple trick: Just drill three holes in a triangular pattern in the bottom of a

MAKING SPACE

Free up space in your shed by getting the garden hoses out of there, at least during the growing season. Take them out to your deck or patio and roll them up inside big planting pots. (This is especially easy to do if your hoses are coiled like telephone cords.) Besides having more room to maneuver in your shed, you'll dodge the hassle of hauling hoses back and forth all the time.

galvanized steel bucket. Then either screw or bolt it to the wall of your shed, with the open end of the bucket pointing out. Coil your hose around the pail, and use the space inside to store extra nozzles and hose-end sprayers.

TRASH IT! In a manner of speaking, that is. Big, clean, sturdy trash cans are some of the best storage helpers you could ever find. Here are three ways to put them to work in your shed—or outside the shed door:

1. Store your garden tools in them for the winter. First, clean your tools and sharpen the blades. Then fill a trash can about halfway full of sand, pour in a quart of mineral oil, and shove each tool, business end first, into the sand. They'll stay sharp and free of rust and corrosion until spring rolls around. (Either a plastic or galvanized can will work for this job.)

2. Use either plastic or metal cans to hold salt, sand, cat litter, or whatever substance you prefer to keep your stairs and walkways free of ice. Just empty your melter of choice into the can, toss in a big scoop, and you're good to go—with no leaky bags to fumble around with.

3. Choose waterproof, plastic trash cans for grass seed, fertilizer, pet food, or anything else that could be damaged by dampness or pests. Pour products that you use regularly, like pet food or fertilizer (during the growing season), directly into the can. To store things like leftover grass seed, simply place the original bag into the can.

COLLECTOR ALERT!

Problem: Your ever-expanding collection of terra-cotta pots is taking over the shelves in your shed. Stacking them would save space, but they're likely to chip or crack when you pull them apart.

Solution: Get some mesh produce bags, like the ones lemons and onions come in. Put a pot in a bag, and nest it inside of another pot. When you've got several pots (in bags) stacked up, tuck the bag on the top into its pot, so you can just grab the mesh when it's time to pull the stack apart.

CHAPTER NINE

THE WORKSHOP AND HOBBY ROOM

I n any home, these hardworking spaces contain mountains of material, equipment, and supplies, both large and small. Some of that stuff is necessary, or at least highly helpful, to the tasks at hand. But let's be honest here—a fair amount of it is nothing but clutter. So get to work de-cluttering and you'll soon be enjoying the fruits of your labor.

NAIL DOWN A PLAN

No matter how big or small your workshop is, you can't get much work done if you have to climb over piles of ski boots, sandbox toys, and broken appliances just to reach your workbench. Or maybe your problem is simply that you have to search high and low every time you need a specific wrench or a certain size screw. In either case, you've come to the right place. With our get-organized strategy, you can whip that shop into shape in no time at all!

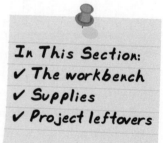

In This Section:
✔ The workbench
✔ Supplies
✔ Project leftovers

SORT

Just like any other room in your house, the workshop tends to attract a lot of things that don't need to be there. To clear them out, start separating the keepers from the intruders.

WHO NEEDS IT? Before you even start rounding up and labeling boxes—much less filling them with stuff that's cluttering up your workshop—ask yourself whether you even *need* a workshop. If refinishing furniture, building tree houses for your grandchildren, or simply puttering around the old homestead is your idea of a grand old time, then the answer is "You betcha!" On the other hand, if it's been years since you've done anything more complicated than hanging a picture or tightening a loose hinge, then clear out your tools and put that space to better use. Turn it into a home gym, rec room, or craft studio—or simply fill it with super efficient storage units so it can help you de-clutter the rest of your house.

SERIOUS SORTING. If you fall into the reluctant do-it-yourselfer category, whittle your tool collection down to a few basic must-haves, like a hammer, pliers, and a couple of screwdrivers (both slotted and Phillips head). Stash them in a toolbox, a plastic bin, or even a spare drawer in the kitchen. Then put the phone number of a good local handyman in your address book, or program it into your speed dial, and you're good to go.

FOR ALL YOU WILLING WORKERS... If you fall firmly into the "I need a workshop!" category, grab some trash bags and a bunch of boxes, and give them the standard labels: Trash, Keep Here, Take Elsewhere, and Donate or Sell. Of course, some of the items in your workshop may be too big to fit in the boxes. In that case, in addition to labeling your containers, divide the floor (or the driveway) into different zones, and allot a section to each of the categories.

FIRST THINGS FIRST. Start your workshop-sorting session the same way you did in the basement and garage: by gathering up any and all hazardous

MAKING SPACE

Attention, all you folks who follow the-fewer-tools-the-better philosophy (see "Serious Sorting" above). Instead of crowding your toolbox with both a claw hammer and a rubber mallet, run down to the local hardware store and pick up a ¾- or 1-inch rubber tip that's called a boot (because it's often used on furniture legs). Tuck it into your tool kit, and whenever you need to do some gentle pounding, slip the boot onto the hammerhead and go to town.

materials. Get rid of oily or greasy rags, dried-up paint, and containers with a thin layer of turpentine or paint stripper in the bottom. Then stash any still-usable containers of paint, cleaners, and solvents in a locked metal storage unit that's away from nearby sources of heat (like your furnace, water heater, or washing machine and dryer).

THE EVICTION PROCESS. Once you've dealt with potential workshop hazards, move on to the rest of the inventory. Clear out everything that fits any of these descriptions:

- It's broken and can't be repaired (or you simply don't want to bother doing the job). This list includes things like cracked safety goggles, power tools with frayed cords, and screwdrivers with chipped heads.

- You can't remember the last time you used it. Or maybe you've *never* used it. Perhaps your mother gave you a fancy jigsaw for Christmas three years ago, but you haven't even taken it out of the box. Or maybe you bought a vise and a miter box for a specific project back in 1995, and they've been gathering dust ever since.

- You have more than you need. Are you hanging on to a second drill or an electric sander just as a backup? Well, forget that idea. The fact is that most power tools are like plant seeds and batteries: Over time, they tend to go bad whether you use them or not, so put any extras in your Donate or Sell box. Or, in the case of hand tools, see whether you can use one or more someplace else in the house (see "Too Many Tools" on page 322).

- It doesn't belong in the workshop. This is a somewhat iffy category. If your dog commonly supervises your projects, then you probably

OUT OF THE BOX

Saving paint for touchups makes sense, but don't add to the clutter by keeping it in the original can. Instead, transfer the paint you want to save to a small, tight-lidded jar or plastic container. (A mayonnaise jar or food-storage container would be perfect.) Attach a label noting the color and the room where the paint was used.

want to keep a bed and a chew toy or two around for him. On the other hand, if he rarely comes into the room, but somehow you've accumulated a drawer full of rawhide bones and tennis balls, toss them into the Take Elsewhere box. Ditto the jump rope your grandchildren left behind on their last visit, the flashlight you normally keep in the car, and the dirty coveralls you should have taken to the laundry room two weeks ago.

DON'T OVERLOOK THE SMALL STUFF. Do you have half a dozen packages of picture hooks crammed into a drawer— even though every framed picture you own is hanging firmly on a wall? If so, then get 'em out of there. (When you acquire any new pictures, you can always buy appropriately sized hooks.) The same goes for boxes of upholstery tacks left over from the ottoman you re-covered three years ago, mini shingles you bought for a long-finished dollhouse, and extra containers of nails that you know you'll never use. Either sell them in a hardware bargain box at your next garage sale, or give them to an organization that will welcome them with open arms (see "Give the Gift of Workmanship" on page 323).

BRUSH UP ON THIS. Got a few soft paintbrushes that you've never used? Well, don't let them take up space in your workshop. Instead, add them to your household cleaning kit. They're ideal for dusting furniture, picture frames, or anything else that has intricate carvings or other nooks and crannies that a cloth-covered finger can't

PACK RAT ALERT!

Problem: Supplies and tools purchased for projects that you think you might tackle as soon as you have time.

Solution: Tuck those things into a box (or several boxes). Label each container with the contents and today's date, and set it aside. As weeks and months go by, you may find yourself reaching for some of that gear. When that happens, store the items in places where you can get at them easily the next time you need them. But after a year has passed, get rid of supplies that you haven't used.

reach. A soft, clean paintbrush also makes a useful addition to your beach bag. It's the perfect tool for giving feet the brush-off before they track sand into the car, and for de-sanding buckets, balls, or shell collections.

TOO MANY TOOLS. If your workshop is like most, it's a good bet that you've got duplicate or even triplicate versions of common tools like hammers, pliers, and screwdrivers. Before you toss the extras into a Donate or Sell box, consider whether you can use them elsewhere in, shall we say, less conventional ways—like these:

MAKING SPACE

If some of your duplicate tools are brand-new or barely used, give them to a young friend or relative who's headed off to college, or moving into his first apartment. Even a dorm dweller needs a few basic tools. A starter kit could include things like slotted and Phillips head screwdrivers (or better yet, a combo tool that has interchangeable heads), a stud finder and level (for hanging pictures, shelves, or coat hooks), a tape measure, a crescent wrench or gripper pliers, and needle-nose pliers.

• Claw hammer. Take it out to your shed and draft it to fight the never-ending war on weeds. Just slide the claw around the stem of a dandelion or other deep-rooted weed at ground level, and rock the hammer's head back just as though you were prying up a nail. That unwanted plant will pop right out, root and all (at least *most* of the time).

• Slotted screwdriver. One of these belongs in your garden tool kit, too. It's perfect for getting stubborn weeds out of hard-to-get-at places, like the gaps between stepping stones or cracks in a sidewalk. If you've got a couple of surplus screwdrivers in your workshop, park one by the door to your house, and suggest—firmly—that all members of the family use it to scrape out caked mud from the treads of their shoes or boots before they venture indoors.

• Needle-nose pliers. If you love fresh salmon, you need a pair of these babies in your kitchen (well washed, of course). They're just the ticket for taking out those annoying, sharp pin bones that don't get removed at the seafood market. All you need to do is rub your fingers over the flesh side of the raw fish. As you encounter each bone, grip it firmly with the pliers, and pull it out in the direction it's pointing. Just don't rip it straight out, or you'll rough up the flesh.

- Broad plastic scraper. Add one to your household cleaning kit and use it to pick up spilled food or other messy stuff (like the results of a pet's upset tummy). The cleanup process will be a lot faster and easier than it would be if you used paper towels or an old rag.

GIVE THE GIFT OF WORKMANSHIP. Extra tools and building materials may be nothing but annoying clutter to you, but if they're in good condition, they're worth their weight in gold to plenty of other people in the community. Whichever home you choose for your castoffs, you'll win in three ways: You'll free up space in the workshop, do a good turn for someone else, and get a tax deduction, to boot! Here's a handful of places to consider:

1. Shelters and other social welfare organizations. The same groups that gladly accept things like food, clothing, and linens also welcome tools and other home-maintenance supplies. They may use the items to perform upkeep on their own buildings, or they may distribute them to needy families to use in their homes. Check with local churches, or look in the Yellow Pages under "Charities" or "Social Welfare Organizations."

PACK RAT ALERT!

Problem: You haven't refinished a piece of furniture in five years, but you're still hanging on to a package of fine-grain sandpaper.

Solution: Take the sandpaper to the bedroom and add it to your shoe-care kit. Then the next time you get a spot or two on your suede shoes (or a suede jacket or purse), gently rub the marks away. And whenever you buy a new pair of leather-soled shoes, use the sandpaper to roughen up their smooth bottoms. That way, you won't find yourself slipping and sliding across the carpet the first time you wear the shoes.

2. Habitat for Humanity. This group has a chain of stores called Habitat Re-Stores that sell donated building supplies and tools, both large and small. To find out if there's one near you, visit www.habitat.org.

3. Vocational schools or the vo-tech department at your local high school. Depending on the curriculum, they may be able to use anything from power tools and jigsaws to miter boxes and unused tubes of superglue.

4. College, high school, or community theater groups. Folks who build stage sets can use just about any kind of tool you can name, as well as building materials, painting supplies, and even excess paint.

Don't overlook the Boy Scouts, Girl Scouts, or 4-H Clubs when you're off-loading used tools. The youngsters can often use hammers, nails, scrap lumber, and who knows what to complete projects that will help them earn merit badges, build parade floats, or make soapbox derby cars.

A WINDOW (SCREEN) OF OPPORTUNITY. When you replaced your screens last year, you stashed the old ones in your workshop, intending to take them to the dump, but somehow you never got around to it. So now's the time to do it, right? Maybe, and maybe not. If you grow flowers or vegetables, those screens could be mighty handy things to have in your garden shed. Here are just a few ways I put retired window screens to work at my place:

✔ Sift topsoil or compost. Just set the screens on blocks, and have at it.

✔ Stop raccoons or opossums from stealing corn and tomatoes. Prop the screens against the cornstalks or staked tomato vines. The hungry varmints will dine elsewhere.

✔ Keep cats out of your container plants. Cut the screens into pieces and set them on the soil in the pot. Water and air will get through, but kitty won't like the feel of the mesh on her sensitive paws, so she'll give your plants a pass.

✔ Protect newly planted seeds from chipmunks, birds, and other seed eaters by laying the screens over the seedbed. Just make sure you take them off at the first sign of little green shoots poking up.

Save Those Scraps!

When you find odds and ends that are left over from a home-improvement project, don't be too quick to trash all of them. Here's a sampling of ways you can put the best of those leftovers to good use.

WORKSHOP LEFTOVERS	WHAT TO DO WITH THEM	HOW TO GO ABOUT IT
Ceramic tiles	Give them to children to use as art material.	Have the kids draw pictures on paper, then glue the drawings to the tiles. Spray the surface with clear acrylic paint to protect their artwork. The result: paperweights or coasters to give as gifts.
Chicken wire	Arrange cut flowers.	Bend a piece of the mesh into a ball and put it in the bottom of an opaque vase. Then poke the stems through the openings.
Concrete paver or stepping stone (at least 12 inches across)	Get rid of gophers.	Lay the paver in the middle of your lawn. Using the wooden handle of a rake or shovel, pound on the paver for two or three minutes twice a day. After three or four days of this, the underground vibrations should drive the gophers to quieter territory.
Hardware cloth	Keep your gardening shoes dry.	Set a 12- to 14-inch square piece of mesh on the ground under the outdoor water spigot. The screen will let the water pass into the soil without puddling up and making a mucky mess for you to step in.
Rubber stair tread	Cover a swing seat.	To help swing riders get better traction on a metal swing and avoid splinters from a wooden one, glue the tread to the seat.
Vinyl floor tiles	Make heavy-duty coverings for shelves or drawers.	Measure the surface, then cut the tiles to fit, peel off the backing, and set them in place.
Wood chips	Deodorize your sneakers.	Put a handful of chips into each shoe and seal it in a plastic bag. Let it sit for a week so the chips can soak up odors. Then discard the used chips.

NEW HEIGHTS WITH AN OLD LADDER. If you have an old ladder with round rungs cluttering up the workshop, you could set it in the Donate or Sell zone. (These old climbing aids are hot collectibles.) Or you could clean it up, paint it, and take it out of hiding, putting it to work as decorative storage. Here's a trio of terrific possibilities:

1. Prop the ladder against a wall in your living room or family room and drape newspapers and magazines over the rungs. You'll have a homey but sophisticated stand-in for the wooden racks you see in library reading rooms.

2. Put it in your bedroom and use it to store and display pretty scarves, necklaces, or hand-stitched quilts.

3. Nix the metal towel rack in your bathroom and replace it with a ladder. (Just be sure to give the wood a coat of waterproof sealer first.)

A STEP UP FOR PLANTS. Do you have a wooden stepladder that's standing unused in a corner of the workshop? Then get that space hog outta there! Take it to the porch or deck, paint it to match the trim of your house, and use it to display your lovely container plants.

MAGIC CARPET SCRAPS. Well, not exactly magic. But if you've recently installed new carpet in your house and you've still got the remnants in the workshop, they belong in the Keep Here box (or zone). Even the smallest pieces can come in mighty handy. Here are just some of the ways you can use them in the workshop and elsewhere around your home, sweet home:

• Cushion your knees. Anytime you have down-and-dirty work to do, like painting or scrubbing a hard-surface floor or weeding the garden, slide a carpet scrap (soft side up) under your knees.

Cut carpet scraps to the right size and use them to line shelves, drawers, toolboxes, or anyplace else you keep heavy or delicate tools and equipment. The thick mat will protect both your belongings and the container they're stored in.

- Dampen noise. To quiet the noisy vibrations of a portable sewing machine, cut a piece of carpet to the right dimensions and simply slide it under the machine.

- Hold your wood. Before you lay a board in place on a sawhorse, lay a strip of carpet under each end. This will keep the board from sliding around as you're cutting it.

MAKING SPACE If you've got a dead magnetic flashlight hanging around your workshop, toss out the lightbulb end, but hang on to the magnetic body. Then attach it to a metal shelf (or even the refrigerator in the kitchen), and use it to hold pens and pencils.

- Keep moving. At the start of winter, stash some good-size carpet scraps in the trunk of your car. They'll provide excellent traction in case you get stuck on icy pavement.

- Protect your bedroom wall. To prevent a metal mattress frame from gouging the plaster or drywall, glue small pieces of carpet to the frame's sharp corners.

- Protect wood and tile floors. Glue tiny pieces of carpet (soft side down) to the bottoms of chair and table legs so they'll glide easily, without leaving scratches or black marks.

ORGANIZE

It's all well and good to clear unneeded stuff out of your workshop. But it still won't be a lean, mean, working machine until you organize it to suit your needs and the space at hand. These tip-top tips will help you do just that.

ZONED FOR ACTION. If your workshop is part of your garage, basement, or other multipurpose space, try to provide a separate area for each activity. You're only asking for a cluttered mess if you have hammers mingling with bottles of laundry detergent, or sandpaper and safety goggles sharing shelf space with your car-washing supplies.

THE MAIN ATTRACTION. The centerpiece of any workshop is, of course, the workbench. But, just as you did at the beginning of your sorting spree, it pays to ask yourself one crucial preorganizing question: Do you really need a workbench? If you tackle only one or two projects a year that demand a sturdy, steady surface, the space-saving answer is "no." Instead, get yourself a couple of strong sawhorses and an old door. Stash the door in the rafters when you're not using it. Keep the sawhorses up there, too, if there's room. Otherwise, hang them from the rafters, or nest them together and put them in the attic, a corner of your workshop, or some other out-of-the-way space.

THINK BIG. If you do a lot of woodworking or major tinkering, make sure you buy (or build) a bench that's roomy enough for the biggest projects you work on. A workbench that's too small for the tasks at hand will just take up space and act like a clutter magnet. If your floor space won't allow for a big bruiser of a bench, consider buying one that attaches to the wall and folds either up or down (depending on the model) when not in use. Some versions even come equipped with built-in pegboard panels or narrow shelves for storage. They're available in tool catalogs and on the Internet in a variety of sizes.

NO PARKING! You say floor space is not lacking in your workshop, but your family members seem to think that any flat surface is a prime parking spot for everything from flowerpots to last week's newspapers? In that case, a foldaway bench has your name written all over it. As soon as you're done using it, you can tuck it clear out of sight.

MESS-MAKER ALERT!

Problem: Sawdust, wood scraps, bent nails, and other dirty clutter make a mess of your workshop, but at the end of the day, it's all too easy to walk away and leave them there.

Solution: Get yourself a workbench on wheels. Weather permitting, you can roll it outside to do your work—and you're not likely to leave all the messy by-products cluttering up your driveway or patio. Just remember to lock the wheels before you start sawing or hammering!

WORKSHOP MUST-HAVES. No matter how large or small your workshop is, make sure your organizing plan includes this handful of essentials:

1. Good lighting. The number and type(s) of fixtures you need depend on many factors, including the kind of work you do, the amount of natural light in your workshop, and (of course) the state of your eyesight.

2. Plenty of electrical outlets. If you're working with existing outlets, keep them clear of furniture or other obstructions, so you can reach them easily. If you're building a new workshop or totally revamping an existing one, the number of outlets you need will be determined by the number of power tools, plug-in lamps, fans, and other electrical devices you use. When in doubt, remember this rule: You can never—I repeat, *never*—have too many electrical outlets.

3. Excellent ventilation. This is critical if you refinish furniture or do other work that involves using paint, solvents, and other chemicals. Even in a shop that has plenty of windows and a garage door, use several fans to provide good airflow.

4. A fire extinguisher. Or several if your workshop is large and you use power tools in more than one location. I hope I don't have to tell you why this is important!

5. A first-aid kit. No matter how careful you are, you're bound to get your fair share of cuts, scrapes, and splinters—not to mention the occasional burn from a hot power tool. So keep a first-aid kit stocked with antibiotic ointment, rubbing alcohol, bandages, and tweezers close at hand.

If you've leafed through any glossy decorating magazine or an upscale kitchen-supply catalog lately, you're probably familiar with GelPro® mats. These gel-filled floor coverings are made of tough-as-nails vinyl, and they do a fabulous job of relieving the pain and fatigue that results from standing on hard floors. Although they're intended to be used in kitchens, they're also perfect for workshops—especially for anyone who has arthritis or suffers from chronic back or foot pain. You can find these wonder workers on the Internet in a variety of sizes, colors, and textures.

CLUTTER BUSTER PRO

Professional organizer Darcy Schatz, owner of Organized Today in the Minneapolis–St. Paul area (www.orgtoday.com), has organized a *lot* of workshops. She says the process doesn't have to be complicated, and you don't need a lot of expensive storage systems. She offers these simple tips to whip the place into shape—so you never have to search high and low for the right-sized nail while wood glue drips on the floor.

☛ Install pegboard and hooks, and hang as many tools as possible on the board to clear your work surfaces.

☛ Draw the outline of each item on the pegboard using a permanent marker. This will ensure that you can put tools back where they belong quickly and easily. Another option: Attach a label to each hook indicating which tool "lives" there.

☛ Hang a notebook and pen on your pegboard. That way they'll be handy for making notes, marking plans, and keeping a shopping list.

☛ To keep building plans and project instructions in clear view, tack them to a bulletin board that's hung at eye level above your workbench.

☛ When you're not using plans and instruction booklets, slide them into clear, plastic sheet protectors and store them in three-ring binders or expandable files.

☛ Free up drawer and work surface space by hanging tool rechargers, hand vacuums, and small power tools on the wall.

☛ Screw hooks into the undersides of shelves and the ends of your workbench, and use them to hold rulers, levels, and anything else that has a hole for hanging.

☛ Store like items together. All measuring tapes and rulers should be in one location, all drill bits should be organized by size and kept in the same location, and all wood screws should be separated from other screw types.

☛ Use small jars or plastic containers for sorting nails, screws, dowel pins, and so forth by size. Label each container with both the contents and size.

☛ Tackle boxes are also useful for organizing small items like washers, screw-eye hooks, tacks, nuts, and bolts.

☛ Hang a broom and dustpan near the garbage for quick cleanups.

☛ Keep clamps close at hand by attaching them to a table leg or along the edge of a work surface.

☛ Think vertically when organizing your workshop. Wall-mounted shelves and bins can store tools and supplies within easy reach while keeping your work space clear. And wall-mounted hooks and brackets are perfect for hanging sawhorses and other large pieces.

☛ Store frequently used tools within easy reach, and stash things you use less often behind or above your work space.

☛ Keep materials you rarely use in stackable bins with lids. Label each bin clearly, and place it on an out-of-the-way shelf.

☛ Use ceiling-mounted storage racks for wood and other bulky items.

☛ Even if your workshop is tiny, wear a tool belt with pockets to keep all your supplies handy—thereby eliminating extra steps.

☛ A toolbox is one of the most important organizational helpers in any workshop. They come in many sizes, shapes, prices, and styles, but even one as simple as an open caddy will go a long way toward ending clutter and saving you time.

☛ If you have a lot of hand tools, organize them in drawers or toolbox compartments by type and size.

☛ Reduce floor clutter—and eliminate tripping hazards—by using retractable extension cords.

GOT IT PEGGED! No workshop is complete without pegboard, and for good reason: This holey wonder can help you organize everything from hand tools and small hardware to sandpaper and cleanup supplies. To make the most of pegboard, first measure your available wall space. Next, take inventory of all the things you need to store. (It's a good idea to lay them out on the floor at about the same distance apart that you'd use to hang them, and then measure that space.) Then visit a home-improvement center and pick up the right-size board, along with whatever hooks, racks, wire shelves, and hanging bins you need to accommodate your gear.

A LITTLE MORE DECORATIVE, PLEASE. If you'd prefer a slightly more polished look in your workshop, consider slat board. It's solid composite board with horizontal slats that accept special hangers. It was originally marketed for use in retail stores, but it's now available for home use. It comes in 4- by 8-foot sheets in numerous colors, and you can find it—along with a wide assortment of bins, baskets, and shelves—at home-improvement and home-organizing stores and on many Web sites. But be forewarned: Slat board costs considerably more than pegboard, but if appearances matter in your workshop (or hobby room), it's worth considering.

OTHER WAYS TO PUT YOUR WALLS TO WORK. The same organizing aids that help you keep other rooms shipshape can be just as effective in your workshop.

Ask Jerry

Q. I don't have room for both pegboard and shelves in my workshop. What can I do with power tools and paint cans that are too heavy for pegboard hooks to support?

A. Get yourself some plastic milk crates and use sturdy hooks to attach them to a wall, with the openings facing out. The crates are strong enough to hold your tools and filled cans, but they'll take up a lot less space than ordinary shelves would.

• Kitchen cabinets. If you've recently remodeled the kitchen, or you're planning to do so, move the old cabinets to your workshop. If you don't have any kitchen cabinets to spare, buy some brand-new ones at a home-improvement store, or look for secondhand models at a flea market, thrift shop, or store that sells used building supplies.

- Open shelves. Either go with simple pine boards on brackets, install wire shelves, or have shelving built to fit your available space. Ready-made bookcases (freestanding or wall mounted) are also available.

- Tall, freestanding cabinets. Buy units that are specially made for workshop storage, or look for vintage, wooden versions at a garage sale or thrift shop.

UP SHE GOES! If your workshop has exposed rafters, lay boards or sheets of $1/2$-inch plywood across them. Instantly, you'll have a place to stash all kinds of stuff that you don't need to get to very often, like lumber, extra pieces of molding, and off-duty tarpaulins and drop cloths.

In any other room in your house, floor-to-ceiling shelves are the be-all and end-all of efficient organizing. But in the workshop, install the bottom shelf at knee height, rather than at floor level. Crouching down to lift power tools or other heavy equipment is inconvenient at best. At worst, you could pull a muscle or throw your back out of whack. Don't get me wrong—I'm not suggesting that you let that floor space go to waste. Just use it for storage containers on wheels (see Collector Alert! on page 334).

Store

We're almost there! Now that you've gotten rid of everything that doesn't belong in your workshop and organized the space, you've reached the final step in your SOS mission: storing your tools and equipment in a way that works best for you.

YOU'VE HEARD THIS BEFORE... And now you're hearing it again. In your workshop, just like any other part of the house, it pays to follow the golden rule for easy, efficient storage: Always keep the things you use most often in places where you can get to them easily. On shelves, whether they're open or in closed cabinets, that's the area between midthigh and shoulder height.

SHELF LIFE. Here are a few more guidelines to keep in mind when you stock your workshop shelves:

✔ Keep heavier objects on the lower shelves and lighter items on the upper shelves.

✔ Whenever possible, use shelves that are only deep enough to hold the contents in a single row. Not only do shallower shelves take up less floor space, but they also help you avoid the hassle of having to rearrange the things in front to reach the stuff in back.

✔ If you must store items two or more rows deep, put the shortest things in front and the tallest in back. This way, you can see at a glance exactly what you've got.

✔ To avoid wasting vertical space, try to confine each shelf to objects of roughly the same height.

HERE'S THE LOWDOWN. When stocking workshop shelves (see Shelf Life above), here's one rule to follow faithfully: Never store liquids like paint stripper, turpentine, or other solvents on shelves above eye level. Why not? Because if you reach for a container and some of the liquid drips or sloshes out, you'll be hit in the face with a chemical that could burn or blind you. Always store chemicals on the floor or on shelves close to the floor, under lock and key.

COLLECTOR ALERT!

Problem: Heavy, hard-to-lift supplies like bags of cement and gallon (or 5-gallon) cans of paint.

Solution: Screw wheels onto mini wooden pallets and attach both ends of a rope to one side to use as a handle. Then set your heavy stuff on top and glide the pallets under wall-mounted shelves or cabinets. When the need arises, just pull a pallet out and roll it (and its load) to the job site. *Note:* A child's wagon will also work for this purpose. If you don't have any retired ones cluttering up your attic, basement, or garage, then consider buying a new wagon at a discount retailer.

A PARKING PLACE FOR PARTS. Muffin tins are terrific for storing small odds and ends in a drawer, but they also make great temporary storage when you have a project that involves keeping track of lots of small parts. I keep one in my workshop just for these occasions. The compartments are helpful for separating nuts, bolts, screws, and what have you, and I can readily see what I have without scattering them all over the place.

A JARRING EXPERIENCE. Looking for a neat, efficient way to store nails, screws, and other tiny pieces of hardware? Well, look no further than this classic trick: Hang a wooden shelf at eye level on the wall behind your workbench. Then gather up a bunch of small glass jars (baby food or small condiment jars are perfect). Attach the lids to the underside of the shelf with a single screw through the middle, so the glass jar will screw up into the cap. Not only will you be able to see at a glance exactly what little doodads you need, but you'll also be able to open the jar with one hand while you hang on to your work in progress with the other!

NO MORE TANGLES. A ball of twine is a workshop essential, but when it's just sitting on a shelf or in a drawer, it seems to tangle itself up as if by magic (at least it does at my house). But I've found a way to put an end to those shenanigans. How? Just store it in a clean plastic container, like the kind that yogurt or tub margarine comes in. Poke a hole in the cover, and feed the end of the twine through it. Drop the rest of the ball into the container, and replace the lid. If you want to be able to just yank at the twine, put a heavy weight (like a stone) in the bottom of the container before you insert the ball of twine. Now you've got twine that stays neat and tidy—and ready to use.

OUT OF THE BOX

The next time you use up a jar of hand or face cream, don't toss out the container. Instead, take it to the workshop and use it to store nails. The little bit of cream left in the jar will keep rust from forming on the fasteners.

CAN THE RUST. Coffee cans are classic storage containers in the workshop, but there's just one problem: When you use them to store things like nails and screws, rust tends to collect on the metal hardware. Fortunately, help is as close as the kitchen. Just toss a teaspoon of baking soda into the can before you fill it up, and you'll bid your rusty concerns good-bye!

HAND-TO-HAND COMBAT. To protect hanging hand tools from rust, use an old rag to apply a thin coat of oil to the metal parts after each use. Make sure you wipe the oil off before using the tool again, or the oily film will collect dust and dirt, and you'll have a real mess on your hands.

HAND-TO-HAND COMBAT, PART TWO. If you keep some or all of your hand tools in drawers or toolboxes, cut a carpet scrap to fit the bottom of the container. Then spray the carpet with a lubricant like WD-40®, and set it in the box or drawer. Your tools will pick up just enough oil to fend off rust. When the carpet gets grungy, throw it away and replace it with a fresh piece that's been sprayed with lubricant.

MESS-MAKER ALERT!

Problem: Sanding belts get creased and even cracked when you store them in a box or drawer.

Solution: Mount a couple of clean, dry paint roller covers on pegboard hooks, and hang the belts around the soft, plump rollers. They'll stay crease-free and ready for action.

LOOK SHARP! Glass cutters and metal scrapers demand slightly different rust-prevention measures. Store these sharpies standing up (blade end down, of course) in a small jar that's got half an inch of oil in the bottom. Wipe the oil off with an old rag before you use the tools. Given this treatment, they'll stay rust-free and rarin' to go for years.

STILL LOOKIN' SHARP. If you want the fine edge of a wood chisel to stay in top cutting form, you need to give it a little extra TLC when storing it. Here are two terrific ways to do that—and cut a little clutter from other parts of the house at the same time:

1. Cut a finger off an old leather work glove or insulated winter glove. Then slide the finger over the business end of the chisel, and tie the opening closed with a piece of twine or an old shoelace.

2. Cut a slice that's the width of the chisel into a hollow rubber ball or an old tennis ball. Then simply shove the tip of the chisel into the ball.

DON'T LET YOUR SAW BLADES MINGLE. A pegboard hook is the perfect place to store circular saw blades. But always put a piece of heavy cardboard or other protective material between the blades to keep them from touching each other. If they rub together, they're more likely to rust, plus they could become dented or worn.

FROM GARDEN DUTY TO GUARDIN' DUTY. Protect the blades of stored handsaws, hatchets, and work knives with pieces of old rubber garden hose. Cut a piece of hose the length of each blade, then cut a slit down one side and slide it over the sharp edge. The tools will keep their cutting power—and you'll be less likely to cut yourself when you reach for them.

ZIP GOES THE SANDPAPER! As soon as you bring a new supply of sandpaper home, pop it into a ziplock plastic freezer bag. Then either toss it in a drawer or attach a binder clip to the bag and hang it on a pegboard hook. When it's safely encased in plastic, the paper will stay dry and last a whole lot longer.

MAKING SPACE

Free up a little more space in the workshop by taking any extra unused batteries to the kitchen and storing them in the freezer. Put them in a ziplock plastic freezer bag, being careful that the terminals don't come in contact with each other. (If they do touch, each one will quickly lose its charge and become worthless.) Before you use the batteries, let them sit at room temperature for 24 hours to activate the chemicals inside.

THE INS AND OUTS OF POWER CORDS. Nothing clutters up a workshop—or makes it more hazardous—than a pile of off-duty extension cords lying on the floor. One way to deal with that problem is to coil each cord up the minute you're done using it, wrap Velcro® or a heavy-duty twist tie around the coil, and hang it on a pegboard hook. But here's a better idea: Replace your old extension cords with retractable versions. They recoil themselves automatically onto sturdy plastic reels, which you can then hang up or set aside neatly on a shelf. You can find retractable extension cords in tool catalogs and on the Internet in a variety of sizes and price ranges.

CREATE A MASTERPIECE

In This Section:
✔ Project supplies
✔ Lighting
✔ Work surfaces

Are you lucky enough to have a whole room that's devoted just to quilting, painting, pottery, scrapbooking, or whatever craft(s) you love? Do you create your masterpieces in a corner of the basement or kitchen? Or do you and your family share a room that's used for everything from your weaving projects to the kids' finger-painting sessions?

If these alternatives sound familiar, then you already know that any creative endeavor generates a mountain of tools, supplies, and finished projects. And that, my friends, can add up to major clutter in no time flat. The solution? Read on for lots of workable ideas to get that hobby room under control.

SORT

No matter what kind of crafts you enjoy making in your hobby room, one thing is for certain: You'll get a whole lot more pleasure out of creating your masterpieces when you have a neat, uncluttered space to work in. In fact, it will probably inspire you to create more. So grab a bunch of boxes, and get to sorting!

THE SAME OLD CROWD. Start your sorting mission by giving the boxes the usual labels: Trash, Keep Here, Take Elsewhere, and Donate or Sell. If other folks in the family also use your hobby room, try to make sorting a team project, with everyone pitching in. Otherwise, assign one box (or more) to each person and tuck belongings into the appropriate carton(s). Then have everyone sort the contents at his or her earliest convenience.

TRASH IT! A whole lot of junk tends to accumulate in even the neatest hobby room. The trash can or recycling bin is the place for everything that falls into one of these categories:

✔ Anything that's broken or worn out beyond repair

✔ Sewing patterns with pieces missing

✔ Dried-out glue, markers, and paint

✔ Parts that once belonged to tools or other implements that you no longer own (like a pedal for a sewing machine that died in 1998)

✔ Anything you can't identify

IT'S A WRAP. Lurking deep in the back of your hobby room closet is a handful of cardboard tubes that once held gift-wrapping paper. (How on earth did *they* get here?) No matter. Just toss them into a Take Elsewhere box—whatever you do, don't trash them. They're perfect for corralling this trio of household items:

• Christmas lights. Just wind the cords around the tube, wrap the whole thing in tissue paper, and tuck it away in your designated light box.

You've just pulled an embroidery hoop out of a drawer, and you haven't done a single stitch of embroidery in years. An obvious candidate for the Donate or Sell box, right? Wrong! Take that hoop to the laundry room, and use it as a stain-removal aid. When you have to treat a spot on something really big, like a tablecloth or a sheet, simply clamp the hoop over the soiled part of the fabric, and then go to work with your favorite spot remover.

- Scarves. Instead of folding them, roll your scarves around the tube.

- Tablecloths. When you fold them, tuck a tube into each fold to keep creases from forming.

Just one word of caution: When you're using this trick for long-term storage of either scarves or tablecloths, put a layer of acid-free tissue paper between the cardboard and the fabric. You can find it at art-supply stores and in catalogs that specialize in archival-storage supplies.

SHARE AND SHARE ALIKE.

Consider your sorting spree a chance to share your passion for a favorite craft with someone who's never tried it. Fill an attractive basket or box with several necessary materials, and add a gift certificate offering some get-started lessons in scrapbooking, beading, quilting, knitting, or whatever. Then give it to a friend or relative who you think would enjoy it. Knowing that someone else will make good use of the castoffs—and might even become a fellow devotee of your pastime—should give you the incentive to dig in and start sorting.

BEEN THERE, HAVEN'T DONE THAT.
Every seamstress or needleworker has had this experience: You purchase a pattern and supplies for a garment or project you plan to make, and the stuff just sits there—

PACK RAT ALERT!

Problem: Your hobby room is filled to the brim with craft supplies, but you can't bring yourself to get rid of any of them because you're certain you'll get around to using them.

Solution: Figure out how long, on average, it takes you to complete a medium-size project. If you're, let's say, a dedicated knitter, how many days or weeks does it normally take you to create a sweater? Use that number as a guideline, and calculate how many projects you can complete in the next two to three years. Next, sort the supplies into piles by project. If you end up with more sweaters, scarves, and afghans than you can possibly get done within the time limit, weed out your least favorite projects until you're at a number that's within reach.

sometimes for years. Well, do yourself a favor: Take a good, hard look at all those materials, and decide which ones you're likely to tackle in the next year. Put them in a box labeled To Be Done and set it aside. In the meantime, give all of the other patterns, yarn, fabric, and what have you to someone who will use them. A nearby senior center, nursing home, or women's shelter would welcome your castoffs with open arms.

DEAL WITH DUPLICATES AND TRIPLICATES. Maybe you got a new sewing machine as a gift last Christmas, but the old one is still cluttering up the hobby room. That falls squarely in the Donate or Sell category. Multiple pairs of scissors? Put the extras in the Take Elsewhere box, and see if you can use them in the bathroom, kitchen, or home office. More spools of white or black thread than you'll use anytime soon? They could be useful in the laundry room (see "Sew What?" on page 213). I could go on and on, but you get the picture.

YARDSTICKS FOR THE YARD. If you have an extra yardstick or two cluttering up the hobby room, don't let those measuring sticks just lie there, taking up space. Instead, cut them into 1-foot sections, and use them as lawn-mowing guide sticks. Sink the sticks into the soil at several spots in your yard because grass grows at various rates, depending on shade, moisture, and other factors. Then mark each one at the line that's one-third over the optimum mowing height for your grass. (That's because you never want to remove more than one-third of a grass blade at any one time.) So, for instance, if your lawn is Kentucky bluegrass, which should be kept at 2 inches in cool weather, mark the sticks at the 3-inch line. When those green blades start brushing the line, haul out the old mower, and give the top inch a trim.

OUT OF THE BOX

Got more bottles of white glue than you need in the hobby room? If so, then take one to the workshop and tuck it into your first-aid kit. The next time a splinter plants itself in your skin, cover the sliver with a thin layer of glue, and spread it over the area. When the glue dries, peel it off. The intruding sliver will slide right out.

USE 'EM OR LOSE 'EM. Are you hanging on to a pile of sewing scraps just because the fabric is too pretty to throw away? If so, don't toss 'em in the trash—but don't keep them cluttering up your hobby room, either. Instead, use them in other projects or give them to someone who will. Even the smallest pieces of fabric can still lead useful "lives." Here's a sampling of possibilities:

• Accessorize. Depending on the size of the remnants, use them to make accessories like hats, scarves, ties, sashes, headbands, or hair bows.

• Create a collage. Turn those snippets into a picture, either on their own or as part of a mixed-media work (as they say in artist lingo) that contains other hobby-room leftovers like sequins, buttons, or fancy paper. Just cut the material into shapes of your choice and paste them onto a wood panel or a piece of archival mounting board. (If this idea sounds enticing, but intimidating, check with your local community college or adult-education center; many of them offer collage-making classes for all experience levels.)

• Make a quilt. Or give your scraps to a quilter who will turn them into a work of useful art. You can bet your bottom button they'll find a happy home, especially if the fabrics are choice silks and velvets.

• Make rugs. Cut your leftovers into strips and turn them into either hooked or braided rugs. (Many quilting, weaving, and fabric shops offer classes in this old-time pastime.)

• Protect your clothes and linens. Sew little pouches and fill them with dried lavender or other herbs that smell terrific *and* repel cloth-destroying moths in drawers and closets.

MAKING SPACE

If you're currently storing hobby supplies in a hodgepodge of small cupboards, dressers, trunks, and other assorted containers, do yourself a favor: Get rid of those odds and ends and replace them with one large, great-looking piece like an armoire, or with a wall of cabinets or shelves. The big, single unit will actually take up less physical space than a bunch of smaller ones—and a whole lot less visual space, too!

- Thrill your cat. Cut out two pieces in the shape of (for instance) a fish, and sew them front to front, leaving one end open. Flip the little pouch inside out, stuff it with high-quality catnip, and stitch it shut. Your favorite feline will jump for joy!

Decorate a dollhouse by turning sewing scraps into pint-size curtains, slipcovers, tablecloths, and wall coverings.

- Trim the Christmas tree. Cut out trees, stockings, or other seasonal shapes, and stitch them together as described in "Thrill your cat" above. But instead of stuffing your creations with catnip, use cotton batting or panty hose. (Otherwise, you'll have Fluffy scrambling through the boughs!) Attach color-coordinated ribbons and hang the decorations on the tree.

- Wrap presents. Use larger pieces in place of wrapping paper and tie them with braid, rickrack, or high-quality ribbon—thereby delivering a bonus gift: the makings of a decorative pillow.

- Wrap presents, take two. Cut shapes out of smaller remnants, and glue them onto plain white or solid-colored paper. Use them simply as decorations, or turn them into gift tags by writing on them with permanent marker.

ORGANIZE

The only right way to organize a hobby room is the way that works best for you. And that depends on the kinds of crafts or other hobbies you use the room for. But regardless of where your creative interests lie, these guidelines will help you make the most of your space.

DIVVY UP THE TERRITORY. If your hobby "room" is actually part of your basement, family room, or other multipurpose space, designate a clearly distinct section for your work surface(s) and supply storage. Simple curtains hung from the ceiling will do the trick, but if you choose your dividers wisely, they can give you storage and/or display space on both sides. Consider these options for creating a room within a room:

- Folding screens. Find or make one with a purely decorative surface on one side, and face that toward the family living area. Line the side facing the hobby room with corkboard, where you can pin up fabric samples, photographs, or other inspiration for your work.

- Freestanding bookshelves or storage cabinets. Space permitting, place two units back to back, so that the one facing the hobby area will hold craft supplies, and the one facing the laundry area will hold detergent, cleaning supplies, and so forth. Or use the one facing the family room to hold, what else? Books!

DIVIDE FURTHER. Do you use your hobby room for more than one kind of craft? In that case, keep (let's say) your loom and weaving supplies separate from your sewing machine and fabric stash. Likewise, if your children or grandchildren use the room for their own creative projects, try to give them a worktable and storage facilities of their own.

NOW YOU SEE IT... If floor space is limited in your hobby room, consider buying a foldable workbench (see "Think Big" on page 328). That now-you-see-it, now-you-don't surface can work every bit as well for cutting quilt patches or laying out pattern pieces as it does for carpentry projects. For the ultimate in

Ask Jerry

Q. I've recently taken up scrap-booking in a big way, and I love it! The trouble is that not only do I not have a separate hobby room, but I also don't have space to spare in the kitchen, bedroom, or anyplace else in the house. How can I pursue my passion without making a cluttered mess everywhere?

A. Learn to be sneaky. Get yourself a folding or rolling table that you can stash in a closet when you're not using it. Keep larger supplies in containers that blend in with the decor, like pretty baskets, trunks, or lift-top ottomans. For smaller items, use boxes and bins that you can tuck away in cabinets or slide under a bed. Then when you've got the time, pull everything out and get scrappy!

CLUTTER BUSTER PRO

Krista Colvin, professional organizer and owner of Organize in Style in Camas, Washington (www.organizeinstyle.com), specializes in helping creative people de-clutter their work spaces. Whether your hobby (or profession) is weaving, sewing, quilting, painting, or scrapbooking, these tips will help to organize your space so it works efficiently—and makes your creative juices flow.

☛ Move your worktable away from the wall so you can easily maneuver around it.

☛ Place your worktable (or easel, loom, or potter's wheel) so that it faces a source of natural light. If there's a window with a beautiful view to inspire you, so much the better!

☛ Great lighting is a must. Experiment until you find the combination of lamps and wall or ceiling fixtures that works best for you.

☛ Choose a light, neutral palette for your furniture and storage pieces. Not only will it make the room look and feel bigger and less cluttered, but it will also let your creations take center stage.

☛ Designate zones pertaining to the various stages of your projects. For example, the Design Zone could contain a sketchbook, color charts, or magazines and books that provide inspiration. The Create Zone would house the tools and equipment used in your work.

☛ Use walls for storage, thereby increasing the amount of floor space available for your working gear.

☛ Keep the things that inspire you to create out in the open, where you can see them. Hang beads, fancy trim, or hanks of yarn from wall racks; stack bolts of colorful fabric on open shelves; and pin postcards, photographs, and magazine clippings to bulletin boards.

☛ Stash more mundane supplies like sewing patterns, glue, and pads of tracing paper behind closed doors or in attractive containers.

☛ Display the fruits of your labor. Not only will they add visual pizzazz to the room, but they will also inspire you to create more.

efficient organizing, choose a model that includes pegboard or shallow shelves for storage.

STAGING AREAS. Some crafts are multistage affairs. If you both design and make hooked rugs, patchwork quilts, or needlepoint tapestries, set up separate areas for each process.

SHOP AT HOME. Before you go out and buy a big piece of storage furniture to organize your craft and hobby supplies, take a tour of your house. You just might find an armoire, bookcase, buffet, or hutch that will work perfectly—that's currently gathering dust in the attic, or cluttering up another room.

BACK TO THE KITCHEN. You've been reading a lot about kitchen cabinets in this book and for good reason: They can be organizing superstars in many parts of the house, and the hobby room is no exception. Look for veteran performers in places that sell used or salvaged building supplies, or splurge on new cabinets at a local home-improvement or building-supply store. Base cabinets with accompanying countertops will give you terrific work surfaces, and their wall-hung mates will hold plenty of supplies.

MAKING SPACE

Don't overlook the walls when you're organizing hobby room space. Whether you opt for pegboard, slat board, or wall-hung cabinets or shelves—or any combination thereof—those vertical surfaces are the most valuable real estate you could ever ask for. So be sure to put it to good use!

STORE

Most crafts and creative hobbies have one thing in common: They require a whole lot of equipment and supplies, which all have to be stored somewhere. But don't fret. Just let your imagination soar, and you'll find all kinds of terrific storage containers—including many that won't cost you a penny.

TOOLS OF THE TRADE. Does the inside of your sewing box look like an earthquake hit it? If so, then transfer your gear to a toolbox, and assign all the little odds and ends to separate compartments. That way, it'll be a snap to find exactly what you're looking for.

IT'S IN THE BAG. If you're like most women I know, you have two or three handbags that you use all the time, and several more that are just gathering dust in the bedroom closet. So move them to the hobby room to hold yarn, quilting templates, and other small gear. You can either set the bags on shelves, or hang them from hooks on the wall or the back of a door.

IT'S IN ANOTHER KIND OF BAG. An over-the-door shoe bag, that is. Hang one (or more) on a wall or on the back of a door, and use it to store rolls of tape, tubes or bottles of glue, packages of beads or buttons, and anything else that will fit neatly inside the handy see-through pockets.

CRAFTY KIDS. If your children or grandchildren use the hobby room for their own projects, stow their supplies in transparent, plastic storage boxes that have lock-down lids and handles. Choose small containers that are easy to carry, and put them on shelves that the youngsters can reach without climbing on a chair—or calling for help.

KEEP OUT! Sewing and other kinds of needlework are not normally considered dangerous pastimes, but some of the essential

Instead of trying to stuff used sewing pattern pieces back into their original envelope—and winding up with a creased, wrinkled, or even torn mess—get yourself a three-ring binder and some plastic sleeve pockets. Then store the empty envelopes and pattern pieces in the pockets (one project per pocket, of course). For works in progress, you can even keep any special notions in the pockets, so they'll be close at hand.

supplies can be deadly in the hands (or mouth) of a small child or pet. So if four-legged or tiny two-legged visitors have even occasional access to your hobby room, store any potential hazards well out of their reach. The no-no list includes needles; pins; beads; buttons; scissors; bottles of paint, dye, and glue; and anything else that's small enough to swallow, sharp enough to cut, or enticing enough to drink.

MAKE IT A GLASS ACT. A great many craft supplies are just too pretty to hide in boxes, baskets, and bins. So why not make your stash part of your decor by showing it off in clear glass jars, bowls, bottles, and even vases? You can find transparent treasures in sizes and shapes that will accommodate everything from teeny-tiny beads and buttons to elegant camel's hair paintbrushes, spools of thread, and hanks of colorful yarn.

ALL IN THE FAMILY. Glass containers aren't the only kind that can turn your hobby gear into a decorative asset. Simply by choosing containers that are in the same color family or are made of the same material, you'll reduce visual clutter and achieve a sophisticated "designer" look at the same time. Consider these options:

✔ Galvanized or stainless steel buckets, baskets, and boxes in a variety of sizes

✔ Boxes that are covered in fabric of the same pattern, different patterns in the same color combo, or one or two solid colors

COLLECTOR ALERT!

Problem: Your button collection is all tossed together in a drawer, so when you need a particular size or color, it takes forever to find it.

Solution: Sort the buttons by size and color, and thread each group onto a separate piece of embroidery floss, matching the color of the floss to that of the buttons. That way, it will take only seconds to find the right size and shade. (Yarn will do the trick, too, as long as the holes in the buttons are big enough for the yarn to slip through.)

- ✔ Baskets of similar styles, but different sizes

- ✔ Wooden boxes

SAFEGUARD YOUR MASTERPIECES.
Attention, quilters! When you need to store any of your creations, it's important to do it in exactly the right way. Otherwise, the fabric could suffer considerable damage, and all of your time and effort will go right down the drain. This is the method professional textile conservators recommend. *Note:* These same guidelines apply to storing needlepoint, cross-stitch or other embroidered work, and anything else that's made of fabric.

1. Get a two- or four-ply acid-free rag box that's big enough to hold the quilt when it's folded into thirds. (They're available at art-supply stores and from Web sites that specialize in archival-storage materials.)

2. Lay the quilt on a flat surface, top side up, and place acid-free tissue paper on top of it. (You can find the paper at the same places that sell archival boxes.)

3. Gently fold the quilt into thirds, keeping the tissue paper in place.

4. Wrap the whole, folded quilt in more tissue paper. When you're finished, every bit of fabric should be covered with the acid-free tissue.

Ask Jerry

Q. *I'm an avid scrapbooker, and I've got dozens of hole punches that make different-shaped cutouts. The problem is that when they're all jumbled together in a box, they look like a zillion pairs of pliers. Whenever I want a particular one, I have to plow through the whole pile to find it. Do you have any clever ideas for storing my crafty punches?*

A. I sure do—and it might help you cut a little clutter from your (or your hubby's) bedroom closet at the same time! Just get an old belt and cut it in half—removing the buckle first. Poke a hole at either end of each half, and hang the two pieces horizontally from hooks, either on pegboard or directly on the wall. Then simply slip the punch handles over the leather strips.

5. Set the quilt in the box, and put it somewhere safe that's free of dampness, pests, and extreme temperatures.

6. Every few months or so, take the quilt out and refold it in a slightly different configuration, so the creases don't become permanent.

TWO BIG STORAGE NO-NOS.
Whenever you store a quilt or other textile, keep these two rules in mind:

• Never store fabric wrapped in plastic. For one thing, it can trap dampness, which will encourage mildew to form. What's more, any plastic that contains polyvinyl chloride (PVC) is likely to cause the material to yellow.

• Whatever you do, don't pin a label to your creation! And make sure there are no pins or needles remaining in the material from the stitching phase. Why? Because those little metal fasteners will leave rust spots and holes in the fabric.

MESS-MAKER ALERT!

Problem: You need to store a quilt in a wooden drawer.

Solution: Whatever you do, don't let that quilt (or any other fine textiles) come in direct contact with the surface of the drawer. All woods contain sulfur, which will gradually cause the fabric to deteriorate. First, paint the inside of the drawer with polyurethane varnish, and line it with clean, 100 percent cotton sheets, acid-free paper, or unbleached muslin. Then wrap up the quilt (see "Safeguard Your Masterpieces" on page 349), and set it into its nice cozy "bed."

CHAPTER TEN

DOWNSIZING

Even if you've relocated many times over the years, moving from larger quarters to smaller ones is never easy. And when the place you're moving away from has been your family's home, sweet home for decades, downsizing can be one of the most challenging and stressful experiences of your life. Trust me: Nothing can make it a barrelful of laughs. But our plan can make the transition go a whole lot smoother.

GETTING READY

The key to successful downsizing is a positive attitude. Don't think of it as casting off generations' worth of cherished possessions. Instead, consider it a golden opportunity to weed out all the extraneous clutter in your life and focus on things that really matter.

In This Section:
✔ Sort: big time
✔ Organize
    for the move
✔ Store in smaller
    quarters

SORT

If you need a little prodding to start your big sorting spree, maybe this reminder will help: The less stuff you have to pack up and transport, the easier your move will be—and the less it will cost you. And that means you'll have more time, energy, and cold cash to enjoy life in your new surroundings. So what are you waiting for? Dive right in!

IT'S NEVER TOO SOON TO START. This simple fact should be a no-brainer, but it's something a lot of folks don't think about: The sooner you start getting rid of things you don't really need or want—or at least deciding what you'll do with them when the time comes—the less you'll have to deal with as moving day approaches. And that will translate into a big reduction in your stress level. If you and your spouse have decided that you'll move to smaller quarters when you retire in a couple of years, the time to start downsizing is now—not a few weeks (or even a few months) before the moving van rolls up to your door.

MORE REASONS TO START EARLY. Getting an early jump on your future move has a few other big advantages:

1. You avoid having to make snap decisions about what to take and what to leave behind. If you wait until the last minute (or even the last few weeks), you could act too hastily and throw something away that you'd really regret losing—and that can't be replaced at any price.

2. You can take your time finding exactly the right home for treasured belongings you're positive you won't be taking, like your grand piano, vintage Chris-Craft speedboat, or big dining room table that's been in the family for five generations.

3. It's much easier on your health, both physically and mentally. Even routine de-cluttering can be hard, tiring work. Just the thought of clearing out an entire house from top to bottom on a tight deadline is enough to make your entire body (including your head) ache. At least it does mine!

4. You'll be giving yourself plenty of time to plan for how to dispose of your unwanted goods. You can schedule a garage sale

PACK RAT ALERT!

Problem: You've got a big house that's filled to the rafters with so much stuff that you don't even know where to start sorting.

Solution: Begin in the basement or attic. Why? Because if your home is like most, those out-of-sight, out-of-mind areas are where the majority of household clutter piles up. And a whole lot of it is nothing but useless junk that you can toss out without giving it a second thought. Those kinds of instant results will give you powerful momentum to use in other rooms in your house.

(see page 359 for some tips), put items on eBay®, and/or donate items to local charities and nonprofit organizations. Start by listing all the furniture, artwork, dishes, and so forth that you think you won't need anymore. Then match them up to the appropriate sale or donation venue.

CLUTTER BUSTER PRO

One of the most challenging aspects of downsizing is getting rid of years' worth of possessions without throwing your memories away. Marilyn Bohn, a professional organizer and owner of Get It Together Organizing (www.marilynbohn.com) in Bountiful, Utah, offers these timely tips to help you cull your belongings, so you can free up your space, your time, and your life—and hang on to precious memories at the same time.

☛ Get rid of the guilt factor. Many people consider themselves the guardians of their family heirlooms—even if they've been in storage for years. Set your mind at ease by giving the heirlooms to relatives or close family friends who will actually enjoy using the clan's treasures.

☛ If you offer an object to someone and he or she refuses it, don't take it personally. The fact that some folks don't share the same love for your possessions, or don't have room for them in their homes, does *not* mean they don't love you.

☛ Before you give any heirlooms away, get together with the recipients and share your memories about the items. Then take pictures of the pieces you especially care about, and put them in a photo album or scrapbook. (Or if you prefer, save them in a file on your computer.)

☛ Make special arrangements for cherished belongings that your loved ones don't want. Either give them to a shelter or library, where they'll be used and appreciated, or donate them to a thrift shop or tag sale that benefits a cause you especially care about. (Many groups, including hospitals, symphony orchestras, and animal welfare groups, maintain full-time thrift shops or hold periodic sales to raise money to support their activities.)

EASY DOES IT. If you don't have a basement or an attic (see the Pack Rat Alert! on page 352), or you're just not ready to tackle such a big area yet, think small. Start your sorting spree in a spare bedroom, large closet, or whatever other space meets these three criteria:

1. It contains a lot of items that are being stored, rather than displayed or used on a regular basis.

2. Much of the contents will likely be stuff that you won't even want to consider taking with you.

3. For the most part, the things you'll have to deal with have little sentimental value. (That will make your take-it-or-leave-it decisions a lot easier and much less stressful.)

OVER MY DEAD BODY! Before you start sorting—and if possible, before you start looking for your next home—make a list of the things you own that give you the greatest pleasure. If you love nothing better than sitting down at the piano and plunking out your favorite tunes, do everything possible to keep that baby, even if it means trading in your big couch for a smaller model, or making the coffee table double for dining. (Don't worry: That won't mean you have to hunker down on floor cushions to eat dinner. In catalogs, on the Internet,

COLLECTOR ALERT!

Problem: Your home is filled with possessions that bring back decades of memories—happy, sad, and bittersweet. Try as hard as you might, you just can't bring yourself to start sorting through it all.

Solution: Ask a close friend or family member for help. Not only will the job be less stressful, but it will also go faster. Choose someone whose company you enjoy, who knows your tastes and how you really live. It should be someone you trust to give an honest opinion about everything from how you *really* look in that red dress to how likely you are to need half a dozen party platters in your new home. And be sure to choose a sorting buddy who makes you laugh because, as the medical gurus tell us, laughter is the greatest stress reliever of all.

and in some furniture stores, you can find very attractive tables that easily adjust from coffee- to dining-table height.)

LIST THE SMALLER KEEPERS, TOO.

Write down everything you simply refuse to leave behind, no matter what, and keep this list handy as you sort through your belongings. Maybe it's your dad's photo album from World War II, the journal your mother kept when she was expecting you, or the souvenir plates you collected on road trips with your children. Granted, you may need to make some trade-offs as you come across things you'd forgotten about. But putting your priorities in writing will be a reminder that all of your possessions are *not* created equal.

GET THE LAY OF THE LAND.

As soon as your new home is lined up, get a blueprint or drawing that shows the exact dimensions of each room, including the garage and any other places you might use for storage. Don't forget to measure the height of the ceilings, as well as the height and width of doorways and windows (including their height from the floor). Then go through your current house and measure each piece of furniture, as well as any other large objects you might like to keep. Knowing which items can fit into the new rooms and which ones can't will make your decision-making process much easier—and allow you to make the best use of your future space.

For older folks who have been in the family homestead for decades, moving to strange new surroundings can be downright traumatizing. If you're helping elderly relatives downsize their lives, this simple trick can make the transition a little easier: Before changing a single thing, take pictures of the inside of their current home. Then after the move, place their belongings in a way that's as similar as possible to the old arrangement. Carry out the plan in as much detail as space permits, from arranging the bedroom furniture to placing books on the shelves and pictures on the walls. The closer you can come to duplicating the old setup, the sooner your loved ones will start to feel at home.

COMING TO TERMS. The sorting categories for a full-scale downsizing will be slightly different than they are for routine de-cluttering. In this case, in addition to your trusty boxes, gather up a supply of labels or index cards to use for items that are too big to fit in cartons. You should have designated containers and ID tags marked Trash, Donate, Sell, Take Along, and Special Handling. That last category is for family heirlooms, treasured collections, or other prized possessions that you'll turn over to relatives, friends, or particular organizations.

JUDGMENT CALLS. The candidates for your Trash boxes (or bags) are the same ones we've talked about throughout this book—anything that's broken and can't be repaired, containers with a solidified layer of who knows what in the bottom, and parts that once belonged to appliances, games, toys, or other things that you no longer own. Special Handling is something only you can define. As for the Take Along containers, anything you truly love and/or use on a regular basis that you'll have room for in your new home definitely deserves a place in the moving van.

GET RID OF IT. When it comes to any belongings that do not have great sentimental value, plan on selling or giving away those that meet the following criteria:

• You won't need it in your future home. For instance, if you're moving to a condo or rental apartment where the management handles all maintenance chores, you won't need many tools.

COLLECTOR ALERT!

Problem: Moving day is rapidly approaching, but you just cannot decide what to do with some of your family's most cherished, and irreplace-able, possessions.

Solution: When in doubt, take them along if it's at all possible. Or leave them in the care of a trusted friend or relative until you can make a decision. Remember: Your goal here is to simplify your life—not to deprive yourself of all the things you hold dear. You can always get rid of things later if you need or want to.

- You have something else that could serve the same purpose. You probably don't need a blender *and* a food processor.

- It's not in good shape. If your coffeemaker is showing serious signs of wear and tear, you may want to leave it behind and get a new one after the move.

MAKING SPACE

When push comes to shove, you can rent or borrow just about anything, from cocktail glasses to canoes. So why crowd your home and your life with stuff that you haul out only once a year, if that?

- It can be replaced. If you cast off your big roasting pan, you can always buy a disposable one when the family unexpectedly decides to drop by for Christmas. But it's a whole different ball game to part with a beloved antique or an original work of art, only to find out it would have fit in your new home after all.

- It'll be easier and/or cheaper to replace it rather than move it. In this case, your decision depends in large part on how far you're moving. If you're only headed across town, then by all means, take that almost-new kitchen trash can. On the other hand, if you're leaving Boston bound for Key West, forget it!

ORGANIZE

When you're downsizing for a move, the organizing process is a little different than it is when you're simply de-cluttering your house. In fact, in this case, you need to organize before, during, *and* after your sorting spree.

PACK AS YOU GO. Before you start sorting, stock up on boxes, tape, and plenty of padding like bubble wrap, packing paper, and/or foam peanuts. Then as you pinpoint items that you want to take along, but don't use every day, pack them up and set them aside. (Be sure to label the box with the contents and the room they belong in.) If you can, designate a guest room or other little-used space as a "holding tank," where the boxes will be out of the way. Prime candidates for early packing sessions include seasonal or holiday decorations, out-of-season clothes, photo albums, and artwork.

GIVE AS YOU GO, TOO. Assign separate areas for things that you'll be donating to charity or giving to friends or relatives—and keep that stuff flowing out of there. Not only will you lessen the chances that you'll change your mind about getting rid of the silver candlesticks that you haven't used since 1985, but you'll also free up room to store the things you will be loading onto the moving van. And take it from me, friends: Once your belongings are packed in boxes, they'll take up a lot more space than they did when they were hanging on the wall or sitting on shelves!

DON'T SELL AS YOU GO. Instead, as you come across potential garage sale items, move them to a certain area (maybe the garage, if there's room). If an item is too big to move easily, or it's still in use, simply attach a Sell label to it. Then go about your business as usual until it's time to set up shop.

NIX THE NEWSPAPERS. If you've been hanging on to piles of papers to use for packing, toss 'em in the recycling bin! Don't use them as padding when you pack, or you'll have a big mess on your hands later on because newspaper ink rubs off on everything it touches. Instead, as soon as you decide to move, notify all your friends and neighbors

If you lack the time, energy, patience, or physical strength to downsize your home, or to help your parents downsize theirs, don't do it—at least not all of it. Instead, get help from a downsizing professional or a moving company that specializes in senior clients. These pros can tackle all or part of the transition, from setting a time line and comprehensive plan for the move to arranging the furniture in your new home and even hooking up electronic devices. To find a downsizing specialist in your area, contact the National Association of Senior Move Managers (877-606-2766 or www.nasmm.com) or the National Association of Professional Organizers (856-380-6828 or www.napo.net).

that you'll welcome their cast-off bubble wrap, foam peanuts, and plain packing paper. It's a good bet they'll be able to supply all you need. If not, you can buy those cleaner, neater packing materials from any moving company, office-supply store, or truck-rental office. *Note:* Whatever you do, don't buy them (or boxes either) from a shipping store—they'll cost you an arm and a leg!

GARAGE SALE ORGANIZING 101. A successful garage sale doesn't just happen. Like any other aspect of successful downsizing (or general de-cluttering), it takes some planning. The better you organize the event, the more stuff you'll get rid of—and the more money you'll have to spend in your new locale. This handful of hints will help:

1. Do some homework. Read the garage sale ads in the local paper, and visit a few sales to get an idea of what's selling and for how much. There's no sense pricing books at $1 each if the going rate is 25 cents.

2. Advertise. Spring for an ad in the local newspaper. Many papers offer special garage sale rates and/or free signs to advertisers. If possible, mention specific categories like garden tools, furniture, or collectible pottery. Whatever you do, don't waste your ad dollars on "miscellaneous."

3. Get help. Besides enlisting willing volunteers to set up tables, price and arrange merchandise, and hang signs around town, be sure to put someone in charge of watching the till—and keeping an eye on any small valuable items that could, um, wander off.

PACK RAT ALERT!

Problem: There's so much stuff to sell that you don't think you could do it in one day or even one weekend—and time is running out.

Solution: Find a local church, school, or civic group that's hosting a tag sale open to outside vendors, and rent a space or a table. The charity benefits from your rental fee, and you get to keep the sale proceeds. Plus, you're all but guaranteed to get a lot more traffic than you'd get at home.

4. Plan for the leftovers. Well in advance of the sale, arrange for Goodwill, the Salvation Army, or another charity to come by at a certain time to pick up everything that hasn't sold. And be sure to tell them the stuff is garage sale surplus because some groups won't accept anything that still has a price sticker on it.

5. Be there. Have you ever gone to a garage sale, only to be ignored by the seller, who's slumped in a chair reading a book or chattering on the phone? Well, I have, and believe me: It sure didn't put me in the mood to spend money! So greet your customers with a smile and a cheery hello, and be ready to interact with them. You'll sell a lot more stuff—and have more fun, to boot.

THINK OUTSIDE THE GARAGE.
Although a garage sale is a terrific way to get rid of ordinary stuff that's filling your house, it's not the way to go when parting with valuables that have real financial worth. If you have much in the way of antiques, original artwork, fine or artisan-made jewelry, or a sizable library of good books, opt for one of these approaches instead:

• Auction it off. For a percentage of the profits, auctioneers will appraise, catalog, stage, and sell your belongings, either in your home or in their gallery. Check the Internet or the Yellow Pages for an auctioneer nearby.

Ask Jerry

Q. *I have a big collection of vintage pottery that I plan to sell before we move in a few months. My husband says I should post it on eBay®, but I think that would be more trouble than it's worth, and it's better to put the collection in our garage sale. Who's right?*

A. In my opinion, you are. It is true that on eBay you'll probably get a few more dollars for each piece than you would at a garage sale. But you have to weigh that against the time it takes to photograph each item, write a description, and post it on the Web site—not to mention the wait for buyers to appear. Then, whenever you make a sale, you'll have to pack the item up and take it to the post office. Plus, you'll have to pay commissions to eBay and PayPal. My advice is to have a garage sale.

- Hold an estate sale. Traditionally, the goods offered at such an event were the belongings (i.e., the estate) of a deceased person. But today, many estate sales are simply fancier versions of garage or yard sales, usually held indoors and offering more upscale merchandise. You can stage the show yourself, but you'll save a lot of time and effort—and probably make more money—if you let a pro handle the job. Like auctioneers, estate agents handle all the work in exchange for part of the proceeds. You can find them in the Yellow Pages and on the Internet.

STORE

Just like organizing, storing your belongings in downsized quarters is something to consider from the first day you know you'll be moving. So before starting your big sorting spree, take a gander at the tips in this section. They'll help you make the most of your future space—and make the weeding-out process easier at the same time.

STORAGE ON THE MOVE. As you go through your furniture, deciding which pieces to take and which to leave behind, pay attention to the ones with storage space, and consider how they can be reinvented in your new digs. For instance:

- A standing iron pot rack in your current kitchen could hold towels in your future bathroom.

- A couple of low bookcases in the living room might make perfect bedside tables at the new place.

- An antique hutch in the dining room could store clothes and linens in a bedroom; supplies in the home office;

OUT OF THE BOX

If you have handmade treasures like a large needlepoint tapestry hanging on the wall, or a small hand-hooked rug that might not make the cut, don't be quick to get rid of them. Instead, find a bench or ottoman with a top that lifts up to reveal a storage compartment below, and use the needlepoint or rug to reupholster the top. (Unless you're a skilled upholsterer, it's best to have a pro do the work.)

or stereo equipment, CDs, and books in the living room.

PUT YOUR COLLECTIONS TO WORK. While you may not have room to display a big collection of cookie jars, souvenir coffee mugs, vintage lunch boxes, or doll-size furniture in your new home, don't be too quick to leave your treasures behind—at least not all of them. Instead, think about how you can use them as decorative storage containers for small kitchen gadgets, office supplies, cosmetics, or anything else that will fit inside.

DOING DOUBLE DUTY. When you shop for new furniture, look for things that perform more than one function. A trunk that doubles as a coffee table is a classic example, but don't stop there. Small chests of drawers can function fabulously as living room end tables or bedroom nightstands. A captain's bed, with its spacious drawers underneath, provides nighttime comfort *and* plenty of storage for clothes, linens, or anything else you want to stash in that handy spot. A dining table that's got a pedestal with shelves or drawers built in can hold an entire cupboard's worth of kitchen gear, in no more space than a standard table takes up.

LIGHT UP. In cramped quarters, small collectibles can add up to big clutter—fast! But here's a bright idea: Latch on to a lamp with a hollow, clear glass base and a lift-off top that can hold beach stones, seashells, marbles, souvenir matchbook covers, or any other mini

MAKING SPACE

I know that big-screen TVs are all the rage these days, but unless you really feel the need to turn your downsized living room into a movie theater, opting for a more modestly sized model will save a whole lot of space. Look for one that will fit into a cabinet, sit on a shelf, or hang on a wall. You can even recess a shelf into the wall, and make a "door" for the opening by attaching hinges to a favorite framed painting—thereby making room for the TV and a cherished work of art at the same time!

treasures you want to keep and put on display. You can find these space-saving show-offs in catalogs, in craft and furniture stores, and (of course) on the Internet.

LOOK OUT BELOW! Just about everybody stores things under their beds. But don't overlook the valuable real estate that's lurking under other pieces of furniture in your house. Coffee tables, end and console tables, dressers, buffets, easy chairs, and couches can all provide handy

CLUTTER BUSTER PRO

Even the smallest home needs an office space of some kind. Brandie Kajino, owner of The Home Office Organizer (www.thehomeofficeorganizer.com) in Vancouver, Washington, offers these tips for making every inch count in your new, more compact home office.

☛ Forget about file cabinets. Instead, get an ottoman or coffee table that doubles as a file drawer.

☛ Keep software CDs, as well as owner's manuals and instructions, in three-ring binders, which can sit neatly on shelves.

☛ Save floor space by using wall-hung shelves, tall freestanding hutches or cabinets, and hanging magazine racks (they're great for holding files).

☛ Go as paperless as you can stand. Have bills and financial statements e-mailed to you, rather than getting paper copies, and scan receipts into your computer. (Just be sure to back up your files!)

☛ Keep it all under control: Spend the last 15 minutes of the day clearing your desktop, so you can start fresh each day. Smaller spaces get cluttered in a hurry, so it's crucial to stay on top of it before it gets out of hand.

☛ Purge your file system at least once a year. (A good time to do this is just after you've paid your taxes.)

hideaways for anything that'll fit into the space. You have four fabulous options for using that storage gold mine:

1. To make use of a roomy, under-table area, simply add your choice of decorative containers. Depending on your taste and how big the space is, wicker baskets, trunks, hatboxes, and vintage suitcases all work well.

2. Forget about decorative containers. Instead, cover the table with a floor-length cloth and simply tuck your stuff in under it.

3. In the case of a coffee or end table with a lower opening, build an open box that's the right size to fit under the table. Paint the box to match the decor, and attach four wheels to the bottom. Add a decorative handle to one side, and you're ready to roll! Books, magazines, CDs, and DVDs are all excellent candidates for this mobile approach.

If your kitchen base cabinets are like most, they are raised 4 to 5 inches off the floor, with a baseboard installed to keep dust from collecting underneath. Well, that board, a.k.a. "toe kick," conceals some mighty valuable real estate. If you cut a section of that board away (or have a contractor do it for you), you can fill the space with shallow drawers that will hold table linens, serving platters and trays, extra flatware, or anything else that will fit inside. Or, forget about drawers and use that shallow area to store a thin, folding stepladder.

4. If the opening is low and concealed by upholstery fabric, as in the case of a couch or armchair, simply slide your storables under the skirt. This kind of space is perfect for flat items like trays, board games, off-duty pictures, or the extra leaves for the dining room table. Just one word of caution: If you have trouble bending down, use that space for stuff that isn't used very often.

DOORWAY TO DREAM STORAGE. The smaller your new quarters are, the more important it is to use every inch of storage space that's available—including the backs of doors in just about every room, cabinet, and closet. So as soon as you've moved in, take inventory of the items that need homes, measure each door, and then go shopping for some of these handy helpers:

- Bulletin boards

- Flat-sided hanging baskets, either wicker or metal

- General-purpose racks

- Hanging files

- Individual hooks

- Magnetic boards and strips

- Pegboard

- Shallow cabinets

- Shallow wire shelf units

- Shoe bags

- Specialized racks and hooks for things like irons and ironing boards, shoes, trousers, and cleaning tools

LOOK UP, TOO. When you're struggling to maximize storage space in your downsized living quarters, it pays to look up as well as down. A shelf installed above a door, or even around a whole room just below the ceiling, is the perfect place to stash things that you don't use very often—like linens, toys, or other gear that you only haul out when your grown children or grandchildren come to visit. (That way, they can climb up on a ladder to retrieve the stuff, and you won't have to risk a fall!)

MAKING SPACE

Turn the back of a door, or even a whole wall, into versatile vertical storage space by giving it a few coats of so-called magnetic paint. Despite its name, the paint itself is not magnetic. Rather, it contains tiny iron particles that create a metallic surface that attracts and holds magnets, in the same way your refrigerator door does. The more coats you apply, the stronger the holding power is, which means you can hang anything from lightweight pictures to sturdy racks and shelves without the use of screws, nails, or tape. This wonder worker is available in paint and hardware stores, as finish-coat paint, primer, or an additive that you mix with conventional paint.

INDEX

A

Accordion files, 161
Adjustable-height tables, 108
Advertising mail, 154–155,
    212
Aftershave lotion, 173
Air fresheners. *See* Deodorizers
Animal beds and bedding, 199,
    294
Ant control, 175
Antibiotics, 169–170
Antifreeze, 285–286
Apothecary chests, 14, 150
Appliance garages, 83
Appliances. *See also specific*
    appliances
        cleaning, 67, 68
        old, 246, 248–249
Archive files, 157–158, 280
Armoires
    bedrooms, 13, 40–41
    hobby rooms, 342
    home offices, 148
    laundry rooms, 226
    as linen closets, 207
Artwork
    displaying, 111–112
    on refrigerators, 44, 50–51
    storing, 114
Attics
    books in, 272
    downsize sorting in, 352
    heirlooms in, 270
    mementos in, 267, 270–
        271
    organizing, 273
    pro tips for, 274–275
    recycling and reusing items
        in, 264–268, 270
    remodeling, 277
    safety in, 275–277
    sorting strategies for,
        263–264, 269
    storage in, 276, 277,
        278–281

what not to store in,
    268–269
Auctions, 360

B

Baby christening dresses, 279
Baby gear, 265–266
Badminton equipment, 292
Bakeware organizers, 74
Baking soda
    freshness test, 89
    uses for, 67–68, 175, 181–
        182, 336
Balls, storing, 303
Barrels, as nightstands, 22
Baseball bats, 267
Baseballs, 303
Basements
    appliances in, 246, 248–
        249
    concrete floors in, 253–
        254, 255–256
    dampness in, 245, 253,
        254, 257
    downsize sorting in, 352
    emergency supplies in,
        254–255
    furniture in, 244–245
    hazardous waste in, 244
    laundry in, 256
    newspapers in, 245–247
    organizing, 252–253
    preventing clutter in, 249
    pro tips for, 258
    as root cellar, 261–263
    safety equipment for, 255
    sorting strategies for, 243,
        247–248
    stairs leading to, 243–244,
        260
    storage in, 255–260
    what not to store in,
        249–250
    windows in, 259–260

as wine cellar, 260–261
Basketballs, 303
Baskets, as organizers, 79, 106,
    113, 166
Bath mats or rugs, 182–183
Bath powder, 174
Bathrooms
    cleaning supplies in, 181–
        182, 189
    cosmetics in, 170–173, 188,
        192, 194
    deodorizers for, 179–180
    displays in, 179
    first-aid supplies in,
        180–181
    fixture replacement in,
        184–186
    guest baths, 196, 208–209
    medications in, 169–170,
        192
    notepads in, 190
    organizing, 187–189
    pro tips for, 196
    recycling and reusing items
        in, 173–179, 183–184
    sorting strategies for, 169
    storage aids for, 186–187,
        190–197
    visual clutter in, 182–183
    wastebaskets in, 189–190
Bathroom scales, 185
Bathtubs, 176
Batteries, 286, 337
Bed linens. *See also* Linen closets
    displaying, 13
    folding, 206
    organizing, 208
    recycling and reusing,
        199–204
    sorting, 199
    storing, 25, 209–210
    vacuum-packing, 207
Bed risers, 24
Bedroom closets. *See also*
    Clothes; Shoes

alcoves as, 35
armoires as, 40–41
back of door, 38–39
clothes hangers in, 29, 38, 40, 41
organizing, 34–38
preventing clutter in, 34
sorting strategies for, 28–33
storage aids for, 39–40
Bedroom decor, 17, 19–20
Bedroom drawers
alternatives to, 13, 14
apothecary chests as, 14
duplicate items in, 3–4
jewelry in, 8–13
out-of-season clothing in, 3
recycling and reusing items in, 3–5
removing bed linens from, 13
sorting strategies for, 1–2, 5–7
storage in, 14–16
Beds
clutter around, 17–21
foot-of-bed storage, 26–27
headboards for, 27–28, 267–268, 308
nightstand alternatives, 19, 21–23
pillows on, 18
storage under, 24–26, 293–294
types of, 25, 27
unmade, 21
Bedside tables. See Nightstands
Beetles and weevils, 201
Belts, 5, 9, 16
Between-the-stud storage, 187, 276, 304–305
Beverages, 43, 48–49
Bicycle wheels, 264–265
Bill paying, 19, 159–160
Binder clips, 139
Binders, for filing, 165–166
Bird nest material, 213
Birthday candles, 233
Boats and boating, 230, 296
Bookcases

bathroom, 186, 187
bedroom, 27
living area, 125, 130
as room dividers, 344
Books
in bathrooms, 197
in bedrooms, 17–18
care of, 107
displaying, 129–130
as measuring device, 112
mildewed, 245
new, 127
organizing, 125–126
sorting, 115–118, 272
valuable, 272
Booster seats, 153
Bracelets, 9–10
Bread boxes, 80
Breads and rolls, 87, 89
Broom handles, 229, 309
Brooms, 97
Bubble bath supplies, 195
Buckets, for storage, 11–12, 98
Buffets (furniture), 61, 101, 236
Building codes, 277
Bulletin boards
home office, 160–161
kitchen, 51, 97
laundry room, 239
pushpins for, 6
workshop, 330
Buoys, 230
Bureaus. See Dressers and bureaus
Business cards, 137–138, 166
Buttons, 12, 348

C

Cabinets. See Kitchen cabinets
Camping gear, 249
Candles, 122, 180, 233
Candle wax, removing, 179
Canisters, 58
Canned foods, 95
Captain's beds, 25
Car batteries, dead, 286
Carbon monoxide detectors, 255
Cardboard boxes, 257, 264, 279

Cardboard tubes, 173, 339
Carpet care, 218, 229
Carpet scraps, 326–327
Cars
cleaning windows, 4
organizing interior, 289–291
protecting seats, 200
pro tips for, 290
storing in garages, 283
Catalogs, 119–120
Cat toys, 343
CD cabinets, 131
CD players, 128–129
CDs
organizing, 126–127
sorting, 115–118
storing, 129, 130
Celery, 47
Chalkboard paint, 97
Chamois cloths, 295
Charcoal, as deodorizer, 266
Charitable donations
appliances, 246
downsizing and, 358
furniture, 102
pick ups for, 122
toiletries, 169
tools and building materials, 323–324
Cheese, 52
Chess and checkers, 128
Chest of drawers. See Dressers and bureaus
Chests and trunks, 110, 266, 280
Children. See also Toys
bathrooms, 191
bedrooms, 41
cleaning supplies and, 98, 181, 238
collectibles and, 109
craft supplies, 59, 91, 347
food storage and, 93
school supplies and papers, 79, 91, 145, 164
teaching to organize, 113, 124
traveling with, 200

Children's items, in attic, 266–267
China, 76
Chinch bugs, 201
Chisels, 336–337
Christmas decorations, 250, 281, 339, 343. *See also* Holiday decorations and supplies
Christmas trees, 200
Cleaning products
    commercial chemicals, 65–67, 98, 181
    green alternatives, 67–69, 181–182
    storing, 97–98, 163, 181, 189, 238
    toiletries as, 174–175
Cleaning rags, 199
Clipboards, 75
Closet doors. *See* Door-hung organizers
Closets. *See* Bedroom closets; Home offices; Kitchen pantries; Linen closets
Clothes
    on bedroom floor, 20
    black vs. blue, 36
    children's, 41, 113
    keeping or tossing, 29–31
    mildewed, 245
    organizing, 13, 34–38
    out-of-season, 3, 25, 31, 41, 277, 278, 280, 281
    recycling and reusing, 2, 3–5, 213
    repairing, 33, 213–214
    static cling, 38
    storing, 16, 279
    washing, 213, 219–221
    washing instructions for, 238
    worn or stained, 212–213
Clothes dryers, 216–217, 227
Clothes hangers
    in bedroom closets, 29, 38, 40, 41
    as hooks, 281
    for table linens, 208
Clothesline, retractable, 221

Clothespin holder, 230
Clothespins, 233
Clutter prevention
    basements, 249
    bedroom closets, 34
    entertainment areas, 124
    garages, 300
    home offices, 141
    refrigerators and freezers, 46
Coffee cans, 336
Coffee mugs, 74, 81, 194
Coffee tables, 106, 108, 110
Coins, 14
Cold frames, 184
Collectibles and knickknacks
    in bedrooms, 17
    dusting, 232
    in kitchen, 61, 80–81
    in living areas, 104, 109, 123
    as storage containers, 362
Color-coding
    children's clothing, 41
    cutting boards, 84
    files, 159
    food storage, 92–93
    plastic storage bins, 258
Compost material
    burying, 85
    dryer lint, 216
    food, 42–44
    newspaper, 247
    storing, 85–86
Computer disks, 166
Computer networks, 136–137
Computers, 134, 135–136, 232
Concrete floors, 253–254, 255–256
Condiments, 46, 49, 95
Contact paper, removing, 178
Cookbooks, 81, 125
Cookie cutters, 58
Cookie jars, 81, 194
Cookware, 73, 74, 230
Corner cupboards, 14
Corn-shucking tool, 177
Cosmetics, 170–173, 188, 192, 194

Counter-height tables, 82
Countertops. *See* Kitchen countertops
County surplus stores, 142–143
Coupons, 155
Crackers, 87
Craft books, 125
Craft supplies, 59, 91, 347. *See also* Hobby rooms
Crayon marks, removing, 178
Credit cards, 160
Crocks, ceramic, 150
Croquet balls, 291–292
Crystal decanters, 268
Cucumber beetles, 295
Cup hooks, 74, 75
Curio cabinets, 109
Curtain tiebacks, 5
Cut flowers, 174
Cutlery holders, for storage, 15, 76, 194, 314
Cutting boards, 69, 83, 84, 85

D

Dairy products, 48, 51
Deer deterrents, 174
Deer ticks, 217
Dehumidifiers, 253
De-icing aids, 232, 317
Deodorizers
    candles, 180
    charcoal, 266
    dryer sheets, 232–233
    polyurethane, 280
    vinegar, 69, 179
Desks
    buying, 142–144
    clearing top of, 133–137
    placement of, 141–142
    sorting drawer contents, 137–141
Desktop carousels, 150
Diamond drawer organizers, 15
Dining room hutch or sideboard, 61, 101, 236
Dining tables, 82, 105, 108
Direct Marketing Association, 120

Dish drainers, 80
Dishes, 60–61, 76
Dish washing, 174
Dishwashing basins, 302
Documents. *See* Paper piles and documents
Dollhouses, 343
Door-hung organizers
    bathrooms, 190–191
    bedrooms, 38–39
    downsized homes, 364–365
    home offices, 148, 149–150
    kitchens, 76, 97
    laundry rooms, 235–236
    linen closets, 205
Downsizing
    garage sales, 358, 359–360
    help with, 354, 358
    maximizing storage and, 361–365
    new home and, 355
    packing strategies for, 357–359
    pro tips for, 353, 363
    sorting strategies for, 351–357
    valuables from, 360–361
Draft blockers, 2
Drain cleaners, 67, 181–182
Draperies, 103
Drawer organizers, 188
Drawers. *See* Bedroom drawers; Desks; Kitchen drawers
Dressers and bureaus
    alternatives to, 13
    as bathroom vanities, 184–185
    in garages, 305
    as nightstands, 21–22
    shared, 8
    storing clothes in, 16
    styles of, 8
Drip irrigation, 231
Drop cloths, for painting, 184
Drop zones, 79, 109
Dryer lint, 216–217
Dryer sheets, 232–233
Drying racks, 225
Dumbbells, 231

Duplicate items
    in bedrooms, 3–4
    in entertainment areas, 115–118
    in hobby rooms, 341
    office supplies, 141
    tools, 322–324
Dust cloths and tools
    bed linens as, 200
    chamois cloths, 295
    hair dryers as, 178
    paintbrushes as, 321
    socks as, 4
DVDs, 115–116, 127–129, 130

E

Earrings, 6, 12
EBay®, 360
Egg holders, for storage, 15
Eggs, 46–47, 48
Electrical cords and cables
    corralling, 144, 173
    storing, 308–309, 331, 338
Electrical outlets, 329
Electronics, in kitchen, 82
Embroidery hoops, 339
Emergency supplies, 254–255
End tables, 111
Entertainment areas
    organizing, 125–127
    preventing clutter in, 124
    recycling and reusing items in, 122
    reducing clutter in, 118–121, 123
    sorting strategy for, 115
    storage in, 127–132
    things to toss, 115–118, 121, 123
Entertainment centers (furniture), 127, 148
Envelopes, from advertising mail, 155
Erasers, 139
Estate sales, 361
Exercise equipment, 18

Expiration dates, of foods
    explanation of, 43
    food-storage guidelines, 49, 92, 95, 251
    grocery shopping and, 87
Extension cords, retractable, 331, 338

F

Fabrics, storing, 349–350
Fabric softener, 229
Fabric-softener sheets, 232–233
Fashion accessories, 3, 5
File boxes, 166–167
Filing cabinets
    alternatives to, 165–167
    alternative uses for, 163
    buying, 163
    organizing, 157–159
    purging, 165
    sorting papers for, 152
    types of, 163–164
Financial records, 162, 274. *See also* Paper piles and documents
Fire extinguishers, 255, 329
Fire hazards, 244, 272
Fireplace mantels, 104
Fireplaces, 103–104, 111, 246
Fire-starter nuggets, 217
First-aid supplies, 91, 180–181, 311, 329
Fishing-tackle boxes, 150, 193, 331
Flashlights, 66, 327
Flat files, 110
Floors, cleaning, 68, 69, 181, 253–254
Focal points, 105–106
Food storage, 57. *See also* Kitchen pantries; Refrigerators and freezers; *specific foods*
Food substitutions, 88
Footballs, 303
Foot-of-bed storage, 26–27
Footrests, 150
Formal wear, 31, 32
Freecycle Network™, 308

Freezers. *See* Refrigerators and
    freezers
Fruit
    cleaning, 68
    storing, 55, 261–263
Funnels, homemade, 231
Furniture. *See also specific pieces*
    arranging, 10, 104–106
    in attics, 281
    in basements, 244–245
    downsizing, 361–365
    family heirlooms, 102–103
    for hobby rooms, 346
    for home offices, 141–144
    keeping or tossing, 99–101
    moving, 4
    new homes for, 101–103
    as storage solution, 108–
        112, 361–365
Furniture pads, 183, 201

G

Games
    in emergency kit, 254
    homemade, 139
    organizing, 113, 121–122
Game tables, 128
Garages
    cars kept in, 283
    flooding in, 297
    hazardous waste in,
        285–286
    narrow, 299
    organizing, 297–300
    preventing clutter in, 300
    purpose and use of, 283
    recycling and reusing items
        in, 291–296
    refrigerators in, 296–297
    vs. sheds, 306–307
    sorting strategies for, 283–
        289, 291
    storage in, 300–305
Garage sales, 289, 358, 359–360
Garbage cans, 79, 245–246, 317.
    See also Wastebaskets
Garbage disposals, cleaning, 69
Garden hoses, 308, 316–317, 337

Garden supplies. *See also* Sheds
    planters and pots, 294–295,
        308, 317
    plant labels, 231
    plant protectors, 184, 204
    plant stakes, 229, 292
    plant ties, 200
    recycling and reusing,
        308–309
    seeds, 309–310
    trellises, 292, 293
    window screens as, 324–
        325
Garlic, 53
Garlic presses, 59
Garment bags, 40
Gas mileage, improving, 283
GelPro® mats, 329
Gifts, 32–33
Gift wrap, 156, 246, 343
Gift wrap tubes, 339
Glass cleaner formula, 259
Glass containers, 348
Glass cutters, 336
Glasses, for storage, 194
Glass tabletops, 106
Gloves, washing, 233
Glue, 341
Gluing techniques, 233
Golf bags, 233–234, 303, 314
Gone Fishin' game, 139
Grocery bags, 60, 189
Grocery coupons, 155
Grocery shopping, 87, 155, 180,
    234–235
Grout, cleaning, 67, 181
Guest baths, 196, 208–209. *See
    also* Bathrooms

H

Habitat for Humanity, 102, 277,
    301, 324
Hairbrushes, 175–176
Hair conditioner, 174
Hair dryers, 177–179, 193
Hair scrunchies, 174
Hair spray, 173
Hammers, 319, 322

Hammocks, for storage, 278, 301
Handbags, for storage, 347
Hands, cleaning, 174
Hanging cupboards, 23
Hanging racks, homemade, 21
Hard hats, in attics, 276–277
Hardware, 289, 335
Hatboxes, 11
Hazardous waste, 244, 285–286,
    319–320
Headboards, 27–28, 267–268,
    308
Heirloom items
    china, 270
    christening dresses, 279
    downsizing and, 353, 356
    furniture, 102–103
    holiday items, 121
Herbs and spices
    freezing, 54
    for pest control, 96, 210
    shelf life of, 95
    storing, 92, 96
Historic documents or items, 280
Hobby rooms
    children's supplies in, 347
    dangerous items in,
        347–348
    duplicate items in, 341
    furniture for, 346
    making space for, 344
    pro tips for, 345
    room dividers for, 343–344
    sewing scraps in, 342–343
    sorting strategies for,
        339–341
    storage containers for,
        346–349
    textile storage in, 349–350
Hole punches, storing, 349
Holiday decorations and
    supplies, 120–121, 209. *See
    also* Christmas decorations
Home-improvement project
    scraps, 325
Home offices. *See also* Paper
    piles and documents
    clearing desktop, 133–137
    in closet, 138

closet in, 145–146

de-cluttering cabinets and
    drawers, 137–141

downsizing and, 363

furniture for, 141–144

making space for, 142

organizing supplies in,
    144–147

paperless, 136

preventing clutter in, 141

pro tips for, 140

storage in, 147–150

Honey, 95

Hooks, for storage

    basements, 256

    garages, 303, 304

    sheds, 315

    workshops, 330

Houseplants, 180, 246, 314

Humidity

    in damp basements, 245,
        253, 254, 257

    food storage and, 94

I

Ice cube trays, for storage, 15

Ice scrapers, 296

In- and out-boxes, 148

Income tax records, 162

Insecticides. *See* Pest-control
    agents and aids

Insect repellents, 233

Ironing boards, 226

Irons, 217–218

J

Jars

    for storage, 94–95, 194,
        331, 335, 348

    as stress-relieving toy, 45

Jelly cupboards, 146

Jewelry

    cleaning, 177–178

    organizing, 8–13

    selling, 6–7

    sorting, 6

Jewelry holders, 4–5

Jewelry mirrors, 10

Junk drawers, 63–64, 76

K

Kitchen appliances, 67, 77. *See
    also* Refrigerators and freezers

Kitchen cabinets

    adding shelves to, 71–73

    dishes in, 60–61

    displaying items from, 61

    doors of, 75–76

    dull knives in, 62–63

    junk drawers, 63–64, 76

    mounting appliances
        under, 83

    organizing, 70–71

    in other rooms, 70, 144,
        236, 277, 301, 332–333,
        346

    plastic containers in, 61–62

    recipes in, 64, 77–78

    recycling and reusing items
        in, 58–60

    sorting strategies for, 56–58

    storage aids for, 73–78

    storage under, 364

    under-sink cabinet, 64–68,
        72

Kitchen carts, 84–85, 148

Kitchen countertops

    organizing, 82–84

    removing clutter from,
        78–81

    small appliances on, 79–80,
        82–83

    storing items from, 84–86

Kitchen drawers, 58, 62–64, 76

Kitchen gadgets and utensils,
    58–61, 73–74, 84

Kitchen islands. *See* Kitchen
    countertops

Kitchen pantries

    adding shelves to, 91

    alternatives to, 89

    organizing, 89–93

    pro tips for, 90

    rescuing food from, 87–89

    rotating foods in, 92

    sorting strategies for, 86–87

    storage aids and guidelines
        for, 94–98

Kitchen sinks

    cabinets under, 64–68, 72

    dish drainers in, 80

    over-the-sink shelves, 83–84

Kitchen sponges, 65

Kitchen tables, 82, 91

Knives, 62–63, 75. *See also*
    Cutlery holders, for storage

L

Labeling guidelines, 274, 275,
    281, 315

Label makers, 157

Ladders, 13, 326

Laminating documents, 280

Lamps and lighting

    attics, 274, 276

    bedrooms, 20

    closets, 147

    hobby rooms, 345

    living areas, 101

    as storage containers,
        362–363

    workshops, 329

Lateral files, 163–164

Laundry baskets, 230

Laundry carts, 224–225, 235

Laundry detergent, 174, 230,
    234–235, 240

Laundry rooms

    in basements, 256

    clean laundry in, 218,
        221–222

    in closets, 227

    counter space, 222

    dryer lint, 216–217

    equipment, 214–218,
        222–225, 227, 237

    organizing, 219

    in plain view, 227

    pro tips for, 224

    purpose and use of,
        211–212

    recycling and reusing items
        in, 213

Laundry rooms (continued)
 repairing clothes in,
   213–214
 sorting clothes in, 212–213,
   218–220
 storage in, 226–227,
   235–240
 utility sinks, 214, 223, 225
 washing clothes in, 213,
   221
Laundry supplies
 organizing space for,
   234–237
 recycling and reusing,
   229–234
 sorting strategies for,
   228–229
 stain-removal chart,
   240–241
 storing, 238–240
Lawn darts, homemade, 264–265
Lawn mowing, 341
Lazy Susans, 21, 49, 188–189
Leather, mildewed, 245
Leftover food, 43, 51, 56
Lettuce, storing, 52
Libraries, 116
Lighting. See Lamps and lighting
Linen closets
 bathroom supplies in,
   206–207
 doors of, 205
 organizing, 205–208
 pro tips for, 202–203
 recycling and reusing items
   in, 199–204
 sorting strategies for, 197–
   199, 204
 storing items in, 208–210
Lingerie bags, 5, 21, 220
Lip balm, 174
Living areas. See also
 Entertainment areas
 artwork, 111–114
 collectibles, 104, 109
 fireplaces, 103–104
 furniture, 99–103, 106–108
 lighting, 101
 storage, 108–111

traffic flow, 104–106
window coverings, 103
Lofts, building, 312
Loose change, 14
Lubricants, 174
Luggage, deodorizing, 233, 266,
 280

M

Magazines
 in bathrooms, 197
 as clutter, 17–18
 in home offices, 152–153
 in kitchen, 78–79
 preventing clutter from,
   124
 storing, 130
Magnetic paint, 365
Magnetic storage bins, 238
Mail, 154–155, 159, 212
Mailing supplies, 146–147
Mantels, 104
Manuals. See Owner's manuals
Meat, when to toss, 44
Mechanical equipment, 255
Medications, 169–170, 192
Medicine cabinets, 145, 192
Mementos, 121, 161, 267,
 270–271
Memorabilia, 271
Mesh laundry bags, 5, 21, 220
Message centers, 147, 234
Mice, 247
Microwave carts, 84
Microwave ovens, cleaning, 69
Milk, storing, 48
Milk crates, 332
Mirrors, 15, 106, 108
Modeling clay, homemade, 217
Mold and mildew, 182, 245
Mop handles, 229
Moth repellents, 5, 210, 218, 342
Motor oil, used, 286
Mouthwash, 174
MP3 players, 118
Muffin tins, for storage, 58, 335
Mugs, 74, 81, 194
Multitools, 63

Murphy beds, 27
Mushroom brushes, 177
Mushrooms, 54
Music. See CDs; Sheet music

N

Nail polish, 178
Nails, rusty, 293
Necklaces, 8
Neckties, 16
Needle-nose pliers, 322–323
Newspapers
 as clutter, 78–79, 124
 as packing material, 358
 recycling and reusing,
   245–247
Nightstands
 alternatives to, 19, 21–23
 clutter on, 17–18, 20
Notepads, in bathroom, 190

O

Office equipment, 134–137
Office space. See Home offices
Office tools and supplies
 duplicates, 141
 miniature versions,
   135
 organizing, 144–147
 pro tips for, 140
 sorting, 134, 137–141
 storing, 147–150
Onions, 53
Ottomans, 110–111, 361
Outdoor gear, 249, 291
Out-of-season clothes
 in bedroom closets, 41
 removing from bedroom,
   3, 25, 31
 storing in attic, 277, 278,
   280, 281
Ovens, cleaning, 68
Over-the-sink shelves, 83–84
Over-the-door racks, 76. See also
 Door-hung organizers
Owner's manuals, 77, 152,
 164–165, 330

P

Packing blankets, 183, 201
Packing materials, 279–280, 357–358, 358–359
Paint, 97, 287, 320, 365
Paintbrushes, 229, 321
Painted-wood surfaces, cleaning, 68
Painting drop cloths, 184
Pallets, 256
Pantry. *See* Kitchen pantries
Paper bags, 60, 189
Paper clips, 139, 164
Paperless office, 136
Paper piles and documents
    advertising mail, 154–155
    clearing off desk, 137
    historic documents, 280
    how long to keep, 154, 162
    organizing, 157–161
    shredding, 155–157
    sorting, 151–153
    storing, 162–167
    vital documents, 162
Paper products, 89
Paper shredders, 136, 155–157
Parking spaces, in garages, 300
Party supplies, 120–121, 209
Pedestal or wall-hung sinks, 184, 186
Pegboard
    home offices, 145
    kitchens, 77
    laundry rooms, 239
    sheds, 312
    workshops, 330, 332, 334, 336
Peppers, 47
Perfume, 173, 193
Pest-control agents and aids
    bed linens as, 200–201
    commercial products, 66–67
    dryer lint as, 217
    dryer sheets as, 233
    herbs, 96, 210
    potatoes as, 247

    removing from kitchen, 66–67
    sachets, 5, 342
    shower curtains as, 184
    tires as, 295
    toiletries as, 173, 174, 175
Pet hair, 232
Pets
    beds and bedding for, 199, 294
    cleaning supplies and, 98, 181, 238
    food storage and, 93
    grooming, 295
    traveling with, 200
Photographs
    displaying, 111–112
    for insurance purposes, 273
    as keepsakes, 32
    on nightstands, 19
    on refrigerators, 44, 50–51
    sorting, 123
    storing, 132
Piano benches, used as nightstands, 23
Pickle jars, 94
Pickle juice, 47
Picture frames, for jewelry display, 12
Pillows, decorative, 18
Pins (jewelry), 10, 11
Plant care, 43, 293
Planters and plant pots, 294–295, 308, 317
Plant labels, 231
Plant protectors, 184, 204
Plant stakes, 229, 292
Plant stands, 307
Plant ties, 200
Plant trellises, 292, 293
Plastic bags, 60
Plastic bottles, 230–232
Plastic containers, 61–62
Plastic eggs, 269
Plastic storage bins, 258–259, 302–303
Plastic storage cabinets, 257–258, 302

Plastic utensils, 58
Platform beds, 25
Plumbing pipes, frozen, 178
Potatoes, 54–55, 247
Pot-lid racks, 58
Pot racks, 73
Pottery bowls, for storage, 12–13, 149
Power cords. *See* Electrical cords and cables
Produce. *See also specific types*
    cleaning, 68
    storing, 55, 261–263
Produce crates, 22, 150
Professional organizers' tips
    attics, 274–275
    book care, 107
    cars, 290
    children, 41, 113
    downsizing, 353, 363
    guest baths, 196
    hobby rooms, 345
    kitchen pantries, 90
    laundry rooms, 224
    linen closets, 202–203
    office supplies, 140
    plastic storage bins, 258
    sheds, 315
    workshops, 330–331

Q

Quantity purchases, 46, 180, 240
Quilt racks, 13, 19
Quilts
    displaying, 13
    making, 32, 342
    storing, 349–350

R

Rafters, exposed, 277, 304, 333
Rag rugs, 200
Raisins, 87
Reach extender, 309
Recipes, 64, 77–78
Recreational equipment. *See* Games; Sporting goods; Toys

Recycling and reusing
  baby gear, 265–266
  bed linens, 199–204
  business cards, 137–138
  clothes and accessories, 2,
    3–5, 213
  computers, 134
  garden supplies, 308–309
  hairbrushes, 175–176
  hair dryers, 177–179
  ice scrapers, 296
  jewelry, 6
  kitchen cabinets, 70
  newspapers, 245–247
  paintbrushes, 321–322
  shower curtains, 183–184
  sporting goods, 291–292
  tires, 295–296
  toiletries, 173–175
  tools, 322–323
  toothbrushes, 176–177
  towels, 199
  wading pools, 293–294
Refrigerators and freezers
  capacity of, 50
  clutter on outside of, 44,
    50–51
  dating food in, 49
  defrosting, 178
  frozen-food shelf life,
    251
  in garages, 296–297
  making space in, 46, 48
  organizing, 48–50
  preventing clutter in, 46
  sorting strategies for,
    42–47
  storing food in, 51–56,
    250–251
  temperature in, 48
  washing inside of, 45–46
Remote controls, 21, 131–132
Room-by-room strategy, 117
Room dividers, 343–344
Room screens, 18, 344
Root cellars, 261–263
Rubber bands, 139
Rubber mallets, 319
Rugs, making, 200, 342

Rust
  preventing, 174, 190, 336,
    350
  removing, 69

S

Safe-deposit boxes, 162
Safety equipment, 255
Safety pins, 234
Salt and pepper shakers, 81
Sandboxes, 295
Sanding belts, 336
Sandpaper, 323, 337
Saw blades, 337
Scarves, 5, 16, 340
School supplies and papers, 79,
  91, 141, 164
Scoops, homemade, 231
Scrapers, 232, 336
Screwdrivers, 322
Seashells, in bathrooms, 179
Seasonal items, 300, 306, 311,
  357. See also Out-of-season
  clothes
Seedlings, 314
Seeds, storing, 309–310
Seed-starting pots, 246–247
Seed-starting test, 309
Sell-by dates, 43, 92
Serving carts, 101
Sewing boxes, 347
Sewing patterns, 347
Sewing scraps, 342–343
Shampoo, 174
Shaving cream, 174
Sheds
  as basement alternative, 252
  dampness in, 311, 313
  first-aid supplies in, 311
  vs. garages, 306–307
  lofts in, 312
  organizing, 310–313
  pro tips for, 315
  purpose and use of, 310
  recycling and reusing items
    in, 307–309
  sorting strategies for,
    306–307

  storage in, 313–317
Sheet music, 116
Shelf life
  cosmetics, 171
  frozen foods, 251
  packaged foods, 43, 95
  paint, 287
  refrigerated foods, 49
Shelves and shelving units
  attics, 274, 276
  basements, 256, 259
  bathrooms, 187
  bedrooms, 19, 28
  downsized homes, 365
  garages, 301–302
  home offices, 144–145
  kitchens, 71–73, 91
  laundry rooms, 237
  sheds, 312, 315, 316
  workshops, 331, 333, 334
Shoe bags, hanging
  bathrooms, 193
  bedroom closets, 39
  hobby rooms, 347
  home offices, 149–150
  jewelry and accessories,
    9, 39
  kitchen pantries, 97
  sheds, 316
Shoe bags, for travel, 5
Shoe boxes, for storage, 15, 129
Shoe holders, for storage,
  192–193
Shoelaces, 5
Shoe racks, 39
Shoes
  on bedroom floor, 23
  care of, 323
  children's, 41, 113
  keeping or tossing, 30, 31
  storing, 39, 40, 41
  wet, 246
Shopping bags, 60
Shopping tips, 87, 155, 180,
  234–235
Shower curtains, 183–184
Shower doors, cleaning, 232
Showerheads, cleaning, 182
Showers, cleaning, 182

Shredded paper, 155–157
Sideboards, 61, 101, 236
Sinks
    cleaning, 68
    kitchen, 80, 83–84
    pedestal or wall-hung, 184,
        186
    utility, 214, 223, 225
    vessel, 185–186
Sink skirts, 183, 184
Skis, 260
Slat boards, 332
Sleep, clutter and, 1, 17
Sliding door security, 229
Small appliances
    cleaning, 68
    on kitchen countertop,
        79–80, 82–83
    storing, 71
Smocks, for beauty treatments,
    200
Smoke detectors, 255
Snacks, 91
Snag repair tool, for clothes, 214
Snow saucers, 292
Social service agencies, 169, 323.
    See also Charitable donations
Socks
    preventing orphans, 5, 221
    recycling and reusing, 4–5
    storing, 16
Sofas, storage under, 112
Sorting categories
    attics, 264
    basements, 243
    bathrooms, 169
    bedrooms, 2, 28
    downsizing, 356
    garages, 285
    hobby rooms, 339
    home offices, 137
    kitchens, 57–58, 86–87
    laundry rooms, 212
    linen closets, 197
    paper piles, 151–152
    sheds, 306
    workshop, 319
Sorting process tips, 7, 117, 358
Souvenirs, 123

Spice racks, 59, 194
Spices. See Herbs and spices
Splinter removal, 341
Sponges, 65
Sporting goods
    recycling and reusing,
        291–293
    sorting, 291
    storing, 250, 257–258, 260,
        303, 304
Spray bottles, 65, 97–98, 232
Spring-tension poles, 236
Squash, 53
Squash bugs, 295
Stain-removal aids, 339
Stain-removal chart, 240–241
Static cling, 38
Static shock, 229
Stemware, 74
    Stereo speakers, 118–119
Storage containers
    from attic, 267–268, 270
    for basements, 257–259
    for bathrooms, 194–195
    collectibles as, 362
    for hobby rooms, 346–349
    for home offices, 149, 167
    for laundry rooms, 226–
        227, 239
    for living areas, 131
    for sheds, 313–314
Stress-reducing toy, 45
Sump pumps, 253
Sweaters, 2, 178
Swimming pool supplies, 306

T

Table linens
    sorting, 204
    storing, 207, 208, 209–210,
        340
Tables. See also Nightstands
    adjustable-height, 108
    child-size, 266
    coffee tables, 106, 108, 110
    counter-height, 82
    dining tables, 82, 105, 108
    end tables, 111

    game tables, 128
    kitchen tables, 82, 91
    storage under, 364
Talcum powder, 175
Teapots, 81
Telephone directories, 153
Telephones, 82, 135, 147
Television carts, 127–128
Television remote controls, 21,
    131–132
Televisions, 115, 362
Temperature, for food storage,
    48, 94
Tent caterpillars, 175
Textiles, 245, 349–350
Tires, old, 295–296
Tire swings, 296
Toasters, cleaning, 68
Toilet paper, 197
Toilet paper tubes, 173
Toiletries, 169, 172–175, 176,
    198
Toilets, cleaning, 182
Tomatoes, 52–53, 200, 295
Tool belts, 331
Toolboxes, 331, 347
Tool caddy, 231
Tool handles, reusing, 309
Tools. See also specific tools
    duplicates, 322–324
    in kitchens, 63
    maintaining handles of, 173
    need for, 319
    preventing rust on, 174,
        246, 336
    sharp, 313
    storing, 300, 313, 314, 315,
        317, 336–337
Toothbrushes, 176–177
Toothbrush holders, 194
Toothpaste, 175
Towel bars, 191
Towels
    on floor, 19, 191
    folding, 206
    organizing, 208
    recycling and reusing, 199
    sorting, 198
    storing, 209–210

Toxic chemicals. *See* Cleaning
products; Hazardous waste
Toys
    household items as, 60,
      184, 204
    storing, 41, 131, 303, 304
    stress-relieving, 45
Traffic flow, in living areas,
    104–105
Trash, from sorting process
    basements, 247–248
    bathrooms, 176
    bedroom drawers, 3
    hobby rooms, 339
    home offices, 138, 159
    kitchens, 44, 58, 86
    laundry rooms, 212, 228
    linen closets, 198
    living areas, 123
    refrigerators, 44
    workshops, 320
Travel
    car organizer for, 291
    with children or pets, 200
    information files for, 158
    toiletries for, 188
Trellises, 292, 293
Trouser racks, 39
Trundle beds, 27
Trunks and chests, 110, 266, 280
Tub Top™, 214
Turkey basters, 59
TV carts, 127–128
TV remotes, 21, 131–132
TVs, 115, 362
Twine, storing, 335

U

Under-bed storage, 24–26,
    293–294
Under-sink cabinet, 64–68, 72

Under-sink organizers, 72, 184
Under-table storage, 364
Use-by dates, 43
Utility sinks, 214, 223, 225

V

Vacuum-packing method,
    207
Valuables, 360–361
Vegetables. *See also specific types*
    cleaning, 68
    storing, 55, 261–263
Velcro™, 21
Ventilation, in workshops, 329
Vessel sinks, 185–186
Video games, 128
Vinegar, uses for, 68–69, 179,
    181–182
Vine trellises, 292, 293

W

Wading pools, 293–294
Wagons, 266–267, 314, 334
Wallpaper, cleaning, 178, 218
Warranties. *See* Owner's
    manuals
Washing machines, 214–216,
    222–223, 227, 237
Wastebaskets, 18, 189–190, 308.
    See also Garbage cans
Water, storing, 255, 259
Water alarms, 253
Watering cans, 231
Web sites, for garage storage
    systems, 304
Wheeled carts
    kitchen carts, 84–85,
      148
    laundry carts, 224–225,
      235

    in linen closet, 206
    serving carts, 101
    for toys, 303
    TV carts, 127–128
Wheeled storage devices, 26,
    334
Wiffle™ ball bat, 229
Wi-fi, 136–137
Window coverings, 103, 183
Windows
    in basements, 259–260
    cleaning, 229, 259
    winterizing, 179
Window screens, 324–325
Wine, opened, 53
Wine cellar, 260–261
Wine racks, 59, 83, 191
Winter squash, 53
Wooden crates, 22, 150
Workbenches, 300, 328,
    344
Workshops. *See also* Tools
    essentials for, 329
    hazardous waste in, 319–320
    organizing, 327, 332–333
    project scraps in, 325
    pro tips for, 330–331
    purpose and use of, 318–319
    recycling and reusing items
      in, 324–327
    sorting strategies for,
      319–321
    storage in, 333–338
    workbenches for, 328

Y

Yardsticks, 341

Z

Ziplock bags, 316, 337